Henry G. Briggs

Nizam

His History and Relations with the British Government - Vol. 2

Henry G. Briggs

Nizam
His History and Relations with the British Government - Vol. 2

ISBN/EAN: 9783337878818

Printed in Europe, USA, Canada, Australia, Japan

Cover: Foto ©Andreas Hilbeck / pixelio.de

More available books at **www.hansebooks.com**

THE NIZAM

HIS HISTORY

AND

RELATIONS WITH THE BRITISH GOVERNMENT

BY

HENRY GEORGE BRIGGS

SECRETARY, BOMBAY MUNICIPALITY

IN TWO VOLUMES

VOL. II.

LONDON

BERNARD QUARITCH, 15 PICCADILLY

1861

CONTENTS

OF

THE SECOND VOLUME.

CHAP. V.

CHAP. VI.

APPENDIX.

APPENDIX A.

APPENDIX B.

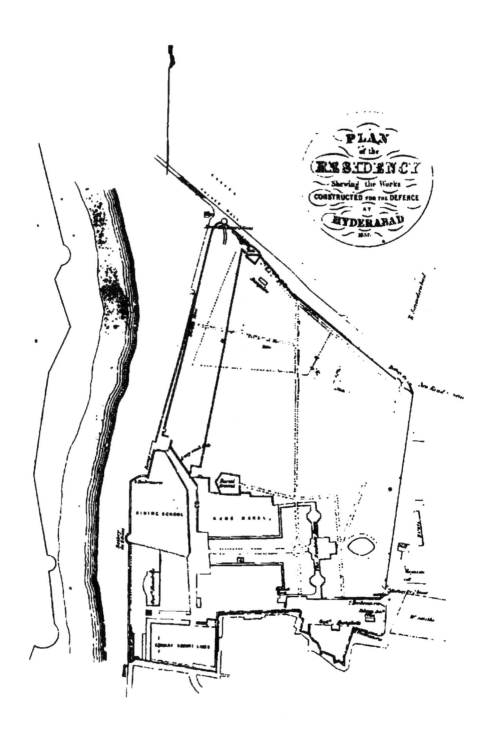

PLAN of the RESIDENCY Shewing the Works CONSTRUCTED for the DEFENCE AT HYDERABAD 1857.

THE NIZAM:

HIS HISTORY

AND

RELATIONS WITH THE BRITISH GOVERNMENT.

CHAPTER I.

BRITISH RESIDENTS AT THE COURT OF THE NIZAM. — TRACE OF EARLIEST
CORRESPONDENCE. — COLONEL FORDE. — GENERAL CALLIAUD. — MR. HOL-
LOND. — MR. GRANT. — MR. JOHNSON. — SIR JOHN KENNAWAY. — GENE-
RAL WILLIAM KIRKPATRICK. — COLONEL J. ACHILLES KIRKPATRICK. —
CAPTAIN SYDENHAM. — SIR HENRY RUSSELL. — SIR CHARLES J. METCALFE.

THE managers of the English Factories on the coast had CHAP.
I.
previously to the death of the great Asoph Jah carried
on intrigues with the subordinate officers of his govern- General.
ment, in furtherance of their views against the French;
but they do not appear to have gained access to the
Nizam direct till the year 1747, when Asoph Jah returned to Aurungabad, leaving Unwoor-ood-Deen, his
deputy, in the Carnatic. Madras was then in the hands of
the French, whose successes threatened the total extinction
of British interests on the coast; while their ally, Nuwab
Unwoor-ood-Deen, turned a deaf ear to their entreaties
for assistance.

In this emergency, Commodore Griffin, commanding the naval force on the station, and the Governor of Fort St. David, despatched two letters, dated respectively the 7th and 9th March, 1747, to Asoph Jah, informing him of the losses which they had sustained, and entreating him, in the name of their sovereign, " to call the Nuwab to an account for his past transactions, and interpose his power to restore as nearly as possible in its original state what had been so unjustly taken from them." The application was favourably received by Asoph Jah, and a peremptory order issued to Unwoor-ood-Deen to chastise the French, to recover his Majesty's sea-port town, and restore the English to their rights. To enforce these orders, a body of horse under the personal command of one of his sons, was detached by Unwoor-ood-Deen to retake Madras; but being foiled in the attempt by the intrepidity of the French garrison, were obliged to return precipitately to Arcot.

In the disturbances that followed the death of Asoph Jah, the English took part with Naseer Jung in opposing the pretensions of his nephew, Moozuffir Jung, who was supported by the French Government of Pondicherry. To remove this competitor, Naseer Jung proceeded direct to the Carnatic, where he was joined by a small body of English troops under Major Lawrence, afterwards better known as Major-General Stringer Lawrence, " the man," according to Lord CLIVE, " to whom his reputation, and of course his fortune, was owing."

On the near approach of the two armies, and on the eve of a battle which was to decide the fate of the two rivals, Moozuffir Jung was suddenly deserted by his French allies, who returned to Pondicherry; and, despairing of success, he delivered himself up to his uncle,

who had him immediately put in fetters. The English
contingent, after remaining a short time with the Soobehdar's army, were withdrawn in consequence of Naseer
Jung having failed to fulfil the terms upon which their
service had been granted to him.

The first Englishman of whom we have any account
who had to deal with the Nizam's government was
Colonel FORDE, and he concluded the Treaty of 1759.
The next was General CALLIAUD, who got the Northern
Circars under the Treaty of 1766. The following Treaty
of 1778 was executed at Madras by an agent of the
Nizam, on behalf of his Highness.

Mr. JOHN HOLLOND was the first envoy to the *durbar*, Mr. Hol-
or court of the Nizam. Mention having already been lond.
made of him, it is now merely necessary to say that he
was a Madras civilian, and sent on this diplomatic mission
by the Government of Fort St. George, who taking umbrage at the notice of their conduct in this proceeding
by the Supreme Government, recalled the envoy. The
Governor-General thereupon interfered and made Mr.
Hollond his representative. Mr. Hollond reached Hyderabad in April 1779; he left upon his promotion to a
seat in the Executive Council of Fort St. George, and
though superseded for a time in the government of
Madras by Lord Macartney, through the influence of the
Board of Control, he eventually did become and retired
as Governor of Madras, but with great odium attached
to his administration.

Upon Mr. Hollond's removal to Madras, he was suc- Mr. Grant.
ceeded by Mr. GRANT, who resigned his office in 1784,
as he did not consider that his instructions warranted
any remonstrance being made against the Nizam resuming
possession of the Guntoor Circar, which had lapsed to the

British Government by the death of Bazalut Jung, the Nizam's brother, in terms of the Treaty of 1778.

Between this period and the arrival of Lord Cornwallis in India, the name of Mr. JOHNSON occasionally appears as on deputation to the Nizam's court. Whether he was the Madras civilian who was removed from Sir Thomas Rumbold's council, or a Bengal civilian, there is no trace; his name is first seen in the month of February 1784. Mr. Johnson was required to press the durbar for the restitution of the Guntoor Circar, as well as to negotiate a settlement of the arrears of peshcush due to the British. "Mr. Johnson," writes an officer competent to offer an opinion, "was directed to assure the Nizam that nothing but the financial distresses of the Government, occasioned by the expenses of the late war, had caused the payment of the peshcush to fall so much in arrears; but that if peace with Tippoo remained uninterrupted, they hoped not only to make arrangements for its regular payment in future, but also to be able within two years to liquidate the heavy arrears due by them.

"During the negotiations arising out of this subject, a proposal was made by the Nizam to the Resident to the effect that the British Government should make over to him their right to the Circars acquired by the Treaty of 1768, on condition of receiving from him an acquittal in full for all arrears of tribute, and a present of money of one crore of rupees. This, together with the subsequent proposal for the surrender of the Carnatic to the Nizam, was strongly recommended by the Resident to the favourable notice of the Supreme Government, by whom it was referred for the consideration of the Court of Directors of the East India Company.

"The steps taken by Mr. Johnson in these negotiations were severely censured by the Court of Directors, as tending to raise expectations in the mind of the Nizam which could not be realised ; and it appears by a letter from the Court, under date the 25th September 1785, that the Government were directed to remove Mr. Johnson from his situation as Resident at Hyderabad."

In 1788 Lord Cornwallis appointed his aide-de-camp, Captain, afterwards Sir JOHN, KENNAWAY as his envoy to the Nizam's court. Captain Kennaway and his brother in the Bengal Civil Service had been brought to the notice of the Governor-General by the Marquis of Lansdowne. "The Kennaways," writes the Marquis, "are friends' friends, being recommended to me by Sir Robert Palk ; but I am glad to hear they have merit, which he assured me they had." Independent of Captain Kennaway becoming known to Earl Cornwallis under such favourable auspices, by the Earl's own showing his present preferment was owing to personal claims. "Captain Kennaway, one of my aides-de-camp," are the words of the Governor-General to the Secret Committee of the Court of Directors, "was at my recommendation appointed (by the Supreme Council) to the deputation (to the Nizam), as a gentleman well acquainted with the country languages and customs, and in whose ability and prudence I could place an entire confidence ;" and subsequently, "I believe Captain Kennaway to be well calculated for gaining the Nizam's good will and esteem, and, at the same time, to discover any intrigues that may be meditated. I propose to leave him some time longer at Hyderabad, to keep a watchful eye upon his Highness's conduct, and to endeavour by every means in his power to establish a confidential and friendly communication between the two governments."

Captain Kennaway left Calcutta for Hyderabad in the beginning of May 1788, but] "the rains and bad roads rendered his journey so unavoidably tedious and difficult that he did not arrive at his destination till the latter end of July." He was instructed to recover the Guntoor Circar and to settle about the arrears of peshcush due to the Nizam by the British Government. The Circar was quietly made over to the Government, but as there was some difficulty in adjusting other matters, Meer Allum was sent on behalf of the Nizam to Calcutta to meet the Governor-General.

In July 1790 Sir John Kennaway concluded, on behalf of his Government, a treaty of offensive and defensive alliance with the Nizam. "The principal provisions of this treaty were that the Nizam should co-operate to the utmost of his power with the English and Mahrattas to humble the power of Tippoo Sooltan; that he should furnish a contingent of 10,000 horse, to be paid by the British Government, and that with the exception of such forts and territories as might fall into the hands of the British Government previously to the appearance of the other parties in the field, the Nizam should receive a third share of all the benefits accruing from the war." This is known as the Tripartite Treaty, as the Mahrattas as well as the English and Nizam were parties to it, and included a mutual guarantee against Tippoo; the manner, however, in which this guarantee was to be realised was left by the treaty to be determined by subsequent regulation. "Shortly after the first Mysore war, Lord Cornwallis, who appears to have been most anxious to have this point properly defined, submitted to both durbars

the draft of a treaty passed upon the principle that
neither party were to assist the other till 'they were
convinced that the party requiring assistance had justice
on his side, and that all measures of conciliation had
proved fruitless.' After a lengthened negotiation the
project fell to the ground, the Mahrattas demanding, as
the price of their accession to the Governor-General's
views, an engagement on the part of their allies to assist them in realising their claims of *chout* on Tippoo's
dominions, while the Nizam wished to secure our interference in a dispute existing between him and that prince
in regard to the Nuwab of Kurnool."

In the war with Tippoo Sooltan in 1792, terminating in
a treaty of peace with that prince, to which the Nizam
was a party, by his minister, Azeem-ool-Oomrah, Sir John
Kennaway rendered such essential aid as to draw the
following paragraph from Lord Cornwallis in his despatch
to the Court of Directors, dated the 4th March, written
in his camp before Seringapatam:—" I have in many
instances derived great advantages from Sir John Kennaway's services in acting as a channel of intercourse
between me and Azeem-ool-Oomrah, but it has proved
peculiarly fortunate that his attendance upon the Minister
put it in my power, at this important juncture, to avail
myself, by naming him as my deputy, of his address and
conciliatory manners in conducting the negotiations to so
happy an issue; and it is very satisfactory to me that I
can equally depend upon the most able assistance from
him, both in obtaining from Tippoo the execution of the
preliminaries and in framing the articles of the definitive
treaty of peace."* Sir John Kennaway was obliged to

---

* Ross' *Cornwallis Correspondence*, ii. 532.

relinquish his appointment and to leave the country on account of ill health in 1793, having been Resident at the court of the Nizam for upwards of five years. He had joined the Bengal army in 1773. In the year 1778 he was appointed Adjutant to the Infantry of the Futtyghur Brigade; in 1781 Persian Secretary to the officer commanding the force sent from Bengal to the relief of the Carnatic; and in 1786 Aide-de-camp to Lord Cornwallis. For his military services under Sir Eyre Coote in the campaign between 1781 and 1784, against Hyder Alee and the French, Captain Kennaway had his name enrolled "for future marks of the esteem and favour of Government." For his civil services he was rewarded with a baronetcy on the 25th February, 1791, by the British Government, and a special annuity of 500*l.* per annum by the East India Company.[*]

Captain WILLIAM KIRKPATRICK, who succeeded Sir John Kennaway, had previously held a similar appointment at the Court of Scindia. Subsequently he was specially selected by Lord Cornwallis as envoy for the first British mission to Nepaul, and he was probably the first Englishman who visited that remote and still little-known court.[†] Of his previous antecedents it is merely necessary to say that he joined the Bengal army in 1773, and not long after was appointed Persian Interpreter

---

[*] Born March 6th, 1758; died January 1st, 1836. Married February 18th, 1797, Charlotte, daughter and co-heir of James Amyott, Esq., M.P.

[†] Various attempts had been made to open commercial intercourse with Nepaul, but they had all failed. At length a dispute having arisen between the Nepaulese and the Lama of Thibet, the latter, whose troops had been repulsed, called in the Chinese, who before long advanced to within a short distance of Katmandoo. The Nepaulese then invoked British military assistance, which Lord Cornwallis declined affording, but tendered his good offices to reconcile the two hostile powers. Before, however, any reply could be given, the Nepaulese made peace, not on favourable

to General Stibbert, the Commander-in-Chief of that
force.

In 1797 Major Kirkpatrick was obliged to leave
Hyderabad upon medical certificate for the Cape of Good
Hope, and while at Cape Town was noticed by Marquis
Wellesley (then Lord Mornington), on his way to India as
Governor-General. For the rest I will quote the testi-
mony borne by that illustrious nobleman in his letter to
the Right Hon. Henry Addington, President of the Board
of Control, under date the 15th January, 1802 :—

" Lieutenant-Colonel Kirkpatrick's skill in the Oriental
languages, his extensive acquaintance with the manners,
customs, and laws of India, are not equalled by any person whom I have met in this country. His perfect knowledge of all the native courts, of their policy, prejudices,
and interests, as well as of all the leading political characters among the inhabitants of India, is unrivalled in the
Company's civil or military service; and his integrity and
honour are as universally acknowledged and respected as
his eminent talents, extraordinary bearing, and political
experience.

" These qualifications recommended him to my particular confidence. He possessed no other recommendation or
introduction to my notice. I fortunately met him at the
Cape of Good Hope on my voyage to India, and I have no
hesitation in declaring that to him I am indebted for the

terms, with China. But the British
Envoy, Captain Kirkpatrick, was still
requested to visit Nayakote, where
the Raja was residing, from whence
he proceeded to Katmandoo, the
capital of the country. The mission
left Calcutta in September 1792,
but did not enter the Nepaul country
till January 1793. They returned
in the beginning of March, having
been received with great cordiality
by the Raja, his uncle the regent,
and all the authorities of the State,
but no immediate benefit arose from
this visit. — Ross' *Cornwallis Correspondence*, ii. 188.

seasonable information which enabled me to extinguish French influence in the Deccan, and to frustrate the vindictive projects of Tippoo Sooltan. He remained at the Cape for some months after my departure for India, and he arrived in India soon after I had concluded the first treaty with the Nizam in 1798. I immediately appointed him to the confidential office of Military Secretary, in which capacity he attended me to Fort St. George during the war with Tippoo Sooltan, and after the conquest of Mysore acted in the delicate and arduous situation of Commissioner at Seringapatam. Having in every great political transaction of my administration derived the utmost advantage from his experience and ability, after the settlement of Mysore, when the vast extension of the empire required a modification of the office of Secretary at Fort William, I appointed Lieutenant-Colonel Kirkpatrick to the political department, because I knew him to be not only better qualified for that office than any other man in India, but to be the only man in India from whom I could hope to receive any important assistance in a department to which so large a share of my particular attention had been devoted at every period of my life, and that I knew I could expect little additional information from any person whom I could place in the office excepting Lieutenant-Colonel Kirkpatrick. . . . . He held the office for a year, during which time many important political measures were accomplished. His health failing in Bengal, I appointed him Resident at Poona in the month of January 1801; he proceeded as far as Madras on his way to Poona, but finding his health still declining, he has been reduced to the necessity of embarking from Madras for Europe."

Major-General Kirkpatrick died many years after these

occurrences, and he bequeathed to his friend and predecessor in office at Hyderabad, Sir John Kennaway, his
valuable collection of Oriental works and manuscripts.
General Kirkpatrick is said to have been possessed of
great literary attainments, besides being a profound
Oriental linguist. He published an account of his visit
to Nepaul, but his more valuable work is a translation of
Tippoo's Letters. [*]

When the Resident proceeded on sick certificate to the
Cape of Good Hope, he left his office in charge of his
younger brother, Captain JAMES ACHILLES KIRKPATRICK.
He was Acting-Resident at Hyderabad when Lord Mornington arrived in India. The zeal, address, discretion,
and firmness evinced by Captain J. A. Kirkpatrick in
bringing to a successful issue the delicate negotiation of
disarming the Nizam's French force at Hyderabad occasioned the Governor-General, upon the resignation of
Colonel Kirkpatrick, to manifest his sense of Captain
Kirkpatrick's merits by appointing him Resident at the
court of the Nizam, and by conferring on him the peculiar distinction of *Honorary Aide-de-camp*—the first
person of the Indian army on whom this honour was bestowed. The Governor-General at the same time recommended Captain Kirkpatrick to his Majesty's ministers as
deserving of some mark of the Royal favour.

Achilles Kirkpatrick, as he is more frequently called,
was drafted from the Madras army, while his two immediate predecessors had belonged to that of Bengal. He
was more than eight years at the Hyderabad Durbar; but
that period is about the most eventful of our connection
with the Nizam. He negotiated the greatest number and

---

[*] Born 1754 and died August 22nd, 1812.

most important of the treaties between the English and Hyderabad Governments. He accomplished the disbanding of the French battalions in the Nizam's service. He was the last Resident who occupied in his diplomatic capacity the garden-house of a native nobleman, and the first who dwelt in that princely mansion which he induced the Nizam to erect for the British Ambassador at his court. He entered upon office when the Nizam's domains had felt the pressure of the Mahratta, when the Nizam was labouring under alarms from the Mysorean Sooltan, when the heir to the sovereignty had rebelled against the Nizam, and when the power and dominion of the Nizam were, as it were, at the very ebb,— and upon his death he left the Nizam with but the Peishwa as his only formidable opponent in the Peninsula. Spite of all these circumstances, sufficient of themselves not to prevent the name of Achilles Kirkpatrick being engraved in the scroll of history, there is a romantic tale by which he is better known in the neighbourhood of his fame. Achilles Kirkpatrick built the zenana on the Residency grounds known as the *Rung Mahal,* lying to the south of the west wing of the great building and immediately between the cemetery and the flower-garden. That he should have had a zenana at a time when it was no offence to morals or society to possess such an establishment, is nothing astonishing ; but it is the spice of romance connected with it, even when begums of Delhi and Lucknow chose to link their fortunes with Christian heroes. At the time the Residency was built, and even up to its occupation by Sir Charles Metcalfe, not a native house lay before it for miles around. It is true there was then the house of Mr. William Palmer, and a little below it that of Sir William Rumbold, now the property of the Church Missionary Society; and there was also a house somewhere about, close to the Residency, where Kirkpatrick was accustomed to pass his nights, which was occupied by his mistress, a native woman of low caste. To this house was frequently sent a young maiden, the grandchild of a Persian gentleman and the great-niece of Meer Allum, who, upon the pretext of the intense heat of the weather, took to sleeping at the doorway of the balcony where Kirkpatrick generally lay of a night during the particular hot season. It is needless to say what followed, but it has been urged, and was so put, as I shall presently show, to the Governor-General that this girl's seduction was a political plot connived at by her mother, a noted profligate and bawd, though the daughter of Akh-ool-Dowlah, a Persian employed by the Nizam as his agent to Lord Harris for the transaction of affairs with the British Government. This Akh-ool-Dowlah, be it mentioned, *en passant*, was a jolly character, being devoid of all table-prejudices, for he used to eat ham and call it English mutton. Kirkpatrick soon took a real liking to Khair-ool-Nissa, for such was the name of the damsel; and to throw decency over the connection, brought her to the Residency, built for her specially the *Rung Mahal*, and there made the usual public acknowledgment of marriage according to Mahommedan ritual, by allowing garlands to be bound about his brow.

Meanwhile Kirkpatrick's enemies were not idle. Judging from themselves, the natives of India believe that Englishmen are as readily influenced in public transactions, or rather permit interference in that way, by women, as in their case. Meer Allum, the Minister, made serious complaints to the Supreme Government of this unhappy connection, and represented its evil consequences both to Kirkpatrick himself and the government of which he was envoy. Meer Allum, it will be remembered, had visited Calcutta, and had closed negotiations most satisfactorily for his master, the Nizam, and in a manner to elicit the unqualified approbation of Lord Wellesley, the Governor-General, so that, it can easily be understood, any complaint coming from such a quarter would not be treated with indifference. Captain John Malcolm, now on the staff of the Governor-General, and erst Kirkpatrick's first assistant, was appointed to institute inquiry into the position of Khair-ool-Nissa, with a special commission in his pocket to supersede Kirkpatrick if everything did not turn out as correct as it should. Malcolm sailed down the Bay of Bengal to Masulipatam, where he found Captain Hemming, the commandant of the Resident's personal escort, awaiting his arrival, with explanatory notes from Kirkpatrick anticipating the inquiry ordered by Lord Wellesley, urging, too, that Malcolm's appearance at Hyderabad would tend to lower Kirkpatrick in the estimation of the public, particularly the natives. Malcolm knowing Kirkpatrick's character, and, as his *aide* only a short while before, not ignorant of the motives which prompted misrepresentation, expressed himself satisfied with the explanations furnished, and returned to Calcutta without proceeding on his journey at all from Masulipatam to Hyderabad.

In September 1805, Colonel Kirkpatrick, with the permission of Lord Cornwallis, proceeded to Calcutta by way of Masulipatam, partly for the benefit of his health, which was somewhat impaired by his long residence at Hyderabad, but chiefly for the purpose of conferring with his Lordship on the political affairs of that court. He reached Calcutta prostrated by a malady of which he died

on the 15th October.* The following order was immediately issued by the authorities of Fort William :—" The
Vice-President and Deputy-Governor with sincere regret
performs the painful duty of directing the last tribute of
military honours to be paid to the remains of that valuable officer and meritorious public character, Lieutenant-
Colonel J. A. Kirkpatrick, of the establishment of Fort
St. George, late Resident at the Court of the Soobehdar of
the Deccan, in which situation he rendered the most important service to the Honourable East India Company."

The following paragraph occurs in the despatch of
Mr. Henry Russell, the Acting-Resident at Hyderabad,
under date November 3rd, 1805, to Sir George Barlow,
Governor-General : — " The intimation of the decease of
Lieutenant-Colonel Kirkpatrick, the late Resident at Hyderabad, was received by his Highness the Soobehdar with
expressions of the most poignant grief, and diffused a
universal gloom over every individual at durbar. The
important public services and the eminent private virtues
of Lieutenant-Colonel Kirkpatrick, were always justly
appreciated at the Court of Hyderabad. He commanded
the confidence and attachment of those with whom he
was connected by the functions of his public office, and
the love and admiration of those who participated in the
happiness of his private friendship. I had long known
the respectability of his public character, and long esteemed the virtues of his mind ; and it was not without a
bitter pang that I directed the last tribute of respect to
be paid to the memory of a man whose loss can never
be sufficiently deplored." The reply from Mr. Edmonstone, Secretary to the Supreme Government, dated No-

* Born in August 1764; joined the Madras army in 1780.

vember 25th, is couched in these terms :—"The Governor-General has received with deep concern and regret the intelligence of the death of Lieutenant-Colonel Kirkpatrick, the late Resident at Hyderabad, whose eminent public services during the long period of time that he discharged the arduous and important functions of that high station, entitled him to the distinguished approbation of the British Government."

On the death of Colonel Achilles Kirkpatrick, Mr. Henry Russell, of the Bengal Civil Service, at the time Assistant, acted as Resident from October to December 1805, until relieved by Kirkpatrick's permanent successor.

Captain THOMAS SYDENHAM was the next Resident at the Nizam's court. Sydenham was one of three brothers who were all special favourites of the former Governor-General. Indeed, Benjamin, the eldest, was always on the staff of Lord Wellesley, and George, the youngest, was his brother Thomas's political agent at Aurungabad. Sydenham was previously Resident at the court of the Peishwa, where he had been preceded by Sir Barry Close, and was succeeded by Mr. Henry Russell.

Captain Sydenham was appointed Resident by Lord Cornwallis, as he had some time previously served as First Assistant to Colonel Achilles Kirkpatrick. There was between the chief and his subordinate, as there generally is between such parties, a difference of political opinion and adherence to different interests in the State, of which this only need be noticed, in the present instance, that while there was personal animosity between Achilles Kirkpatrick and Meer Allum, Sydenham had a high regard for the Meer; and again, while Kirkpatrick had procured a pension of 700 rupees a month for his moonshee, Azeezoola, from Government on the score of usefulness in promoting the treaties respectively of 1798 and 1800, Sydenham looked upon the man as corrupt, and his first act in taking charge of the Residency was to dismiss Azeezoola. Although Kirkpatrick's moonshee was dismissed by Sydenham, he pursued the system which prevailed of communicating with the Nizam's court through native agency, and a new set of men, not so respectable nor efficient as the former, took their places, till they in their turn were dismissed by Henry Russell, who succeeded Sydenham in the Residency, and brought in a new staff, the relations of Azeezoola, who were dismissed in a short time for corruption and political intrigue.

The three great acts of Sydenham's administration were —*first*, the supercession of the Nizam's authority to place it uncontrolled in the hands of Meer Allum. The assent of the Nizam was extorted from his timidity, and in conjunction with it; *secondly*, the dismissal of Raja Mohiput Ram from the city to his command on the frontiers, a position almost equal in power to that of the Minister. From thence again Raja Mohiput Ram was banished for corresponding with Holkar to Shahpoor in the Shorapoor district, by the co-operation of the English Government. He retired to the place of his exile with an army of picked men from his forces, above 3000 strong, principally of Arabs, Rohillas, Scindians, and Sikhs; he plundered the neighbouring Mahratta country and the zumeendaree of Shorapoor to maintain his military retainers, gave battle to the Nizam's troops which were sent out against him to put down these practices, and defeated them. He was expelled the Nizam's territory by English troops, and fled to Holkar, against whom having rebelled, or rather mutinied, for the recovery of his pay and arrears, he was attacked by Holkar's troops and was killed. Meer Allum died; and the *third*

CHAP. I.

Captain Sydenham.

great administrative act of Sydenham was assisting at the appointment of a new minister, in which he conducted himself with intemperance towards the Nizam. Sydenham desired that Shums-ool-Oomrah should be invested with the office, and the Nizam wished Mooneer-ool-Moolk; concession was made by the English Government to the Nizam's wishes, but the appointment of Mooneer-ool-Moolk was made nugatory of any evil which might have proceeded from it by his being bound down by a written engagement to take no part in the administration, but to be content in the enjoyment of a stipend of about six lakhs of rupees (60,000*l.*) per annum. The authority of the government was vested in Raja Chundoo Lall, under the designation of the Minister's Deputy.

The Nizam's objections to Shums-ool-Oomrah were that, in the first place, he was not a Sheeah in religion, nor a Syud by birth; secondly, that he was allied to Ferridoon Jah, his Highness's brother; and thirdly, that he was at the head of the Paigah party — an office that had always been maintained by the sovereign of the Deccan, as a counterpoise to the power of the Minister; and that the possession of that office was consequently ineligible to the premiership, as he would thereby engross the whole power of the State, civil and military.

To the first objection Sydenham replied that the selection of a minister should be regulated by political considerations alone, and could have no relation to the religious tenets of the different candidates. The second objection he endeavoured to repel by referring to the altered circumstances of the State, and the absence of all danger from his brother's rivalry, while his Highness's throne was sustained by the arms and resources of the British empire. To the third objection, Sydenham ob-

served that there was no longer any necessity to secure
the obedience of the officers of Government by employing
them as checks on each other, as it was now in the power
of the Nizam to keep them all in due subordination;
besides which, the British alliance, he remarked, had
wholly altered the relative condition of the Paigah chieftains. Formerly, the chief of the Paigahs was entrusted
with the care of his Highness's person, was foremost in
battle, and led his troops on all services of danger or
desperation. Now the case was changed; for the British
detachment, in fact, formed the Paigah party of the
Nizam's army, where that confidence was placed which
had formerly been reposed in the Paigah corps.

Sydenham resigned in consequence of a public censure
inflicted upon him for the part he took in the officers'
mutiny of 1809, disclosed by his letter to his friend
General Sir John Doveton, commanding the subsidiary
force then stationed at Jaulnah, who, on his trial, submitted to the court, as part of his defence, Sydenham's
letter. That letter inculcated that it was a wise policy
in a chief, when he could not control his forces, to
appear to take part with them, and gradually to wean
them back from their disaffection to their pristine loyalty.
Sydenham was hardly dealt with by the reprehension of
Lord Minto. He proposed to his Lordship the difficult
task of publicly cancelling his censure, as the only condition on which he would retain office. This his Lordship
would not do, though he pressed Sydenham strongly not
to resign. Sydenham was a high-minded man; and his
Lordship's private expressions of regard and confidence
were not considered satisfactory *amende* by him. He
quitted office, as well as the service; and while in England
was always at the elbow of Lord Wellesley.

Captain Sydenham was graceful in his person, and surpassingly so in his manners and address; in fact, there was an air of elegance about him not to be mistaken. He conversed easily with every person, without fearing any encroachment upon his dignity. He was a man of considerable abilities and extensive reading, possessing the accomplishments usual to well-educated gentlemen, and prominently the characteristics belonging to a high-minded English gentleman. He was incapable of being actuated by sinister motives, of double dealing, or of committing a mean action. His intercourse and his table were free of all form; he conversed to amuse and to give pleasure to his auditors — in short, he was as Resident, unlike other Residents, more the English gentleman than a functionary of the Indian Government. His wife, unmistakingly an elegant woman, was the widow of Captain Bunbury, brother to Sir Charles Bunbury, and had been maid of honour to the Duchess of York. Mrs. Sydenham died at Hyderabad, and it is to the mausoleum over her that I allude in the chapter treating upon the British Residency.

Captain Sydenham took up his appointment as Resident towards the last days of December 1805; and his stay at Hyderabad in that capacity occupied a period of four years and a half, when he made it over to Captain Charles Russell, of the Bengal army.

I cannot refrain, upon closing this biography, from quoting the testimony of Lord Wellesley's respect for the memory and services of the two brothers Sydenham — Benjamin and Thomas — written more than a quarter of a century after these proceedings. I am obliged, for the beauty of the passage, to quote it entire, as written in Major-General Sir Patrick Ross's copy of *The Marquis Wellesley's Despatches.*

"Hurlingham, April 4th, 1837.

"I trust that these volumes may be interesting to Sir Patrick Ross, for whom I entertain great respect and esteem, not only personal, but from recollection of his worthy father's, Major-General Ross's, services in India during the memorable war in Mysore; nor can I forget the same respectable officer's uniform and active support of my administration, of which an honourable testimony is recorded in the first of these volumes.

"Lady Ross also will take an interest in the recital of transactions in which I derived the greatest advantage from the affectionate attachment and zealous services of her excellent, amiable, and accomplished brothers.

"Captain Benjamin Sydenham was for years my most intimate, confidential, and faithful friend to the hour of his premature, and by me ever-lamented death. He was my principal reliance and support in all difficulties and dangers; and he is entitled to a large share of the merit of whatever success has attended me in public life. His loss was, and is to me, irreparable; nor can my affectionate regret for him be diminished while any power of memory shall remain. Of Captain Thomas Sydenham's talents, accomplishments, and integrity, I must ever retain the highest estimation, with the strongest gratitude for his continued friendship and assiduous services.

"To the remaining branches of a family so justly endeared to me, may these pages recall and confirm those sentiments which are warmly cherished in my heart.

"WELLESLEY." *

Captain Russell officiated as Resident from June 1810,

* Martin's *Wellesley Despatches*, iv. App. R. 678.

c 3

to March 1811, when his brother, Mr. HENRY RUSSELL, was appointed to the office.

From my narrative it will have been seen that Sir John Kennaway, the two Kirkpatricks, and Sydenham, were all military men, and of like rank when sent to the Court of Hyderabad. Mr., afterwards Sir Henry, Russell was the first of the Bengal civilians who were Residents at Hyderabad. With the exception of General Fraser, Mr. Russell was the longest in office,— more than nine years. He had, however, been assistant to both Colonel Achilles Kirkpatrick and Captain Sydenham, and, as already stated, held the ribbons for the brief interval of three months between the retirement of the one from, and the accession of the other to, office; to use his own words in the letter that he addressed the Court of Directors of the East India Company in 1824, he "was employed at Hyderabad from first to last for upwards of twenty years." Sydenham had retired from office with the declaration that he considered the disorders of the Nizam's government to be "too deeply rooted and too widely extended to admit of any remedy short of placing the administration of the country under the control of the Resident;" and years afterwards, when the discussion occurred at the East India House in connection with the dispute between Sir Charles Metcalfe and the house of Messrs. William Palmer and Company, consequent on the loans to the Nizam, and it was hinted that this evil originated with Mr. Russell, so as to provoke from him the letter already noticed, he writes: "I protest against being held in the most remote degree responsible for the disorders of a government with which not only I was not empowered to interfere, but with which I was prohibited from interfering. It was a fundamental rule of our policy, repeatedly insisted upon in the orders both of your Honourable Court and of your Government in India to abstain from all interference in the internal concerns of our native allies. I was employed at Hyderabad from first to last for upwards of twenty years, and I affirm that during the whole of that time no influence or interference was exercised by the Resident in the domestic affairs of the Nizam's government. In questions of foreign policy, in measures affecting the safety of the government, and generally in matters in which our own interests or the common interests of the alliance were involved, we always did and always must exercise that influence which essentially belongs to the relative condition of a protected and protecting state. But in the management of his country, the collection and distribution of his revenues, the control of his local officers, and the command, payment, and employment of his whole army, with the exception of that part to which English officers were attached, no influence whatever was exercised by the Resident; and the Nizam's government was as much an independent state as if the alliance with us had not existed." KAYE, in his *Life of Lord Metcalfe*, has so happily described Mr. Russell's career, that it leaves me no room to do otherwise than to quote the passage. "An abler man than Mr. Henry Russell has seldom gone out to India. He seems to have seen clearly, from the first, the wrongs under which the unhappy country was groaning. He declared, in one of his earliest despatches to Government, that it was 'in so lamentable a condition that it could not long continue to endure the extortions which were practised upon it by the avarice and rapacity of its governors.' He was, indeed, continually describing in language so vigorous and eloquent that it is a pleasure to read his despatches, the diseases which were entering into the State and making the whole one mass of corruption. But it may be doubted whether his talents were of the kind best suited to the work that lay before him. He said, years afterwards, that he did not make the disorders which had so long been destroying the Hyderabad State, but found them there ready-made—a heritage from his predecessor. He found them, and it is but right to say that he desired and endeavoured to remove them."

The chief charge against Mr. Russell is, that he allowed that portion of the local army to which English officers were attached to grow " into formidable dimensions." "At all events," says the biographer of Lord Metcalfe, " whilst Mr. Henry Russell occupied the Residency the contingent became, in all essential respects, a British force, paid in some manner or other, directly or indirectly, from the treasury of the Nizam." One brigade was baptized, in honour of the Resident, the *Russell Brigade*.

Be this as it may, Henry Russell was the most accomplished, if even charged with being the most parsimonious, of the Residents at Hyderabad. He was the son of the Chief Justice of the Supreme Court at Bengal by his second wife, sister of the last Earl Whitworth, and succeeded his father in the baronetcy in 1836. While Resident at Hyderabad he married Mademoiselle Mottet, the daughter of a French gentleman of Pondicherry.

In the month of April 1820, Mr. Russell had written to Sir Charles (then plain Mr.) Metcalfe, the Political Secretary to the Governor-General, " that he purposed to remain at Hyderabad until the commencement of the following year, and that he earnestly hoped his correspondent would be his successor." The two gentlemen were on terms of intimate friendship and familiarity.

They were connected, indeed, by marriage. Mr. Russell was a first cousin of Theophilus Metcalfe's wife.[*] The thought of handing over his office to such a man as Charles Metcalfe afforded him, both upon public and on private grounds, the liveliest satisfaction; and even when such a transfer seemed to be remote, he spoke in glowing terms of the situation. "I always thought," he said, "that you would regret the change from Delhi to Calcutta. It can hardly be long before you are placed in Council; but if this should be the case, and you should continue desirous of returning to your own line, I should be delighted to deliver this Residency into your hands. You will find an excellent house completely furnished, a beautiful country, one of the finest climates in India, and, when the business which now presses has been disposed of, abundance of leisure to follow your personal pursuits. My original intention was to go home at the end of this year, having made a sort of promise to my father to be with him by the time he is seventy, which he will be in August twelvemonth. These measures of reform will detain me; but by the end of next year matters will be so completely set a going in their new train, that I shall certainly go then." Metcalfe at this time, however, had set his mind upon the illusory kingship of Central India, with Malwa for his capital, that Sir John Malcolm had pictured to his fancy, rather than take up the position of Envoy to the Court of Hyderabad. He communicated an outline of the plan of the great Central Indian project to Mr. Russell, and was answered in the following terms, under date the 26th May, 1820.

[*] "My eldest brother, Theophilus John, was yesterday married to a charming young woman, Miss Hannah Russell" (March 2nd, 1804), niece of Sir Henry Russell, one of the judges of the Supreme Court of Calcutta.—Kaye's *Life of Lord Metcalfe*, i. 85.

"My dear Metcalfe, — The project mentioned in your letter of the 10th instant has made an alteration in my views, or rather, it has done away·the alteration I had before made in them, and restored them to what they originally were. Until lately my plan always was to go home at the end of this year; and nothing could have induced me to remain .longer but the wish of not only carrying the reform of the Nizam's affairs into complete effect, but also of placing it on so firm a footing as to prevent a clumsy successor from injuring the work, or a hostile or illiberal one from depriving me, after I am gone, of that share of credit to which I may be justly entitled. Now, everything that experience and local knowledge enable me to do better than another person, will have been done by the end of this year. The foundation has already been substantially laid. The Minister knows as distinctly as I do what is to be done, and by what means it must be accomplished. The reduction of establishments has been arranged and is in progress; our interference and the objects and effects of it are known and felt throughout the country; and by the end of the revenue year, in September, all the talookdars will have been chosen and appointed, and the necessary new engagements framed and executed between them and the Government. In short, the whole of the new system has been discussed and matured, and put in action. In the course of the year, therefore, my first wish will have been accomplished; and the second will be effectually secured if, at the end of it, I can deliver the Residency into such hands as yours. In point of magnitude, your situation in Malwa will certainly be superior to this Residency; but you may do as much real good and acquire as much real importance here, as you could do there.

The office now proposed for you will be made great by
adding many things together; at Hyderabad it will be
compact and considerable in itself, and will afford, for
several years to come, an ample field for the exertions of
a man of talent and benevolence. As to personal convenience, there can be no comparison. In Malwa you will
have no time to yourself, and you will either be wandering about the country, which is always irksome when
it is perpetual, or you will have to build and furnish a
house, at the expense of certainly not less than a lakh of
rupees, out of your private fortune. At Hyderabad,
after the first six months, when you have looked thoroughly into everything, you will find, compared with
what you have been accustomed to, little to give you
trouble; at least half of your time will be at your own
disposal; and you will step at once, without care or
expense, into a house completely furnished and provided
with every accommodation. Upon the point of honour,
surely you need give yourself no concern. Colonel
William Kirkpatrick was appointed from your present
office to the Residency at Poona; and even if there were
no precedent of that kind, you might be content to
measure with Sancho's rule, 'Wherever you sit will be
the head of the table.' You say yourself that you think
you should prefer Hyderabad to Malwa, if you had your
choice of the two at the same time. My principal fear,
therefore, is lest you should suppose that by coming into
this arrangement now, you would be consulting your
own inclinations in the smallest degree at my expense.
But a man may be trusted to judge for his own happiness. Be assured that there is quite as much of selfish-
ness in my proposal as you could possibly desire. No
galley slave ever laid down his oar with greater joy than

I shall feel at laying down this Residency, whenever I can do so with justice to myself and with a conviction that I leave the public interests in the hands of an able and upright successor. As it was, it was a sacrifice, and a great one too, for me to resolve on staying so long; and I know that if you succeed Malcolm this year, you will be engaging in plans and measures which will effectually prevent your coming to Hyderabad hereafter. If, therefore, you can be prevailed upon to think the arrangement agreeable to yourself, and do not foresee any serious obstacle in the way of its accomplishment, you can at once intimate to Lord Hastings my wish to retire, and propose to him to nominate you my successor. As I should like to leave Hyderabad in November, so as to be ready to embark at Madras or Bombay by the first ship that sails after Christmas, it is desirable that no time should be lost in doing whatever you may be resolved upon. My end would of course be defeated unless you were to secure the appointment for yourself at the same time that you announce my intention of vacating it. Indeed, I would not resign after all, if I found that any other person was intended for my place.

"Believe me ever, my dear Metcalfe, most sincerely yours,

"H. RUSSELL."

So Sir CHARLES METCALFE resolved to proceed to the court of the Nizam, and he submitted the proposed arrangement to the Government. The arrangement was at once sanctioned, and on the 10th November he embarked on board the "Hattrass" for Masulipatam, accompanied by Lieutenant Hugh Barnett, who was appointed his second assistant, and Mr. Richard Wells, of the Bengal

Civil Service, third assistant. The "Hattrass" cast anchor in Masulipatam roads on the 16th, and on the 18th of that very month of November Metcalfe and his party proceeded by dawk from Masulipatam to Hyderabad. There Metcalfe found Russell awaiting him. The next item of information must be taken from his own memoranda.

CHAP. I.

Sir Charles Metcalfe.

"Saturday, the. 25th, having been fixed upon for my presentation to the Nizam, the ministers, Mooneer-ool-Moolk and Raja Chundoo Lall, came to the Residency in the morning about ten o'clock, according to custom, to pay their compliments to me and invite me to wait on the Nizam. They remained some time at the Residency, and during their stay produced a note from the Nizam, of which the following is a near translation :—

"'Mooneer-ool-Moolk Bahadoor and Maharaja Chundoo Lall will go to-morrow to Saheeb Jung Bahadoor's (Mr. Russell's) residence. Let the pending negotiation regarding taking and giving between the above-mentioned Bahadoors be settled, in order that there may not be any injury after the departure of that gentleman. This matter is at the responsibility of the talookdars and Abbas Alla Khan.'

"If I were to explain this note myself, I should conceive it to allude to the pending unsettled negotiation regarding the partition treaty, and to be dictated by an apprehension that a new Resident might come forward with new demands, or might urge those already discussed and declined. It was, however, urged by the ministers as having a more general meaning, and as proceeding from a fear lest matters formerly settled should be ripped open for fresh discussion. Friendly assurances were given without hesitation on the point; but it was pointedly impressed on them that these assurances had no reference to the pending treaty, which, being avowedly unsettled, was fully open to discussion. The ministers took leave of us and went to the palace with their suite. They had been numerously and respectably attended. Not long after, Mr. Russell and myself, attended by the gentlemen of the Residency and others who wished to see the Nizam, proceeded to the palace, where, after being met in the usual manner by the ministers, we were received by the Nizam. He was, it is said, unusually affable and talkative, though he did not certainly talk much. To what this might be attributed—I mean his uncommon affability—I cannot pretend to say. After remaining with him about a quarter of an hour, we received our leave and came away. The gentlemen who were introduced presented *nuzzurs*, which struck me as an unusual practice, never having heard of such at any native court except the king's. The style of the durbar and the dresses of the court were plain; the palace itself not grand."

Metcalfe was not the man to shirk work, and he buckled on his harness at once, though " there were dinners and balls and suppers—race ordinaries and lotteries in which he was expected to take a part." He had at his elbow Mr. Sotheby, the first assistant to the Resident, and he had the benefit of Mr. Russell's counsel and assistance until that gentleman's departure for England. Metcalfe jotted in his journal not long after, " On Christmas-day gave a dinner, ball, and supper to the society of Hyderabad, Secunderabad, and Bolarum." Inferior to Russell in aptitude for writing a despatch, and devoid of the advocate's skill in representing a case, a more hard-working, patient, persevering, honourable representative than Charles

Metcalfe the British Government never had. But the
early training of Metcalfe ill-fitted him for the post he
now occupied. He had been the boy-political, as his
father was wont to call him, with Lord Lake, who
allowed him very much his own way, and his position
was not only an exceptional one with Lake's force, but it is
passing strange that it did not turn his head. Still a very
young man when employed on the mission to Runjeet
Singh, and concluding a treaty of offensive and defensive
alliance with the lion of the Punjaub, one can understand
his "consciousness of power" and his pretensions of
fitness for any office. Earlier than either of these incidents was his rupture with Colonel Collins, the Resident
at Nagpore, to whom he had been appointed assistant.
The envoy at the Court of Scindia was Metcalfe's father's
"old friend, Jack Collins," who would for that father have
put up with a good deal from the son; and though Mr.
Kaye endeavours to smooth apparent difficulties between
the Resident and his assistant, yet he says, "Collins stood
upon his position and he stood upon his age. He exacted
a deference which the youth was slow to concede; he
claimed a superiority which was not willingly acknowledged. The boy thought the man arrogant and domineering. The man thought the boy forward and pre-
sumptuous. . . . . Charles Metcalfe was doubtless fond
of arguing, and King Collins did not like being argued
with by a boy of seventeen. This, in a few plain words,
seems to have been the cause of their rupture." Some
estimate may be formed of Colonel Collins's character from
the following extract of a letter to Metcalfe written after
their misunderstanding :—"Pray let me hear from you
sometimes. Be assured that I shall ever feel warmly interested in your success in life, and consequently must

be desirous of knowing how you get on. Remember, also, I am your banker as well as your sincere friend."

It will therefore be seen that Metcalfe early acquired a sense of his own personal consequence, and this feeling engenders strong prejudice. He had been an amanuensis of Lord Wellesley, and had written from dictation instructions to every political representative in British India, and he had also held the political portfolio to suggest, to advise, and to direct. He laid the flattering unction to his soul that purer-minded diplomatist than himself never lived, and it was true in a certain sense — from the medium with which he regarded things ; but no man felt more keenly anything that came between the wind and his nobility. So when he came to Hyderabad, he came to act up to the part which necessarily belonged to his office — " as Resident at Hyderabad, he would be Resident indeed !" He intended great reforms : he attempted them, and in trivial instances realised them. But when he came to Hyderabad he found that there were others who were as great as he — that there were three Kings of Brentford. The history of the firm of Messrs. William Palmer and Company I have made the subject of a special chapter ; but it is here only I can properly mention that at the time when Metcalfe joined the Residency, Mr. William Palmer lived in what he called a " huggur-muggur " style : his table abounded with every luxury obtainable, and glittered with vessels of gold and silver — there were never less than thirty guests daily at his house. The splendour of that day seems fabulous to our generation, but the men who saw it refer to it with no ordinary pleasure to expose the humdrum, paltry trifles of the present day on which we pride ourselves. A little beyond Mr. Palmer's house was what was called Rumbold's Kotee, the residence of Sir

William and Lady Rumbold. The elegance and taste of
their dwelling, the fashion, and, more than this, the charm
of female society which prevailed there, could not otherwise than make it the rendezvous of Hyderabad.   Within
that circle, too, was Miss Ross Lewin, a young lady who had
been the belle of Calcutta, and who, it was reported, had refused the hand and fortune of Mr. John Adam, the councillor
of Calcutta and bosom friend of Metcalfe.   If the parties
at the Residency were thinned to hear music and the song,
or to take part in the conversation in which the ladies at
Rumbold Kotee excelled, is it at all surprising they should
have preferred agreeable amusement to the stately, perhaps supercilious notice and official conversation of the
Resident?   Metcalfe was essentially proud, and his pride
could not brook this preference — worse still, this preference played upon his nervous system so as to partake of
the character of a disease.   The partners in the house of
William Palmer and Company—Mr. William Palmer and
Sir William Rumbold—proceeded on a visit to the Nizam's
minister, and crowds recognised their palkees and saluted
them; they were not only familiarly known to them, but
their masters were in the books of the firm, and they
salaamed as their masters would have done and would
have wished their servants to do.   The Minister alone had
to deal with the Resident: what wonder, then, if in the
Resident's progress through the city only an occasional
hand salaamed to him?   If ever any feeling possessed a
man, it was that of mortified pride which beset Metcalfe;
hence his second assistant Barnett's remark to one of
Palmer's house, that the people at the Residency were
nobodies.   Hence one can easily understand his bile, his
bitterness, his malignity at the house of Messrs. William
Palmer and Company, " the plunderers of the Nizam;"

hence, we presume, the following letter to John Palmer, the brother of William — one of his oldest friends : — " I rejoice that your health has been perfectly recruited by your late trip.   Mine is very good, and I am as happy as any man can reasonably expect to be; I should be perfectly so were it not for one thing : but you are the last person whom I ought to trouble on this subject, for unconsciously you helped to create the mischief which I deplore.   Habits, however, of old confidence will prevail. I allude to the plunder of the Nizam by William Palmer and Company, in league with an unprincipled minister.   I do not object to merchants making good bargains for themselves.   But when the resources of the State are sacrificed by a profligate servant, without any regard to the interests of his master, as the purchase of the support of the Governor-General through the influence of an individual, it is bribery in the most horrible degree, and the misery of it will be long felt by this suffering country. Had I known what I now see before I quitted Calcutta, nothing should have induced me to come here.   Being here, I must do my duty, and make myself as cheerful as I can be in a very disagreeable predicament."   Such was the eloquence of a distorted brain ; had he seen that in transferring the debt of William Palmer and Company to the British Government he was not only shifting the burden, but the sins imputed to William Palmer and Company to that government, he would have been startled — he not only shifted existing sins, but made that government usurious, unrelenting creditors !   Sir Charles Metcalfe's biographer has made an elaborate effort to vindicate the reputation of his hero from much of the abuse that was showered upon him while living in connection with his Hyderabad administration, some of which must, however, attach to his name so long as it is coupled with that of Messrs. William Palmer and Company. At this lapse of time, when facts and circumstances can be coolly reviewed, the unbiassed mind will give that great mercantile house credit for more ingenuity and discernment than has ever been allowed it, and will forgive Sir Charles Metcalfe many deplorable errors which he perpetrated, impressed with a sense of his official purity of character and his lofty pretensions of his position; neither he nor his friends will attempt to justify that grievous mistake by which he made his Government take the place of William Palmer and Company.

Metcalfe left Hyderabad early in August 1825, for Calcutta, on his way to Delhi, where he had been appointed Resident by Lord Amherst, the Governor-General. He then became a member of the Supreme Council, and retired from India after having for a season officiated as Governor-General, and for a time reigned as Lieutenant-Governor of the North-West Provinces. On his return to England he was selected by the ministers of the Crown for the appointment of Governor of Jamaica, and his successful administration led to his being made Governor-General of Canada. He was raised to the peerage as Baron Metcalfe, of Fern Hill, in the county of Berks, and he survived his honours long enough to return to England, and to be buried in the family vault of the Metcalfes, in the parish church of Winkfield, near Fern Hill. On the marble tablet in that church occurs the following passage in that inscription, penned by Lord Macaulay to the memory of Charles Theophilus, first and last Lord Metcalfe: — " A statesman tried in many high posts and difficult conjunctures, and found equal to all." *

* Born at Calcutta January 30th, 1785; died September 5th, 1846.

D 2

CHAP. II.

CHAP.
II.

Mr. Mar-
tin.

Mr. WILLIAM BYAM MARTIN, of the Bengal Civil Service, succeeded Sir Charles Metcalfe as Resident of Hyderabad. Civil servants had now superseded military men as politicals at the courts of the "Country Powers," as independent native governments were then called; all the fighting work had been done, and it was only writing that had to be performed; any plea or pretence would serve to justify the nomination to lucrative offices of men who seemed destined to enjoy the loaves and fishes. So early as 1802 the Court of Directors had taken objection to Lord Wellesley's nomination of Colonel William Kirkpatrick as Political Secretary to the Supreme Government, on the ground that his military commission disqualified him for a civil office, according to the spirit of the Act of Parliament; though Lord Wellesley showed in his reply that "established practice warranted the appointment of military officers to diplomatic situations, and on extraordinary occasions (such as the settlement of recent conquests or cessions) to various other important civil stations." Lord Wellesley took grave offence at this expression of the

Court of Directors, but the principle of excluding military officers from civil appointments ever after took effect.

Mr. Martin was appointed to the Residency by Lord Amherst, and joined in September 1825. He came from either the Suddur Dewanee Udhalut, or the Board of Revenue at Calcutta; but the most remarkable circumstance in his previous career was that he had been one of the assistants to Mr. Parr, the Resident at Amboyna, when that gentleman was murdered in his bed by Malays, and when also his wife was rescued from a similar fate by the other assistant, Mr. Charles Murray. I must also mention another important fact, very honourable to him, that Mr. Martin was one of the first and most distinguished of all the students, even with Sir Charles Metcalfe, in that college of Fort William founded by the wisdom and foresight of Lord Wellesley.

The officials of the Residency, excepting Captain Barnett, gave Mr. Martin a high character, eked out by the mention of his great abilities and the important situations he had held; but in private circles, though he was not denied these advantages, he was not much esteemed. The dislike of Barnett will be understood, when I mention that Martin was averse to him as one of Metcalfe's offshoots, and in consequence to him was loud in condemning Metcalfe and his writings. Martin laughed at Metcalfe's expression in reference to William Palmer and Company, "that the atmosphere was affected with their corruption." Barnett's communication to Metcalfe only led to an unprofitable correspondence between the latter and Martin. Martin broadly ridiculed other passages in Metcalfe's Hyderabad writings, but particularly the allusion to the connection with Henry Russell "being hallowed by recent affliction." The opposition policy which seems to mark succeeding Residents was never so obvious as in this particular instance.

Sir Charles Metealfe had substituted English agency for the moonshee communication with the Durbar; and though Mr. Martin had come to Hyderabad without his moonshee, to whom he was known to be partial, his assistants, Messrs. Ravenshaw and Colvin, were known to be able men. Mr. Martin, however, transacted business without their assistance, and reverted to the system which obtained in the days preceding Metcalfe, of giving an entire support — conformable to the directions of his Government — to Raja Chundoo Lall, which was considered right. The moonshee soon made his appearance, and his influence was unbounded with his master, as every manner of confidence was reposed in the man. In the first instance, the keys of the treasury were taken from Captain Barnett, the first assistant, to his evident mortification, and given to the moonshee; and then he was employed in Mr. Martin's multifarious communications with Raja Chundoo Lall and Mooneer-ool-Moolk.

Of this moonshee I may now say that — it is a self-evident proposition — like all other natives, he was corrupt; but, unlike all other natives, he was so openly and defyingly. The whole of Mr. Martin's staff detested him, and the feeling towards Mr. Martin was not very different. They had heard and knew the moonshee to be corrupt; they had no proofs to bring him forward, and they did not dare to seek for the proofs which would have enabled them to do so. The moonshee received bribes from Raja Chundoo Lall and his rival Mooneer-ool-Moolk; and he disgusted Chundoo Lall by the support he acquired at times from Mr. Martin for the objects of Mooneer-ool-Moolk, though opposed to the views of Raja Chundoo Lall.

At this time, Mooneer-ool-Moolk was being sued in the
courts of Hyderabad by the trustees of William Palmer
and Company; and to defeat this suit he offered the
moonshee a bribe of a lakh and a half of rupees, and of
this sum 50,000 rupees were paid on the instant as earnest
money. Meanwhile, Raja Chundoo Lall, dissatisfied with
the moonshee's connection with Mooneer-ool-Moolk, kept
advising the trustees of William Palmer and Company
of his corrupt proceedings against them — among other
facts mentioning the receipt by the moonshee of the
50,000 rupees, but refusing to give any proofs or any
clue to lead to them. The trustees of William Palmer and
Company charged the moonshee with corruption; and a
commission, consisting of Mr. Ravenshaw, Mr. Colvin, and
Captain Stokes, was appointed to try the case. The
charge was proved, and the moonshee dismissed. A
good deal of curious matter was revealed during the
trial. The trustees of William Palmer and Company
asked that the moonshee should be suspended from office
pending the trial, and that Mr. Martin should not lead to
a notion of his influence by seeing him, as he did daily,
which obstructed their procuring necessary evidence. It
appeared by evidence on the trial, that Mr. Martin after
this saw his moonshee every night before going to bed.
Two questions were put by the commission to Mr.
Martin: 1st, whether he had assisted to borrow a large
sum of money for Shahyar-ool-Moolk, giving some sort
of guarantee to the transaction by affixing his seal and
signature to the bond; and 2nd, whether he had at the
same time given his seal and signature to an engagement
formed anew by Shahyar-ool-Moolk to pay an old debt
due to the estate of Umeen-ool-Moolk, to which his brother, Mooneer-ool-Moolk, administered. To the first

question Mr. Martin answered in the affirmative, alleging
that his Government had enjoined the Residents to give
their support to the family of the Minister, Aristo Jah,
of which Shahyar-ool-Moolk was a member. (*Query.*—
Was the sort of support given by Mr. Martin to Shahyar-
ool-Moolk in the line of his instructions?) In regard to
the other question, Mr. Martin had no recollection. But
the wukeel of Mooneer-ool-Moolk, giving his evidence to
show that Mooneer-ool-Moolk was not frittering away the
estate of Umeen-ool-Moolk, contrary to the injunctions
which the trustees had procured Mr. Martin to give
Mooneer-ool-Moolk, produced uncalled for the bond of
Shahyar-ool-Moolk, to show that the money had not been
frittered away, inasmuch as payment had been guaranteed
by the signature and seal of Mr. Martin. On the second
reference to him on this subject, Mr. Martin said he could
not account for his conduct, but supposed that he had
acted under the requisition of the Minister, Raja Chundoo
Lall. There was contradiction throughout in Mr. Martin's conduct; but it may be understood, if one believes
that he acted almost invariably under the influence of his
moonshee. Mr. Martin borrows money for the accommodation of Shahyar-ool-Moolk. He guarantees payment
of an old debt of Shahyar-ool-Moolk to the estate of
Umeen-ool-Moolk, which he had resisted for years. This
was certainly not for Shahyar-ool-Moolk's accommodation? Important as this circumstance was, Mr. Martin
had forgotten it, and referred to Raja Chundoo Lall to
refresh his memory. Chundoo Lall's reply gave the character indelibly to the transaction; his answer is vague
and unintelligible, and written in bad and ungrammatical
Persian. Mr. Martin directed the commission to try the
case and give no opinion. This was overruled by Lord

William Bentinck, who expressed himself dissatisfied — I cannot say whether he did so officially — by the want of fairness evinced by this circumstance.

One charge of the trustees of William Palmer and Company was that the moonshee had acquired enormous wealth. The books of Mohunund Ram and Poorun Mull were called for, through whom payments were made, I must continue to say, to the moonshee. This, the wily minister saw, would expose his corrupt transactions at the Residency; and he sent word to the trustees that on condition of their not calling for the books of Mohunund Ram and Poorun Mull, he would put direct proofs of the corruption of the moonshee in their hands; Chundoo Lall did so, and the books were not called for. Shurf-ood-Deen Khan, his agent at the Residency, having remonstrated with Chundoo Lall for not giving a more strenuous support to the moonshee, was answered very impatiently, " I cannot degrade and ruin this Government for the protection of a moonshee." The moonshee was dismissed, and Mr. Martin transferred, in disapprobation of his conduct (vide *Mandamus Papers*) to Delhi. He requested his government to be allowed to retain the Residency till the rains were over — a short period of two months : this was refused him, — strong testimony to evince how very much his conduct was disapproved.

On the death of Mooneer-ool-Moolk, his son, Suraj-ool-Moolk, conveyed to one of the trustees the documents in his father's handwriting, in which one entry was made of 50,000 rupees having been paid to the moonshee by two payments of 25,000 rupees each, and the purpose for which it was made was stated, viz., to defeat the claims of William Palmer and Company. Mr. Martin had aspersed their trustees for the part they had taken in the

prosecution of the moonshee, and Major Oliphant, Military
Secretary to the Resident, as well as one of the trustees, to
vindicate himself and colleagues, sent the document to Lord
William Bentinck, to show the extent of the injury they
had sustained by the conduct of the moonshee. Lord
William Bentinck forwarded the paper for verification to
Colonel Stewart, who procured in regard to it the attesta-
tion of Suraj-ool-Moolk, Raja Chundoo Lall, of Shurf-ood-
Deen Khan who had paid the one sum of 25,000 rupees,
and of the soucar who paid the other sum.

Mr. Martin stayed but a short time at Delhi, where he
was said to roll in wealth, and then went home. Much
about the period of the occurrences I have just noticed,
he was appointed by the Home authorities a member of
the Council of the Supreme Government, and had taken
his passage to India. This intimation was rapidly followed by another that he had relinquished his purpose of
coming out, in consequence of an aunt having assigned to
him an allowance of 5000*l.* a year.

A circumstance had occurred, previously to the matters I have related, deserving of notice. Lord William
Bentinck had enjoined Mr. Martin not to employ his
moonshee in his communications with the Nizam's
government, but an English officer of his staff, which in-
junction had, to appearance, been obeyed without producing any diminution of the moonshee's influence at the
Nizam's court. The then Nizam being on his death-bed,
several moonshees of the Residency busied themselves
in preparing an account of the geniture of some of the
princes, as if to balance their claims to the throne. This
was done though there could not be, and there was not,
any question raised by the public to the validity of Naseer-
ood-Dowlah's right to the succession. The intrigue, either

got up by Raja Chundoo Lall or by the moonshee, with
or without the participation of Mr. Martin, was too shal-
low to escape detection of the motive. It was intended
by alarming Naseer-ood-Dowlah to make the most out
of him, and accordingly, on the death of Secunder Jah,
the moonshee, in breach of the orders of his Government, was sent by Mr. Martin to the palace. Rumour
says he brought away from it a lakh of rupees,—of course
in gold; others, more competent to offer an opinion,
besides myself, disbelieve this rumour. The manner of
presenting this money was gauche, and the sum too
small.

The Mandamus Papers express in strong terms Lord
William Bentinck's opinion of Mr. Martin's conduct. His
Lordship attributes to him a want of judgment, and
declared that his despatches, which could not be surpassed
as specimens of scholastic writing, were in every other
respect entirely unsatisfactory. I refer to the Mandamus
Papers as pithy, though I consider them not to be expressions of all that Lord William Bentinck thought and
felt towards Mr. Martin.

Mr. Martin is said to have been mean-looking in appearance; his manners were gentlemanly, not after the
fashion of gentlemen in England, but of the form which
prevails in India—there was something of a mannerism.
Of his principles nothing can be said. He was distrusted
by every man on his staff, who lived on barely civil terms
with him. Amongst them must not be included Captain
Byam, of the Madras Artillery, who originally was in the
Hyderabad Contingent, but was removed to the staff of
Martin in some nondescript capacity of third or other
assistant not well known. Captain Byam was a man of
high principles and honour, and from what I have already

stated, it will be easily understood that he regarded Mr. Martin with gratitude and attachment. Major Moore, the Military Secretary, kept well with Mr. Martin, which is significant of nothing,—he would have kept well with any Resident.

It will not be a bad summing up of Mr. Martin's diplomacy to say that that which was at first considered to be support of Raja Chundoo Lall by him was afterwards found to be subserviency to Chundoo Lall's views.

Mr. Martin left Hyderabad in August 1830, before his successor could join the Residency, and during the interval, Mr. Ravenshaw, of the Bengal Civil Service, his first assistant, officiated as Resident.

Colonel JOSIAH STEWART, of the Madras army, was nominated by Lord William Bentinck to the Residency, and took up his appointment in November 1830. He was one of Sir John Malcolm's numerous protégés, and had accompanied Sir John in his second embassy to the Court of Persia. In 1817 Stewart was an assistant to Malcolm when they entered Central India. He was then employed at Bhopal, for two years acted as Resident at Gwalior, and subsequently became Political Agent at Jeypoor.

Colonel Stewart, while at Hyderabad, was called upon to transact many affairs of importance, and in all he acted soberly and quietly. He was submissively obedient to his Government, and I cannot trace his having taken the initiative in any diplomatic measure,—indeed, he seemed fearful of undertaking responsibility; hence an apparent want of energy, and the occasion of the common expression of his time that, " there was a Resident at Hyderabad but the Residency had gone to sleep."

Colonel Stewart did not hesitate to declare that he was

appointed to Hyderabad to see justice done to the firm of
William Palmer and Company. Unquestionably he did
no injustice; but as Sir Charles Metcalfe was in the Council
of India, no influence was used by Stewart to procure that
firm either right or justice but in obedience to the strict
letter of his orders, and those orders were framed in such
a cold-water spirit that little could be expected to come
out of them, and but little was obtained.

Colonel Stewart supported Chundoo Lall's administration, from a conviction that there was no man in the
country better fitted for the post of Premier; but it was
impossible that a partiality for that minister personally
should not have been engendered by their intercourse.
The very worst thing said of Colonel Stewart in respect of
this partiality is, that a swindle of Chundoo Lall's having
been brought with some warmth and reprobation to his notice, instead of feeling disgusted at the trick, he expressed
himself amused at the cleverness with which it was performed. Is it possible that this amusement might not
have been occasioned by the manner in which the communication was made to him?

Colonel Stewart was directed to tell Naseer-ood-Dowlah,
the Nizam, that, unlike his father, he was left free to act
in his own affairs; the context being that he might as he
pleased retain or dismiss Raja Chundoo Lall. Naseer-ood-
Dowlah had no objection to the Raja; on the contrary,
considered himself indebted to the Minister for his quiet
succession to his rightful patrimony. Raja Chundoo Lall's
administration was complained of at the same time, and
the Nizam further informed, that if the Minister did
not ameliorate the condition of the country in two years,
the British Government would recommend his dismissal. The Nizam, faithful to his benefactor, retained Raja

Chundoo Lall in office; and though upon the expiry of the two years the British Government recommended the dismissal of the Minister, the recommendation was not accepted by the Nizam.

Colonel Stewart, though a man of ordinary manners, and possessed of the common cast of countenance, was pleasing-looking—the expression inviting confidence. His mind was not comprehensive nor his information above mediocrity, but there was a soundness in his reasoning, and a plain honesty in his manners calculated to satisfy those who heard him. Imputations were made against him by some of the Indian newspapers for jobbery perpetrated in certain appointments in the contingent, but Colonel Stewart was undoubtedly a man of strict probity. Some estimate may be formed of his character and administration from the remark made to me of his time by one competent to form and offer an opinion:—"The Residency was a quiet stream, passing between its banks without any observation; if it did not overflow to give fertility to the adjacent soil, there was at the same time no fear of a devastating inundation."

Colonel Stewart was a Persian linguist, and had translated the *Memoirs of Jehanghir*, the Mogul Emperor. He lost his right arm in the Persian Gulf, and with the left not only shot snipe with facility, but conducted the whole of his lengthy and heavy correspondence.

Colonel Stewart retired in January 1838. The first assistant, Major Cameron, of the Bengal army, officiated as Resident until his death, which occurred in the month of May of that year. In the interval between Major Cameron's death and General Fraser's arrival at Hyderabad, Brigadier Tomkyns of the Bengal army, who was attached to the local force, was appointed by Lord Auckland, then Governor-General, to act as Resident.

Major-General JAMES STUART FRASER, of the Madras army*, assumed charge of the Residency in September 1838. General Fraser was promoted by Lord Auckland from the Residency at Travancore to that of Hyderabad. He had commenced his public career by serving on the personal staff of Colonel Keating, upon the capture of Mauritius, otherwise known as the Isle of France; and was successively Private Secretary to Sir George Barlow, Governor of Madras; Deputy-Secretary to Government in the Military Department; Town-Major of Fort St. George; Commandant of Pondicherry; Agent for the Settlement of the Affairs of the Netherlands Government; Special Agent for Foreign Affairs; Special Political Agent with the Force employed against Coorg; Secretary to Government in the Military Department; and Resident successively at Mysore and Travancore.

General Fraser continued in office until January 1853, when he was bullied out of it by Lord Dalhousie. He was an upright and independent statesman, and would not lend himself to any unscrupulous act for the smile or frown of the Governor-General. Lord Dalhousie wanted General Fraser to take the initiative in respect of the basis of the Treaty of 1853, by which all sorts of cessions of country and payments of unliquidated balances of account could be brought about. General Fraser asked for distinct instructions; it did not suit the policy of the Governor-General to be distinct in that way. Truth to tell, the Resident was left to exercise his judgment by

* Appointed in 1790.

anticipating the wishes of the Governor-General, and an honest man found this course next to impracticable. But there have been few bolder or abler men, who, similarly circumstanced, have been able to hit the nail on the head so well as General Fraser did. General Fraser may have been careless or indifferent in the employment of facts, but he was right beyond dispute, not only in the principles he laid down for himself but in the application of them; added to these, he possessed unquestioned ability in the use of his pen. At a dinner party given at the Residency, he had made some remark that "for the use he had been for the fourteen years he was at the Residency, he need not have been sent there at all." The remark appeared in one of the Madras newspapers a few days after it fell from his lips; and General Fraser was not the man to deny the thing that was true, when called upon to say whether the assertion had been correctly reported. So when evil days came upon him, as his friends believed (and such evil days happen to be the political capital of some men and the proudest heritage to their family), General Fraser did not palter with his sense of honour or duty; he wished to know clearly whether the Nizam was to be asked to have his possessions coloured red, a policy which his conscience smote him as being not correct, but which was notoriously the policy of the Governor-General of that day. What mattered it, then, to Lord Dalhousie what he said to General Fraser? He accused him "of ambitious greed," which the General might fairly have retorted upon his Lordship; but, like another hero, General Fraser felt that "all was lost save honour," and accordingly resigned in January 1853. General Fraser carried out great reforms while Resident at Hyderabad, not the least of which was the remodelling of the Contingent Force, together with

the abolition of the designation hitherto used, the Nizam's
Army.

It was not difficult for an unyielding temper like that of
Lord Dalhousie to find out the pliant instrument for his
purposes, and for the nonce he selected Colonel; now
Major-General, JOHN LOW, C.B., then the representative
of the British Government at the Court of Scindia.
Colonel Low was the most obedient of all functionaries ;
he knew but the will of his masters ; and to the general
public his name had been long familiar as a political hack.
He came to Hyderabad in the month of March 1853,
and left in the month of September following to take
his seat as a member of the Supreme Council of India.
Within that short period of six months he had got the
Nizam to ratify the most odious treaty the British ever
concluded with that prince, which our pride should never
have thought of proposing, and for himself the highest
office that had been attained by an officer of the army to
which he belonged. Colonel Low landed at Madras in
July 1805, and commenced his career as aide-de-camp to
Sir John Malcolm in the campaign in Central India, to
whom he was afterwards an assistant in the Political Department. He held for many years the appointment of
commissioner with the ex-Peishwa Bajee Rao at Bithoor,
who adopted the Nana Sahib of Cawnpore infamy.

In December 1853, Mr. GEORGE ALEXANDER BUSHBY, of
the Bengal Civil Service, entered upon his charge as Resident to the Court of the Nizam. He had gone through
a long, an useful and honourable career, and for years
occupied the high post of Secretary to the Government of
India. He had been in 1822–23 at Hyderabad as first
assistant when Sir Charles Metcalfe was Resident. He
now came to sit in his master's chair. Prior to this he had

held the appointment of Governor-General's Agent in the Saugor and Nerbudda territories, with Gwalior, Jhansi, and Bundlecund under him. Lord Dalhousie just then had determined to place all Central India under one political officer, so when Hyderabad became vacant by General Low getting into the Council of India, Mr. Bushby was sent there, and his appointment doubled up and put under Sir Robert Hamilton. Just three years after Mr. Bushby became Resident at the Nizam's court, he sank under the conjoint influences of climate, age, and the long delay in attempting that change so materially necessary to a European constitution. In December 1856, the mortal remains of Mr. Bushby were interred in the Residency cemetery: a block of white marble marks the site. The small church of Bolarum — the prettiest in all India for its external appearance and its interior arrangements — contains a slab to Bushby's memory, erected by his admiring friends.

His successor was at the time Resident at Baroda in Goozerat, at the court of his Highness the Guicowar, from which he was summoned to take up the appointment where he had officiated in the interval between General Low's departure and Mr. Bushby's arrival.

Colonel CUTHBERT DAVIDSON, C.B., landed at Calcutta as a military cadet in 1826, and was posted to the 66th Regiment Bengal Native Infantry—since Ghoorkas—in which he rose. He was aide-de-camp to Lord William Bentinck, Governor-General of India; subsequently served on the staff of his brother-in-law, the right honourable Sir Robert Grant, G.C.H., Governor of Bombay, and was then attached to the Hyderabad Cavalry Contingent, a regiment of which he afterwards commanded. He was temporarily attached to the Residency of Hyderabad in 1846, and permanently in 1848. He had been appointed Resident at Baroda on the death of Colonel Duncan A. Malcolm — an appointment that he did not hold for quite three years, when he was called back to the scene of many years' employment and to the highest seat that a functionary could hold at Hyderabad.

No Resident, however, has had to deal with such evil times as seem to have overtaken Colonel Davidson. Not six months after taking office he had to put the Residency in a stage of siege, and though one of the kindest-hearted men, yet he has been marked for assassination. The attack on the Residency has been dealt with separately as a general rise on the Government; I have now to recount the particulars where the attempt was to injure an individual. As rebellion was being suppressed throughout India, Lord Canning had felt that some system of policy should be pursued, if not more conciliating than that hitherto pursued, at least having some regard to the feelings and prejudices of our native allies. His Lordship thereupon placed himself in communication with his various political representatives, offering suggestions and inviting observations thereon. The Nizam's was a particular case, and Colonel Davidson preferred a personal interview to ascertain the views and wishes of the Governor-General; so, with his Lordship's approval, the Resident proceeded to Calcutta by way of Masulipatam. Colonel Davidson returned to Hyderabad from his official visit of six weeks late on the evening of the 8th March, 1859. The following morning it was arranged that he was to be at the Nizam's durbar on Tuesday, the 15th of that month, to present a *chureetah* from the Governor-General. Colonel Davidson arrived at the court at the usual hour of eleven o'clock, and the interview with the Nizam seemed to him to be a most pleasing one, considering that his Highness was still suffering from the effects of an attack of severe illness: the Resident had the further duty to give the Nizam a general assurance that the British Viceroy would not forget recent services.

Upon the Resident gaining the courtyard, after walking out of the durbar room arm-in-arm with Salar Jung, the Minister, and attended by their respective suites, one Jehangeer Khan, a Rohilcund Patan; discharged the contents of a carbine loaded with slugs at Colonel Davidson, which fortunately missed him, and then the fellow advanced upon the Colonel with a drawn sword. The firing and advancing were the work of a moment, but, like a flash of lightning, the next moment swords flew from their scabbards; Captain Hastings Fraser, the second assistant to the Resident, with naked sabre, passed in front of his chief to shield him from any further murderous intent, and that gallant deed was responded by the followers of the Minister, who at once fell upon the miscreant and cut him to the ground. Two of the slugs, after passing Colonel Davidson, hit the right thigh of one of the dewan's retinue, who had been walking immediately behind Colonel Briggs, the military secretary: the injury was instantly attended to by Dr. Smith, the Residency surgeon. Meanwhile the noise attending the scuffle, and the unusual uproar of the great crowd which collects on these diplomatic occasions, alarmed the Nizam, who returned to his reception room, into which the Resident had been drawn from the crowd. The Nizam expressed great solicitude for Colonel Davidson; his concern was manifest not only in his face, but by the orders he issued without the intervention of official of any kind. He sum-

moned his body-guard, and required the prompt incarcera-
tion of the associates of the villain whose life had paid
for the audacity of his offence. In the course of an hour
Colonel Davidson was induced to return to the Residency
upon the entreaties of the Nizam, escorted by his Highness's
household troops, and accompanied by two members of
the family of Shums-ool-Oomrah, as hostages for the safe
conduct of Colonel Davidson and his suite. So they quitted
the durbar; but the entire way that they passed through
the city, every available patch of ground, whether inside
or outside, or on the top of a house, upon which a human
being could stand and see the passing procession, was
occupied; and willing as the most benevolently-disposed
may be to believe that this immense mass of humanity
was influenced partly by curiosity and partly by sympathy
for the intended victim, there were, I am told, in this mass,
faces that did scowl as well as sneer at the British retinue,
and hearts regretting the frustrated issue of the adventure
of that morning. Jehangeer, the poor wretch who was
slaughtered by the dewan's followers, was a fanatic with
a previous bad character, but was at this time in the
employ of Tegh Jung, the son of Ikhtidhar-ool-Moolk and
grandson of Shums-ool-Oomrah, whose mother was the
sister of the late Nizam : his family is otherwise connected
with the present Nizam by several intermarriages.

This incident was reported a few days after by the
Resident to Lord Canning, and elicited a reply from Mr.
R. Simson, Under-Secretary to the Government of India,
dated Fort William, the 2nd April, 1859, No. 1511; for
the following extract from which I am indebted to his
Excellency Salar Jung :

" I am directed to acknowledge the receipt of your
despatch, dated the 19th ultimo, No. 40, and, in reply, to

acquaint you that the Governor-General in Council has read with deep interest the account given therein of the event which occurred upon the occasion of your visit to the Nizam on the 15th idem.

" 2. His Excellency in Council congratulates you warmly upon your providential escape from the attempt which has been made upon your life.

" 3. Whether it was your life alone that was sought may be uncertain, but the fact that the shot was fired when you were arm-in-arm with the Nizam's minister, and not at the minister singly, although he had been lately within the assassin's easy reach, is sufficient proof that you were the chief, if not the only object of his violence.

" 4. It is satisfactory to the Governor-General in Council to observe the anxious concern with which this atrocious crime was regarded, not only by the Nizam and his ministers, who acted in accordance with the well-proved friendship which his Highness has habitually evinced towards the British Government, but by the whole of his Highness's court and retinue, and by a great part of the populace of Hyderabad.

" 5. All that you describe the Nizam to have done upon this occasion redounds to his Highness's honour ; his Highness's conduct has been dignified and calm, and the measures taken through his ministers were, so far as they went, prompt and judicious.

" 6. But the Governor-General in Council, speaking in all friendship, desires to warn the Nizam that the event of the 15th ultimo is no light matter. The British Government holds the person of its representative sacred from all insult or violence. To no court which cannot give protection to the representative of the Governor-General will his Excellency trust the life and honour of a British officer.

It therefore behoves the Nizam, in order that no cause for an interruption of the present relations of the two governments may occur, to take the most vigorous measures to prevent the recurrence of so lamentable an act as that which has now been perpetrated.

"7. The criminal is beyond the reach of justice. It may be that he was a single fanatic, without instigators or accomplices. But it is incumbent upon the Nizam's government to use the utmost diligence to ascertain whether this be so or not; and if there should be reason to suppose that others remain who are actuated by the same spirit and entertain like designs, to take precautions accordingly. It must be clearly understood by the Durbar that they are responsible for the safety of the British Resident within the Nizam's territory."

Very recently the press of Western India has charged Colonel Davidson with implicitly carrying out the views of the Bengal Secretariat, and a Calcutta journal has insinuated the very contrary. The press of the Indian peninsula has charged Colonel Davidson with a strong leaning to make Hyderabad, as it were, a dependency of the Madras Government, whereas those who can offer an opinion will say that he has introduced not only the Bombay Survey, but a Bombay officer as Commissioner in Berar — the great cotton district; he has also always urged that half of the Hyderabad country is, in respect of language, trade, and geographical position, a part and parcel of Bombay, and in proof of this last fact has opened up the new road between Sholapore and Hyderabad. If a man's acts can testify to his sincerity of purpose, these would go far to show not so much how groundless, but how venomous some of the assertions advanced by the Indian press happen to be. That press does not seek to

CHAP.
II.

Colonel
Davidson,
C.B.

Resident's
salary.
promote a public good or remedy a public evil, but, guided by those who pull the strings behind the curtain, asperse private character either to gratify malice or for some sordid purpose.

Up to the time of Lord William Bentinck, who went out to India as Governor-General to apply the financial shears to all incomes, the British Resident at the court of the Nizam drew monthly 8000 rupees, made up of salary 3000 rupees, and table allowance 5000 rupees.

The Resident's present salary is 5500 rupees per mensem, and the Commissioner appointed to revise salaries proposes it to be prospectively reduced to 4333 rupees per mensem, as will be seen from the report subjoined hereto; but this is a mistake, from the many calls on the Resident's purse as the head of the local administration, as the European society is now very large, and will increase about Hyderabad, Secunderabad, and Bolarum. Besides this, it is bad policy to show the natives retrenchments of this kind ; for, if we cannot respect our own officials, and treat them with that liberality to enable our countrymen to look up to that official with respect, what are we to expect from others? I must not omit to mention that there is a certain sumptuary allowance for the Queen's birthday, and for other occasions included in the present consolidated salary of the Resident, but the amount is alone known in that unmistakeable mystery known as the Indian Account Department.

This chapter would be imperfect if I did not notice the assistants to the Resident. The first of these was Lieutenant Stewart, of the Bombay army, who was appointed Assistant to Sir John Kennaway. He was attached to the army of 1792, before Seringapatam, and upon his death

Colonel William Kirkpatrick appointed his brother Achilles his assistant. Upon Captain Kirkpatrick succeeding his brother as Resident, Captain, afterwards Major-General, Sir John Malcolm, was nominated Assistant in the following terms by the Governor-General :—

The Earl of Mornington to Captain Malcolm.

"Fort William, September 20th, 1798.

" Sir,—The office of Resident at Hyderabad having become vacant by the resignation of Colonel Kirkpatrick, I have this day appointed Captain Kirkpatrick to succeed him ; and it afforded me great satisfaction at the same time to have it in my power to nominate you assistant at that court, having learned from my brother* that in a letter to him you had stated that such an appointment would be acceptable to you.

" In conferring this appointment upon you, I have been governed by no other motive than my knowledge of the zeal, activity, and diligence with which you have pursued the native languages and of the political system of India ; and I take this opportunity of expressing my satisfaction at your having made choice of a situation in which I am persuaded you will render essential service to the public, and satisfy your honourable desire of distinction.

"I wish to see you previously to your proceeding to Hyderabad, and as soon as it may be convenient to you after you shall have received this letter. There are many circumstances relative to the political system of India which it is proper you should learn as early as possible ; it will also be advantageous to the public service that you should thoroughly understand my opinion on various

* The Duke of Wellington, then Lieutenant-Colonel Wellesley.

points with a degree of accuracy which cannot be conveniently stated in writing. I therefore hope that you
will contrive to visit Calcutta soon after the receipt of this
letter.

"I shall by this day's post apprise Lord Clive of your
appointment, in order that the necessary steps may be
taken for procuring you leave of absence from the establishment of Fort St. George.

"I am, &c.
"MORNINGTON."

Somehow or another Malcolm got the intimation of his
appointment contained in this letter before he received the
letter itself, and instead of proceeding to Calcutta he went
on to Hyderabad. Not long after he joined the Governor-
General as Military Secretary, and he rose, step by step,
after being twice Envoy to the Court of Persia, to be
Governor of Bombay. He was a wonderful man, much
belauded in his time and even since; but we must rightly
attribute his extraordinary physical performances to that
bodily strength he possessed, which made him laugh at a
climate to which others, for want of that strength, have
succumbed.

When Malcolm left, Thomas Sydenham took up his
place at the Hyderabad Residency, and as a second
assistant was considered indispensable, Henry Russell was
placed in the new appointment that had to be made.
The latter, however, was only a few weeks with Sydenham, and returned to Calcutta, when he was appointed
to the Arcot Commission, and Captain Charles Russell,
who commanded the Resident's escort, officiated for his
brother Henry. Henry Russell came to reign at Hyderabad, and Charles took up the post of First Assistant, and

another brother, Frank, of the Bengal Civil Service, took up that of second, which, after a short time, he resigned. Frank Russell was replaced by Hans Sotheby, also of the Bengal Civil Service. Metcalfe reigned in Russell's stead, and Sotheby, his first assistant, was immediately after appointed Governor-General's Agent at Moorshedabad. Barnett, a Captain in the Bengal army, came round with his master from Calcutta, as second assistant (and succeeded Sotheby as first), along with two young civilians as third and fourth, by name respectively Wells and Bushby. When Martin occupied the chair, Barnett, though his first assistant, it will already have been seen, had none of his master's good feeling on account of the sympathy with Metcalfe; Ravenshaw and Colvin, both of the Bengal Civil Service, were respectively second and third assistant; and Captain Byam, a connection of the Resident, fourth assistant. Barnett died at Aurungabad, and his subordinates rose in the office thereby. With Colonel Stewart, Captain D. A. Malcolm, of the Bombay army, was first assistant, an office which he also held under General Fraser, until removed to the Baroda Residency. Captain Newbold, who has attained celebrity in India as a geologist, was for a time first assistant to General Fraser, until obliged to leave for change of health for the Eastern Archipelago, when Captain Davidson acted for him. Major Davidson was first assistant to both General Low and General Fraser. Major Thornhill was previously first assistant to Mr. Bushby, as he is now to Colonel Davidson. Captain Barrow, of the 5th Madras Light Cavalry, was for a time second assistant to Mr. Bushby as well as to Colonel Davidson, until promoted at Lucknow; he was succeeded by Captain Rose Campbell, of the 32nd Regiment Madras Native Infantry, obliged to

CHAP.
II.

Assistant-
Residents.

leave on sick health, and followed by Captain Hastings Fraser, of the same establishment, who, during Major Thornhill's short absence in England, has officiated as first assistant.

The Resident and other Officers in Hyderabad.*

Revised
official
salaries.

Formerly, besides the salary shown in the margin, Rs. 5000 per annum was granted to the Resident as a table allowance. This was discontinued in 1834. The Resident has charge of the political relations between the British Government and his Highness the Nizam. In 1853 the civil administration of the districts assigned by his Highness, by the treaty of that year, was vested in the Resident, but he was relieved of nearly all the duties connected with the charge in 1856, by the appointment of a Judicial and Financial Commissioner. The Resident has the control of the Hyderabad Contingent.

RESIDENT.

Salary per month . . .	Rs. 5,500
,, per annum . . .	66,000

This is a very responsible post, but not so responsible as the post of Chief Commissioner in the Punjaub or Oude. I have proposed to give the Chief Commissioner in the Punjaub a salary of Rs. 50,000 per annum, and a sumptuary and travelling allowance of Rs. 10,000 per annum. To the Governor-General's agent in Rajpootana I have given Rs. 42,000 per annum salary, and a sumptuary and travelling allowance of Rs. 10,400 per annum. I think a salary of Rs. 45,000 per annum, and a sumptuary and travelling allowance of Rs. 10,000† per annum, would be suitable for the Resident at Hyderabad.

The first assistant to the Resident at Hyderabad receives per mensem Rs. 1652. 1. 11, as follows:—

1ST ASSISTANT.

Salary	Rs. 1,612	11	1
Office Rent	40	0	0
Per mensem . . .	1,652	11	1
Per annum . . .	19,832	5	0

* From the Report of the Commissioner for the Revision of Civil Salaries and Establishments throughout India.—No. 61.

† Sumptuary allowance	.	.	Rs. 7600
Travelling allowance	.	.	2400

Assistant	.Rs. 750	0	0
Superintendent of Police at Chudder Ghaut	662	11	1
Assistant in the Thuggee Department .	200	0	0
Office Rent	40	0	0
	Rs. 1652	11	1

The two offices last mentioned are paid by the Nizam's Government. The Resident represents that the duties are arduous. The assistant has charge of the treasury and the conduct of much correspondence with the native government, as well as with the authorities of Madras and Bombay. The Resident is of opinion that the allowance is not, on the whole, disproportioned to the duties performed, and he is opposed to any reduction.

It is very desirable that the Resident at Hyderabad should have the assistance of an officer of ability and experience. The charge of Rs. 750 per month only falls on the British Government, but the aggregate allowance is more than is paid to officers with similar responsibilities elsewhere. I have already proposed that the Rs. 200 per mensem paid in the Thuggee Department should be retrenched, and I think the salary may be reduced to Rs. 650 per mensem, which, with the allowance of Rs. 662. 1. 11 as Superintendent of Police, will make the salary of the assistant Rs. 1312. 1. 11 per mensem. If an office can be provided for the assistant the office rent should cease. The Resident writes :—" There are few political agencies, perhaps, in which the duty is so unintermitting, and requires more judgment and care, than the office of first assistant at Hyderabad, who is also the administrator in police matters at Chudder Ghaut, as well as in local civil matters, for the settlement of which he is frequently called on to convene punchayets, and arbitrate differences occasionally involving large sums of money and values of property. He has also a jail to look after, and the care of prisoners before their committal and after their conviction." The salary proposed will still nearly equal that of the political agent in Kutch (Rs. 16,800 per annum), and will exceed that of the agents in Mahee-Kanta, Rewa-Kanta, and Hurrowtee (Rs. 14,400 per annum).

The office of second assistant, to which is attached a salary of *Rs.* 600 per mensem, was created on the transfer of the assigned districts in 1853. The Resident proposed that, on the appointment of a Judicial Commissioner, the second assistant should be attached to that officer. There does not appear to be occasion for this. The duties of Judicial Commissioner in the assigned districts will not be more arduous than in the Punjaub and Oude. The Judicial Commissioners in those provinces have not assistants. I think the second assistantship should be abolished.

2ND ASSISTANT.

Salary per mensem	. . . *Rs.*	600
„ per annum	. . .	7,200

This office was created in 1856. The causes for its creation are to be found in the letter addressed by the Most Noble the Governor-General to the Honourable Court of Directors, dated the 8th of October, 1855. His Lordship wrote:— "The facts which have been brought to notice in this report, and the experience we have already gained, have satisfied me that the districts cannot be efficiently governed by the Resident alone. The political duties of the Resident render it highly inexpedient that he should ever be long absent from Hyderabad. Recent events which have been reported by the Resident confirm strongly the opinion which I have just expressed of the necessity for the constant presence of the Resident at the capital. But if the Resident be constantly present at the capital, it is impossible that he should efficiently superintend and control those districts which are distant. Appeals from the Deputy-Commissioners become a fiction, and supervision is no more than a name. The management of the assigned districts must, according to the treaty, be vested in the Resident; but I consider it to be proved essentially necessary that a Commissioner should be appointed, who, under the Resident, should exercise control over the district officers in all respects. The chief power of civil administration should practically be exercised by this officer. His

JUDICIAL AND FINANCIAL
COMMISSIONER.

Salary per mensem	. . . *Rs.*	3,500
„ per annum	. . .	42,000

functions will be very onerous and laborious. He must be a, selected officer of proved ability and of large experience in civil office. Under these circumstances, I consider that the salary given to the Judicial and Financial Commissioners in the Punjaub, namely, *Rs.* 3500 a month, is the lowest salary which ought to be sanctioned for the office."

The creation of the new office was sanctioned by the Honourable Court in their despatch, dated the 5th March, 1856.

By the orders of the Supreme Goverument, dated the 15th May, 1856, the duties and responsibilities of the Judicial and Financial Commissioner were regulated as follows : — " The Resideut to be responsible for the administration of the assigned districts, and to possess plenary authority aud control in all departments of the administration. In the departments of civil and criminal judicature, police and revenue, the primary authority to be exercised by the Commissioner. All trials in which the Judicial Commissioner may pass and record a capital sentence, to be submitted to the Resident, and without his concurrence no such sentence to be executed. The Commissioner to pass ordinary contingent charges to the extent of *Rs.* 500. The Commissioners in all departments to be subordinate to and subject to the authority of the Resident, who will hold in respect of the assigned districts the same position as that of the Chief Commissioner in the Puujaub and Oude. The Commissioner to be charged with the direction and control of civil and criminal justice, and to be the ultimate judge in all cases of a judicial character. His decisions to be ordinarily final, but the Resident to be vested with a discretion to call for the papers of any civil or criminal case, and pass such orders on it as may seem fit. The Commissioner to receive appeals from the orders of the Deputy-Commissioners, and his orders ordinarily to be final. In cases committed to his court as a court of sessions, the Commissioner to pass sentence of imprisonment for life in transportation beyond seas, or for any shorter period. In all cases not involving a sentence exceeding niue years' imprisonment, or in which the accused may have voluntarily confessed his guilt, the Commissioner to try the case on a view of the record of the

Deputy-Commissioner's Court, and pass sentence without summoning the parties and witnesses. In appeals from orders in criminal cases, the Commissioner may enhance the punishment awarded by the lower court, and reverse sentence of acquittal whenever he may see fit. The Commissioner to have the superintendence of all matters relating to the district or the rural police, the management and control of jails, the establishment and management of public ferries, and the introduction and management of town duties. On these subjects the Commissioner's orders to be final, but he is to obtain the Resident's approval of any important circular he may desire to issue on any matters falling within his cognizance. The local funds to be primarily under the Commissioner, who will have authority, subject to the concurrence of the Resident, to sanction expenditure not exceeding Rs. 10,000 on any one work. In his capacity of Financial Commissioner, the Commissioner to exercise much the same powers as are exercised, by the Sudder Boards of Revenue — to direct and superintend the revenue administration in all its branches. Whenever regular settlement may be commenced, the Commissioner to have the entire direction and control thereof, subject to such advice and restrictions as he may receive from the Government of India and the Resident. The Commissioner to sanction finally all intermediate summary settlements, and to sanction remissions of balances and refunds of revenue, and excise wrongly demanded. The Commissioner to receive appeals from all orders passed by Deputy-Commissioners in the Revenue Department, and to call for the record of any case whenever he may consider it expedient; to dispose of all claims to grants of land rent-free under ten acres, whenever he may be of opinion that such holdings should be re-leased for the lives of the incumbents; to grant tuccavee for the construction of wells, or other works of permanent utility, to an extent not exeeding Rs. 500 for each work. The Commissioner to deal in the first instance with all questions connected with revenue surveys, and settlements, stamps, excise, pensions, reporting the more important to the Resident for his orders, or for submission to Government. In regard to pen-

sions and pensioners, the Commissioner to exercise all the powers
that reside in the Sudder Board of Revenue, North-Western
Provinces. The Commissioner to sanction extra or temporary
establishment for a period not exceeding six months. The
Commissioner to refer for orders all important matters, and all
such as may involve ultimate heavy expenditure, such as all
questions regarding projects for the extension of irrigation, for
the preservation of forests; for developing the resources of the
country, for the construction of new and extensive lines of
roads, for the construction, alteration, and repair on a large
scale of public buildings, for the introduction of educational
measures, and such like."

Such are the powers vested in this officer. They are extensive, but the responsibility is less than the responsibility attaching to the Judicial and Financial Commissioners in the Punjaub.
The office may be, in some respects, more onerous than that of
a Commissioner in one of the largest divisions of the Punjaub
or Oude. A salary of *Rs.* 36,000 per annum will secure the
services of one of the best men in the Madras Civil Service. I
would fix that sum, with a travelling allowance of *Rs.* 10 per
day when absent from head-quarters.

The Deputy-Commissioners, as in the other non-regulation
provinces, have authority in
all departments. As civil
judges, they have the jurisdic-
tion of judges under the new
code of procedure, and hear

4 DEPUTY-COMMISSIONERS.

1 at	. *Rs.* 18,000
2 at *Rs.* 14,400 each . .	28,800
1 at	12,000

appeals from the Assistant-Commissioners and other subordinate
tribunals. As criminal judges, they have the powers of magistrates in the regulation provinces, and also special authority to
try session cases, and submit the record to the Judicial Commissioner for his orders. In the Revenue Department they can
dispose of all cases, subject to appeal to the Financial Commissioner. The under-written statement shows the population,
area, land revenue, &c., of the assigned districts :—

	Area in square Miles.	Population.	Land Revenue.	No. of Persons paying Revenue direct to Dep. Commissioner.	Receipts of Treasury.
			Rs.		Rs.
North Berar -	6400	9,50,000	15,50,507	81,871	25,40,492
South Berar -	8228	5,13,566	7,50,531	54,506	7,70,786
Nuldroog -	6292	4,97,000	8,21,589	40,868	13,97,184
Raichore Doab	6100	5,31,798	9,69,691	67,623	13,38,575
Total -	27,020	24,92,364	40,92,318	2,44,868	60,47,037

The district of North Berar is equal to any district in the Punjaub or Oude, and I see no reason for assigning a less salary than has been allotted to first-class Deputy-Commissioners in those provinces, namely, *Rs.* 23,000 per annum. The remaining three districts are larger than second-class districts in the Punjaub, to which a salary of *Rs.* 18,000 has been assigned. I cannot propose to give the Deputy-Commissioners of the districts of the South Berar, Nuldroog, and Raichore less than has been proposed for second-class districts in the North-Western Provinces, namely, *Rs.* 20,000 per annum.

The Assistant-Commissioners have power to try civil suits up to *Rs.* 1000; as magistrates, to pass sentence of two years' imprisonment and fine of *Rs.* 1000; and as revenue officers, to exercise such functions of the Deputy-Commissioner as he may delegate to them. In order to place these officers on a footing with assistants in other non-regulation provinces, there must be—

6 Assistant-Commissioners.
Salary of each per mensem *Rs.* 600
„   „   per annum   7,200

1 at	9,600
2 at *Rs.* 7800 . . .	15,600
2 at *Rs.* 6000 . . .	12,000
1 at	4,800
Total	*Rs.* 42,000
Average per annum	*Rs.* 7,000

The first-class extra assistants have power to try civil suits to the amount of *Rs.* 1000, and exercise the powers of joint magistrates. The extra assistants of the second and third classes can try civil suits

12 EXTRA ASSISTANTS.

2 at *Rs.* 7200	. . . .	*Rs.* 14,400
4 at „ 4800	. . . .	„ 19,200
6 at „ 3000	. . . .	„ 18,000

to the amount of *Rs.* 1000, and in the magisterial department exercise the powers of assistant-magistrates under the Bengal code. To place these officers on a footing with extra assistants in the Punjaub or Oude, they should be paid as follows :—

1	9,600
1	7,800
1	6,000
3 at *Rs.* 4800 . . .	14,400
6 at *Rs.* 3000 . . .	18,000
Total . .	*Rs.* 55,800
Average per annum . .	*Rs.* 4,500
Or, per mensem . .	*Rs.* 387

The average in the Punjaub is *Rs.* 381 per mensem, in Oude it is *Rs.* 377, in the North-Western Provinces *Rs.* 378.

Besides the officers above enumerated, there appears to be a Superintendent of Police, with a salary of *Rs.* 700 per mensem, and Tehseeldars exercising judicial powers, but I have endeavoured in vain to procure satisfactory information respecting [*] them. Under date the 23rd October, 1857, the Commissioner of the assigned districts wrote :— ". I find it almost impossible to afford the information which is requested by the Commissioner ; at any rate, it could only be prepared at a cost of labour which would seriously impede the duties of my office. The establishment of these districts has long been in a state of transition. The courts of the Meer Adil and the Moonsiffs have been abolished, and Tehseeldars have been vested with judicial powers for the decision of cases up to *Rs.* 300. The whole system is under revision. It appears, then, to me that it

* Appendix, Nos. 141 and 142.

would be useless for me to attempt to describe changes which have taken place in offices, many of which have been abolished, or are about to be immediately abolished."

Under these circumstances, I can carry revision no further, for I cannot procure the information required.

The result of the alterations recommended will be an increased expense of *Rs.* 1800 per annum.

	Existing Scale.	Proposed Scale.
Resident *	*Rs.*60,000 0	*Rs.*55,000 0
1st Assistant †	10,952 6	15,752 6
2nd Assistant	7,200 0	
Judicial and Financial Commissioner	42,000 0	36,000 0
1 Deputy-Commissioner	18,000 0	23,000 0
1 Ditto	14,400 0	20,000 0
1 Ditto	14,400 0	20,000 0
1 Ditto	12,000 0	20,000 0
1 Assistant	7,200 0	9,600 0
1 Ditto	7,200 0	7,800 0
1 Ditto	7,200 0	7,800 0
1 Ditto	7,200 0	6,000 0
1 Ditto	7,200 0	6,000 0
1 Ditto	7,200 0	4,800 0
1 Extra Assistant	7,200 0	9,600 0
1 Ditto	7,200 0	7,800 0
1 Ditto	4,800 0	6,000 0
1 Ditto	4,800 0	4,800 0
1 Ditto	4,800 0	4,800 0
1 Ditto	4,800 0	4,800 0
1 Ditto	3,000 0	3,000 0
1 Ditto	3,000 0	3,000 0
1 Ditto	3,000 0	3,000 0
1 Ditto	3,000 0	3,000 0
1 Ditto	3,000 0	3,000 0
1 Ditto	3,000 0	3,000 0
Total . *Rs.*	2,85,752 6	2,87,552 6
Deduct existing scale		2,85,752 6
Increase per annum . *Rs.*		1,800 0

* The sum of *Rs.* 55,000 shown in the proposed scale for the Resident includes a sumptuary and travelling allowance of *Rs.* 10,000 per annum.

† This officer draws also *Rs.* 2400 per annum as an assistant in the Thuggee Department, which is to be retrenched, and *Rs.* 480 per annum, which is likewise to be retrenched, if office room can be provided for him.

CHAP. III.

THE British Residency occupies an area of several acres. The grounds lie on the north bank of the river Moosee, and between the two handsome bridges known as the old and new; the former constructed under the superintendence of Colonel Oliphant of the Madras Engineers, and the latter designed by Captain Buckle, also of the Madras Engineers, but built under the superintendence of Mr. Marrett, a skilful architect in the employment of the Nizam.

The Residents formerly occupied one of the garden houses of the Minister of the day; but Colonel Achilles Kirkpatrick suggested the propriety of a building to be permanently appropriated to this object. Writing to Lady Clive, in October 1799, while passing through Hyderabad on his way to Persia *viâ* Bombay, Sir JOHN MALCOLM says :—" I will conclude this letter by relating an anecdote connected with this projected edifice (the Residency) that will satisfy you the princes of the East do not lose much of their valuable time in the study of geography. Major Kirkpatrick, the Resident at this court, wished to obtain a grant of two or three fields to erect this structure upon. He requested the engineer of the English force stationed at Hyderabad to make an

CHAP. III.

Situation.

CHAP.
III.
———
Situation.
exact survey of the spot; and when this was finished
upon a large sheet, he carried it to the Durbar, and
showing it to the Nizam, requested he would give the
English Government a grant of the ground. The prince,
after gravely examining the survey, said he was sorry he
could not comply with the request. When the Resident
was retiring, not a little disconcerted at the refusal of a
favour which he deemed so trifling, Meer Allum (the
Minister) said to him with a smile, ' Do not be annoyed.
You frightened the Nizam with the size of the plan you
showed him. Your fields were almost as large as any of
the maps of his kingdom he had yet seen. No wonder,'
said the Meer, laughing, ' he did not like to make such
a cession. Make a survey upon a reduced scale, and the
difficulty will vanish.' The Resident could hardly believe this would be the case ; but when, at his next
interview, he presented the same plan upon a small card,
the ready and cheerful assent of the prince satisfied him
that the Meer had been quite correct in his guess at t e
cause of his former failure." * In due course the building
was proceeded with, and completed by Lieut. Samuel
Russell, of the Madras Engineers.

Descrip-
tion of
building.
Sir James Mackintosh, while Recorder of Bombay,
visited his friend Captain Sydenham at Hyderabad, in
December 1808, and notes in his Diary: "The Residency
is the most elegant house which I have yet seen in India.
In the front is a very noble portico, formed by Corinthian
pillars. It is sixty feet in length, and nearly as lofty as
the house. From this porch you go into a hall of the
same length, and formerly of the same height, but now
divided by Captain Sydenham into two stories. . The

* Kaye's *Life of Sir John Malcolm*, i. 100.

support of the ceiling requires so many pillars that the lower hall may now be called a colonnade; but the columns are beautiful, and have a very fine effect. At each end is an oval room, thirty-six feet by twenty-four. One is a dining-room, the other a library and family drawing-room. At the corners are four smaller square rooms, office, billiard-room, &c. Above stairs, the same distribution is exactly repeated, comprising a drawing-room sixty feet by forty. The whole of both floors is uniformly carpeted, glazed, *sofaed*, &c., with English furniture, and in the handsomest style of London. In short, this house is Oriental only in its magnificence; it is perfectly English in its comforts.

On the 24th July, 1817, Sir John Malcolm found himself again approaching Hyderabad, on the circuit of the Political Residencies in the Peninsula, to which duty he had been deputed by Lord Hastings, the Governor-General of that day. In his journal-letter to Lady Malcolm, Sir John writes:—" I had left the representative of the British Government at this court, fifteen years ago, lodged in the house of a native nobleman, which was pleasant from being surrounded with small gardens and fountains, and had been sufficiently modified by improvements to be rendered a tolerably convenient European residence. You may conceive my surprise to approach a palace — for such the present mansion of the British Resident of Hyderabad may well be termed. It is only surpassed in splendour and magnitude by the Government House at Calcutta. That at Madras cannot be compared to it. You enter through a lofty and fine-arched gate, and approach through a garden laid out more in the Oriental than European style. The body of the house has much the appearance of the Government House at

Calcutta, but on a smaller scale. It contains the public rooms; and you may judge of their size and splendour when I state that the dining-room is sixty feet long and forty feet broad, and that the drawing-room upstairs is sixty feet long, forty feet broad, and upwards of twenty feet high. This room, with two adjoining ones that are connected with it by arched doors, form a most splendid suite of apartments. You may judge of the style in which it is furnished when I tell you that the chairs and couches are all covered with crimson velvet, with massive gilt arms and backs; that it is lighted by twenty-four girandoles and five lustres, and that the central one, which was made by Blade, and is considered the finest ever seen, cost 950l. in England. Such is the centre part of this fine building. The wings, which are removed by a terrace of about forty yards, consist each of an ante-room, a sitting-room, a bed-room, and closet. They are upon the same elevation as the dining-room, and are connected by separate stairs with office below. These wings are excellent houses. The sitting-room is thirty-six feet by twenty-four, and the others are in proportion. They are furnished in a plain way, and are quite to my taste. The palace I have described was built and furnished by the Nizam, and is kept up by him, as is much of the other parts of the state of the Resident."*

The chairs and couches, the girandoles, lustres and mirrors, were originally in Carlton House; but the Prince Regent wanted to sell off this furniture, and the Directors in Leadenhall Street of that day required some political concession, so the East India Company pur-

---

* The present Nizam is disposed to refurnish the house, and it is to be regretted that his caprice is not gratified.

chased this furniture at the price wanted by the Prince
of Wales, and made the Nizam pay for it.

There is a miniature model of the proposed building in
the flower garden attached to the zenana on the grounds,
from which it would appear that instead of the drawing
or reception-room upstairs, a balcony was merely intended,
very much after the fashion of a building in Shums-ool-
Oomrah's *baradheree*, designed and executed by some
Frenchman. But the alteration into a room has been
quite an improvement, and the boarded floor, which has
been attacked by white ants, is about being replaced by
a flooring to rest upon iron girders, as a more substantial
and less costly substitute than teak beams.

The northern front of the building, which is the entrance for European visitors, consists of an open flight
of steps, leading to a portico, paved with alternate squares
of black and white marble, and the pediment is supported
by six composite pillars. Level with the floor of the
portico, on each side of the flight of stone steps, is a
strong wall, on which is recumbent one of those grotesque
figures very frequently mistaken for the Sphynx, but
really half woman, half lion, or anything else one might
please to fancy. In the pediment are the royal arms in
relievo.

The southern, or back view, is more imposing, but it is
a departure from the design intended by the miniature
model. A small porch opens upon the offices on the base-
ment floor, where is also the treasury constantly guarded
by a party of native soldiers. But if not proceeding
into the offices, stone stairways open upon each side and
alight the visitor upon the landing-place which leads into
what is called the billiard-room, directly in front, or to
the wings right and left of the building. Otherwise the

grand stairway of this vestibule conducts the visitor into the reception-room above, and while ascending the eye catches on either side, in fitting receptacles, rare pieces of sculptuary of Venus rising from the Sea, and the Apollo Belvidere. In the niche half-way, where the stairway breaks into one on either hand, there is another piece representing Leda and the Swan. These works of art were introduced by Sir Henry Russell.

This is the principal building in what is called the Residency, and is occupied by the Resident himself, with the guests that he may have putting up with him. But the grounds contain separate dwellings for the whole of the suite, consisting respectively of the First and Second Assistants, the Military Secretary, and the Surgeon, as well as the Commandant of the Resident's Escort, now an honorary office, but in former years one of considerable emolument.

On the grounds are quartered a detachment of cavalry, who make the body-guard of the Resident on state occasions, and a large number of native soldiers of the line, who furnish the details for day and night guards at all points of the Residency.

The Residency is worth a visit at any time, and the present occupant has been at considerable pains to improve the grounds. There is an orchard, as well as a flower and vegetable garden; there is a dove-cot, and some fine specimens of deer; there are Goozerat cranes, and two great turtles, said to be very old, one showing in its shell the mark of a bullet fired forty years ago by Colonel John Sutherland to test the strength of that shell; there is the zenana, with its fountain within and fountains without, that Achilles Kirkpatrick built for his Indian wife, and its queer decorations of fruits, flowers, birds,

and beasts, as well as the military cavalcade attending the
native prince and European envoy, curiously introduced
and extravagantly bedaubed with rude colours on the
walls; and there, last not least, is the cemetery where lie
Mr. Bushby, the Resident — Major Cameron, who died
while officiating as Resident — Colonel Eric Sutherland,
Military Secretary to the Resident—Mrs. Sydenham, under
a handsome mausoleum overshadowed by the umbrageous
tamarind tree, and the children of several persons either
belonging to or living in the neighbourhood of the Residency.

I must now ask my good reader to remember specially
that there is no opening or gateway for a good part of the
southern or city side of the Residency grounds, as it
overhangs the bed of the Moosee, and that chiefly towards
the end close to Oliphant's bridge; but at the end near
the bazaar now being built on the way to the new
bridge, there is a sort of lane between the Residency wall
and the wall of the garden of one Dilsook, — at this end
there is a gateway with a native guard.* Then along
the western wall there was a gate where a Martello tower
has been erected within the last three years; another
gate a little higher up leading into the *Pootlee Bowree* — a
tank frequented for water by people in the vicinage
during the hot months — and a third gate which looks
down the road to Secunderabad; but all these gates run
along the thoroughfare used by the people from the city.
It is necessary for me to be so circumstantial, for my
reader to understand the narrative I will presently enter
upon: interesting as that Residency is for its construction

---

* Grindlay, in his *Sketches*, has   caricature at the present time.
a view of this, which would be h

CHAP.
III.

and all other particulars attending its history, surpassing every story connected with it is the attack made on that Residency on the 17th July, 1857.

The Attack.

The revolt—for mutiny most assuredly is a misnomer —broke out in Bengal on the 11th May, 1857; the intelligence reached Hyderabad at the end of that month. The subsidiary force quartered at this time at Secunderabad, about five miles from the British Residency, consisted of—

EUROPEANS. — One troop Horse Artillery.
One Battery, and
One regiment of Foot.

NATIVES. — One troop Horse Artillery.
One regiment Cavalry.
Five regiments Infantry, each 1000 strong.

Tantia Topee had his emissaries about the city of Hyderabad urging the people to join them against the Feringhee, but old feuds and unhappy reminiscences of the Mahratta neutralised their purpose. As it was, Colonel Davidson was hourly being telegraphed by politicals from the north of Central India to as far south as Travancore to keep them alive of passing occurrences and to hold to the last, conscious that if the capital of the Nizam went, the whole Peninsula would soon rise. The native mind was in a state of ferment, and it merely required some powerful house or great chief to create a flame, to make that flame a blaze from the Bay of Bengal on the one side to the Indian Ocean on the other, and to extend as far south as Cape Comorin.

That our own politicals should not only feel alarm, but entertain anxiety for the turn matters might take, one can readily understand : not so the real or pretended sympathy of natives, not British subjects, to urge the Resident to fly from his post. Colonel Davidson, from the very onset, had trustworthy information that the fanatical spirit which prevailed in the city was strong against his Government and his country; he knew that a *jehud* (a vow of fidelity to any cause, which requires to be taken by 360 persons, to assimilate it in number to the days of a lunar year) had been taken to repeat at Hyderabad the scene of Cawnpore; he was even made aware that he was specially marked for assassination, and he was told, by those who knew the men under their command, that every Sepoy of every arm of our military force had been tampered with, and was ready to turn upon us by joining any successful body of insurgents. Admittedly there was not a European who had made so many native friends as Colonel Davidson; his kindness to them was proverbial, and of that nature which lays a man under personal obligations for the rest of his life. Such kindness and weakness of purpose are to the native mind synonymous; they could not identify with that benevolence of spirit a loftiness of character which would imperil life itself rather than for a moment be supposed to depart from what was considered a sense of duty. So, upon the first outbreak of the rebellion, his native friends warned him repeatedly that he was not only marked for assassination, but a price put upon his head. Finding these hints made no impression in inducing the Colonel to alter his usual course of life, these natives at last sent an old man whom he had known for upwards of twenty-five years, and whom it was thought he greatly trusted. After long Oriental circumlocution, this ancient worthy addressed the Resident in these terms: "Many here desire well for you, and that you should escape with your life. Flee, then, at once across the Krishnah, out of the Hyderabad territory, for the life of every other European is doomed." Such was the insidious language, under the guise of friendship, to induce a benefactor to take that step which should not only blast his reputation, but imperil the safety of his countrymen. Those only who know the quiet, courteous manner of the Colonel can well conceive his reply :— "I have taken a fancy to lay my bones at Hyderabad. If open force be used, I will fight to the last ; and if my life be attempted secretly, you will perhaps get some one here whom you will like worse than you say you have done me. Rest assured, however, that the British Government will hold the Nizam responsible if harm come to the Resident." *

In the midst of these difficulties, Lord Elphinstone, the Governor of Bombay, made a requisition for cavalry, in which it was weak, for the Central India Force that had just taken the field under the command of Sir Hugh Rose, and without hesitation Colonel Davidson gave him the whole of the 3rd Hyderabad Contingent Cavalry; and when the political horizon was looking still darker, he parted with one half the cavalry he then had—a wing each of the 1st and 4th Contingent Regiments. Subsequently he sent to join General Whitelock's force a squadron of the 2nd Cavalry, a troop of the 12th Lancers, and a squadron of the 7th Madras Light Cavalry. Colonel Davidson also allowed the 6th Madras Light Cavalry to march from

---

* Captain EVANS BELL, in his letters from Nagpore on *The English in India*, says : — "The Resident at Hyderabad was begged by several native noblemen in the city to go to Secunderabad, the military cantonment, only four miles from the Residency, as a place of greater security ; but he replied that he was attached to the Residency by many old associations, and had a particular fancy to be buried in the garden. It is extremely probable that this advice was not really given to him with friendly intentions, but to try and create a panic which might spread among the Madras troops."

Jaulnah and join Lord Clyde, substituting in place of that corps a small detachment of local cavalry.

It was getting on well now for the middle of June, and men no longer spoke in bated breath of the large assemblies that met on the *Joomma* (the Mahommedan sabbath) at the *Mecca Musjeed*, or great mosque; for the tidings from Hindoosthan were daily worse and worse—that the tide of disaffection, and mutiny, and ruin was rolling dead against us. What wonder, then, that cravens should assume the natural *rôle* of the bully? The troops at the Residency were now reinforced, and consisted on the 16th of July of—

Three guns Madras Horse Artillery (Native).

Two guns and two mortars, with detail of artillery of the Hyderabad Contingent.

One troop Hyderabad Contingent Cavalry.

Twenty-five troopers, Madras Light Cavalry.

Two hundred Madras Native Infantry.

These troops were disposed of wherever it was thought likely an attack would be made, especially towards the river face ; and the arrangements were such as to ensure easy communication with each military post. The officers employed under the directions of the Resident were—

Lieutenant-Colonel S. C. Briggs, the Military Secretary, commanding the whole.

Captain George Holmes, commanding the Madras Horse Artillery.

Captain Allan Scott, commanding the guns of the Hyderabad Contingent.

Captain Bradley, 24th Regiment N. I., commanding the escort of Madras troops.

Major Thornhill and Captain Campbell, respectively First

and Second Assistant to the Resident, acted as volunteers.

On the memorable Friday the 17th July, Salar Jung, the Minister, sent a note to Colonel Davidson, at about one o'clock in the afternoon, saying the crowd had quietly dispersed from the Mecca Musjeed without any commotion, and that the report that the Jehud would be proclaimed that day—which had been made to the Resident, and communicated by him to the Minister in the early morning —was evidently false. At a quarter to six in the evening, a messenger was hurriedly despatched by Salar Jung to Colonel Davidson, with a verbal communication that 500 Rohillas had broke loose from the city, headed by Moolvee Alla-ood-Deen and the notorious Rohilla leader, Torabass Khan, followed by an immense mob of insurgents, with a request that the Resident would defend himself till the Minister had assembled the Nizam's troops. The insurgents soon waved to and fro; the western thoroughfare and the road leading towards Secunderabad seemed an ocean of human faces, exhibiting ferocity in its worst forms. Every gate of the Residency grounds had been closed, and every means of access bristled with bayonets. The Resident at once took the attitude of defiance—he scorned that of mere defence —with men whom he never trusted and he did not now fear to meet. The Rohillas proceeded to occupy the two large upper-storied houses * with terraced roofs, belonging to two Soucars by name Ubbu Saheeb and Jey Gopall Dass, facing the western wall of the Residency, and just across the thoroughfare of which mention has been made, thinking by this means to command entrance into the grounds : the garden of Dilsook was also occupied in force by the

---

* These were blown down immediately after the attack on the Residency was over.

insurgents. They made the gateway opening upon the Pootlee Bowree one of the points of attack, and almost tore off its hinges the gateway a little below; but their great card apparently was to be played from the Soucars' houses. The firing directed from those houses immediately they were entered was very heavy for about twenty minutes, till it became dusk. Captain Holmes's guns then commenced playing, and the European officers were fully alive to check any attempt of treachery on the part of their own people. Dropping-shots were now continued by the insurgents throughout the night, until four o'clock in the morning, when a volley was fired, it is supposed, while the insurgents were evacuating the houses with the connivance of the Arabs sent by the Minister to prevent their escape into the city; for they dug a hole in that direction, and there is little doubt that before daybreak they were safely lodged in their hiding-places in that very city. Thirty-two men were killed and wounded by the fire of the Madras Horse Artillery guns. The rabble continued hovering about the Residency all the night long: they had been completely dispersed by daylight on the 18th July.

After the night's attack, the Resident's escort was reinforced by 200 European infantry, the other three guns at Secunderabad of the troop of Madras Horse Artillery, and a complete troop of the 7th Madras Light Cavalry. Sand-bag batteries were erected along the river-face of the Residency, and bastions improvised at desirable points; but these were replaced, as soon as possible, by more permanent constructions, although still military works of a temporary nature, to command every approach to the Residency.

It is possible that had any of the Moglaee princes or

nobles of Delhi taken the initiative, instead of Tantia Topee in stirring insurrection, Hyderabad must have given way. I firmly believe that the opportunity was alone wanting to make Hyderabad go like Delhi, Lucknow, and other Mahommedan cities; it was simply by maintaining a firm attitude while the populace and seditious were waiting to see how affairs progressed elsewhere, that enabled the Resident to tide over the storm.

Of the leaders of this assault on the Residency, Moulvie Alla-ood-Deen was soon after caught and sentenced to transportation — a sentence which he is undergoing in the Andamans, and Torebass Khan was shot by the native government upon refusing to surrender after escape from confinement.

There was a second attempt made to have the people rise upon Europeans not quite two years afterwards, but the emissary was detected in good time. In the month of April 1859, Major Murray, C.B., apprehended, near the Fort of Randhar, one Rung Rao Pahgay Brahmin, who was travelling about the country with two treasonable documents, one a proclamation and the other a sort of general encyclical letter. The proclamation was concealed at the back of a native barber's shaving-glass, always circular in form and never larger than to fill the palm of a hand. This proclamation invited all princes, chiefs, and people in the Deccan to rise and join the Nana's army, which was said to be in full march towards Poona, and called on all to unite in the destruction of the Feringhee, detestable for being the conqueror and ruler of their dominions.

Rung Rao was tried by the Resident for treason, as being the Nana's emissary. The man freely admitted that he was endeavouring to raise troops under the order

of the Nana, to whom he had been deputed by the late
Sonajee Pundit, a Mahratta Brahmin, formerly head of
the Nizam's revenue dufters, from which appointment he
had been dismissed, and was under surveillance for
malversation in office. The Resident passed the sentence
of death, which was commuted by the Governor-General
to transportation for life to the Andamans, where he died
not long ago.

Perhaps it would be desirable to know what the Resident himself thought and wrote upon this matter, and
this we can only gather from his Administration Report
for 1858-59 of the Hyderabad Assigned Districts, now a
mere name, since the chief portion has been returned to
the Nizam under the Treaty of the 7th December, 1860.
Writing in this report to the Supreme Government, under
the head of "Political," Colonel Davidson says:—

"This section necessarily will, in the Administration
Reports of other provinces entirely under British rule, be
the most interesting and entertaining to the general
reader, as the dry statistics of the preceding chapters will
find no place under this head; but such remarks as can
be made on the political state of merely the assigned
districts, would obviously add little of value to the information contained in this report, while a fair and impartial
review of all the political events that occurred at Hyderabad during the two momentous years of 1857-58 would
most probably give umbrage to the government of a
reigning prince, who has proved himself our most faithful
ally.

"Under these circumstances, it is clearly better at
present to abstain from any discussion of the causes that
led to results hostile to British interests in the Hyderabad
territory; but as the political occurrences at Hyderabad

itself, and in the Nizam's territory, cannot altogether be separated from the assigned districts, as every movement that occurs at that metropolis vibrates throughout all the surrounding country, all that seems necessary to say here is that the most prominent acts of revolt, viz., the mutiny at Aurungabad, the attack on the Residency, the rebellious risings at Shorapoor and Copal, the proposed invasion of the Deccan by Tantia Topee and the Rao Saheeb, and the insurrection of the Arabs and Rohillas when Rissode and Nelingah in the assigned districts were plundered, were each and all promptly met by British troops and suppressed with equal determination, energy, and success.

"It would lengthen this report too much to explain how this was so happily achieved; but in contrasting the condition of Hyderabad during the rebellion of 1857 with other provinces of the Indian Empire, whose administration were entirely under our own officers, it should never be forgotten that one of the greatest sources of uneasiness the British authorities there had to contend with was that the whole resources of the State were not under their own immediate control, and however friendly the executive of the native government was, it might at any instant have become powerless, as was repeatedly nearly the case, under the influence of some popular and fanatical cry, calling for the destruction of the infidels and the extermination of all Christians with their friends.

" The state of Hyderabad and the Nizam's dominions was no doubt most critical, and a source of constant alarm throughout the two last years to the neighbouring governments, and entreaties for early intelligence were received from the surrounding authorities from all quarters. Still peace, seemingly unhoped for, to the surprise of every one, was maintained at Hyderabad, and that, too, in spite of the elements of insurrection being there as rife, and if not more so, yet at least in an equal degree as in any other part the most troubled in India.

" The insurrectionary movements in the Mahratta States of Holkar and Scindia, except as a general means of excitement to subvert our power, were never regarded with any favour at Hyderabad; indeed, a general Mahratta movement, having a probability of success, would have at once enlisted on our side the old hereditary and ever-cherished 'Moglaee' animosity against their former and national foe, the Mahrattas, and there is no doubt the Nizam and his own immediate army would have been easily induced to take the field in our favour on such an event and in such a cause.

" Gwalior fell, and was retaken without a sign, except a few passing remarks at Hyderabad, and although a rising in favour of Tantia Topee was latterly planned by emissaries sent by the Nana, it, as far as it went, was only joined by some of the most impoverished and desperate characters of the Durbar, while the Deccan Mahommedans of the contingent were perfectly willing, as of old, to be led against Scindia and Holkar, which they believed was the case when they first took the field to join the Bombay troops in Malwa.

" While this was the feeling towards the Mahrattas, it was very different in regard to the Mahommedan cause; every eye was turned towards Delhi and Lucknow, and news of every kind was eagerly sought and paid for. Disastrous rumours of the wildest kind, hostile to the British Government, were prevalent and always acceptable to the fanatical and warlike classes of the population; letters of the most treasonable and seditious character were intercepted from Aurungabad, Bhopal, Ahmedabad, Belgaum, Kurnool, and Mysore ; and there cannot be a doubt that, had a popular leader arisen, Hyderabad would have been speedily in a state of insurrection as it had already been of sedition, but fortunately no one of rank, wealth, and position could rise after the unsuccessful attack on the Residency in July 1857, which was the culminating point of our troubles at Hyderabad, and also as it was plain to all that the British Government were determined to fight the battle to the last and at all hazards, wherever insurrection showed itself.

" The attack on the Residency was repulsed by the troops under the command of Major Briggs, 31st Madras Native Infantry, and had been expected and provided for a month previously. What its probable results would have been, if successful, cannot be better described than in the evidence of Colonel Montgomerie, C.B., of the Madras Horse Artillery, given before the Commission for the organisation of the Indian armies, with this exception, that he speaks in laudatory terms of the detachment of three guns of Madras Horse Artillery, whereas this was due to the whole detachment of about 400 native troops : — 'Only last year, when a body of Mahommedan fanatics from the city attacked the Residency at Hyderabad, a detachment of Madras native horse artillery stood staunch, and instead of wavering in their duty, opened their guns on the insurgents, although men of their own creed. Had this detachment not stood firm at this critical moment, it is perhaps not too much to say that the whole of the Nizam's territories might have been in revolt; and the south of India, from Cape Comorin to the Nerbudda, in a blaze.

" While it is thus evident that there was no absence of

rebellious feeling at Hyderabad, still it was enabled at
the most critical turn of our fortunes to furnish its quota to the troops rallying at the call of the Government of India, in June and July 1857; and a strong brigade, consisting of artillery 12 field-guns, cavalry 1204 sabres, and infantry 1200. In short, half of the contingent were pushed into the field. The achievements of this force in the central India campaign, under Major-General Sir Hugh Rose, who called the cavalry, in his despatches, the 'wings of his army,' and at the battle of Bandah, under General Whitelock, require no comment here, as they are already inscribed on the annals of India.

" The letters of the men of the contingent cavalry, mostly Mahommedans of the Deccan, to their friends and families in the city, when in the campaign, descriptive as they were of desperate encounters with the army, and tales of uninterrupted victory to the British arms, did more as political engines to expose the true state of the contest than all (although derived from authentic sources) that could be urged by the British authorities. Theirs were considered inventions of the enemy, the braggadocio of the Hyderabad troopers was received as gospel, and satisfied the disaffected that the game to subvert British supremacy in India was already ended.

" The assigned districts, during the last two years, have within themselves preserved profound peace; the people have shown no desire for a change of rule, but, on the contrary, a decided preference for that under which they are now peaceably and prosperously living.

" The utmost dread was shown on the approach of the rebels to the northern frontier of Berar, under Tantia Topee, in November 1858; and every one, high and low, displayed eagerness in assisting the military in placing the great commercial town of Oomraotee in a state of defence. Moreover, in both districts of Berar, the villagers, when the gun bullocks were knocked up by rapid marching, yoked their own, and assisted in bringing the artillery and ammunition into camp. Supplies were readily furnished to the British troops, whether contingent or others. Wherever marching through the country this was invariably the case, not in the assigned districts alone, but all throughout the Nizam's dominions. Indeed, from the numerical strength of the several detachments, large armies may be said to have passed through the Hyderabad territory, and with hardly one instance of serious complaint of being badly supplied by the country people. In addition to this, and in illustration of the friendly feeling towards us, emissaries of the Nana and other rebel leaders were seized and delivered up to justice through the instrumentality of the people of the country.

"All this, in a political point of view, and that a principality under a native government containing a population of ten millions, the adult part of which all go armed, remained quiet, cannot be too highly appreciated, or form a subject of too much congratulation, as peace was maintained when we were supposed in this part of India to be most dangerously situated; and Hyderabad, described lately by the highest military authority at Madras*, not only did not turn against us, but gave us the assistance by its brave contingent, under British officers, at the time of our greatest need."

---

* "Hyderabad (city) can, at any moment, send forth 75,000 armed men. It is to Southern India what Delhi was to Northern India. All in this quarter look to the Nizam and his capital; and general insurrection here would, I cannot but think, spread like wildfire throughout the Madras Residency and to Nagpore."

CHAP. IV.

THE disbanding of the French battalions, under the command of M. Piron, in the service of the Nizam, had been accomplished ; but the important information obtained in that object by the Governor-General during his brief stay at the Cape of Good Hope, together with his despatch to the President of the Board of Control upon the subject, are worthy of perusal, and will be found in the Appendix.

Malcolm carried to Calcutta, and laid at the feet of the Governor-General, the colours of the annihilated French corps. More grateful trophies there could not be to the heart of Lord Wellesley. Such of the men as were not incapacitated from further exertion, by age or other infirmity, were drafted into the infantry battalions commanded by Colonel Finglass, who has been already referred to. Scarcely, however, had the French officers been relieved from their command, when war with Tippoo Sooltan was proclaimed by the Governor-General, after every negotiation had failed to prevent such an evil. " The British army, under General Harris, took the field. The Nizam was to aid us with an auxiliary force. Malcolm, who had arrived at Madras by one of the vessels which was to carry the Governor-General and his suite to the southern coast, was despatched from Madras to expedite the advance of our allies. The subsidiary force, under

Roberts and Hyndman, which had awed the French party into submission, was pushed forward, with a large body of the Nizam's troops under Meer Allum, to the Mysore frontier. On the 19th January, 1799, Malcolm joined the force. The duties which devolved upon him were, to communicate continually with the Governor-General and the Commander-in-Chief; to supply them with full and detailed information respecting the components, the organisation, the discipline, and the temper of the Nizam's troops; to hurry on their march; to control their excesses; to communicate with the chiefs of the country through which they passed; to obtain supplies for the army; to direct the councils of Meer Allum, the Nizam's general, who commanded, in behalf of his master, this auxiliary force; and, finally, to restrain the soldiery from breaking out into open mutiny.

"This last was no easy task. Among the infantry battalions of our allies were a large number of the men of the old French corps. Malcolm found them in a state of disorder, for which it appeared to him that the only permanent remedy was the appointment of European officers to the command of the different battalions. But the men were wrought upon by their native leaders, and declared that if such a measure of interference were carried out, they would march back to Hyderabad with all their guns, arms, and ammunition. Here, then, was a danger to be encountered which might well have perplexed an older and more experienced soldier. The alarming intelligence was brought to Malcolm at midnight; before daybreak, he waited upon Meer Allum, and urged upon him, in the strongest terms, the necessity of peremptorily ordering the guns and magazines to be sent forward under the protection of one regiment, and to direct the others to

march onward in the usual manner. The orders were sent,
but the regiments hesitated. So the Nizam's cavalry were
drawn up on the flank of the infantry line, whilst Colonel
Roberts's corps, which had overawed the French battalions
at Hyderabad, took up a position which could have reduced the recusants, had it been necessary to proceed to
extremities. Still there was procrastination. Some of the
native leaders were eager to delay the settlement of the
dispute till the evening. So Malcolm conceived that the
time had come for the abandonment of all delicacy and
reserve, and for a direct personal interference, such as, he
said, under less pressing circumstances, he might not have
been warranted in exercising. He offered his services to
Meer Allum; said that he was ready to carry the Minister's
orders into immediate execution; and, on receiving a full
consent to the proposal, mounted his horse and rode into
the lines of the mutinous battalions.

"His determined bearing had the desired effect. He
ordered the Sepoys to fall in; and they obeyed. He directed one regiment to move forward with the guns and
the stores, and the others to march in the order determined;
and his commands were not resisted. The men, indeed,
responded to the word with a ready acquiescence, which
showed that they had been misled by some of the chiefs
in the Nizam's camp. The success of his English friend
delighted Meer Allum, who at once importuned Malcolm
to take command of the entire infantry force. Other
European officers were appointed under him; and thus
brought back to a becoming state of discipline and order,
the services which the regiments rendered contributed
greatly to the success of the campaign.* In Meer Allum,

* With a view of rendering them   ing the utmost advantage from their
as efficient as possible, and of deriv-   services, they were arranged into bat-

who appeared rather in the character of an ambassador than of a military commander, Malcolm found one whose heart was in the cause, and whose energies were put forth honestly and manfully to promote it.

"To this confederate force, consisting, as it did, entirely of native troops, it was considered expedient to attach a European regiment. The corps selected for this service was his Majesty's 33rd, which had been stationed at Vellore. It was in excellent condition; its perfect discipline and soldierly appearance had attracted the attention and elicited the commendation of General Harris, who had recognised in the commanding officer all the qualities essential to secure the efficiency of the troops under his charge and the confidence of the authorities above him. It happened that about this time Colonel Roberts had expressed a desire to be relieved from his command: so the lieutenant-colonel of the 33rd Regiment was appointed to lead the Nizam's detachment in his stead.

"The appointment was one especially calculated to give satisfaction to our allies, to flatter their pride, and increase their confidence. For the great name and high connections of the new commanding officer were second to none in India. His name was Arthur Wellesley. Few may have suspected then that he was destined to become the foremost man of the age; but all knew that he was the brother of the Governor-General. It was this circumstance which rendered the appointment so acceptable to Meer Allum

talions commanded by British officers and the whole placed under the command of Captain John Malcolm, whose zeal and ability, added to a perfect knowledge of their language and customs, rendered him peculiarly qualified for this situation. To Captain Malcolm's command were attached two troops of native cavalry, clothed, accoutred, and disciplined in the same manner as the Company's regiments.—BEATSON's *War with Tippoo.*

and so flattering to the Nizam, that history may well afford to sink the question of military seniority which it involved. . . . . The allies marched upon the capital of Mysore. The result belongs rather to general history. 'On the 4th of May,' wrote Malcolm to Lord Hobart, ' all our labours were crowned with the completest victory that ever graced the British annals in India. A state that had been the rival of the Company's Government for nearly thirty years was on that day wholly annihilated.' Seringapatam was taken, and Tippoo Sooltan was slain.

" In a general order issued to the troops on the breaking up of the Grand Army, the Commander-in-Chief acknowledged in befitting terms the services rendered by the Nizam's force, and subsequently, in a letter to the Governor-General, called the especial attention of Lord Wellesley to the zeal and activity, the combined energy and judgment, which had characterised the successful exertions of Captain Malcolm to give the utmost effect to the alliance : —

" ' The body of his Highness the Nizam's contingent force being about to separate from the army,' wrote General Harris on the 9th June, ' I have the honour to enclose to your Lordship a copy of an order I thought it proper on this occasion to issue to the troops under my command.

" ' Captain Malcolm, Assistant to the Resident at Hyderabad, through whom my communications with Meer Allum Bahadoor were necessarily conducted, has at all times during the campaign, in which he took a very conspicuous part, made the requisite arrangements for the co-operation of the contingent in a manner which reflects the highest honour on his abilities, and which strongly marks his zeal in the public cause. His peculiar talent for conciliating the Sirdars of the allied force, and directing their exertions to objects of general utility in a manner foreign to their habits of service — his activity in applying the unconnected power of resource possessed by the contingent in aid of the general wants of the army, and the important assistance which he gave with the corps of his Highness the Nizam's regular infantry, under his immediate orders, in occupying posts for the security, and covering parties for the supply, of the army during the siege of Seringapatam, are points of valuable service which it is incumbent on me to point out, as entitling Captain Malcolm to the particular notice of his Lordship in Council.'"

It might interest the reader to know the nature of the materials which constituted the European officers of the Nizam's contingent force at the very opening of this century. I have not been able to ascertain their salaries, nor the exact extent of their commands, for their battalions consisted very unequally of from 200 to 1000 men. I give the names according to the grade of their pre-eminence, not marked by official rank, for the Government gave none but by the estimation — very ill-judged — of the native community. Amongst the whole there was but one man — and I make the statement upon valuable authority — who had been bred a gentleman, the son of a Dr. Gordon, on the Madras establishment, and of a Pondicherry lady, his wife. Captain Gordon had been well educated in England, and was a gentleman in principles, in morals, and in manners. His house at the French Gardens was the frequent resort, from the agreeableness of the family, of Captain Sydenham, the Resident, than whom, as the reader is already aware from what I have said elsewhere, there was not a more elegant man or of greater conversational powers, as he was in other respects highly accomplished.

The leading person in 1800 in the Nizam's service was Colonel Don Clementi de Avila, a Spaniard; and the following commanded the several regiments :—

Major Johnstone, an East Indian.

Captain Don Torribio Paulo Denis, a Portuguese and an officer attached to the Goa Brigade of his Catholic Majesty.

Captain Joseph Gordon, already mentioned.

Captain Freeman, an East Indian.

Captain Joachim Fonsea, a Portuguese of Pondicherry.

Captain William Palmer, an East Indian.

Captain Guest, an Englishman.

Captain Bridges, ditto.

Colonel Drew, also an Englishman, who was attached to the troops of Salabut Khan, a Jagheerdar; and

Captain Elliot, an East Indian.

The following are the names of those who were considered in the.light of subalterns :—

Captain Vincente, a Spaniard.

Captain Blake, an East Indian.

Dr. Silvestre, a Portuguese.

Signor Joachim, ditto.

José De Nunes, a Goa Portuguese.

Mr. Key, an Englishman.

Mr. Kullick, ditto.

Mr. Joachim Smith (or Schmidt), an East Indian, of Dutch extraction.

Mr. Plightdodo.

Mr. Marten, a Portuguese.

There were several East Indians holding this grade, with the exception of a German and a Frenchman; the name of the latter I have not been able to obtain, and the former was familiarly and only known as Papa George, as he was considered the father of the contingent service. I should perhaps have mentioned two other officers, Captain Harding and Captain Douglas, who were in Colonel Finglass' brigade, which was raised as a counterpoise to Raymond's; they were both Irishmen. The first is an historical name; he was killed at Sindree Lonee, in the battle between Holkar and Scindia, in command of a brigade of Holkar's force, whose service he had entered. Holkar complimented the memory of Captain Harding by telling Colonel Close, the British Resident at Poona, that, " though he had won the battle, in losing Harding he had lost his right arm."

In respect of this local force, I should wish no mistake to be made. The Government gave no military rank to its officers. The rank which I have given in the foregoing list to the several parties was assumed respectively by each, and admitted by the Government; that is to say, they were so addressed by the ministers and high functionaries of the State. Mr. William Palmer, for instance, took the rank of captain from the native officers of his regiment — the 14th Battalion — and he glided into his majority by being brigade-major to Colonel Stevenson, commanding the subsidiary force during the Mahratta war of 1802–3. In the department of the Nizam's infantry, Captain Palmer's duty was to convey, on an occasion rarely occurring, his commands to the officer commanding the Nizam's army, and, if considered necessary, to make reports to him. Most of these gentlemen occupied the grounds known as the French Gardens — remarkable at the time for the beauty of its women, mostly from Goa, and equally so for their good conduct.

Before proceeding into the general history of the
Nizam's contingent, I may as well quote here the opinion
of the Governor-General to the Home Government in
March 1799, regarding that portion which attended at
the fall of Seringapatam.

" This force, under the general command of Meer
Allum, formed a junction with the army on the 19th of
February, and it is with the greatest satisfaction that I remark to your Honourable Court the beneficial effects which
the (East India) Company have already derived from the
recent improvements of an alliance with the Court of
Hyderabad. The Nizam's contingent actually arrived in
the vicinity of Chittor in a state of preparation for the field
before General Harris was ready to proceed on his march
from Vellore."

In October 1800, Major J. A. Kirkpatrick concluded
that treaty with the Nizam by which his Highness commuted the money subsidy hitherto paid in defrayment
of the expenses of the British troops employed in defence
of his country, for the territories since known as the Ceded
Districts; and engaged to furnish, in the event of a war
between the contracting parties, a force of 6000 infantry
and 9000 cavalry. This levy was first employed, in conjunction with the Hyderabad subsidiary force, under
Colonel Stevenson, against the Mahratta confederacy in
1803.

On the death of Nizam Alee Khan, in August 1803,
notwithstanding the hostile designs of parties to excite
commotions in the State and to disturb the regular order
of succession in support of Furreed-oon-Jah, the younger
son, Secunder Jah, upon gaining the musnud, afforded
vigorous co-operation with his British allies against the
common enemy. The power of the Court of Hyderabad,

stimulated by the British Resident, proved eminently useful, and contributed to the speedy as well as successful termination of the war in the Deccan.

The Nizam's troops, consisting of artillery, cavalry, and infantry, were now located in Berar, having their head-quarters at Aurungabad. The cavalry were of two descriptions — Circaree and Jagheerdaree. The Circaree cavalry, by far the most numerous, were composed of small parties raised and commanded by different Sirdars. The whole system was faulty in the extreme. The head of a paigah would let out his party for a certain sum per horseman, for which sum horse, rider, arms, accoutrement, and ammunition were engaged to be furnished. Every casualty was to be borne by the owner, so that it was the interest of the horseman to avoid everything that would endanger the safety of his horse. A muster master was appointed, but it was soon found that he not only imposed upon the Government himself, but connived at the imposition of others. The muster roll of the Circaree cavalry gave 7150, and of the Jagheerdaree 4340. Many of these horses had no existence but on paper. Of the Jagheerdaree cavalry about 1800 belonged to Salabut Khan, about 900 to Soobhun Khan, and the remainder, in small parties of from 20 to 100 horsemen, to different inconsiderable Jagheerdars.

Of the infantry there were about 3000 irregular and about 5000 regular. The irregular infantry were Circar troops except one small corps of about 700 men belonging to Nuwab Shums-ool-Oomrah. Of the regular infantry two battalions of about 900 men each belonged to Salabut Khan, and the remainder were called the Nizam's establishment of regular infantry.

In the year 1804 a proposal was made to the Nizam to

maintain a regular establishment of the Silladar Cavalry, similar to the Mysore Horse. After some negotiation the Nizam consented generally to the plan, but as he objected to all those parts of it by which alone the efficiency of the establishment would have been insured, the proposal was necessarily abandoned; since, without some satisfactory arrangement for the regular payment of the troops, they would not have been at all superior to any other party of horse in the Nizam's service.

As may be supposed, the whole system of the Nizam's military establishment was defective. The only way in which our influence could be usefully exerted was in keeping their numbers complete, in getting them more regularly paid, and in suggesting plans for their disposition and employment.

The irregular infantry were fit for nothing better than the duty of sebundies, nor could anything better be expected of men whose nominal pay was five rupees a month, and that paid irregularly.

The two regular battalions belonging to Salabut Khan were very respectable corps. They were commanded by an Englishman of the name of Drew, who had a few other Englishmen employed as officers under him. The men were dressed like our Sepoys, and armed with our muskets, and, what was of much greater importance, they were regularly paid.

The Nizam's own establishment of regular infantry was to us the most important part of his whole army. It consisted of six battalions, nominally of 800 men each, divided into two brigades, each brigade commanded by a European officer called a Major, with a European Adjutant to each battalion. The men were dressed and armed like our Sepoys, and their establishment of native officers was nearly the same as that maintained in our own native corps. Part of this establishment is said to have been brought to a respectable state of discipline; but in consequence of the withdrawal of all supervision and control, they soon lost not only the benefit of every improvement they had previously gained, but acquired most of the defects to which an establishment of the kind under a native government is liable. They are described as being at one time incomplete in numbers, loose in discipline, badly armed, and irregularly paid.

To make these establishments really effective, the Resident, who had early applied himself to the organisation and discipline of the Nizam's troops, recommended that the number and respectability of the European officers should be gradually increased, the men well paid and regularly disciplined, supplied with arms and accoutrements from our own stores, and the general superintendence and control over the whole vested in a British officer, who should exercise the necessary degree of personal authority, and keep the Resident constantly informed of their real condition.

As no encouragement was then given to continue this proposed reform, the Resident seems to have confined himself to inducing the Nizam's government to introduce some system of regularity in the organisation and payment of a few of the battalions at Hyderabad.

Of the troops at the capital there were two battalions, with a small number of guns in the old French lines, commanded by Major George Gordon. After his violent death, effected in cold blood by a rebel, his brother, Major Edward Gordon, succeeded to the command. These troops do not appear to have been in any way subject to the orders of the Resident, but under the direct control of the Nizam's Minister, by whom they were paid. In 1812 they mutinied for their pay, tied up their commanding officer to a gun, and threatened to blow him away, unless their pay was given them, together with a free pardon for their offence. Both were promised. Funds were sent from the Residency treasury. But the chief mutineers were punished, as the Resident considered that no promise should be held good which was exacted under such circumstances. After this the battalions were reformed, taken under the protection of the Resident, and located in a new cantonment near the old French foundery.

This brigade, subsequently designated the " Russell Brigade," out of compliment to the Resident, was permitted to purchase, under certain arrangements, ammunition and stores from the Company's arsenal at Secunderabad. The brigade consisted of nearly 2000 men, together with a train of one 24-pounder, four 6-pounders, and two 5½-inch howitzers.

In 1813 Mr. Russell induced the Nizam's government to allow him to disburse the pay of one battalion from the proceeds of the peshcush, and to extend the same arrangement to the second battalion as soon as it was completed.

The attention of our Government was now directed to effect a reduction in the Nizam's irregular battalions, and to supply their place with corps formed on the plan of the " Russell Brigade." While these arrangements were in progress for the organisation of the " Russell Brigade," the Nizam's regular infantry in Berar was placed under the general control of the political agent in that quarter, who was assisted in his military duties by a staff-officer under the designation of Brigade-Major. Captain Sydenham was the political agent, and Lieutenant Parker, of the Madras Cavalry, his Brigade-Major.

The regularity with which the political agent succeeded in prevailing on the local government to pay the troops in Berar was in itself an object of first-rate importance; and the arrangements which he made for mustering the men, filling up vacancies, and supplying stores, were also highly judicious. The political agent in Berar acted of course under the orders of the Resident of Hyderabad.

The Resident, whose heart was in reform, was desirous that the whole of the six corps of regular infantry should be kept complete in numbers, and in every respect put upon an efficient footing; but as much time would necessarily be required for the adoption of the plan to its fullest extent, and as many difficulties stood in the way, it was wisely determined, so as to avoid the danger of undertaking too much at once, to introduce the system gradually—to limit the immediate measures of reform to the four battalions which composed the first and second brigade—and to transfer the remaining battalions to the exclusive authority of the native officers of the local government.

The battalions which were the best disciplined were the first equipped, and ammunition for the ordnance and small arms was now for the first time supplied from the Company's arsenal, though the supply was very judiciously restricted to those corps which, in all other respects, were in a complete state of discipline and equipment. The condition of these corps might be traced in a great measure to the support which they had received from our political authorities, but still more to the individual character of their commanders. The class of men, too, were widely different, depending of course upon the care that had been taken in recruiting and selecting them, for the rate of pay was everywhere the same. The Russell Brigade was formed out of the finest men that Hindoosthan could produce, while most of the other regiments were recruited with less care. Some of them were composed of the refuse of the old French corps, others again of the personal adherents of their several commandants, while it was well known that in some of the regiments their numbers were to be found only on paper.

In 1814 Lieutenant Hare of the Bombay army was appointed to the command of the Russell Brigade, and at the instance of the Minister, Raja Chundoo Lall, European officers were in due course appointed to the small bodies of artillery and cavalry attached to the force.

This brigade, under the energetic measures of Mr. Russell, and through the skill and assiduity of Captain Hare and the officers under him, attained, as we shall have occasion to show, the highest state of efficiency, and formed the basis upon which the whole of the contingent was subsequently organised.

In September of the above year the following order was published to the troops, remarkable only as being the first order issued on their new organisation :—

" The divisions at present denominated cohorts shall be equally divided into two regiments, each to be completed to the following establishment : —

" EUROPEANS.	— Commandant					1
	Adjutant					1
	Serjeant-Major					1
	Quarter-Master Serjeant				1
NATIVES.	— Soobehdars					10
	Jemadars					55
	Havildars					50
	Drummers and Fifers				20

Buglers	8
Packallies	10
Naiques	53
Sepoys	800
Total	1007

ATTACHED.—	
Armourer	1
Blacksmith	1
Bellows' Boy	1
Carpenter	1
Chuckler	1
First Dresse	1
Second Dresse	1
Dhobis	10
Hujjams	10

" It being supposed that all European officers attached to a corps of this kind are already conversant with their duty in every respect, regulations which of course would approach as near as possible to his Majesty's or those laid down by the Honourable East India Company for the government of their troops are rendered unnecessary. It is also expected that unanimity, the essential support of discipline and subordination, which is so necessary in every person engaged in the military profession, shall exist in the corps.

" As soon as the regiments are formed, it is to be hoped that emulation between the two corps will take place. The state that a corps is in with regard to discipline must redound to or detract from the military charac-ter of the officers attached to it, although it is in the service of an ally of the Honourable Company; yet the sanction and support given to it by the lending of its officers, authorises that strict mode of discipline intro-duced into their native army, and for which their officers are at all times accountable, in whatever situation they

may be placed. Among all nations every individual with
an army is subject to the rules and regulations adopted
by that army."

During the year 1815 the reform of the Russell Brigade
was prosecuted with great industry and perseverance. . A
brigade-major was appointed in the person of Captain
Jones of the Madras army. Other nominations and
appointments were made to the European ranks of both
commissioned and non-commissioned. A code of articles
of war was authorised by the Nizam's government, and
other useful regulations introduced for the discipline and
well-being of the force in all its branches. The men
were ruled by the best of all rules, the fear of punishment and the hope of reward. Of the native officers we
find the services of some "dispensed with by his Highness
the Nizam;" others, again, promoted for "gallant conduct." Nor were the interests of the whole as a body
disregarded, for a proportionate increase was made to the
pay of each grade, from the soobehdar to the private,
respectively.

About the middle of this year the brigade was ordered
into the city to suppress a disturbance created by the
princes. Moobariz-ood-Dowlah, the Nizam's youngest
son, had proceeded to the extremity of seizing and confining a servant of the Residency. Captain Hare's brigade
with two guns were accordingly ordered into the city.
As the force approached the prince's house it was fired
upon; for the houses on both sides of the road were
occupied by armed men, who offered a determined and
formidable resistance. The brigade pushed on reso-
lutely, and with their guns blew open two of the gates;
but they found that within which offered still greater
obstacles than the gates without; and after a severe con-

test and an ineffectual attempt to penetrate into the prince's house, the force was under the necessity of retiring, but not without considerable bloodshed, and the death of an officer belonging to the Resident's escort.

The Nizam acted with great determination on the occasion. He enforced his orders for imposing an effectual restraint upon the violence of his sons, directed measures to be taken for apprehending and punishing their associates, and in the end removed the princes to the neighbouring fort of Golconda. Under the immediate sanction of the Nizam's own authority, tranquillity was soon restored to the city.

"The following," writes Mr. RUSSELL, in addressing Captain Hare, "are extracts from despatches which I have received from Mr. Secretary Adam, in reply to my reports on the subject of the service on which a detachment of your brigade was employed on the 20th August : —

"'The Governor-General perused with concern your report of the loss sustained by Captain Hare's brigade in the attack on Moobariz Jung's house ; and his Lordship especially laments the death of Lieutenant Darby. The failure of that plan cannot in any degree be ascribed to the conduct of the brigade, or of Captain Hare, who, as well as the other officers and the troops under his command, merit his Lordship's approbation for their steadiness, perseverance, and gallantry under very trying circumstances.'

"I have great pleasure," adds Mr. Russell, "in being the channel of communicating to you this honourable testimony to the conduct of a corps in whose welfare I shall always feel the warmest anxiety, from private inclination as well as public duty."

The year 1816 gave an invalid and pension establishment to the Russell Brigade. The subjoined extract of
the Resident's letter on the occasion deserves a place here,
as expressing sentiments highly honourable to his feelings,
and as showing the interest Mr. Russell continued to take
in the child of his adoption. " Having," concludes Mr.
Russell, " the honour and prosperity of the brigade chiefly
at heart, I rejoice at this arrangement, as I do at every
measure which contributes to the advantage of the native
officers and men composing it. I request you will
assure them of my constant protection and support. I
shall always watch over their interests with the cordial
anxiety of a friend; and I expect of them, in return, that
they will cultivate a proper sense of the benefit they
enjoy, that they will emulate the spirit of their European
officers, and that they will distinguish themselves by the
faithful and zealous discharge of their duties both in
quarters and on service."

To give importance to the occasion, a salute of nineteen
guns was fired from the artillery, a *feu de joie* from the
infantry, and all prisoners were released from confinement,—a compliment paid as much, perhaps, to the
Nizam's minister, from whom the boon ostensibly ema-
nated, as to the occasion itself.

Captain Hare appears to have understood the character
of the native soldier. He took every opportunity of
encouraging them by kindness and consideration, stimu-
lating their pride, and animating them by the hope of
reward.

As an indication of it, the following order was issued
on the occasion of his brigade parading for the first time
with the Hyderabad Subsidiary Force : —

"The commanding officer requests commandants will

communicate to the officers and men under their command his entire approbation of their conduct and soldierlike appearance on parade the first time they have had an opportunity of appearing under arms with British troops, and hopes they will proudly support the good character and opinion which they have gained. He, in consequence, directs that there be no parades for exercise for eight days from this date."

In this year, Lieutenant Sotheby * of the Bengal Artillery joined the Russell Brigade as commander of the artillery, being the first artillery officer appointed to the contingent. Of Lieutenant Sotheby, then a young officer, little could be known; but his intimate knowledge of all professional details soon became conspicuous, and made him invaluable in his new position. Without any facilities but such as were derived from his own personal exertions, he had everything to form and everybody to instruct; and nothing but the most active zeal and most untiring industry (for he was a painstaking man of laborious and minute arrangement), could have enabled him to overcome the difficulties against which he had to contend. Under this able officer the Nizam's artillery was originally organised; and to him is chiefly to be ascribed whatever merit may be due for the state of efficiency which the ordnance department in all its details is acknowledged to have attained.

Towards the end of the year the Resident inspected the brigade, when Mr. Russell, who cannot be made to speak too often, expressed himself in the following terms :—

" I have sincere pleasure in assuring you of the grati-

---

* Now Major Sotheby, C.B., retired list.

fication which the performance of the Russell Brigade at the review yesterday morning afforded me. Their appearance and movements were in every respect as good as could be either expected or desired. To me, who have frequently witnessed their progress and discipline, and who know the skill and industry which have been employed in their improvement, this was only a confirmation of the opinion I already entertained; but I heard several experienced officers, who were on the ground, and who had not had the same opportunities of knowing the brigade that I had, unanimously speak in the highest terms of their proficiency. I request, therefore, that you will accept my congratulations and my thanks, and that you will have the goodness to convey the expression of my applause to all the officers and men of the brigade."

CHAP. IV.

Constitution of, and services.

In the same year (1816) the subject of a reform of the Nizam's cavalry was brought under the notice of the Supreme Government. For the incursions of the Pindarries required that some vigorous measures should be adopted for the protection of Berar. As the Pindarries were famed for their proficiency in the art of running away, so it became essential to organise troops that could run after them; for rapidity of movement was all that was necessary in the contest with those plundering adventurers. Irregular cavalry, efficient, and equipped for rapid movement, were the description of troops required; since the constitution of regular troops unfitted them for competing with the quick and desultory excursions of the Pindarry Horse.

The Nizam's own establishment of cavalry, as it existed in Berar, increased the evils which it was employed to suppress. The troops were as much dreaded by the peaceable inhabitants whom they were sent to protect, as were the Pindarries ; and the province itself suffered infinite distress from their depredations. The resources of the country were neglected, the poorer people oppressed, and the military force capable only of mischief. Such were the evils of the native system, requiring the strenuous interference of our political and military authority to check. Some parties of the Jagheerdar cavalry were nevertheless susceptible of improvement as having a better description both of men and horses ; these it was proposed to select, to form them into light and efficient troops, and to remodel them upon a new and improved system under European control.

The general principles were to provide for the immediate organisation of 7500 cavalry in Berar alone. Raja Govind Buksh, who then exercised chief authority in Berar, was called upon to furnish the greater portion. Some reluctance was at first shown ; but after a rather lengthened discussion the Raja acceded to the propositions of the Resident, which were negotiated by Captain Sydenham with great zeal and intelligence, — qualities that were conspicuous throughout the whole of that officer's proceedings. The Raja consented to furnish a body of 5000 cavalry for the protection of Berar against the Pindarries ; but as that number could not be immediately organised, the party of Mysore Horse then in the Deccan were retained for the defence of Berar ; for they were of a superior description to the Nizam's own cavalry, being composed of men who had learned in the school of Hyder and Tippoo the duties of light troops.

The portion of the Jagheerdar horse were to be furnished, the greater part by Salabut Khan, and the remainder by other parties in Berar, to be under the orders of Nuwab Futteh Jung Khan, a leader of approved courage and fidelity, and a near connection of Salabut Khan.

The Jagheerdars and others were required to pay their troops with punctuality; and as the greater portion of them belonged to Salabut Khan, it was anticipated, from the arrangements already introduced by that chief, that a regular system of payment might be depended on. No change was necessary in regard to the payment of the Mysore Horse, as funds for that purpose were already provided from the Resident's treasury, and the amount repaid by the Raja of Mysore. The troops were guaranteed the continuance of their long-established usages and customs. The pay of each silladar horseman was fixed at forty Hyderabad rupees. Every horse killed or disabled on service was to be paid for by the State; and other beneficial arrangements were introduced, which made the situation of both native officers and soldiers more advantageous, more creditable, and more secure in every respect. With all classes the proposed plan was extremely popular; and the service soon became, as it has been ever since, one of much request among natives of respectability and character.

The next point for consideration, and one requiring much circumspection, was the selection of a European officer possessing the various qualifications necessary to the efficient discharge of the delicate and arduous functions of the chief command of the party; for, although for ordinary and internal purposes the command might still be exercised by the native officers, yet the cavalry would neither be placed upon a respectable footing, nor maintained in efficiency, nor employed with any advantage to the State, unless commanded and led by European officers.

Alluding to the description of officers required with irregular cavalry, Mr. Russell, as we gather from a small publication at the head of this article, thus expresses himself: —

"He would have to .lead and direct them on all occasions, to guide them by his knowledge, and encourage them by his example; and, above all, he would have the difficult task of surmounting the prejudices of caste and religion, and reconciling the men to act with cheerfulness under his authority. But for this duty, difficult and complicated as it is, I have no hesitation in recommending Captain Davis. The integrity of his character, his known gallantry and enterprise, his temper and experience, his habits of personal activity, his acquaintance with the language, manners, and prejudices of the natives, and his skill in their peculiar modes of horsemanship, eminently qualify him for such a charge."

The direct superintendence of the troops in Berar had been previously vested in the political agent there; but in 1817 the system was modified, and the cavalry and infantry were respectively placed under the immediate command of two officers of the Company's service specially selected for the duty—the general control and direction of the whole still remaining with the chief political officer on the spot, whose authority was to be exercised on the same principles which regulated the authority of political Residents over officers commanding subsidiary forces.

Major Pitman of the Bengal army, who accompanied Mr. Elphinstone in his mission to Kabool, was nominated to the general command of the Nizam's regular infantry in Berar. The war which was close at hand prevented any immediate reform; but at the close of it he com-

menced with rather a severe hand — forcing some of the
old European officers to retire on pensions, replacing
them by Company's officers, and driving most of the old
men out of the ranks, but producing thereby a result
which raised the regiments to a level with those in the
Company's service.

Captain Davis, who had previously commanded one of
the battalions of the Russell Brigade, and who, as we
have just shown, had been strongly recommended by the
Resident, was appointed to the command of the cavalry
brigade, composed of four risalahs of 1000 each. To
Captain Davis was left the execution of all the details for
carrying out the proposed plan of reform in the cavalry,
and that nothing might impede the progress of the good
work, he was allowed by the Governor-General to select
his own instruments to aid him in the important and
difficult undertaking. The undermentioned officers were
accordingly appointed :—

Lieutenant H. B. Smith . . . . *Madras Army.*
Captain Pedlar . . . .⎫
Lieutenant Wells . . . . . .⎬ *Bombay Army.*
Lieutenant John Sutherland . . .⎭

Through the exertions of Captain Davis and his officers,
this force, on the breaking out of the Pindarry campaign,
was considered sufficiently organised to take its place
with the army under Sir Thomas Hyslop. Their services
throughout the war were "most exemplary," and afforded
an opportunity of showing the discernment which had
guided Captain Davis in his selection of the officers to
serve under him.

In the same year a small regiment of native cavalry of
300 men was organised on the plan of our regular

CHAP.
IV.

Constitu-
tion of, and
services.

cavalry, attached to the Russell Brigade, and the command of it given to Captain Jones the Brigade-Major.

The plan of lending English officers to discipline the troops of our native allies was at one time considered of very doubtful policy, and was at first proceeded on with caution; but after a time, the ground being supposed safe, it gradually enlarged, and in the end extended throughout the Nizam's regular army. But this reform was not effected at once, nor without difficulties that might not have been overcome but for the enlightened views of the British Resident, who then watched over our interests at Hyderabad, directed and supported as he was by a corresponding spirit at the presidency.

On this subject we find among the Hyderabad papers the following letter from the Home Government under date the 3rd April, 1814 :—

"In our despatch of the 23rd December, 1813, we apprised you of our intention, at a future period, to communicate our sentiments upon the subject of encouraging our allies to form regular battalions, disciplined after the European methods, and commanded by British officers."

2. "We have subsequently given to that subject all the attention which its importance required; and, upon full consideration, we are led to apprehend more danger from the extension of the European system of military discipline amongst the troops of the native powers, than we can expect to derive from their services.

3. "To the superiority of European discipline, is to be attributed the establishment of the British empire in India; and, in proportion as that discipline is extended amongst the natives not in our service, we must consider the power we have acquired exposed to hazard.

4. "The various contingencies which occur in the

conduct of the affairs of so large an empire as we possess in India, have at all times made it advisable to avail ourselves of the assistance of native troops, not actually in our service, and to place them, upon such occasions, under the command of officers belonging to the Company's army.

5. "But we look upon the adoption of such temporary expedients in a very different light from the establishment of a system formed for the express purpose of introducing European tactics, in all their regulations and details, into the armies of any of the native governments.

6. "In extending our subsidiary alliances, we have not been insensible to the risk of increasing our native force, beyond that proportion of European troops which ought always to accompany every augmentation of our Indian army; but we felt, at the same time, that there were circumstances connected with those subsidiary alliances, which counterbalanced the evil they were, in some degree, calculated to produce.

7. "The subsidiary force absolutely constitutes a part of our own army, is entirely under our own control, and can be changed, or even withdrawn, at the discretion of our own Government; and although it is supported at the expense of our allies, affording them protection and authority whilst in amity with us, it gives them no strength in the event of hostile disposition.

8. "It appears to us, that the proposed plan, without the advantages which have been stated, is liable to all the objections which can be urged against the subsidiary system : and whatever weight may be due to the opinions that have been brought forward in its support, the possible consequences of its establishment we deem of a magnitude sufficient to deter us from authorising its

further encouragement; particularly with reference to the artillery,—an arm in which it ought to be our policy not to extend the knowledge of it to the natives.

9. "You will observe, by their military despatch of the 8th November, 1814, that the Court of Directors are thoroughly impressed with the necessity of preventing the absence of our European officers from their regimental duties. The gradual reduction which they have ordered in the number :of those officers, in itself constitutes a sufficient reason for not allowing them to serve with the native powers."

Again in January 1818 :— "The doubts," the Court observes, "which we have formerly expressed, as to the policy of encouraging, generally, the princes in amity with us to maintain large bodies of regular infantry are by no means removed."

The Court appear to have had in mind the failure of a similar scheme in 1775, when the assistance of British officers being granted to discipline the Oude troops, it was found necessary in less than two years to discontinue the plan, for the following reasons recorded by Warren Hastings on the 5th May, 1777 :—

1st. "The superior pay and emoluments enjoyed by the officers in the Nuwab's service, excited murmuring and dissatisfaction among those who remained in the Company's service, and by discouraging their zeal and attention to their duty, tended to the general relaxation of discipline.

2nd. "The want of effectual checks had been deeply felt, the principle of moderation which should actuate the conduct of officers in their public disbursements, having been found to have little influence when the expense was defrayed by a state on which they had no natural and

permanent dependence. Hence the burthen had become
too enormous for the Nuwab to bear.

3rd. "The service having been too remote for the
British Government to observe all abuses in it, local interests were acquired, and opportunities of making undue
advantages afforded.

4th. "The officers employed on this service being
exempt from the articles of war, the British Government
had no further influence over them than such as was
created by a dread of losing their profits, which alone was
insufficient to restrain excesses proceeding from the same
principle."

In June of this year, when Sir Thomas Hyslop, the
then Commander-in-Chief of the Madras Army, assumed
the general control of political and military affairs in the
Deccan, the Nizam's army was supposed to consist
nominally of about 70,000 men, though probably not
more than two-thirds were actually kept up; and even of
that proportion the only useful part were the reformed
horse, and the establishment of regular infantry, and those
only because they were paid, clothed, and armed through
British influence, and controlled by the ability and exertions of British officers.

The reformed horse, consisting of 4000 men, under
Captain Davis, were stationed in different parts of Berar.
Its organisation had now been completed. And the gallant affair which had recently taken place in Candeish
afforded practical proof of the value of the services which
might be expected from it. A party of 600 men under
the personal command of Captain Davis, after a rapid
march of fifty miles, charged a body of Prembukjees'
adherents, near four times their strength, strongly posted,
and prepared to receive them. The enemy was almost

immediately broken and repulsed, leaving some hundreds killed and badly wounded on the field. Both Captain Davis and Captain Pedlar, the only one of his European officers who had then joined him, received severe wounds.

The Nizam's establishment of regular infantry, as before stated, consisted of six battalions with artillery attached to them, of which two were stationed at Hyderabad, and four in Berar.

The two battalions at Hyderabad composed the Russell Brigade, commanded by Captain Hare. The men were chiefly Hindoos, natives of Hindoosthan. They did no duty in the city, nor with any other troops in the Nizam's service. In name alone did they belong to the Nizam. They were paid regularly every month from the Resident's treasury, and considered themselves as Company's troops. For all practical purposes they were as much so as those on our own immediate establishment, and could be made quite as useful; for under Captain Hare the Russell Brigade had by this time attained the highest state of efficiency.

The four battalions in Berar had not had the same advantages as the Russell Brigade. They were well spoken of, and when employed on service had done their duty. They were commanded by European officers, and disciplined and equipped like our own troops. Three of the battalions were said to be in good order, but the fourth, of which the command was at that time vacant, was from various circumstances not in such good condition as the other three. Captain Seyer, of the Bengal army, who had highly distinguished himself in the Nepal war, in which he was severely wounded, was subsequently appointed to this vacancy. From this and Major Pitman's appointment great advantage was anticipated, and ultimately the Berar Infantry became part of the present contingent.

There were besides, the troops under Salabut Khan, a chief who had always been distinguished for his attachment and fidelity to our interests. They consisted of 1500 horse and 2000 infantry, paid from the produce of the jagheers held by him under the Nizam's government in the neighbourhood of Ellichpoor. Salabut Khan's horse, although not equal to the reformed, were the next best in the Nizam's service.

The infantry composed a brigade under the command of Captain Lyne of the Company's army. The men approached in discipline to our own troops; but the inveterate abuses which existed in the corps, the number of officers and men whom it had been found necessary to discharge, together with an irregularity in their payment, had prevented so great an improvement being accomplished as might have been desired. They were in consequence not in a condition to act as regular troops with our army.

All that could be expected therefore of Salabut Khan's cavalry and infantry was that they should defend that part of the Nizam's territories contiguous to Ellichpoor.

No brigade in India was more highly disciplined or more complete in appointments, camp equipage, and bazars, than the Russell Brigade. It accompanied the army to Malwa in 1817, composed part of Sir John Malcolm's division at the battle of Mehidpoor; and the records of that day show that no corps was organised on better military principles, or better performed its duty.

" The Commander-in-Chief," as we gather from a General Order of that day, "notices in the highest terms of

praise the steadiness, courage, and discipline of * * * *
and the Russell Brigade under Major Hare." And among
those officers who in General Orders received the public
thanks of the Commander-in-Chief, we find the names of
Captain Hare, commanding the Russell Brigade; Captains
Larride and Currie, commanding the 1st and 2nd Regiments, Russell Brigade; and Lieutenant F. S. Sotheby,
commanding the artillery, Russell Brigade.

Most of the other regiments co-operated with divisions
and detachments of the British army. The Ellichpoor
Brigade served with Colonel Deacon's detachment, Major
Fraser's regiment with Major Pitman's, Captain Blake's
with Major Davis. But none of those corps approached
in discipline to the Russell Brigade; nor, with the exception of Major Fraser's, and perhaps Captain Blake's, were
they disciplined in a degree to admit of their taking their
place even in brigade.

During this year the reformed troops were frequently
employed against the strongholds of bands of freebooters
known by the names of Naiks and Bhils, who had long
infested the province of Berar, and whom it was strongly
suspected the local officers of the Government secretly
encouraged in order to share in the plunder. The gallantry of Jemadar Shaik-Kader-Buksh, with a party of
200 reformed horse, was conspicuous. Dismounting his
small party, he stormed and carried a strong ghurry,
sword in hand. The troops under Major Pitman were
successfully employed in reducing the fort of Urjingaum,
and detachments under Major Fraser and Major Elliot
respectively were employed at different times in similar
operations, and always with equal success. A party of
reformed horse, under Lieutenant John Sutherland, likewise distinguished itself against the garrison of Newas.

The gallant conduct of Lieutenant Sutherland and his party was thought deserving of being brought to the notice of the Governor-General ; and in order to encourage and confirm the spirit of emulation which the example of Captain Davis and his European officers had infused into their troops, the Resident forwarded letters both from himself and Raja Chundoo Lall, to the several native officers of the party, who were respectively addressed by the title of Khan and Rae, applauding their gallantry and good conduct on the occasion.

In March 1818, the following order was issued by Brigadier-General Sir John Malcolm :—

" Brigadier-General Sir John Malcolm cannot allow the separation of so large a party of the Russell Brigade from his force as that ordered to march to-morrow, without expressing his great satisfaction with the conduct of the corps since they were first placed under his orders.

" The Russell Brigade have received the thanks of his Excellency the Commander-in-Chief,—the reward due to their discipline and gallantry on the 21st December.

" It remains only for Brigadier-General Malcolm to state, that since they formed part of his division he had uniform cause to observe that state of excellence which it has attained. He also offers his best thanks to Captains Larride and Currie, commanding the two battalions of the brigade, and to Lieutenant Sotheby, in charge of the ordnance. He has, in the course of the service, had frequent occasions to observe and applaud the zeal and activity of these officers. The Brigadier-General must also express his particular thanks to Surgeon Mickle of the brigade, for his great attention to the sick and wounded. He also begs that Brigade-Major Tucker, and the other officers of the brigade, will accept his best acknowledgment for their officer-like behaviour throughout the campaign; and begs that his thanks may be conveyed to the native commissioned, non-commissioned, and privates, for the cheerful alacrity with which they have uniformly performed their duty as soldiers during a period of trying service."

As we ought not to deprive the Russell Brigade of any of its justly-earned laurels, we must add to that of others the testimony of the Most Noble the Governor-General to its efficiency and good conduct.

"The return of the Russell Brigade," writes Mr. Secretary Adam, in addressing the Resident, "to the dominions of his Highness the Nizam affords the Governor-General an opportunity of which he gladly avails himself to express his entire approbation of the services of that valuable corps during the operations of the late campaign, and the cordial gratification his Lordship has derived from the honourable testimony borne to the merits of Captain Hare and the officers and troops under his command by his Excellency Lieutenant-General Sir Thomas Hyslop and by Brigadier-General Sir John Malcolm, under whose orders the Russell Brigade has been acting since the return of Sir Thomas Hyslop to the Deccan.

"You are requested to bring to the particular notice of his Highness the Nizam's government the just and favourable sense entertained by the Governor-General, and by the officers under whose immediate command it has acted, of the gallantry, conduct, and efficiency of the Russell Brigade, and communicate these sentiments to Captain Hare and the officers and men composing the Russell Brigade."

During this year (1818) Captain Pedlar had the satisfaction of adding to the reputation of the reformed horse, by bringing to notice the individual gallantry of the native

offieers of his risalah in an affair at Nagpore. Each native
officer was rewarded by being addressed, on the part of
Government, by a title one degree superior to that which
he had hitherto held.   The services on another occasion
of Shaik Zoolfikar Alee were distinguished by the approbation of the Governor-General, and rewarded by his being
promoted to the rank and pay of First Jemadar.

After the termination of the Mahratta war in 1819,
Mr. Russell continued to pursue the system of assimilating
the several portions of the force with one another, and the
organisation of the Nizam's army began in consequence to
assume a more regular and consistent form.   The benefits
of the pension establishment, which had for some time past
been enjoyed by the Russell Brigade, were, in March 1818,
extended to the regular infantry in Berar.   The whole
system up to this period appears to have been anomalous
in the extreme, especially in regard to the pay of the
European officers, which was fixed by no rule, but dependent apparently on the degree of interest which the individual possessed at head quarters ; though with reference
to the class of officers in the service, it was probably found
necessary on the introduction of officers from the King's
and Company's army, to fix their pay with reference more
to their qualifications than to the position and rank they
individually held in the service.

The Resident, in reply to Major Pitman's suggestions
in regard to the pay of the European officers and an
increase to the men belonging to the force, draws a curious
distinction between the two classes.   "The pay of a lieutenant," says Mr. Russell, " ought not to be less than 350
rupees per mensem, and that of ensign not less than 250
rupees per mensem ; but the increase of pay, both to the
European and native commissioned officers, ought to be

conditional, and not absolute, the addition being granted to such an extent and in such instances only as the commanding officer may think proper to recommend. The increase of pay to the non-commissioned officers and sepoys is absolute, and is to be granted to them immediately."

Towards the end of the year Major Pitman was summoned to the Residency to aid with his advice and experience in the completion of certain arrangements which the Resident was desirous of making for the improvement of the contingent; for the whole system, from various causes, was found to be so defective as to render it necessary to remodel the whole.

In the Russell Brigade, which was under the immediate supervision of the Resident and regularly paid from his treasury, the system had been assimilated, in a great measure, with that in force among our regular troops. But in Berar the troops had to a certain extent been considered as a separate body, under the control of Raja Govind Buksh, the governor of the province, with whom it rested to provide funds for their payment, and to whom all questions of a general nature, such as the pensioning of officers, accepting their resignation, and other matters connected with the general duties and concerns of the establishment, were referred. The conduct of Raja Govind Buksh had for some time past been a constant source of complaint on the part of the Minister; and in the changes now about to be made, an opportunity was taken to lessen the Raja's power, by withdrawing the troops in a great measure from under his control, and dispossessing him of the districts which had been made over to his management for their payment.

On the 1st of January, 1819, the orders for the reorganisation of the force were promulgated. The principal alterations in the existing system were as follows :—

. · The force was divided into two commands, north and south of the Godavery. Major Pitman was retained in command of the Nizam's troops north of the Godavery, which included the whole service, cavalry, artillery, and infantry, with the exception of the Russell Brigade.

To the command of the Russell Brigade, Major Doveton, of the Madras army, was appointed. It consisted of Captain Hare's brigade of infantry, a small regiment of regular cavalry maintained by a European officer on a contract (including the pay of native officers) of fifty rupees a month for man and horse, a company of artillery, and a small corps of engineers.

The increasing magnitude and importance of the Nizam's military establishments is supposed to have been the cause of the appointment of two field officers from the Company's army to the general command of the two principal branches of it; but as in these two nominations two brigadiers were given to one brigade, Major Doveton's appointment was thought superfluous, and as it cost the Nizam's government some 60,000 rupees a year, might have been dispensed with. . His nomination, moreover, was viewed as a direct supercession of Major Hare, who had long exercised the command, and who was perfectly competent to do so. But both Majors Doveton and Pitman were officers of a superior stamp, whose employment communicated a high professional tone, calculated to elevate the character and the respectability of the service.

A new system was at the same time established for the payment of the troops in Berar. The funds, instead of being provided by Raja Govind Buksh, were to be thenceforward furnished by the Minister under a special engagement entered into with parties at the capital. The Berar establishment, therefore, like that of Hyderabad, though still employed in the same portion of the Nizam's territories as before, were in future to be dependent immediately upon the Minister, instead of being subject as heretofore to the control and authority of Raja Govind Buksh.

Major Pitman was directed to exercise his command on the same principles on which the general command of a collective body of troops would be exercised in the Company's service. Regular reports and returns were to be made to the Resident, from whom the officers commanding the two divisions would, from time to time, receive their instructions. They were, likewise, to correspond with the Resident on all points connected with the general duties and concerns of their respective commands. And to prevent the possibility of any inconvenience to the public service, the officer commanding in Berar was directed to comply with any requisitions he might receive from the political agent at Aurungabad, in cases which would not conveniently admit of the delay of a reference to Hyderabad.

All communications with the local government were to be conducted, as before, through the political agent, who was also to be kept regularly acquainted with the distribution and movements of the troops.

Leave of absence to the native officers and men was to be granted as before at the discretion of the officer commanding, but all applications for leave of absence to the European officers was required to be forwarded to the Resident, who would refer the same to the consideration of the Minister.

The regular troops were to be governed as heretofore by the code of laws then in force. With regard to the reformed horse, Mr. Russell makes the following remark in conveying his instructions to Major Pitman :—" In cases relating to these men a different course must necessarily be pursued. Troops which are irregular in their constitution cannot be governed by the same rules of discipline to which regular troops are subjected. Towards this part of the establishment, therefore, the same course which has hitherto prevailed must be pursued in future. In ordinary cases the personal authority of the officer commanding the horse, or of the commandant of risalahs under him, will be sufficient for the reprehension of the offenders; on more serious occasions he may be discharged, and in the instance of any flagrant crime, the criminal must be delivered up to the officers of the Nizam's government to be judged according to their own laws."

The two irregular battalions under Major Freeman, which were then considered as invalid corps for the rest of the establishment, although generally employed on miscellaneous duties under the local officers of the Nizam's government, were now withdrawn from under their control, and transferred under the new arrangement to Major Pitman's authority.

The Ellichpoor Brigade, forming the contingent of Salabut Khan, had hitherto been considered separate from the rest of the regular force, and little interference had in consequence been exercised in any of its details.

On the death of Mr. Drew, a local officer in the immediate service of Salabut Khan, Captain Lyne, of the Madras army, was, at that chief's particular request, nominated in 1815 to the command of the brigade; but on the decease of that officer the practice of consulting

Salabut Khan seems to have been discontinued, as Major James Grant, of the Madras army, a distinguished cavalry officer, was appointed direct by the Governor-General. He commenced a reform, but with rather a sparing hand. He had not the heart in time of peace to deprive old soldiers of their bread; but still the reform was in progress, when, on the death of that lamented officer, it was in a very short period of time carried into complete effect by Captain Seyer who succeeded him.

The troops were not destined to remain idle. In the beginning of this year (1819) a force under the personal command of Major Pitman, but totally unconnected with the late war, was directed to assemble to the northward of Nandair with the design of taking possession of the late Peishwa's district of Umurkhair, to suppress the insurgent naiks in the neighbourhood, and generally to establish the authority of the Nizam's government over the unsettled districts in that quarter.

The force consisted of two battalions of the Russell Brigade, a field battery and small battering train, the 3rd Battalion of Berar Regular Infantry, and a party of the reformed horse.

Of the insurgents the most important was Nousajee naik, whose principal hold was Nowah, a place of some strength about twenty miles from Nandair. Under the apprehension of an attack, he had collected a large Arab force. From him, therefore, some resistance was anticipated, and preparations for a siege were made accordingly.

A short detail of the operations may not be uninstructive, as showing what may be achieved by talent and perseverance.

Nowah, although small in size, was strong of works. In shape, an oblong square with a bastion at each angle, and one on each side of the gateway. The outworks were a faussebray, covered way, ditch and glacis. The principal gateway was protected by an outwork in which guns were mounted. It was altogether an excellent specimen of fortification, as strong perhaps as a square fort of its size could under any system be made; and the arrangement of the traverses, the glacis, and the clear esplanade around the fort, indicated that the skill of others than natives of India had been employed in its construction.

The only mode of reducing the fort was by regular approaches.

The force took up a position before Nowah on the 8th January. On the 10th a mortar battery was commenced, about 600 yards from the north face of the fort, when the enemy advanced and fired upon our working party. He was immediately driven back into the fort by Captain Hare, with two companies of the Russell Brigade. This battery, and one for our 18-pounders, one hundred paces in advance of it, were completed during the night. Both began to play at sun-rise the following day, with considerable effect, silencing the enemy's guns, and knocking off the defences.

On the evening of the 11th, positions were established to the right and left of our batteries, and within 300 yards of the place; and a 6-pounder and a mortar-battery were constructed in front of the east face, distant 350 yards.

On the night of the 13th the enemy made a sortie, and attempted to pass our post on the right. He was quickly driven back by three companies of the Berar Infantry, under Lieutenant George Hampton, a high-spirited young officer, who had only joined the service two years before.

During the night of the 14th an 18-pounder battery

was advanced to within 250 yards of the fort, and lines of communication were formed between our several advanced positions.

On the 15th, the enemy being very troublesome, a few shells were thrown with considerable effect. From this time up to the 18th the besieged attempted no annoyance, seeming not to understand or to care for our operations.

On the 19th the garrison kept blue lights burning nearly the whole night, and occasionally threw stones from a mortar. About ten o'clock an attempt was made by the rebel chief, Howaji, with a party of horse, to surprise our camp from the rear; but the sentries being on the alert, the piquets soon turned out, and after a little firing he retired, and was pursued some miles by Lieutenant Sutherland and a party of reformed horse, but owing to the darkness of the night he effected a safe retreat.

On the 20th a party from the garrison made a sortie, driving in the working party and destroying a little of our work, but the guard of the trenches obliged them to retire. The fire from the garrison was exceedingly hot, and some loss was sustained.

On the 21st the enemy made a desperate sortie, and, sword in hand, attacked our working party at the head of the sap, but was very soon driven back to the fort.

On the 23rd one of the three Europeans attached to the engineer was mortally wounded.

On the 25th the sap had reached the crest of the glacis, where a 6-pounder battery was established, and two mortars were brought into it. On that night the engineer commenced his mine, which was completed on the 29th. The day of the 30th was employed in battering, and in the evening the breaches assumed a very respectable appearance. Shells and grape were thrown into them during the night.

On the 31st, the breaches being reported practicable, orders were issued for the assault. At two o'clock in the afternoon the mine was sprung. Under cover of the smoke and dust, Ensign Oliphant rushed forward and planted the ladders. The next instant Captain Hare with the Grenadiers, supported by Captain Currie and his light infantry, mounted the breach, fortunately before the garrison had recovered from their consternation,— for there were preparations on the top indicating determined resistance; while George Hampton, in all the pride of youthful strength and courage, bounding so far ahead of his men as to be nearly cut off, carried with his flank companies the enemy's works to the right. In a few minutes the inner fort was carried, and in the course of an hour the whole of the enemy's works were in our possession, with a loss on our side of four killed and seventy-one wounded.

The Arabs continued to defend themselves for a considerable time between the two walls, with the exception of about 200, who fled from the gate of the fort. They were immediately attacked by Lieutenant Ivie Campbell, who commanded a party of infantry posted for the purpose of intercepting them; and nearly at the same time they were charged by Captains Davis, Smith, and Lieutenant Sutherland, with different parties of the reformed horse, so that not a man of the enemy escaped.

The garrison consisted of more than 500 Arabs; of these 100 were taken prisoners, more than eighty of whom were dreadfully wounded, and upwards of 400 dead bodies were counted.

The severe example made of the garrison, although much to be deplored, was not only necessary but unavoidable; and was the means perhaps, in the end, of

CHAP.
IV.

Constitution of, and services.

K 2

lessening the effusion of blood, as deterring the rebel garrisons of other places from offering similar resistance.

Our loss during the whole siege was twenty-four killed and 180 wounded; among the latter were six European officers.

"Major Pitman" (so runs the brigade order of the day) "congratulates the detachments on the fall of the fort; and although he feels obliged to every officer and soldier for their exertions during the siege, his thanks are particularly due to Captain Hare of the Bombay establishment, and the gallant men who stormed the breach.

"It having been an object of primary importance to prevent the escape of the garrison, the services of the reformed horse were of the greatest use for that purpose; and to their watchfulness and zeal during so many successive nights the commanding officer attributes the failure of the many attempts made by the enemy to leave the fort.

"Major Pitman therefore requests Captain Davis to make known these his sentiments to the officers and men under his command.

"Major Pitman cannot conclude without offering to Ensign Oliphant of the Madras Engineers the expression of his unqualified approbation for the skilful display of his professional abilities in the siege of Nowah. To his zealous and indefatigable exertions Major Pitman considers himself chiefly indebted for the opportunity which has been this day given to the gallant troops under his command to make such an example of the enemy."

Nor was the approbation of the Government of India withheld.

"Your despatch of the 5th February," says the Secretary to Government in addressing the Resident, "relating to the capture of Nowah and other operations has been submitted to his Excellency the Governor-General in Council. His Lordship in Council has noticed with the highest satisfaction the distinguished conduct of Major Pitman and the force under his command.

"His Lordship in Council especially applauds the patience and scientific mangements of the siege of Nowah, which is exceedingly creditable to the judgment of Major Pitman; it has excited his Lordship's most marked commendation from its being an instance in which we have availed ourselves of superiority of skill to avoid unnecessary exposure of brave men.

"The merits of Captains Seyer, Davis, Hare, and Ensign Oliphant, have also attracted the particular approbation of his Excellency in Council; and the conduct of the storming party and all the troops engaged in the operations reported in your despatch, is considered to be highly honourable to themselves and the corps to which they belong."

The siege and capture of Nowah deserve some special reflections. Nowah was perhaps the only instance during the Mahratta war of a siege being artfully prosecuted, and, when examined closely, deserves to be held forth as a model of universal practice. It was a bold design on the part of the engineer; for, with only three Europeans and a small working party of seventy men, all more or less ignorant of siege operations, few, with such inadequate means, would have undertaken a regular siege. But the talents of the engineer were of a nature that rose with his difficulties, and the result fully justified his daring mode of proceeding; for, notwithstanding the obstacles opposed by the strength of the place, and the obstinacy of the garrison, the reduction of the fort was effected according to the rules of art and science, without a single instance of failure or disaster. Ensign James Oliphant * of the Madras Engineers, a bold and daring young officer of great skill and enterprise, who conducted the siege, possessed military knowledge extensive both from experience and study, having completed his education at Chatham, where Colonel Paisley had early discovered talents indicating future distinction.

The siege of Nowah belongs especially to the history of the Nizam's contingent; and this must be our excuse for bringing it so prominently forward. Nor would we in the present day withhold from the youthful military aspirant an example so prolific of instruction; for, although to create anything from nothing is what has been and always will be impossible to man, yet to obtain great results with small means is what may be done with much talent, zeal, and perseverance; and the siege of Nowah is an example of it.

The complete success at Nowah was attended ultimately with all the beneficial consequences which were anticipated, and the authority of the Nizam's government was restored in a tract of country which, against every effort of his Highness's irregular troops, had maintained a successful rebellion for twenty years previous. Tranquillity was restored, but there have been no rewards for those whose courage and exertions produced it. It is true that "Mehidpore" and "Nowah" are displayed upon the colours and appointments of the regiments which had the good fortune to be employed on those occasions; but there has been no decoration commemo-

* Afterwards a director of the East India Company.

rating these services bestowed upon the officers and men of the Nizam's contingent.

In April of this year (1819) Mr. Russell, ever mindful of the interests of the troops, obtained for them, in consideration of their "exemplary conduct in the field," further indulgence from the Nizam's government. The soldier was to receive, when rice became dearer than ten seers for the rupee, compensation in money equal to the difference between that rate and the market price — the calculation to be made on that rice called the third sort in the bazaar of the cantonment, and at the rate of one seer a day for each fighting man.

The attention of the Resident was directed at this period to the state of affairs at Ellichpoor, where the proceedings of Futteh Jung Khan, before referred to as a connection of Salabut Khan, were of so extraordinary a nature as clearly to prove a systematic design on his part to subvert the authority of Salabut Khan, and usurp the whole rights and possessions of the family. As the troops were the servants of Salabut Khan, and as he had always been encouraged to look to us for support, it became necessary that we should give him and his family our active and efficient protection, and not allow the troops, in a case where they could not remain neutral, to become an instrument in the hands of Futteh Jung Khan for the perpetration of his nefarious designs. The force of Futteh Jung's authority alone enabled him to carry his measures to the extent he had done; and as that authority rested principally upon the belief that he could command our support, it was peculiarly incumbent upon us to remove that impression and vindicate the rights we were bound to protect. The first thing to be done, therefore, was to extricate Salabut Khan from the degrading state of thraldom into which he had been betrayed, and to secure him and his family against the imminent danger with which they were threatened.

The execution of the necessary measures was confided to Captain Seyer, through whose admirable address, unaided by military force, though troops were placed at his disposal, Salabut Khan's affairs, together with the general political arrangements of Ellichpoor, were brought to a satisfactory conclusion; Futteh Jung Khan being removed from Ellichpoor, and Salabut Khan restored ultimately to his legitimate authority.

An opportunity was now taken of extending our interference to Salabut Khan's contingent, and placing the troops of which it was composed under our more immediate control.

In January 1820 the Ellichpoor Brigade was accordingly constituted a portion of the Berar division under Major Pitman, to whom Captain Seyer was directed to address his reports and returns on all points connected with his brigade. But on subjects not military he was to correspond, as heretofore, direct with the Resident.

The whole of Salabut Khan's troops, according to Captain Seyer's representation, were in such an inefficient state as to render it necessary to remodel the whole establishment. European officers were accordingly appointed, and parties of volunteers from the six infantry corps were transferred to the brigade for promotion in the newly organised battalions. A small party was at the same time sent from the reformed horse to serve as a basis for the formation of the new risalah.

The infantry were formed into two battalions of 650 rank and file each. The pay of the private soldier was increased, and fixed at from seven to eight rupees per mensem when first entertained, and nine rupees after four years' service. Clothing and knapsacks were to be furnished by Salabut Khan. The benefit of rice money and of the invalid and pension establishments were in like manner extended to the brigade, in order to place them on the same footing as the regular troops.

In regard to the cavalry of the Ellichpoor contingent, an arrangement was made by which Salabut Khan was to maintain a new risalah of 600 men, at forty Hyderabad rupees for each man and horse per mensem — in consideration of which a tacit acknowledgment would appear to have been conveyed, that in resigning to us the brigade as newly constituted, all interference on our part was to cease over the remainder of his quota, which was to be left solely under his own personal control, without so much as inquiry being made as to the mode in which it was maintained.

A reduction of useless establishments in the Nizam's own army was effected during this year to the annual extent, it was stated, of between twenty-two and twenty-three lakhs of rupees. Among these reductions were included 305 horse and 500 foot on Raja Chundoo Lall's own personal establishment, and 237 horse and 250 foot on that of his brother, Raja Govind Buksh. All recruiting was suspended, except in the regular and reformed troops, which were to be kept up at their full strength. The annual charge of the contingent was at that time computed at thirty-six lakhs, not including the establishment of Salabut Khan, which was maintained by a jagheer estimated at fourteen lakhs of rupees.

This year was productive of numerous benefits to the officers of the service. A table allowance of 500 Hydera-

bad rupees a month was authorised to each of the commandants of the Hyderabad and Berar divisions, and an
additional monthly allowance of 200 rupees to each of
the following officers: — The commandant of the Russell
Cavalry, the commandant of each battalion of the Russell
Brigade, the commandant of artillery, the brigade-major
of the Russell Brigade, and the surgeon of the Russell
Brigade. Commandants of battalions and risalahs throughout the service having under their orders two or more
complete corps, were authorised to draw superior batta
at the rate of 200 Hyderabad rupees a month, and
officers exercising the temporary command of divisions
were to draw an additional allowance of 500 rupees a
month.

A new and superior rank of native commissioned
officer was established for the Russell Brigade, denominated Soobehdar-Major. The number in the division
was limited to four, one to the regular cavalry, one to
the artillery, and one to each battalion of infantry, with a
brevet pay of twenty-five Hyderabad rupees a month in
addition to the ordinary allowances of the Soobehdar of
a company.

Towards the latter end of the year a new organisation
of the irregular brigade at Aurungabad took place. The
two battalions composing it were brought on the strength
of the Berar division, in order that they might be improved in their condition and rendered fit for the performance of useful duty as veteran corps. Such of the
native officers and men as were found capable of doing
duty were formed into a garrison battalion and employed
in the protection of the districts on the north-west frontier
against the Bhíls. The other, an invalid battalion, was to
consist of men who, having been invalided from the re-

gular corps were still capable of light and easy duty. Their services were to be limited to the furnishing of guards in the Aurungabad city and the neighbouring villages. Such men also as by age or infirmity were incapable of doing any duty whatever were to be transferred to this battalion as pensioners.

On the 1st December, Mr. Russell, on relinquishing the duties of the Residency, took leave of the troops in the following letter to the address of Colonel Doveton:—

" On the occasion of my taking leave of the Hyderabad division of the Nizam's troops, with which I have been so long and so intimately connected by the sentiments of private friendship as well as by the duties of my public station, I request you will yourself accept my cordial thanks, and that you will express to the officers and men under your command the deep sense I entertain of their zeal, exertions, and spirited discharge of their duty on all occasions. The distance at which I am about to be placed from you will in no degree lessen my interest in your welfare, and you will always retain individually and collectively my warmest solicitude for your honour and prosperity."

One of the first measures of Sir Charles Metcalfe was an act of justice to the Nizam's local officers.

Up to the period we are now treating of, servitude in the Nizam's army alone was considered as nothing. A commission in the King's or Company's army supposed everything, was a substitute for everything — was, in short, the measure of an individual's merit. The want of a commission in the British army supposed a disqualification which no amount of professional talent could remove. The continuance of such a system would have doomed the Nizam's captains to the perpetual superiority of King's or Company's lieutenants and ensigns of time present or to come.

To remove at once this defect in promotion, the Resident publicly announced, "That in the Nizam's army all situations are open to officers of merit, and that when the requisite qualifications exist, the want of a commission from the King or Company will not be a ground of exclusion."

Concurrently with this announcement, the following regulations for the better adjustment of the rank of the European officers were published in General Orders:—

" The European officers in the Nizam's regular army, including the reformed horse, will rank in the following order:—

" 1st Class. — Commanders of divisions.

" 2nd Class. — Commanders of brigade, and general or division staff, being field-officers in the King's or Company's service.

" 3rd Class. — Commanders of corps, and general division, or brigade staff, being captains in the King's or Company's service.

" 4th Class.—Captains and officers of any higher rank in the King's or Company's service, not included in the preceding classes.

" 5th Class. — Captains in the Nizam's service.

" 6th Class. — Lieutenants in the King's or Company's service.

" 7th Class. — Lieutenants in the Nizam's service.

" 8th Class. — Ensigns in the King's or Company's service.

" 9th Class. — Ensigns in the Nizam's service."

The Resident, sensibly alive to the imperfections of this arrangement, was not so visionary as to expect that every

onc would be pleased with the place assigned to him; CHAP, IV.
wherefore, in anticipation of the feeling which subse-
quently manifested itself, he made an appeal to the officers Constitu-
of the service in the following terms :— tion of, and services.

"It is feared and deeply lamented that this arrangement must in some measure wouud the feelings of several
officers, by placing above them others who have been
hitherto below them in rank; but it has been found impossible to reconcile the claims of all, or to devise any
scheme wholly free from objections of a similar nature.
The plan now promulgated has been adopted in a belief
of its general justice and expediency. It is hoped that
even to those on whom it may have in some respects a
disadvantageous effect, it will also be found otherwise to
operate with eventual benefit, and that those who in the
first instance suffer by it, will see that the general good
has been the object in view, and repressing the feelings
of dissatisfaction to which any unfavourable change may
naturally give rise, will accept the assurance which is
hereby freely and cordially tendered, that their present
unavoidable disappointment will not be forgotten in future
arrangements, and will be acknowledged to constitute an
additional claim to consideration on all proper occasions."

These regulations remained in force until 1823, when
they were partially modified. They again underwent
various changes and modifications at a subsequent period, and to them we shall take occasion to refer, as we
proceed.

In 1821 the corps of Russell Cavalry was disbanded.
The Ellichpoor Brigade was again made a distinct command, Captain Sir John Gordon appointed to the command
of the Ellichpoor Horse, and his prior office of Quarter-

master abolished. The Quarter-Master of Brigade of the Hyderabad division was also abolished. A judge-advocate was appointed to the Nizam's army in the person of Captain Godley; and as several circumstances pointed out the indispensable necessity of an increase of officers to the cavalry, a second officer (for there had been only one before) was nominated to each of the cavalry corps.

In the following year, the pioneers serving with the several divisions were formed into a corps of engineers, and placed under the command of Captain Oliphant. It consisted of two jemadars, four havildars, six naiks, and seventy-five privates. Their uniform was green with black facings, subsequently changed to scarlet. This corps has proved itself eminently useful on many occasions, particularly in improving the irrigation of the country and in the construction of public works, of which the bridge over the Moossee river need only be named. A European adjutant was subsequently appointed to the corps. In 1837, its designation being changed, it was placed under an officer of the infantry branch, and formed into a pioneer corps, for employment on the roads, construction of travellers' bungalows, and for other useful purposes. In 1846 the corps was disbanded.

In June, 1823, an ordnance-driver company was established for the Hyderabad division, and a new organisation made in the cattle establishment and in the detail of gun and store lascars.

In July the office of medical store-keeper was abolished, and the duties transferred to the Residency surgeon; the salary of the office reverting to the State.

In 1824 several officers were temporarily withdrawn, consequent on the Burmese war. At the end of this year the station of Hingolee was separated from the Aurungabad division and formed into a distinct and independent command, to which Captain Hare was appointed with the rank of Major. In the following year the office of the superintending surgeon was established; and the benefit of furlough to Hindoosthan conceded to the native soldier, in the proportion of ten to every hundred men.

The several corps which hitherto had remained stationary were now ordered to be relieved by one another, and a new designation was given to them. The cavalry corps were numbered from one to five respectively; the companies of artillery from one to four respectively; and the infantry regiments, instead of being designated, as before, according to the division or brigade with which they were serving, were numbered respectively from one to eight.

In arranging numerically the order of the infantry regiments, the Resident considered it due, as a just tribute of his respect for the " brilliant services " of the Russell Brigade, to assign to the two regiments composing it priority of numbers; they were accordingly designated the 1st and 2nd Regiment Nizam's Infantry, or 1st and 2nd *Russell's*, respectively, while the other regiments took their numbers with reference to the periods at which they had been respectively raised.

Another improvement was the publication throughout the contingent of " General Orders by the Resident on the part of the Nizam's government," instead of, as heretofore, carrying on public duty by means of official memoranda which had but limited publication.

In 1826 the designation of " Military Assistant " to the Resident was changed to " Military Secretary." The office of " Commissary of Stores " was created and given to Captain Sotheby, together with the charge of the " General Depôt " which had recently been formed.

In February of the same year the Resident's approbation was conveyed to the Engineer Corps in the following terms : —

" Captain Oliphant having reported the completion of the canal which has been excavated for the purpose of opening a communication between the river Moosee and the tank at Hoossain Sauger, and having brought to the Resident's notice the meritorious conduct of the officers and men of the corps under his command, the Resident deems it incumbent on him to express, in the most public and formal manner, the sense which he entertains of the benefit which has been derived to the public service both from the professional skill, ability, and unremitting exertion which have been manifested by Captain Oliphant in the progress and completion of this important work, and also from the spirit of zeal and alacrity with which the officers and men of the corps under his command have been animated, and which have uniformly characterised their exertions during the period of sixteen months in which they have been employed in the prosecution of it.

" As a mark of his distinguished approbation of their services on this occasion, the Resident is pleased to authorise a donation of 300 rupees to be presented to the corps; and as a further testimony of his satisfaction, the Soobehdar is promoted to the rank of Soobehdar Major."

In the following year the Medical Depôt was again removed from the Residency to Bolarum, and the office of Store-keeper re-established. The designation of the several commands, which had heretofore been " Brigades," was changed to " Divisions," and commanders promoted from the rank of Major to that of Lieutenant-Colonel, which it was determined was thenceforward to be the rank of officers in that position.

In February of this year a third officer, under the designation of Adjutant, was appointed to the several cavalry
corps ; and a few months afterwards, regulations, having
for their object the change of costume from the native to
European, were established for the officers and men of the
cavalry brigade.

Numerous other innovations, opposed and unsuited to
the habits and customs of the men, proceeding from
a spirit of intemperate zeal for the improvement of the
brigade, together with an over-anxious desire to transform
the native horseman into a regular disciplined soldier, had
taken place in the cavalry during the two preceding years,
producing serious discontent, which, operating with other
exciting causes, burst into open mutiny, and led to an
event of a painful and outrageous character.

The real motives to mutiny are not always discoverable.
In this instance they were to be traced to a series of acts,
some of them tyrannical, others imprudent, all of them
opposed to the spirit of the engagement under which the
men entered into the service.

One of the most prominent was the mode and severity
of punishment, another the harsh and harassing system of
drill and discipline. These, combined with other causes
of dissatisfaction, proceeding from disproportionate stop-
pages from their pay on account of various articles of
equipment provided at their expense, and which had frequently undergone capricious alterations, together with
innovations in dress, distasteful both on account of the
expense as well as from the nature of some of the materials, produced a feeling of irritation which was inflamed
into open mutiny by the violent and indefensible conduct
of an European officer in ordering two men to be forcibly
shaved, and publicly declaring that all who did not volun-

tarily remove their beards should suffer the same treatment.

On the following morning a party of one regiment were found drawn up in a state of mutiny, demanding with arms in their hands their immediate discharge from a service in which they had been exposed to such indignities. Colonel Davies rode to the spot. The mutineers signalled him off, advising him not to approach them in their then exasperated state. With that fearless confidence which characterised him on every occasion of danger, he heeded not their advice, but rode up to the party alone and unattended; when, while in the act of endeavouring to reclaim his deluded men to a sense of their duty, the gallant Davies was shot through the body by the ringleader, when the rest followed up the outrage by cutting him almost to pieces. The mutineers were instantly charged by a party of their own comrades who had been drawn up near the spot, and most of them put to instant death; for the mutinous spirit was confined to the few only who were immediately concerned in the perpetration of the outrage.

Such was the amiable private character of Colonel Davies, and so much was he beloved by his men generally, that his death (had it happened under ordinary circumstances) would have been a cause of general sorrow. As it was, it was met with a general burst of horror, as honourable to the unhappy victim as it was indicative of the feelings of the men, for not only had his gallant bearing won for him their admiration, but his conciliatory disposition, his justice, and his attention to their wants on all occasions, had ensured him also their affection.

Immediately after this the whole system of the cavalry was reorganised, all objectionable regulations were re-

scinded, and the several corps remodelled, when the brigade, under the able and judicious management of Major
Sutherland, soon regained its former credit and reputation.

At the end of the year a gold medal, bearing a suitable
device and inscription, was presented to Soobehdar-Major
Chyte Singh and Soobehdar-Major Chota Singh, of the 1st
Regiment Infantry, in consideration of their long services
and uniform meritorious conduct; the latter having gained
his promotion for planting the colours of his regiment on
the bastion of Nowah.

In 1828 the Court of Directors prohibited the employment of any more local officers in the Nizam's service. In
the same year the establishment of privates of corps of
infantry was fixed at 700, and no man under five feet five
inches was allowed to be entertained. In the following year the establishment was again reduced to 640
privates.

Up to this period the contingent had been virtually a
sort of plaything for the Resident and a source of patron-
age to his friends. Things were now to take another
direction, and a few simple regulations laid the axe to
the root of every sort of abuse.

In 1829 several privileges heretofore exercised by the
Resident in connection with the service were withdrawn
by the Governor-General, who directed that no original
appointment to the service or promotion in it was thenceforward to take place except under the authority of the
Supreme Government. A new scale of pay and allowances was at the same time established for the European officers, on the principle of assimilating their rate
of emoluments with that of corresponding situations

in the Company's army, and in order that there might be no mistake, the pay tables common to the three presidencies were directed to be taken as the guide, and in cases of difference the rates in use in the Hyderabad Subsidiary Force were to be adopted.

Retrenchment did not stop with the reduction of pay and allowances. Its operation was extended throughout the service, and in January 1830, the appointments of Superintending Surgeon, Medical Storekeeper, and Surgeon to the Durbar, Principal Commissary of Ordnance, and Judge-Advocate-General were abolished, and the offices of Brigade-Major and Paymaster of the Ellichpoor and Hingolee divisions united. Officers whose appointments were abolished were allowed to resume the situations which they previously held, their successors in those situations making way for them and returning in like manner to the situations which they before occupied, and so on downwards.

By the abolition of these appointments and by the reduction of the allowances of others in the civil as well as military department, an annual saving of nearly three lakhs of rupees was effected in the two following years.

In 1832, in consequence of the repeated failure of Nuwab Namdar Khan to pay the troops of the Ellichpoor division, for which he held a jagheer, having been confirmed on the death of his father in 1824 in all the family privileges, the jagheer for the payment of the troops was resumed by the Nizam's government, and the payment of the Ellichpoor division transferred to the Minister's own authority, thus placing the Ellichpoor force, which had by degrees become assimilated in other respects, precisely on the same footing as the rest of the Nizam's regular cavalry.

In 1833 the office of Bazaar Master in the several brigades was discontinued.

. In the same year the Nizam's service lost one of its oldest and best officers. The late Lieutenant-Colonel Seyer was an irreparable loss to the Nizam's army. His acquaintance with the history of the Indian army and the character of the soldiers of whom it is composed, his extensive military research and acquaintance with the armies of other countries, rendered him a fit person to be consulted in the management of the Nizam's, and an officer to whose sound judgment and discretion its direction might safely be left.

In 1834 a warrant-officer under the designation of quarter-master was authorised for each field-battery, a measure highly expedient and useful, and which has tended much to the benefit of the artillery branch of the service. This class of warrant-officers should be allowed to draw horse allowance. They cannot do their duty either on parade or on the march without being mounted. As it is, their duty is always performed on horseback, but as no allowance is granted for the purpose, they virtually keep a horse at their own expense for the performance of their public duty. This, we conceive, only requires to be brought to notice to be rectified. There being, moreover, only four of this class, we cannot suppose that so small an addition to the public expenditure would be any obstacle to the adoption of so just a measure.

During this year the Minister was very importunate to get rid of the expense of the garrison and invalid corps. Among other schemes, he proposed to commute the money payment to the invalids by a grant of land in perpetuity to. each man, but it was found impracticable, for, on proposing the arrangement to the men themselves, they with one accord declined the offer; so the proposal fell to the ground.

In consequence of the abolition of the appointment of Judge-Advocate-General in 1830, the Resident had frequently had occasion to solicit the opinion of the Deputy Judge-Advocate-General of the subsidiary force on points connected with the proceedings of courts-martial, as well as on other matters connected with the character and discipline of the Nizam's army. Under a conviction of the importance of his legal advice, and from the same considerations which have given rise to this appointment in other armies, and to enable the Resident to call officially for advice in cases of difficulty, the Judge-Advocate-General of the subsidiary force was, under the sanction of the Supreme Government, appointed in 1835 legal adviser to the Resident on such questions as he might find it necessary to refer to him.

In 1836 the much-desired boon of furlough to Europe was conceded to the local officers, with permission to return to their several appointments. When it is considered that this class of officers are deprived of the benefit both of a pension and retiring fund, of Lord Clive's fund, of the military funds, together with other advantages possessed by the Company's officer, and that they have only the Nizam's service to depend upon for their support and maintenance, the extension of this indulgence to them cannot be viewed as unreasonable.

In November 1837 it was notified to the Nizam's army that henceforth Company's officers would only be entitled to promotion to the rank of Captain in the Nizam's army (unless previously promoted in their own service), in twelve years from the date of their being admitted on the strength of the establishment to which they may belong,

and not as heretofore in twelve years from the date of
their nomination by the Court of Directors or first commission, as Cornet or Ensign.

An increased rate of pay was, in January 1839, authorised to the native commissioned officers in consideration
of the exemplary conduct which for a series of years had
marked the career of that respectable class in the Nizam's
service.

An indulgence was about this time conceded to the
private soldier, in extending the annual leave of absence
to men to visit Hindoosthan from six to eight months. No
trifling boon when the distance is taken into consideration, as well as the unhealthy season of the year at which
the men were before obliged to return.

In July the warrant and non-commissioned officers of
the service were stimulated to greater exertions by the
increased promotion held out to them in the following
General Order : —

" In order to hold out still greater encouragement to
the warrant and non-commissioned officers of his Highness
the Nizam's army to display that zeal in the performance
of their duties which must ever lead to promotion, and
to the approbation of their superiors, General Fraser has
been pleased to direct that there be a Deputy Assistant
Commissary at each of the undermentioned stations of
the army, viz., Hyderabad and Ellichpoor, independently
of Aurungabad.

" Though General Fraser is happy on this occasion to
find that no objection exists to the nomination of the two
senior conductors to the rank of Deputy Assistant Commissary, he desires that it may be distinctly understood
that in no case will he consider seniority alone to constitute

a sufficient claim for promotion, unless it be when the claim of merit may be equal between the candidates."

At the end of this year the office of Superintending Surgeon was revived and a senior surgeon authorised at each division of the army in the person of the senior medical officer of the division.

In 1839 a medical school was established at Bolarum for the education of pupils intended for the subordinate medical grades of the Nizam's army. The object of the school was to give a high tone and more scientific character to the professional education of the medical subordinates than had previously obtained. This institution continued for seven years, when, as its advantages did not correspond with the expectations under which it was originally established, it was in 1846 superseded by a similar institution at the Residency, but totally unconnected with the Nizam's service.

The object of the present institution is the diffusion of sound medical knowledge among the respectable natives of the country generally, but more particularly of those residing in and about the city. The benevolent views of the Resident were seconded by the Nizam's government, who cheerfully placed the means of accomplishing them at his disposal. Under the zealous and able instruction of Dr. Maclean, the Residency surgeon, this excellent and useful institution is improving every day, and there is every reason to believe that in its result it will be most beneficial to the people, as rendering them independent of European aid, and in time removing their prejudices against European practice. The cost of maintaining such an institution must be small, compared with the large amount of good which, from its locality, it is calculated to produce among the native population.

In June 1840, the garrison and invalid battalions were disbanded.

The battalions had, for a long time previous, ceased to answer the ends for which they were originally formed, while the expense of keeping them up had been a constant source of complaint with the Minister. The abolition of them was therefore of advantage in every point of view. The European officers, and such of the native officers and others as were entitled to pension by the regulations of the service, were transferred to the pension establishment; and such men as were considered fit for duty were transferred to a new company designated the hill rangers, then authorised to be formed, and to be located in the hill districts between the Nizam's and the Company's territories for the preservation of the peace, and for reducing to order those amongst the bheels and other inhabitants of the hill country who were found to be constantly plundering their more peaceful neighbours. By these arrangements a considerable saving was effected.

Towards the end of 1841 it was notified that all European commissioned, warrant, and non-commissioned officers, serving with the Nizam's army, shall be ruled and governed by the Mutiny Act and Articles of War in force for the East India Company's European troops, subject to certain modification and alterations.

In the beginning of 1842 the Bolarum force was ordered into the neighbouring cantonment of Secunderabad in consequence of the insubordinate proceedings of a portion of the native troops composing the subsidiary force. A detail of these proceedings is unnecessary in this place, nor is it our wish to dwell upon events of so discreditable a character. It is a much more gratifying duty to record praise than censure; and the exemplary conduct of the

Madras Artillery, European and native, and of the 1st Madras European Regiment, on that occasion was most conspicuous, and drew forth from the Government the expression of the highest praise. The admirable conduct and soldier like behaviour of the native artillery cannot be too highly extolled nor too often recorded, for not only did the F. troop horse artillery and B. company golundauze "stand forward in the most prompt and praiseworthy manner to maintain subordination," but their comrades at the head-quarters of the regiment, on hearing that a disturbance was likely to occur, wrote up to them to maintain the honour of the corps by obeying their officers and submitting to the orders of Government. The Madras Government marked its sense of their good conduct by permitting the whole of the men composing those two detachments to reckon three years' additional service. Both officers and men may well be proud of each other, proud also of belonging to so distinguished a corps.

Order and discipline were at length restored without any actual outbreak, when the Nizam's troops returned to their own cantonment, but it is undoubted that the result might have been different, if one less firm or less able had been employed, for the crisis demanded promptness and energy, and he who assumed the command on and for the occasion fortunately possessed those qualities, and knew besides how to create them in others.

In April of this year, consequent on the formation of the new cantonment of Lingsoogoor, a revision of the establishments of the artillery and ordnance department took place. The field batteries were reduced from six to four guns each, and the golundauze from a hundred to eighty men a company. The field batteries were ordered to be maintained in a state of the most perfect efficiency, ready to move at the shortest notice.

In 1843 some modifications were made in the cavalry branch of the service. The 5th Regiment, which had been maintained on the principle of regular cavalry, was formed into an irregular corps transferred to the cavalry division and rendered subject in every respect to the same rules and usages as the other four regiments.

In 1847 a new cantonment was established at Wurungul.

Towards the close of this year the numerical strength of the privates of the several infantry corps was reduced from 640 to 600.

In the beginning of 1848 an alteration was made in the dress of the European and native officers of the cavalry. The ulkhaluq and mundeel turban were substituted for the European dress of the European officers. We have no doubt that there were good and sufficient reasons for this change; but as it involved young officers in debt, by rendering useless to them their previous dress and appointments, which some of them had only recently and at great expense furnished themselves with, it would certainly have been more to their interests had the change not taken place. Let us never forget that changes and even advantages may be purchased at too high a price.

The contingent, as at present constituted, consists of five regiments of cavalry, eight regiments of infantry, four companies of artillery with field batteries attached, and a corps of hill rangers, together with an efficient medical department, and arsenals at the principal military stations, equipped with siege-ordnance, ammunition, and stores of every description. In numbers the force may be thus detailed:—

Cavalry	2750	fighting-men.
Artillery . . .	725	ditto.
Infantry	5752	ditto.
Hill Rangers . . .	170	ditto.
Total of all native ranks	9397	

The European officers, of whom there are eighty-four, are distributed as follows:—

	Lieut.-Colonels.	Majors.	Captain-Comdts.	Captains.	Lieutenants.	Surgeons.	Asst.-Surgeon.	Total.
Military Secretary	0	1	0	0	0	0	0	1
Officers commanding Divisons .	2	3	0	0	0	0	0	5
Superintending Surgeon . . .	0	0	0	0	0	1	0	1
Brigade-Majors	0	0	0	5	0	0	0	5
Paymasters (in course of absorption)	0	0	0	2	0	0	0	2
Cavalry	0	0	1	8	6	4	1	20
Artillery	0	0	1	4	0	0	0	5
Infantry	0	0	8	22	7	8	0	45
Total .	2	4	10	41	13	13	1	84

There are besides thirty-seven European warrant and non-commissioned officers, and a medical staff of fifty-five subordinates.

The Nizam's cavalry are too well known to require any description in this place. Their superiority over all other irregular cavalry is generally admitted; for their pay being handsome, a higher degree of efficiency, both in horses and accoutrements, is required,—which makes the service better and more efficient than the irregular cavalry of the presidencies. The native horsemen themselves are everywhere much the same, and, when they are well treated, devoted to their officers. The great difference observable in the conduct and behaviour of these men will generally be found to arise from the character CHAP. of their commander, and from his mode of treatment. IV. The Nizam's regiments are at all times in a condition fit Constitution of, and for immediate service, complete in horses, arms, appoint- services. ments, bazaars, &c., ready to take the field at the shortest notice, without requiring aid from the Government, or any further assistance than that furnished from their own bazaars.

It is to be regretted, we think, that greater encouragement is not given to the men of the Deccan to enter this branch of the service. We have always understood that the Nizam's cavalry were originally formed with a view to give employment to a large number of men, generally of good birth and respectability, but of reduced circumstances, who were roaming about the country in idleness, ready for any sort of mischief, and who might be thus converted, from being a source of trouble and annoyance to the Government, into cheerful and useful subjects. If, therefore, only as an outlet for the discontented, we would venture to suggest that every inducement should be held out to the men of the Deccan, of character and respectability, to enter the Nizam's cavalry, in preference to the present system of recruiting indiscriminately. The cost of this branch of the service is nearly one half of the entire contingent; but that its real utility to the State compensates the Nizam's government for the immense outlay, we may perhaps be allowed to doubt. We are constrained, therefore, while admitting their efficiency, and even their superiority, to express our opinion that so large a body of cavalry are nearly thrown away in the Deccan. For all useful purposes one half of the present force would be amply sufficient. It is out of all proportion to the other arms. For the last thirty years the regiments have never

taken the field together; and we have it on the best authority, that they cannot participate where they might be
made very useful in the stirring scenes on the distant
frontier, in consequence of their superiority of pay over
the Bengal Irregular Cavalry; a distinction, however, warranted by the state of the two countries.   In the Deccan
almost all articles of consumption are dearer than in Hindoosthan, and a proportionate difference in the pay of the
military has consequently always existed.   At the time
when the Mahratta armies traversed India from the Tum-
buddra to the Indus, it was at all times usual to reduce
the pay of the military on the day on which they crossed
the Nerbudda, proceeding to the northward; and, in the
same manner, the pay was always increased on the armies
crossing the same river to the southward.   We have, then,
a large, efficient force of cavalry, part of which might well
be spared from the Deccan, but which cannot, from circumstances, be employed elsewhere, at a cost to the
Nizam's government of nearly eighteen lakhs of rupees
per annum.   To this we have but one answer, as to other
questions of similar import:—the Nizam cannot afford it.
This is the language of necessity, which cannot be spoken
too often.   Two regiments might certainly be spared from
the contingent; but as these are not times for disbanding
troops, they might be transferred, under some suitable
arrangement, to the Bengal presidency.   The field artillery
is considered as efficient as it can be under the present
system of draught.   The equipments are complete, and in
high order.   The golundauze are well trained and instructed.   We have witnessed them, with a battery of six
guns, fire, dismount the guns, sit down, mount the guns,
and fire again, in less than *one minute and five seconds;*
and we doubt if this can be surpassed.   We are not partial

to such displays, inasmuch as it fatigues the men unnecessarily, and too often injures them; though when a thing is to be done, we like to see it well done. There is little to object to in the Nizam's artillery, except in the draught cattle; but field artillery drawn by bullocks, however excellent in other respects, *must* become, under difficulties, an incumbrance instead of an assistance to any army. We are not at this time of day going to insult the understanding of the reader by detailing with tiresome repetition all that has been written on this question. Enough that the superiority of horse draught is acknowledged, and is now being practically manifested in the Madras army, as it has long been in that of Bengal. We would rather see two horse than four bullock batteries, on the principle that whatever portion of artillery is kept up should be made efficient in every respect. The quality rather than the quantity should be attended to. The guns drawn by horses to *clear* the way, instead of being drawn by bullocks to *stop* the way. The infantry corps are considered in every respect equal to the regiments of either of the presidencies, with this exception—that they have not the same number of European officers. The men are chiefly from Hindoosthan. The Nizam's army has always been a favourite service with the Hindoosthanees, for although removed to a greater distance from their homes, they have a corresponding advantage in respect to furlough. From their frugal habits they often save money enough to enable them to return to their families after eight or ten years' service,—thus giving the State the benefit of the best years of their life. This we conceive cannot be too much encouraged, for the expense of drilling and training a recruit for the ranks is incomparably less than that which is inflicted on the

State by an extension of the pension list. The comfort
of the soldier is besides consulted, and no man is made
unhappy by being forced to remain in a situation against
his inclination. The men are admirably drilled and disciplined. The arms and accoutrements are supplied from
the Government arsenals; the clothing, which is of a
superior description, from the Presidency, and two companies of each regiment have percussion muskets. In
their internal arrangements they are regulated by the
same principles which prevail in the Company's army.
This, although a good deal, is not saying everything.
There is nothing of the *real* business of the soldier in all
this. It is not the appearance at parade, nor being expert
in certain exercises, than can make a man a soldier. It
is but a very small proportion of the force that can boast
of the experience of field service. Their real utility
remains therefore to be tested, though we have no doubt
that when the day of fighting shall arrive, every branch
of the force will perform the same valuable service as did
the Russell Brigade in its early days. We have always
been of opinion that, in a staff service like this, the
principle of selection and not of seniority should influence
the nomination to the higher commands. The importance
of having for these responsible posts only men of temper
and understanding must be so obvious that no considerations of seniority or length of service should lead to the
advancement of those who are wanting in these essentials.
In these remarks we claim to be understood as having no
desire to exalt one class at the expense of another. We
are not unmindful that there are some individuals among
the old officers of the service, whose zeal and worth it
would be difficult to over-estimate. Than the first and
second "Russell's," under their old and zealous com-

mandants, there are not perhaps two finer native regiments in the Indian army. But it is of systems that we
are treating, not of individual cases. At present there is
no safeguard, of sufficient efficacy to prevent the higher
ranks being officered by persons who shall be wanting in
the qualifications for command. We have known more
than one officer in command of a regiment and on staff
employ not only deficient, but illiterate. These allusions
can no longer wound the feelings of the living. They
were promoted, not for their qualification, but because
they were senior. To have passed them over would have
been an invidious task. The first and only consideration
for the higher commanders, we conceive, should be fitness. The qualifications to be sought for should consist
in something more than the mechanical operations of the
parade. Men qualified in every respect should be selected
of decided mental ability, at least respectable general
acquirements, and of a temperament capable of producing
and preserving harmony with discipline, for every one
knows how freaks of power, always the growth of a little
mind, tend to irritate and to destroy unanimity. Such
are the men we would see advanced to the higher ranks
of the Nizam's army. The service should be one of
selection. Qualifications should be sought for, and *wherever* found, cherished; and instead of conferring appointments merely on account of seniority, *merit* should have
its true place; for constituted as that army is, we
conceive it to be neither safe nor consistent with a just
regard to the interests of the public service to regulate
the nomination to the higher ranks by any other principle.
Much has been written in regard to the staff of the contingent. We are not of those who think it too large.
Concentrate the force, and one brigadier might suffice, as

CHAP.
IV.

Constitu-
tion of, and
services.

in the neighbouring cantonment of Secunderabad; but, dispersed as the troops now are, supervision is not only necessary, but indispensable. These commands, moreover, involve peculiar important political duties unknown to officers in similar positions in the Company's army. The Nizam's army is at present cantoned as follows :—Ellich-poor, Aurungabad, Mominabad, Goolburgah, Hingolee, Bolarum, Warungul, Mucktul, and Lingsoogoor, with the hill rangers at Boldanah to protect that part of the hill country. A glance at the map will show that from one or other of these positions, each portion of the Nizam's dominions is within a few days' march of the control of the regular troops, and it may be observed that the contingent, although prepared to set against external enemies, is chiefly required to check the various tributaries and powerful zumeendars who are subject to the Nizam; and who, in the absence of regular troops, would not only in many instances resist the orders of Government, but would constantly be resorting to arms to decide quarrels among themselves, to the great injury of the Nizam's subjects and to the detriment of the revenue.

By the Treaty of 1853 with the Nizam, the Hyderabad contingent is a British auxiliary force, consisting of four regiments of cavalry, 600 strong of all ranks, six infantry regiments of 800 rank and file, and four batteries of 100 men each. They were thus distributed at the end of 1860:—

Stations.	Artillery.	Cavalry.	Infantry.
Bolarum	4 guns.	Wing.	Regiment.
Lingsoogoor	2 guns.		Ditto.
Mominabad	—	Regiment.	
Hingolee	Battery.	Wing.	Regiment.
Ellichpoor	Ditto.	Ditto.	Ditto.
Jaulnah	2 guns.	Squadron.	Detachment of one wing.
New station, near Mulleapoor in West Berar	4 guns.	Regiment.	Regiment.

At the time of writing, I hear that Mr. Temple, of the Bengal Civil Service, has been specially charged by the Governor-General to reduce even this force, which really is, after all, too large for any object; but the measure, I fear, will prove distasteful to those most interested in its maintenance.

N.B.—With a view to explain the frequent use of the plural pronoun in this chapter, I must mention that the greater portion of it is from the article in the *Calcutta Review* referred to in the Preface of this work.

CHAP.
IV.

Constitu-
tion of, and
services.

CHAP. V.

THE FIRM OF MESSRS. WILLIAM PALMER AND COMPANY. — ITS ORIGIN
AND DECLINE. — THE TREATMENT OF MR. PALMER BY THE BRITISH GO-
VERNMENT.

CHAP.
V.

Mr. Pal-
mer's pa-
rentage.

IN the year 1799 — the very time that the map of India
attached to the *Wellington Despatches* so accurately de-
fines the then limits of the Nizam's dominions — a young
East Indian of not more than nineteen years of age
arrived at Hyderabad.   He had had the advantage of the
best education that an academy in England could afford,
and it was his good fortune to be the eldest son of General
Palmer*, by that Begum of Lucknow whose features have
been transmitted to canvas by the brush of Zoffany, and
whose names are still blended in the portraiture of the
early English in India.   General Palmer was at one time
the British Resident at the Court of the Peishwa at
Poona.   Indeed, during a long period of years, General
Palmer filled many of the most important stations in
India, with the highest honour to himself and advantage
to his country, while the virtues of his private life endeared him to all who had an opportunity of approaching
him.   So, when this great man died, the following order
was issued by the Government of India : —

* Born 1740, and died 20th May, 1816.

"Fort William, May 24th, 1810.

"His Excellency the Right Honourable the Governor-General in Council has received, with sentiments of the deepest concern, the melancholy intelligence of the decease at Burhanpoor, on the 20th instant, of Lieutenant-General William Palmer, of the Honourable Company's service.

"The character and distinguished political services of Lieutenant-General Palmer have been repeatedly noticed by the Supreme Government in terms of the highest approbation and applause ; and the loss must be felt with proportionate regret. His Lordship in Council, as a peculiar mark of the sense entertained by Government of the merits of this able and upright public officer, and as a testimony of respect due to his memory, is pleased to direct that seventy-six minute guns— corresponding with the age of the deceased — be fired this evening from the ramparts of Fort William ; the flag being hoisted half-mast high.

"G. W. GARDINER,
"Secretary to Government Military Department."

Two of General Palmer's sons — the elder by his English wife — founded the houses respectively of Palmer and Company, at Calcutta, of which John Palmer was the chief; and of William Palmer and Company, at Hyderabad, in the Deccan, of which his younger brother William was the head. Their names might have been known, or have passed into oblivion, with other commercial firms which existed at the time, but for the celebrity given them by Sir Charles Metcalfe, who liked the brother at Calcutta, whom he had long intimately known, and who quenched the light of the man at Hyderabad, whom he did not absolutely dislike, but felt and found to be an obstacle in his orbit as a political luminary.[*] I might be accused of attempting fiction in writing in this manner, but I cannot do better than adopt the very language of Sir Charles to Lord Hastings, the Governor-General, in September 1821: — " Mr. John Palmer has been my much-esteemed and warm friend for the last twenty years ; and Mr. William Palmer himself is one of those men so amiably constituted by nature, that it is impossible to know ever so little of him without feeling one's regard and esteem attracted."

Mr. William Palmer arrived at Hyderabad after the French battalions in the Nizam's service had been disbanded, and while the Nizam had in his employ a motley crew of Germans, Spaniards, Italians, and Portuguese, to organise the rabble known as his army. Some idea may be formed of the character of these Europeans when I mention that Murray, a deserter from the English ranks, commanded a corps, and that for the sake of his personal safety, to prevent the British Resident getting at him, he never went about without a guard of fifty men! Gardner, afterwards in Runjeet Singh's service, was for a time in the Nizam's employ ; but as he was intriguing against the English, the Resident, under instructions from Calcutta, was ordered to seize him, which Colonel Kirkpatrick did, but the guards allowed him to escape. He was recaptured at Poona by General Palmer, while travelling in a woman's cart, where the curtains are always down for the sake of concealment.

---

[*] " As Resident at Hyderabad he would be resident indeed," p. 428. To Lord Hastings, Metcalfe writes : —" I must act up to the part which necessarily belongs to my office."— KAYE's *Life of Lord Metcalfe*, i. 428.

Mr. William Palmer was the first British subject who entered the Nizam's force; he soon rose to the position of Brigadier, and proved his daring and talent in some military engagements. With all the partisanship that may be charged to the able and accomplished biographer of Lord Metcalfe, I may quote even what is thought to be his reluctant testimony to the character of Mr. Palmer, when he says to " good courage and excellent abilities " he has the credit of having " rendered considerable service to the State by supplying, when at a distance from Hyderabad, information to the British Resident (Captain Sydenham) relative to the outlying districts and the neighbouring native states; and he was sometimes employed to negotiate with the rebellious subjects of the Nizam." * Palmer was one of the officers who escaped, at the cruel butchery, on the 12th February, 1818, by Mohiput Ram, of the Nizam's troops, to tell the tale of the cowardly conduct of the cavalry on the occasion, and to furnish the *matériel* of the British Resident's despatch to the Governor-General.

Palmer's life would seem to have been crowded with incidents even in this brief space of ten years. Whatever the occasion, I find that in August 1810 he has retired from the Nizam's service, is in one of the bungalows at the British Residency, has established " the great mercantile house," according to KAYE, of William Palmer and Company, and is carrying on that business in the bungalow aforesaid. The house then consisted of William Palmer, his brother Hastings; Bunketty Doss, a Hindoo soucar of Guzerat; Samuel Russell, and William Currie. It is

* KAYE's *Life of Metcalfe*, i. 372. Major Joseph Gordon was killed, and Captains Bridges, Foxman, and Henry Burgh were those who escaped with Palmer.

necessary now to my narrative to give an account of these different parties, to a right apprehension of their position, in view to following circumstances which I shall have to relate in order of time. Hastings Palmer, as I have already said, was a younger brother of both John and William. He was a man of a gay, sociable disposition; and all that the public have ever known of him, besides the fact that in early life he had, been an indigo planter and a partner with Mr. Charles Hampton in an estate close to Moorshedabad, which he gave up to join his brother William and this latter particular partnership, is, that Sir Charles Metcalfe "accepted without hesitation, as a personal favour from him, the loan of a house at Aurungabad, which he occupied till he could otherwise accommodate himself." In October 1860 Hastings Palmer paid the debt of nature, and he lies interred at the cemetery on the grounds of the British Residency, a little distance from his early acquaintance, Bushby, the Second Assistant to Sir Charles Metcalfe. Bunketty Doss was reported to be a millionaire; at all events, his credit was so large that he could at a moment command any amount of money of his countrymen. Owing to the similarity in name, Samuel Russell was said to be a brother of Charles and Henry Russell, respectively Residents at Hyderabad; but he was no connection. Samuel Russell had been a lieutenant in the corps of Madras Engineers, and while in the service was sent to Hyderabad to build the present British Residency. He had got as far as Poona, on his way home with Captain Sydenham upon his resignation of office, when Mr. Henry Russell, who had been transferred from the Court of the Peishwa to that of the Nizam, brought him back from Poona to Hyderabad. Samuel Russell then resigned the service of

Government, and joined the firm of William Palmer and
Company. Mr. Henry Russell, the Resident, embarked
some money in Samuel Russell's share, of which the senior
partner knew nothing at the time, but he became aware
of the fact some six months afterwards, as well as that
Henry Russell drew profit in proportion to his contribution. From these circumstances, Henry Russell was
imputed by the friends of Metcalfe in the battle that was
waged at the India House in Leadenhall Street, to be a
partner in the house of William Palmer and Company; but
he was never so. . Samuel Russell left the firm in 1813,
with about twelve lakhs of rupees, the half of which he had
brought into the house. William Currie was a surgeon
on the Madras establishment, and held the appointment
of surgeon to the British Residency; he was an avouched
partner in the house, as all civil surgeons of the East
India Company, up to the year 1840, were allowed to
trade. Dr. Currie brought two lakhs of rupees as his
share to the house.

In 1816 the house obtained a licence from the Supreme
Government of India, in compliance with certain requisitions of an Imperial Act of 1797, to legalise its transactions.

As curiosities, both in a literary and commercial sense,
I reproduce the letter from the Government of India to
William Palmer and Company furnishing the instrument
asked for, together with copy of that instrument :—

Letter from Secretary to Government to Messrs. WILLIAM
PALMER *and* COMPANY, *Hyderabad.*

" Gentlemen,—1. I am directed to acknowledge the
receipt of your letter of the 27th June, requesting the

CHAP.
V.

Partners in
the firm.

consent and approbation of his Excellency the Governor-
General in Council to your doing the several acts from
which you would be restrained by the 37th Geo. III. cap.
142, sec. 28, unless consented to and approved of by the
Governor-General in Council in writing.

" 2. The Governor-General in Council being satisfied
that the interests both of the dominions of his Highness
the Nizam and of the Honourable Company will be promoted by the success and security of your commercial and
pecuniary transactions, as explained in your letter, has
been pleased to comply with your application. I am accordingly directed to transmit to you a writing, under the
signature of the Governor-General in Council and the seal
of the Honourable Company, signifying the permission of
the Supreme Government for your performing the acts
above referred to, with no other reservation than that it
shall be at the discretion of the British Resident at Hyderabad for the time being to satisfy himself regarding the
nature and objects of the transactions in which you may
engage under the permission now accorded.

" I have, &c.

" J. ADAM,
" Secretary to Government.

" Fort William, 23rd July, 1816. "

Instrument, &c. &c.

" Whereas the Right Honourable Francis Earl of Moira,
Governor-General of and for the Presidency of Fort William in Bengal, in Council, has taken into his consideration
the benefits resulting to the government of his Highness
the Nizam, and to the commercial interests of the territories of his said Highness and of the neighbouring provinces of the Honourable the East India Company, from
the transactions and dealings of the firm of Messrs. Wil-

liam Palmer and Company, established at Hyderabad, in the territories of his said Highness, and is of opinion that the maintenance and extension of the dealings and transactions of the said firm of Messrs. William Palmer and Company are a fit object of the encouragement and countenance of the British Government ; these are to certify to all persons whom it may concern that the said Governor-General in Council does hereby, in writing and by virtue of the power in him vested by a certain Act of Parliament made and passed at Westminster on the 20th day of July, in the year of our Lord One thousand seven hundred and ninety-seven, entitled ' An Act for the better Administration of Justice at Calcutta, Madras, and Bombay, and for preventing British Subjects from being concerned in Loans to the native Princes in India,' give his consent and approbation to the members of the said firm of Messrs. William Palmer and Company at Hyderabad, doing all acts within the territories of the Nizam which are prohibited by the said Act of Parliament to be done or transacted without the consent and approbation of the Governor in Council of one of the governments of the United Company of Merchants of England trading to the East Indies first had and obtained in writing, until the said consent and approbation shall be in like manner in writing withdrawn. Provided, however, that the said firm of Messrs. William Palmer and Company shall at all times, when required so to do by the British Resident at Hyderabad, for the time being, communicate to the said Resident the nature and objects of their transactions with the Government or the subjects of his said Highness the Nizam.

"Given at Fort William this Twenty-third day of July, One thousand eight hundred and sixteen.

"To Messrs. WILLIAM PALMER and Co., Hyderabad."

The partners then in the firm of William Palmer and Company were as formerly, William Palmer, Hastings Palmer, Bunketty Doss, William Currie, and the following additional partners who were brought into the house : Sir William Rumbold, the second baronet and grandson of the first — that Sir Thomas Rumbold, the notoriously corrupt Governor of Madras. Sir William had studied for the bar, and though he came out to India without a profession and without an aim beyond that of improving his personal fortune of 8000*l.* a year, he was most certainly not a penniless adventurer, as malice has described him, nor with any false pretensions, particularly so as he had come out to India with the family of Lord Hastings. To high natural abilities which he had cultivated, he possessed a knowledge of the fashionable accomplishments of the day, great address and ready command of polished language. In long years afterwards, when difficulties had set upon the firm, and he felt that his personal honour was assailed by the calumnies propagated by the enemies of the house of William Palmer and Company, he took up battle for his partners, and it was remarked by one of the first lawyers of the day (Lord Tenterden), in respect of the war thus waged, there were not twelve men in England who had the talent and spirit together to give the annoyance that Sir William Rumbold did to the Court of Directors of the East India Company. Sir William Rumbold had married a ward of Lord Hastings, had accompanied his Lordship to India, and though he put into the house for his share two lakhs of rupees (20,000*l.*), he was asked to join it only in consequence of his connection with the Governor-General's family. The share that was given Sir William was originally offered to Mr. John Palmer, who declined it, but proposed Sir William, at the time at Delhi.

Hans Sotheby was the next new partner in the house.
He was a Bengal civil servant, and at the time First
Assistant to the Resident. From feelings of personal regard, Mr. William Palmer gave Sotheby a small share for
a contribution of half a lakh of rupees, which Sotheby
borrowed by Palmer's influence through Bunketty Doss,
the native partner.

Charles Lambe was the last partner. He was a surgeon
in the Nizam's army, and from that circumstance was acting in attendance upon Sir Charles Metcalfe, the Resident,
when Dr. Currie was away.

Upon the negotiation of the sixty-lakh loan with the
Nizam's government, Mr. W. Palmer asked Mr. Sotheby
to retire from the house, in consequence of his official
connection with the Residency, giving him a bonus of
Rs. 50,000, besides returning the contribution of that
amount he had made upon joining the firm. Immediately
after Dr. Currie retired with a fortune that he had acquired, yielding 3000*l.* sterling a year. The remaining
partners continued in the house until its failure.

Messrs. William Palmer and Company were the first
merchants at Hyderabad who pressed commercial enterprise with any vigour or carried it to any important result. They proved by experiment the practicability of
navigating the Godavery 400 miles through the interior,
and thus conveying at once by water to the sea-coast both
the cotton of Berar, which had before been carried by
land to Mirzapore, and the produce of the teak forests of
Ramgear and Palooncha, which had hitherto been inac-
cessible to Europeans. They also applied themselves to
the introduction of British manufactures into the Nizam's
country, and succeeded in promoting their consumption
to an extent which was scarcely expected. Through this
firm the houses of many of the principal natives were

furnished with a variety of costly English commodities; our plain and printed muslins were brought into general use, and Sir Henry Russell says that he has seen the ministers and many persons of rank at the Nizam's court dressed in English muslins and English shawls. William Palmer and Company likewise embarked in the great timber trade. An extensive establishment was formed by them both in the forests on the Godavery and at Coringa, the seaport at the mouth of the river. Captain Charles Tylor, of the Royal Navy, was employed by them as their principal agent, in which capacity he built a ship of their timber at Coringa, and considerable expense was incurred by them for several years in the prosecution of the undertaking.

William Palmer and Company initiated the Godavery Canal, and Colonel Sir Arthur Cotton, with that generosity peculiar to great minds, gives them the credit of being the pioneers of that great work which for the last twenty years he has not now unvainly pressed upon the attention of the British public.

Messrs. William Palmer and Company were, moreover, the great bankers of the country. This was not the original intention : the first idea was to club their own money and to employ that money in developing the resources of the country and opening up a commerce with the English manufacturer ; but subsequently they received deposits upon which they allowed 12 per cent. per annum, and lastly, they became the creditors of the Nizam.

Sir Charles Metcalfe came to Hyderabad and discovered that this great house advanced money for state purposes to a foreign prince for 24 per cent. per annum, and he then reports to his Government that, " With this single

exception of the high rate of interest, which he hopes to
see lowered, as its continuance is not consistent with the
financial prosperity of the Nizam's government, he does
not observe anything in the transaction of the house requiring interference or restraint on the part of our Government." Again : " The enterprise of such a commercial
establishment, and the efforts which it would make for its
own benefit, must tend, he conceives, to promote the prosperity of the country ;" he thinks " it desirable in every
point of view that this house should be as unfettered in its
transactions as any other commercial concern, and that
vigilance on our part should be exercised not with a view
to restrictions on the proceedings of the firm, but solely
in order to guard the interests of the Nizam's government
and our own in those transactions in which they might be
at variance with the interests of the house." But Sir
Charles soon altered his tone, for, when speaking of the
same establishment not long after, he says : " The atmosphere was tainted by their corrupt and unnatural influence," and that it was doubtful " whether the house or
the Resident was the real representative of the British
Government." He sought and accomplished the ruin of
that house.

Messrs. William Palmer and Company were barred of
their claims on the Nizam's government to the amount of
upwards of 20 lakhs of rupees, the British Government
settling the difference. The Nizam's minister, if even
disposed to settle the deficiency, was prohibited at his
peril from doing so ; the transactions of the house were
branded with the most opprobious terms by the Government of India, and Mr. William Palmer himself was
stripped of the allowances which his services had earned.
The house could not contend with such difficulties; it

CHAP.
V.

Sir C. Met-
calfe's
views.

collapsed in the most honourable manner — it paid at once 25 per cent. on all demands, and left the balance for settlement upon the collection of outstanding accounts.

All this may have occurred and may have become of the things that were but for collateral circumstances which contributed to the entire subject being reviewed by the proprietors of the East India Company. On Wednesday, the 3rd day of March, 1823, when it was proposed at a general court of proprietors at that India House in Leadenhall-street, now about passing into a myth, " adequately to reward the Marquis of Hastings for the splendid and glorious results of his government in India," an amendment was carried in the following terms :—" That there be laid before the Court all correspondence and other documents to be found in the public records of this (the East India) House which regard the administration of the Marquis of Hastings, and which may enable the Court to judge of the propriety of entertaining the question of any further grant to the noble Marquis "—this amendment involving, besides particulars of the Mahratta and Nepaul wars, inquiry respecting the loans made by the house of Messrs. William Palmer and Company to his Highness the Nizam. It may be as well, perhaps, to give the resolution entire as moved by the Honourable Douglas Kinnaird, a banker, as it will go to show the high estimation in which the services of that nobleman were held and the notice previously taken of them, and the further intention desired to be expressed of such services :—

" Resolved, That this Court recurring with undiminished pride and gratification to the repeated occasions on which the distinguished services rendered to the East India Company by the Most Noble the Marquis of

Hastings, have been under its consideration, and more especially to the 20th day of December, 1816, and to the 3rd day of February, 1819, when the unanimous thanks of this Court were successively voted to his Lordship for the planning, conduct, and conclusion of two splendid military achievements; and which were again more especially acknowledged and rewarded by a grant of 60,000*l.*, unanimously voted to the Marquis of Hastings and his family on the 5th of May, 1819; and further adverting to the unanimous expression on the 29th of May, 1822, of this Court's high sense of the political and military talents displayed by the Governor-General during nine years' administration of the supreme power in India, as well of its deep regret at having then learnt his determination to return to Europe, is of opinion that the time is at length arrived when the splendid and glorious results of the Marquis of Hastings' government, to the financial prosperity, and to the permanent tranquillity of India, ought to be adequately rewarded, as they are fully appreciated by the proprietors at large, in common with their applauding countrymen, both in Europe and in Asia.

"That it be therefore referred to the Court of Directors forthwith, to take into their consideration, and to report to this Court the means and the measure of such a pecuniary grant, for the approval of this Court, as may be at once worthy of our gratitude for the benefits received, and of the illustrious personage who has so mainly contributed to the reigning tranquillity of their empire, and the financial prosperity of the Company."

The papers connected with these proceedings were printed, and appeared in two years' time, and then followed the discussion in the India House. Mr. Henry Russell considered his character assailed by the expres-

sions of Sir Charles Metcalfe, and the conduct of the
Court of Directors, who presented themselves to the
proprietors, fortified with legal opinions against the rate
of interest levied by the house of William Palmer and
Company. The debate lasted for six days, and upon the
second day, the 18th day of February, 1825, the following formed part of the proceedings. Mr. Russell so fully
and clearly states the case, that it spares me a recapitulation of the particulars.

" Mr. Poynder.— I merely desire to have the resolution of the 3rd March, 1824, read.

" The Resolution, in the following words, was then read
by the Clerk :—' That there be laid before this Court all
such papers and documents respecting the loans made by
Palmer and Company of Hyderabad, to his Highness the
Nizam, as may enable this Court to decide on the merits
of any claim which the Marquis of Hastings may have
on the further liberality of the Company.'

" Sir John Doyle.— My intention in rising, Sir, was to
address you on the question before the Court, but as I
observe an hon. proprietor (Mr. Russell) has risen with
the same object, and with a claim preferable to mine, for
he means to speak in defence of his own character, I
therefore willingly waive my right of precedence, and
give way to the hon. proprietor.

" Mr. Russell then rose and said,— Sir, when this debate began on Friday last, I had not the honour of being
a member of this Court ; nor should I have been so now,
but for the terms in which my name was mentioned on
that occasion. Sir, I do not complain of the passages
which were read from the printed papers, for them I had
seen, and, so far as I thought necessary, I had answered.
. But, Sir, I do complain of the introduction of the opinions

of the Attorney-General and the Company's counsel, into the speech of the hon. Chairman. Sir, the facts which formed the basis of those opinions are either assumed and asserted to exist, or they are hypothetically stated for the purpose of explaining what the law would be if the facts were proved. If they are asserted to exist, the assertion has been made not only without adequate grounds, but without any grounds,—not only without proof, but without evidence: it has been made upon the bare statements and insinuations of individuals, who can be considered in no other light than as partisans deeply committed to one side, and deeply interested in advocating and enforcing their own particular view of the question. If the facts are hypothetically stated, then they are entitled to just as much weight, and to no more than any hypothetical conjecture of any hypothetical person on any hypothetical occasion, which, in plain English, is to no weight at all. The object of an opinion of counsel is to explain the law upon the point at issue; and to suggest the ground to be taken, and the course to be pursued in bringing the question to trial. But, Sir, when your counsel tells you that you have no ground to stand upon; that you cannot venture into Court; that you dare not look a jury in the face, is his opinion to usurp the force of every form and order of judicial function? Is it to supply the place of accusation, proof, conviction, and punishment? Is it to be made the vehicle and instrument of libel? Is a man on such grounds to be denounced to the world as the dupe or the abettor of a conspiracy to defraud? The proposition is not to be tolerated; and if the ground on which I stand is English ground, I have only to state it to expose it to universal abhorrence. I protest against both the principle and the practice. The opinion of

N 2

counsel is necessarily confined to a partial and limited view; it is framed upon the case which is laid before him; and if I were allowed to frame my own case, and the power now assumed were given to a mere opinion of counsel, I would undertake to usurp the possession of any estate in England, and to lay the character of any individual prostrate in the dirt. When the vote for printing the Hyderabad papers was passed near a year ago, I applied to the Court of Directors that I might be allowed to have access to them for the purpose of vindicating my own character. There could no longer be any pretext for concealment. The publication had been ordered, and some of the papers were actually in the printer's hands. I thought that if my request were not granted, from bare justice at least, it should be granted out of consideration to an old servant. If that request had been granted, I should have transmitted my vindication to the Court of Directors, and it would have been printed by them along with the other papers. In that case I should have been spared much that I have since been called upon to do, and I should not have been required on the present occasion to trouble the Court with the various details into which I am now about to enter. I have, Sir, read and examined the papers with as much diligence and attention as any member of this Court, and certainly with advantages of local knowledge and experience which nobody but myself can possess. The Company's counsel has said that the charges alleged against the house of William Palmer and Company cannot be proved. Now, Sir, I will undertake to disprove them on the evidence of the papers printed by the Court of Directors; and I stand here prepared to vindicate the transactions with which my name has been mixed up against the aspersions that have been cast upon them. If those transactions has been such as they have been represented, my voice would have been the first and the loudest to be raised against them. The main charge is, that the sixty-lakh loan negotiated by W. Palmer and Company in 1820 was a fraud and a fiction. The Company's counsel has assumed that it was from first to last a fictitious transaction, and that the parties engaged in it were guilty of a conspiracy to defraud. With that charge, Sir, I shall begin. It has been advanced on two grounds : it has been asserted both that the loan was composed of unsanctioned balances, which were transferred for the purpose of covering them with the sanction of the British Government, and that no cash payments whatever were made on account of the loan. Now, Sir, I undertake to show, and any gentleman who has made himself acquainted with the accounts among the printed papers will recognise the accuracy of my statement ; first, that when the loan began, the house of W. Palmer and Company had not one shilling of unsanctioned balances on their books against the Nizam. And, secondly, that the loan was mainly composed of actual advances in cash. The arithmetical details into which I am about to enter, I take from Sir W. Rumbold's letter to the Court of Directors ; but I desire it to be understood that I do not take them on the credit of the writer alone. I have myself verified the calculations, and I now state them on my own voucher of their accuracy. At the time the negotiation of the loan was entered into, the house of W. Palmer and Company had three separate accounts with the Nizam's government. It has been objected, I understand, that the transactions of the house were entered in more accounts than one ; but that was unavoidable.

The accounts were not kept according to the pleasure of the house, but to suit the financial arrangements of the Nizam's government. Different transactions had originated at different times; they were to be charged upon different districts, or to be provided for by different persons; and if they had all been entered in one account at first, the Minister would have had to distribute them into different accounts. It was more convenient to him, therefore, that they should be entered at once in the accounts to which they severally belonged. Those three accounts were, the Berar Suwar account, the Aurungabad account, and that called the Hyderabad account: the first of them related to the expenses incurred by the Nizam, in equipping and bringing into the field a body of irregular cavalry, which he organised at my recommendation, at the time when the war with the Pindarees and Mahrattas was approaching. Now, it is quite evident, that unless adequate provision had been made for the support of these troops, their services would have been of no avail. The great misery of the troops of native governments in India is, that they are not regularly paid, and are consequently in want of food. This constitutes the great superiority of the British over the native troops; for the first being assured of regular pay, act with more steady and determined valour, and more perfect discipline. The same means which were applied so well to the British troops, have been, with equal advantage, provided for the native troops of India; and the result has been, that we have, at this day, in our Indian territory, whole regiments composed of black faces, ready to stand or fall with officers who have white ones. So much for the first account. When this transaction began, I reported it to Government. I will not trouble the Court by reading that with which, I presume, most of its members are already acquainted. I mean, the answer of the Government approving the proposition. Sir, I know not whether there be now in Court any military officer who served in this campaign, with any branch of the Deccan army; but if there be, to him I confidently appeal, to bear testimony to the services of those troops. I would ask him whether, on every occasion, they did not conduct themselves like brave and active soldiers?

"Colonel FITZCLARENCE (afterwards Earl of Munster) here observed:—Mr. Chairman, after the appeal which has been made, I cannot, as an officer who served in India at the period in question, omit this opportunity of stating, that I never, in my life, saw better or braver troops.

"Mr. RUSSELL continued:—I am much obliged, Sir, to the gallant officer for the honourable testimony he has thus borne to the excellence of those troops. This particular corps, though it formed one body of the Nizam's cavalry, was yet composed of a vast number of small parties (as all the troops of the native princes are), each under a separate command, and receiving pay from its own immediate proprietor. These were, perhaps, fifty or sixty in number, and many of them did not possess the funds necessary for the regular payment of the men. I therefore prevailed on the Nizam's Minister to take upon himself the immediate payment of the troops, and to settle with the several subordinate officers in the best manner he could. This method was not only the most simple and easy in itself, but it was the only one by which regularity could be secured. It would have caused the Minister great embarrassment if those accounts had been

mixed up and confounded with others. I now come, Sir,
to the Aurungabad arrangement, which originated thus:
Captain Sydenham, the political agent in Berar, had repeatedly complained that the troops were not paid regularly; and, Sir, from my own experience, I was convinced
that if they were not paid well they would not fight well.
Captain Sydenham proposed to Mr. Palmer to enter into
an agreement for this purpose. Mr. Palmer stated it to
me; observing at the same time, and I gave him credit
for the statement, that in adopting the arrangement he
did not anticipate any immediate advantage to his establishment; but as the measure would be useful to the
service and acceptable to the English Government, he
probably might, on that ground, be considered entitled
to future support. The money in this case was to be
raised by assignments on certain districts in the Nizam's
territories. These troops belonged to Berar, and it was
necessary that the accounts relating to them should be
kept separate. The only remaining account was that of
Hyderabad, which comprised all the various miscellaneous
payments made to the Minister at Hyderabad. By the
printed papers, it appears that on the 16th of February,
1820, when the loan began, the balances on their account
were as follows:—

Balance due to the house
  at Aurungabad . *Rs.* 19,50,826 6 6
Do. for Berar Suwars . 18,36,825 12 3
                             37,87,652 2 9

And on the Hyderabad account, instead of there being
any balance due to the house by the Minister, a balance
is due by the house to the Minister, of—rupees 1,36,620
12 9. The Aurungabad arrangement did not appear to

give satisfaction, and long discussions took place in Council respecting its expediency. The result was, that I was
directed to call on Mr. Palmer for a statement in figures
of particular parts of the accounts. Sir William Rumbold
was at this time at Calcutta, and on hearing of the demand,
he addressed the Government, protesting against the principle of calling upon a mercantile establishment to give
up its accounts, to be discussed, recorded, and transmitted
to England. This was Sir W. Rumbold's opinion; but
Mr. Palmer thought differently. He said, that if a discussion was to be raised, this was the very point on which
he should wish to invite it; and that instead of confining
himself to the limited information which had been called
for, he was desirous of being allowed to transmit through
me a complete and detailed copy of all the accounts.
'I know,' he said, 'that serious discussions have taken
place in Calcutta, upon our affairs, but I am so perfectly
satisfied of the justice and integrity of these transactions,
that if they will not stand the test of examination, nothing
will.' These accounts, Sir, were forwarded by me to
Calcutta, and they were subsequently sent back to me,
with directions to return them to Mr. Palmer. It appeared,
however, that before this they had been circulated amongst
the members of the Government, and they had evidently
been examined; for when they came back to me I observed some pencil marks on the backs of them, which
proved that some person had taken the trouble to examine
and compare them. Now, although these accounts were
laid before the Government of Calcutta, and the arrangement approved, yet it has since been asserted that the
rate of interest was not known. This, Sir, is utterly incomprehensible; for the accounts current were accompanied by detailed interest accounts; and at the top of

every page the rate of interest was particularly specified
at full length. And Mr. Fendall, in one of his minutes,
expressly states the interest on the Aurungabad account
to have been 24 per cent. If Mr. Fendall recorded this
at the Board, and his statement passed without remark
or observation, — if the rate of interest was exhibited at
the top of every. page, could it be said that the Government were kept in the dark as to the grant? When the
loan was made there were due to Palmer and Company,
from the Minister on the Aurungabad and the Berar Suwar
accounts, as I have stated, rupees 37,87,652 ; but on
the Hyderabad account, the house owed the Minister
1,36,020 rupees, and they held at the same time *tunkas*
or assignments, which were afterwards realised to the
amount of rupees 10,56,711 ; the two sums making a
total of rupees 11,92,742, which, deducted from rupees
37,87,652, left a balance on the actual account of rupees
25,94,910, as due from the Minister to Palmer and Company in February 1820 ; and no portion of this balance was
an unsanctioned balance. The Government knew for what
the money had been paid ; they knew to what purposes
it had been applied ; and they knew the rate of interest
which was charged by the house. The Aurungabad and
Berar Suwar accounts, on which these 25 lakhs of rupees
were due, had not only been sanctioned by Government,
but they had been sanctioned at the interest of 24 per
cent. What benefit then, I ask, could the house of Palmer
and Company derive from the transfer of these balances to
the loan? The only effect of such a transfer would be a
loss to them of 6 per cent. without the bonus of $3\frac{1}{2}$ per cent.
with it. To the Nizam it was a decided advantage, and
not an injury, that the balances should be transferred ;
his advantage being manifestly proportioned to the reduc-

tion in the rate of interest. Having said thus much to
show that the loan was not composed of unsanctioned
balances, I will now advert to the elements of which it
was composed. It is asserted in the correspondence
printed in the Hyderabad papers, that no cash payments
were made on this loan, — that it was totally and utterly
a fiction, — and that, in fact, nothing had been paid on
it; but it will be seen on referring to the accounts in
pages 620, 621, 622, 623, and 624 of those papers, of
·which a summary is given at page 26 of Sir W. Rumbold's
letter, that upwards of 38 lakhs of rupees were paid in
cash. These payments comprehended the period from
the middle of February to the end of August. But it has,
I understand, been contended, that the payments, during·
the first three months, ought not to be included in this
account of the loan, as the sanctioning of Government was·
not applied for until May. Sir, the making of the loan is
one thing, and the sanctioning of it another ; and it by no
means follows, because the house did not discover until
May that the Government was prepared to entertain their
application for a sanction, that, therefore, they may not have
made conditional advances on account of the loan in the
preceding months of February, March and April. But, Sir,
even admitting that May is to be taken for the beginning
of the loan, only 5 lakhs will·be excluded, and even then
it will appear that the actual cash payments made in the
months of May, June, July and August, amounted to no
less a·sum than 34 lakhs of rupees. I cannot allow this
objection to be reasonable ; but even admitting that it
were so, the accounts still furnish a complete and satisfactory answer to the charge, that the loan was fictitious,
and that no cash payments whatever had been made.
Allow me, Sir, here to call the attention of the Court to

one remarkable fact, which, I think, will clearly prove that the loan was a real and substantive transaction, and in no respect fictitious: — In Sir William Rumbold's letter, page 27, an account is given of the advances made by Palmer and Company to the Nizam, in the years 1815, 1816, 1817, 1818, and 1819, being the five years preceding that in which the loan was made. It appears that in that period, a sum of rupees 42,41,542 was advanced by the house of Palmer and Company to the Minister, being at the average of rupees 8,48,308 in each of those five years, or rupees 4,24,154 in each half year; while, in the six months of the loan, from February to August 1820, a sum of upwards of 40 lakhs of rupees, ten times the amount of the former average, was advanced. If the loan were not the cause of this tenfold increase of payments, as compared with former years, it must be accounted for in some other way; and I should be glad to learn, Sir, in what other manner it can be accounted for. As yet I have not heard of any attempt of the kind being made. Nor did this increased rate of advances occur after the loan. It began with it, and ended with it, and belonged exclusively to it. I have already shown, that in the six months from February to August, Palmer and Company had paid, in cash, a sum of 38 lakhs of rupees to the Nizam's Minister; and it is not a little remarkable, that when that Minister was called upon by Sir C. Metcalfe to state what sums he had received from the house, he mentioned the identical sum of 38 lakhs. I know not any reason the Minister could have had, at that time, for giving a false or fabricated account of the transaction. No cause whatever has been adduced to warrant the supposition, that he spoke on that occasion anything but the truth. At two subsequent periods, the Minister gave the same ac-

count of the sum received by him in cash. He always
stated that this was the actual amount of the cash-pay-
ments which he had received at Hyderabad on account
of the loan. When first called upon, he gave an account of the application of 67 lakhs of rupees ; and this
assertion was eagerly laid hold of, as a proof that his
statement was incorrect. How, it was contended, can
any reliance be placed on the statement of a man who,
having alleged that he had raised a loan of 60 lakhs,
of which 8 were bonus, renders an account according
to what he had expended, 67? Sir, the error was not
in the Minister who made the statement, but in those
who misunderstood it. I appeal to two gentlemen eminently skilled in the Persian language, whom I see within
the bar, to support the accuracy of my assertion,
that there is no word in that language which bears the
limited and technical interpretation which we annex to
the term 'loan.' *Qurz*, which signifies 'debt,' generally,
is the word which would be used, and which, unquestionably, was used by the Minister on the occasion now
referred to. (Mr. Edmonstone and Col. Baillie intimated
their assent.) The account he rendered was an account,
not the application of the sixty-lakh loan, but of the
whole of the sums which I had, at various times, borrowed from Palmer and Company. In this statement it
appears by the printed accounts that he was quite
correct. When he was afterwards asked how much had
been received, and he understood the inquiry to relate
specifically to the loan, he answered, that he had received—

At Hyderabad . . . *Rs.*	38,54,957	1	9
At Aurungabad	13,45,042	14	3
Making	52,00,000	0	0

To which, if eight lakhs of bonus be added, there was, at once, the whole amount of the loan. It was, however, discovered by Sir C. Metcalfe, that the Minister some time afterwards explained, in an account of his reductions, that he had applied eleven lakhs to paying off the arrears due to troops discharged. From this, Sir C. Metcalfe chooses to infer, that because the Minister had applied eleven lakhs to that particular purpose, therefore he had applied nothing to any other purpose, and that for any good end, eleven lakhs were the whole amount of the loan. Consequently, in the progress of objections, the first was, that the loan consisted of too much; the second, that it consisted of too little; and soon afterwards it was asserted, that it consisted of nothing at all. Now, really, Sir, when gentlemen assume the province of judging, and come forward confidently, on occasions like the present, where the fortunes, and, what are still dearer to them, the characters, of individuals are at stake, it is intolerable that they should be suffered to proceed upon these crude, vague, and inconsistent conjectures. (Loud cheers from the left side of the Court, and a cry of order from the opposite side.)

"Mr. RUSSELL, apparently supposing that the cry of order was addressed to him, said, 'That he conceived he was entirely in order;' and was proceeding to justify his course, when

"A PROPRIETOR (Sir J. Sewell), rose on the right side and said, 'You are perfectly in order, sir. You are speaking very much to the purpose; and our only wish is, that we may not be prevented from hearing you.'

"Mr. RUSSELL resumed. — What I meant to say, Sir, was, that when we see persons objecting in different ways to the same transaction, it is reasonable to conclude

that their objections, which are inconsistent with one
another, are also inconsistent with the truth. In addition
to the 38 lakhs of rupees, 49,275 rupees were charged to
the Minister in the account of the loan for jewellery, and
97,513 for miscellaneous purchases. These sums run
through the same six months I have already spoken of.
The amount of them is so inconsiderable, that it can have
no effect in mitigating the loan. Yet, even supposing it
were deemed objectionable that the sum charged for
jewellery and miscellaneous articles should be included,
and that the whole payments were required to have been
made in money, was there anything which could have
been done with greater facility? What could be more
easy than to pay rupees with one hand, and afterwards
receive them back for the articles in question with the
other? The sum charged for jewellery is less than half
a lakh of rupees; and even to that small amount it must
not be supposed that Chundoo Lall bought the jewels for
his own use and applied them to bedizen himself or his
wife. Any gentleman in this Court, who happens to have
seen that Minister, will admit that no man ever dressed
more plainly. He generally wore a simple white dress,
with plain leather shoes, divested of everything like
glitter or ornament. On particular occasions of ceremony
at Court, in order to show his respect to the Nizam, he
wore a string of pearls, such as was hardly suited to one
of his own servants even. The jewellery was purchased
for, and was disposed of, according to the Eastern custom
on public occasions. Articles of jewellery are denominated *ruccums*, and are given as presents to those who
appear at the Minister's or at Court, whether on occasions
of business or courtesy; and a man's consequence is estimated according to the number of them which he receives.

Whenever we speak of presentations at Court, we say that a man has met with a gracious reception. In the East it is said that he received so many *ruccums*, and by that number the character of his reception is determined. These jewels are considered, to all intents and purposes, as a branch of the public expenditure. An office is kept in which these jewels are preserved and registered; and it is part of the duty of the Minister to provide a proper supply. As to the other charge for miscellaneous articles, it is made up principally of purchases of cloth and glass. The glass was, I suppose, chiefly for the Minister's own use; the cloths were probably for presents. The whole of these charges are, however, so inconsiderable, as not to weigh a feather, compared with the general amount of the loan. I have now, Sir, I trust, given a sufficient answer to the two objections. First, that the loan consisted entirely of unsanctioned balances; and next, that it was a loan without cash payments. But it has been objected to that transaction, that the Minister having professed to raise it for the purpose of reform, did not, in point of fact, apply any portion of it to that purpose; that it was not only fictitious in its character, but nugatory in its result. Sir, that objection, even if it was valid, would not apply as a charge against Palmer and Company. The money which they agreed to pay to the Minister, they were unquestionably bound to pay him; but they were in no respect answerable for his subsequent application of it. That charge, if it applies to anybody, applies to me. It was my business to watch as far as I could the expenditure of that money, and to see that it was devoted to objects immediately connected with the reduction of expense. Against me, accordingly, it has been objected, that in the month of September, only one month after the completion of the loan, I reported that 23 lakhs of rupees had been applied by the Minister to the reduction of the Nizam's expenses. I was at that time most conscientiously of that opinion. I declare upon my honour, that when I received that report from the Minister, I believed it to be true; I also declare, now, that I still do believe it to be so. The Minister had not deceived me on previous occasions of great magnitude, and I had no reason to believe that he would gratuitously deceive me in that instance. But if there was any deceit in the case, I was not the only person deceived; for a considerable time afterwards Chundoo Lall told Sir C. Metcalfe, in answer to his inquiries, that he had made a further reduction to the amount of 16 lakhs more, making in the whole a reduction of 41 lakhs. Sir C. Metcalfe was not inclined to believe the statement, but Chundoo Lall challenged him to the proof. He said, 'Those people whom I have discharged are naturally discontented. There is a list of the parties I have reduced, and the commanders who suffer by the reduction are not likely to tell falsehoods in my favour. The men are at your door; if you doubt what I tell you, examine them. I challenge the strictest investigation into the truth of what I assert.' These were the words he used; — and if the course he pointed out was not adopted, — if his statement was not repelled, — he is surely entitled to credit. Sir C. Metcalfe has shown no such reluctance to undertake offices, which would be painful to other persons, as to justify the belief that if he could have thrown Chundoo Lall's assertion into the dirt he would not have done so. He said, indeed, that he did not believe Chundoo Lall's statement to be accurate, but still he admitted that he believed a considerable reduction had taken place, though he could not state to what amount. Another objection made to the loan was, that it consisted of a transfer from one account to another. Now, I cannot perceive how that fact can be urged as an objection at all. If the entries in one account are bad, the transferring them to another will not change their character and make them good; and if they are already good, the mere act of transfer will not make them bad. Shall it be said of a merchant, who retires to his office when the business of the day is over to post the entries into his ledger, that he does so for the purposes of fiction and dishonesty, and that the act of transfer is fraudulent, merely because every entry that he inserts in the ledger had previously been entered in his journal in some other account? Sir, I assert, and I defy contradiction, that your own loans in India are made precisely on this principle. There are many gentlemen in Court, who know the mode in which those loans are conducted. Persons are appointed to receive subscriptions, and a distant day is announced for closing the loan. When the subscriptions are made, acknowledgments bearing interest are given to the parties, and when the proper period arrives the whole are combined. Interest is added to principal, and the entire sum is transferred from the account in which the details were originally entered to the general register of public debt. What I ask is the difference between the transfer which took place in the books of Palmer and Company, and that which takes place in these transactions? Palmer and Company were to advance a certain sum of money. They were not to do this all in one day, but as the Minister with whom they contracted wanted the money or might choose to call for it, they were to make the payments. Of course they made the entries as they made the payments; and when the whole had been

paid, they transferred it in one sum to a separate account,
not to an old account, but to a new one, of which it formed
the sole and exclusive basis. This is what they did, and
this is what they ought to have done. The interest which
. Palmer and Company charged on their transactions has
been much objected to. I am not at all surprised to hear
such an objection as this in England; it is always difficult
to convey to persons in one country an adequate conception
of the usages which prevail in another. The country, too,
where those transactions took place is not near us; it is at
the distance of half the globe, and differs essentially from
us in every particular of customs, habits, usages, and
manners. The charge of interest has been specifically objected to, first, on account of what is called an exorbitance, and secondly, on account of its alleged illegality.
Now, Sir, exorbitance is altogether a relative term; it is
precisely the same as the term dearness, as applied to
commodities. The rate of interest is exorbitant or moderate, and commodities are dear or cheap with relation
to their value, not at distant places, but at the same place.
By this scale are the charges of Palmer and Company to
be measured. If they charged 24 per cent. interest when
the Nizam might have obtained money elsewhere for 23
per cent. then the charge was exorbitant; but if the rate,
whatever it was, was the lowest the Nizam had ever paid,
and the lowest at which he could then procure money, as .
I firmly believe to be the fact, then the charge was only
fair and moderate. The charge has also been called a
monstrous charge, and, compared with what money may
be had for in England, it certainly does appear so. Gentlemen on the 'Change in London would no doubt stare, at
hearing of 17 or 18 per cent. interest, though I dare say
they would be glad if they could get such an interest for

their money. Sir, as I understand the word 'monstrous,' it means something unusual and extraordinary — a deviation from the established course. Thus, for example, 24 or 18 per cent. would be a monstrous charge in London, and 5 per cent., by a parity of reasoning, would be a monstrous charge at Hyderabad, where such a rate was never yet heard of, and, what is more, where it never will be heard of. But, Sir, be relative rates what they may, I contend that the lowest rate of interest practically known in the country where this loan was negotiated cannot be considered monstrous. As to the bonus, it must be considered as part of the interest, which in this case it raised from 18 to $20\frac{3}{4}$ per cent. It made an addition of $2\frac{3}{4}$ per cent. to the interest, and gave a sum of about 2 per cent. on the principal of the loan. This has been charged against the House of Palmer and Company as inordinate profit, which the partners had realised and shared *instanter*. It was called the 'booty,' which they are said to have actually received and put into their pockets. Now, Sir, I say, notwithstanding these bold assertions, that it is impossible for any man to read these papers, and not perceive at once, that not one single shilling of the bonus has been realised to this moment. The assignments for discharging the interest, and gradually paying off the principal, were 16 lakhs of rupees a year. One half-year's instalment had been paid, and it was hastily concluded by Sir C. Metcalfe, when he saw the figure '8' at the head of the sum credited by the house, that those eight lakhs were the identical bonus. If errors of this kind are committed; if misrepresentations of this nature are promulgated, what reliance, I ask, can the Proprietors place on the general accuracy of those who fall into such palpable mistakes? I do not mean, Sir, that they with whom

these mistakes originated, intended to send forth false
statements; but nevertheless, such as they were, they did
send them forth to the world sanctioned by their authority, and they were calculated to mislead those whose
province it was to act as judges. Surely it is very hard,
that individuals who had not erred, should be punished
for the mistakes of others. The loan, I have already said,
was to consist of 52 lakhs of rupees, and was to be repaid
within a given time with 60 lakhs. Therefore the first payment which the house received was in liquidation of the
sum which they had actually advanced, and so on with each
successive payment, until the whole sum of 52 lakhs was
repaid: then, and not till then, could they arrive at the eight
lakhs which were intended as a bonus. This bonus has
been spoken of as if it was something abominable and
atrocious in its very nature; as if the name alone stamped
on it a character of reprobation; as if nothing of the kind
was ever before heard of. It is held forth as a sort of
bugaboo. It is pointed at as ' the head and front of offend-
ing,' on the part of Palmer and Company. But I beg of
hon. Proprietors to remember how few loans of any kind
are made without a bonus. If the Court will look at their
loan of 1818, which was made in the very same month with
the contract of Palmer and Company for paying the Nizam's troops at Aurungabad, they will find that it was raised
at Hyderabad on terms which gave, on 60 lakhs of rupees,
a bonus of 7 lakhs and 80,000 rupees, which was within
20,000 of the bonus on the loan contracted for the Nizam
in 1810. In 1819 another loan was raised by the Company, which gave a bonus at the rate of 5 lakhs and
20,000 rupees on the gross sum of 60 lakhs. It is therefore quite evident, that the fact of bonus or no bonus had
nothing whatever to do with the integrity of the loan.

The amount is the thing to be considered. If that was such as to make the terms higher than those on which the Nizam had raised money before, or could obtain it at that time, then indeed the charge of taking exorbitant interest would not be ill-founded; but if those terms were at as low a rate as the money could be advanced, then the bonus must be allowed to be fair and just. Sir, I beg to refer the Court to the printed letter of Sir Wm. Rumbold, where they will see that on examining the books of Palmer and Company, the trustees found that they themselves had paid 18, 20, and sometimes 24 per cent. on the money borrowed by them to make that loan to the Nizam. Why then shall a mercantile body be charged with dishonesty and fraud in a transaction on a portion of which they actually received a lower rate of interest than they them- selves were obliged to pay? If they could have raised the money at a lower rate, it is to be presumed, that for their own sake they would have done so; but the soucars, the native bankers, well knew that the house could not command sufficient funds, and would be obliged to seek assistance from them, and they naturally took advantage of that circumstance. Palmer and Company were in conse- quence compelled to submit to the demands of these men, and to pay 24 per cent. for money on which they charged the Nizam, bonus and all, only $20\frac{1}{2}$ per cent. Sir, I will beg permission of the Court to go back a little in my statement, as I find I have omitted one important feature of the arguments which have been advanced to show that the loan was fictitious. When the accounts, with an ac- cusatory statement, were sent to Government, it was ad- mitted to be equitable that Palmer and Company should be allowed to make their defence. It was deemed just they should be heard, not before the Government came to a

decision, for it appears that they had already made up
their minds as to that point, but before they proceeded to
the infliction of punishment. It appears, however, that in
this respect the Government altered their determination.
Summary justice they thought most advisable, and accordingly we find that on the 31st of July, 1823, they declared their definitive sentiments without having waited
for any explanation. Sir C. Metcalfe, however, when he
received the order to call on the house for an explanation,
did so in the following letter : —

"'Gentlemen,—It appearing from your accounts, that at
the time when you obtained the sanction of the British
Government for a loan of 60 lakhs of rupees to the Nizam's
government, that transaction was effected by a transfer of
52 lakhs from your former Hyderabad account to a new
account, with the addition of 8 lakhs bonus as a compensation for the reduction of interest on the said 52 lakhs, from
2 per cent. per mensem to 1½ per cent. per mensem ; and
there being no appearance of any payment at that period,
which can be considered as a loan of 60 lakhs, or any other
specific sum, I am directed by the Hon. the Governor-
General in Council, to call on you to state whether the
conclusions above noticed, as drawn from your accounts, be
correct or otherwise, or to furnish any explanation of that
transaction which you may judge to be satisfactory.' The
answer of Messrs. Palmer and Company to this letter was,
'We beg to submit to you, for the consideration of the
Right Hon. the Governor-General in Council, that the
whole of the loan of 60 lakhs of rupees was not a transfer
of an old account, but was a new loan negotiation, and
was supported by the several payments in cash or otherwise, which followed the balance of rupees 463,979 : 2½
anas, as exhibited in our accounts.' Here, then, is a clear,

distinct reference to a certain sheet of the accounts, which answers to page 620 of the printed papers. Such, Sir, was the call and such the answer. Now for the comment. This is to be found in page 743. There, Sir C. Metcalfe, observing on the answer of Palmer and Company to his letter, thus expresses himself: 'Their reply is similar to every production that comes from that quarter — shuffling and evasive, and in my opinion completely confirms the conclusion before drawn respecting that fraudulent transaction.' Really, Sir, I know not what Sir C. Metcalfe wished those gentlemen to do. When called upon to explain the payments of which the loan consisted, how could they do so with more distinctness than by saying: 'If you will wet your thumb and turn over the account until you come to a certain page, at that page you will find the particulars of the explanation you desire'? Will it be credited that Sir C. Metcalfe took not the smallest notice of that distinct and conclusive part of their answer?

"Mr. POYNDER. — Sir, I beg the hon. Proprietor will take the trouble of reading a little more of Sir C. Metcalfe's letter, and perhaps he will there find the reasons for his conduct fully explained.

"Mr. RUSSELL. — I have no objection. Sir C. Metcalfe proceeds to say — 'Instead of stating what sums they did actually advance on account of that pretended loan, they argue that it ought to be inferred that there must have been a loan to the Nizam's government, because they were themselves obliged to obtain funds. This is by no means a necessary conclusion; for, having above 60 lakhs locked up in the hands of the Nizam's government, and having still to feed, for their own advantage, the Minister's lavish waste, and having also to supply, for their own profit, the wants of others, with whom they had dealings, there were abundant reasons why they should endeavour to obtain additional funds. The assertion, that a sum of between 4 and 5 lakhs is all that can be considered as a transfer of old debt, does not require any comment. How they could venture on such an assertion in the face of their own accounts, is utterly incomprehensible. The pretence, that the transfer of the whole balance of 20 or 21 lakhs, on account of Berar Suwars, was equivalent to a cash payment, is too preposterous to require remark. In the document herewith transmitted, Messrs. Palmer and Company state, that the bonus of 8 lakhs was intended to cover them from eventual loss, on account of their exclusive responsibility. In their accounts it was represented as compensation for reduction of interest. I apprehend that their explanation cannot be deemed satisfactory; I shall, therefore, proceed to execute the instructions which I have lately received regarding them.' I am very glad the hon. Proprietor gave me an opportunity of reading this despatch at length; because it proves what I must otherwise have asserted on my own authority, that Sir C. Metcalfe did not allude to the statement of Messrs. Palmer and Company. That statement was, that if Sir C. Metcalfe would turn to a certain page in the accounts furnished, he would there find the items of which the loan was composed. Of all the modes that could be devised for giving the Government clear information on this subject, that which was adopted by Messrs. Palmer and Company appears to me to have been the very best. When they were interrogated, they said, 'Turn to such a page, and you will find the desired information.' If Sir C. Metcalfe, having done this, could have shown either that there were no such entries, or that they were entries not connected with the loan, his objection would have been fair and reasonable ; but as it is a statement contained in the letter of Messrs. Palmer and Company it is passed over without a word of notice. Another charge made against the interest of the loan is, that it was wholly illegal. On this subject I must observe, that the question of illegality is still a most important point. It is not yet decided whether the rate of interest taken within the Nizam's territory does or does not come within the scope and operation of British law. One opinion is held by the legal authorities in India — a different opinion is entertained by the legal authorities at home. The former say, it does not come within the scope of the law — the latter maintain that it does. I do not mean to contend that the opinion of the law-officer in India is the true one, but I will say, that, when conflicting opinions arise — when Mr. Strettell at one period, and Mr. Spankie (whose opinion is a most elaborate one) at another, declare that the law does not reach contracts entered into in the Nizam's territory, it is too much to accuse Messrs. Palmer and Company of having wilfully acted in an illegal manner. It cannot escape observation, that Mr. Strettell's opinion was not surreptitiously obtained by Palmer and Company for the purpose of enabling them to defend themselves, after having acted improperly. When they applied for the license of Government, to make loans to the Nizam, the Government knew it would be necessary for them to demand more than 12 per cent. interest. A letter was therefore addressed by the Senators to Mr. Strettell, requesting his opinion as to the legality of such a proceeding. Though the letter itself is not amongst the printed documents, fortunately the answer to it is. Mr. Strettell there states that he has no doubt whatever of the law on the subject. In his opinion, the parties had a right .to take more than

12 per cent. Therefore, Sir, even supposing his opinion
to be erroneous, and that of the learned Counsel in this
country to be right, still, so far as the conduct of Messrs.
Palmer and Company is concerned, their justification is complete. In a moral point of view they have done no wrong,
for they acted under the best advice they could procure;
and, even in a legal point of view, it has not yet been proved
that they were not right. I have always understood it to be
the practice of the highest judicial authorities in England,
where parties act under the advice of Counsel, although
they may be in error, to deal with them in the most len-
ient manner. The circumstance of their having sought
legal advice, so far as punishment is concerned, is never
lost sight of. The uncertainty of the law on this subject,
has been alluded to by Mr. Canning in a speech delivered
by him in the House of Commons, when he was about to
undertake the Governor-Generalship of India. Amongst
other subjects connected with the administration of Indian affairs, that right hon. gentleman appeared to have
turned his attention particularly to this. He said, in
speaking of it, 'The law is so doubtful on this point, that
it requires a declaratory act to set it at rest;' and he
called on his right hon. friend, the President of the Board
of Control, to introduce a bill for the purpose of defin-
ing it. If, then, Mr. Canning, and Mr. Strettell, and Mr.
Spankie, entertained such opinions of the law, can any un-
prejudiced person condemn Messrs. Palmer and Company
for the course pursued by them? I must contend, whether
the transaction were legal or illegal, that, having acted under such circumstances as I have stated, the justification of
Palmer and Company on this point, is decisive. But, if it
be culpable to proceed in this way, then, Sir, I must observe,
that very high authorities must be arraigned for a similar

error; for such authorities have been guilty not only of suffering individuals to take more than 12 per cent. interest, but of presenting much more than 12 per cent. to be awarded. To understand this, I wish the Court to look at the extracts from the Bengal Regulations of 1793 and 1803, given at pages 8 and 9 of Sir W. Rumbold's letter. Those regulations stand in the place of the statute law of this country. They are, in fact, the statute laws of the Bengal Provinces. They were framed for the guidance of the Judges in the Courts of Judicature beyond the town of Calcutta; they are drawn by the law-officers of the Crown and the Company, passed by the Governor-General in Council, registered in the Supreme Court of Judicature, and laid yearly upon the table of the House of Commons. The 15th Bengal regulation, framed in 1793, directs the Courts of Judicature not to decree higher or lower rates of interest than the following:—If the cause of action shall have arisen before the 26th March, 1780, on sums not exceeding 100 rupees, 37½ per cent. per annum — on sums exceeding 100 rupees, 24 per cent. per annum. If after the 28th March, 1780, on sums not exceeding 100 rupees, 24 per cent. per annum. The Bengal regulation (34) of 1803 seems to have had exclusive reference to the territories then recently acquired from the Nuwab of Lucknow. It directs, that where the cause of action shall have arisen before the 10th Nov., 1801, on sums not exceeding 100 rupees, the interest shall be 30 per cent. per annum, and on sums exceeding 100 rupees, 24 per cent. per annum. The first of these regulations was passed twenty years after the 13th of Geo. III. which is now contended to have limited the rate of interest over all India to 12 per cent. — and the second regulation was framed thirty years after the passing of

that Act, ten years later than the 33rd of Geo. III., and
six years later than the 37th of Geo. III.; yet it directs
the Judges in the Company's Courts to decree 30 per cent.
per annum, in some cases, and 24 per cent. per annum
in all others where the debts were incurred before the
10th Nov., 1801, in the territories which the Nuwab of
Lucknow had then ceded to the Company. I contend,
Sir, that the territories of the Nuwab at that time, and of
the Nizam at present, are similarly situated. If, in 1793
and 1803, a higher rate of interest than 12 per cent. were
sanctioned—if the Judge were then desired to award 30
per cent. interest in territories similarly circumstanced
with those of the Nizam at present, why should those who
now require a larger rate of interest be visited with
reproach and vituperation? Why should you confound
ignorance of the law with a wilful determination to do
wrong? If the Act of the 33rd of Geo. III. had been
supposed to restrict the rate of interest all over India,
neither of the regulations I have quoted would ever have
been framed. If that Act had been construed to extend
to the territory of the native prince, the regulation of
1803 would not have been sanctioned. Sir, I now come
to a part of the subject which is personal to myself. In
order to vilify the house, and give an unworthy character
to its transactions, it has been insidiously alleged that I
had an interest in its concerns. In the very first page of
a letter to the Court of Directors, which I published some
months ago, I declared the fact of my having confided a
sum of money to the care of Mr. Samuel Russell, an old
and intimate friend, who had resided for many years at
Hyderabad, and had been in the habit of employing his
own friends in the market there. Circumstances of that
kind are of every-day occurrence in all countries, where

individuals intrust the management of their money to those private friends who are more conversant with such matters, and have more leisure for attending to them than they have themselves. Why did I withdraw that money? Because I thought that the transactions in which it was likely to be employed were objectionable; not in themselves, for I neither did nor do think them so, but objectionable for me in my situation to partake in. When did I withdraw it? At the very time when a substantive establishment was about to be formed, and when, if profit had been my object, it could have been employed with increased advantage and security. And how did I withdraw it? In so abrupt a manner, and accompanied by a course of such peremptory measures, as to produce a rupture not only with Mr. Palmer, but with my own old friend, who, not thinking the reason I assigned sufficient, could not be persuaded but that my real purpose was to injure them. If I had been influenced by undue partiality, should I have acted in a manner to produce a rupture with my friends? If I had entertained any apprehension of their power to injure me, should I have provoked them to open hostility, and have encouraged them to assail me if they could? There are, I believe, gentlemen now in Court who were at Hyderabad at the time, and I challenge them to say that my rupture with Mr. Palmer, and his hostility to me, were not open and notorious. It has also been asserted that my brother, Mr. Charles Russell, was connected with the House, and that he continued connected with them up to the day of his leaving India. To this assertion I have a very short answer—it is totally unfounded. I do not see that it has anywhere been attempted to show that I had any interest of any kind, direct or indirect, in any of the transactions which have

been made the ground of censure on the house. If any
such insinuation has been made, I now meet it personally,
as I have before met it in print, by a solemn, total, unqualified denial. It has also been urged, that the Nizam
might have procured money elsewhere at a more moderate
rate of interest. I assert, however, on the ground of
twenty years' experience at Hyderabad, that he could not
have procured money from any other person at a lower
rate of interest. As to the Aurungabad transaction, which
I believe to be the largest the house ever had with the
Nizam, it appears in page 17 of Sir W. Rumbold's letter,
that, in four years, from 1818 to 1822, the actual payments made by the house amounted to 111 lakhs of
rupees; and that, on the sum so advanced, the charges of
the house, of every description, amounted to 6 lakhs and
43,000 rupees, being less than a charge of 6 per cent. on
the net payments. If gentlemen will turn to the accounts,
they will find that, in 1820 and 1821, the house not only
made no charge of interest, but sustained a charge of
interest themselves; the payments of the Nizam at those
periods having exceeded their advances, they gave him
credit for the overplus. To prove, however, more completely, that the Nizam could not have borrowed money
at a lower rate, I beg the attention of the Court to a
transaction which occurred in 1820. An attempt was
then made to contract a loan of 6½ lakhs of rupees for
the Raja of Nagpore. The Resident there wrote to the
Resident at Hyderabad, requesting that he would invite
proposals for a loan to that amount. He did so, and the
lowest offer was 24 per cent. It should be known, too,
that the loan was to be transmitted by the Resident at
Hyderabad to the Resident at Nagpore, and that repayment was to be made at Hyderabad. Here, then, in ad-

dition to 24 per cent., was the charge of transmitting the loan to Nagpore, and afterwards, when the payments came round, of sending the money back to Hyderabad. If, under a regular guarantee, the two Residents could not raise money for less than 24 per cent., why should it be supposed that the Nizam could have procured it at a more moderate rate? The Nizam's government had no credit. The moneyed men reposed no confidence in it. One reason, which is to be found in the printed papers, will sufficiently show why. When Chundoo Lall was negotiating about the payment of the Nizam's debts, Sir C. Metcalfe said to him, 'You have provided for the house of Palmer and Company, but here is money due to the native bankers; how do you mean to pay them?' 'Pay them!' answered the Minister, 'why, I don't mean to pay them at all! They have received interest over and over again, and I'll pay them no more!' Under such a system as this, was it likely that individuals would lend money without the guarantee of the British Government? I think, Sir, this argument is conclusive, in opposition to the assertion that the Nizam could have raised money at a cheaper rate in some other quarter. I will now refer to another instance in which it was found impossible, even by Sir C. Metcalfe himself, to raise money at a moderate rate of interest. From the statement contained in Sir W. Rumbold's letter, it appears that 'the Dookan, or house of Mootee Chund Ram, of the Begum Bazaar, Hyderabad, advanced a sum of 80,000 rupees to the Minister, on the Resident's guarantee; but he arranged matters so as to acquire $5\frac{1}{2}$ per cent. for a two months' loan.' This is at the rate of no less than 33 per cent. per annum. The charge did not appear under the head of interest. That course he avoided by giv-

ing bills at a premium of one per cent. whilst they
were marketable at a discount of 2½ per cent. This
sum of 3½ per cent., with 2 per cent. interest, gave
the amount I have stated. In this instance the small
sum of 80,000 rupees was actually borrowed at an
interest of 33 per cent. per annum — and yet gentlemen talk of the ease with which loans might be procured at a moderate rate. I now beg to refer the
Court to page 40 of Sir W. Rumbold's letter, in which
the result of Sir W. Metcalfe's efforts to raise money,
after the Aurungabad contract was put an end to, is described. Sir C. Metcalfe, in one of his letters, observed
that 'The Aurungabad arrangement had been effected at.
a considerable charge to the Nizam's government, which,
with proper management, might have been avoided.'
How, then, when that arrangement was at an end, did Sir
C. Metcalfe proceed? When he found it necessary to
borrow, he exerted his best diligence, and yet it appears
that the task turned out to be a very difficult one. The
picture he draws of the result of his endeavours on that
occasion is most striking. It is contained in a passage of
Sir W. Rumbold's letter, and with permission of the
Court I will read it : — 'An end having been thus put to
the Aurungabad contract, Sir C. Metcalfe, of course, pursued that method, in providing for the payment of the
troops, which, in his judgment, ought to have been followed originally. He did, no doubt, the best he could
both for the Nizam's government and for the troops;
yet what was the result of his experiment? At the
expiration of a year and a half, in November 1823, he
himself described it in the following remarkable terms : —
"The payment of the regular troops has been effected
only by incessant attention on our part. At first I trusted

to the Minister's positive assurance, that he had actually supplied the requisite funds; but it at length appeared that a portion of the troops had been for five months without receiving any pay, and that, in some instances, *the recruits had fainted in the ranks from the want of wholesome subsistence.* It became necessary to give more direct attention to this subject; and partly by continual urgency, partly by persuading the native bankers to advance money at 12 per cent. interest, and partly by occasional recourse in emergency to the extreme measure of advancing cash from the Treasury, on the security of the peshcush, the troops have latterly been paid with tolerable regularity. The subject will, however, continue to require incessant attention, for no reliance can be placed on the most solemn promises of Chundoo Lall; and if the payment of the troops be left to his management, without continual inquiry and urgency on our part, the arrears will rapidly increase, until the pressure become insupportable for the troops, and relief impracticable on the part of the Government.' I wish the Court to recollect the particular crisis of the Company's affairs, when Messrs. Palmer and Company entered into the Aurungabad arrangement, which was perfectly effective. We were then in the midst of the most perilous war which we have ever waged. The danger did not arise from the hostility of avowed enemies, but from the treachery of hollow friends. The Courts of Poona and Nagpore declared against us. In every quarter danger was to be apprehended. Alarm and insecurity were universal, and Hyderabad was the only capital that remained true and faithful to its connection. I feel myself justified, Sir, in claiming the merit of this. No false modesty shall deter me from doing so. By my personal influence, and by the manner in which I directed the applica-

tion of his resources, I kept the Nizam faithful to his
engagements, and made him a useful and active ally. It
it is not to be supposed that he did not partake of the
general feeling. He was unquestionably wavering; and
if I had held up my finger it would have been sufficient
to turn him against us. In 1818, when the Aurungabad
contract was made, money was so scarce that the bankers
of Calcutta were borrowing even on deposits of Government paper, at 12 per cent. In 1823, when, with great
difficulty, and with the security of the English Resident,
Sir C. Metcalfe borrowed from the native bankers a very
small sum at 12 per cent., profound peace prevailed
throughout the whole of India, and money was so abundant, that in Calcutta, the houses of agency allowed only
6 per cent. on fixed, and 4 per cent. on floating balances.
It appears, then, that in 1823 — when no extraordinary
difficulties existed, in the midst of a profound peace — Sir
C. Metcalfe (who could scarcely get food for his fainting
soldiers) was obliged to pay at Hyderabad, on a small
sum, an interest of 12 per cent., being double the rate
charged at Calcutta at that period. What valid objection,
then, can be alleged against the terms of the arrangement
made by Palmer and Company in 1818, when the same relative proportion of interest prevailed between Hyderabad
and Calcutta? If, in the midst of the war of 1818, I
had suffered the troops to be so ill-paid and fed as to be
fainting in the ranks, what co-operation could they have
afforded to the Company's forces? And what, Sir, would
have been said to me, if I had been called on to account
for such a state of things? I should have had to stand
before you this day to answer for my conduct. I do not
mean to say, Sir, that we could not have fought without
the aid of the Nizam's forces; but, without them, we

must have contended at great disadvantage, and a protracted warfare most probably would have ensued. If a speedy conclusion had not been put to hostilities, we would have been subjected to the expense of lakhs, nay of crores of rupees, in carrying on a number of consecutive campaigns. A time of war is not the time to expose great interests for the sake of petty expenses, and to hazard the prolongation of hostilities while you are higgling for a few rupees. I now contend that the money was borrowed at as cheap a rate as it could be procured for, and more could not be expected. I have been accused of negligence in not particularly reporting the nature and objects of Messrs. Palmer and Company's transactions to Government. Sir, I deny the charge. Some surprise has been expressed, that I did not act in conformity with the order of the Directors. But, Sir, that order did not reach Hyderabad until I had left the place. In point of fact, however, I had reported the particulars of those transactions; — they were distinctly exhibited in the three accounts to which I have before referred. The Berar Suwar's engagement was laid by me before Government, and approved of and sanctioned by them. The Aurungabad contract, exhibiting the rate of interest at 24 per cent., was laid before Government in complete detail. As to the Hyderabad account, it was of so miscellaneous a nature, that, unless a daily account were made out, it would have been impossible to explain all the items it contained. An outline was, however, furnished to the Government, quite sufficient to put them in possession of the nature of those transactions: and, on the balance of that account, I have shown that at the time the loan negotiations were entered into, the house had not a claim on the Nizam for one single rupee. As an answer to the charges which have been alleged against Messrs. Palmer and Company, I shall now, as a matter of justice to them, point out some of the advantages of which their transactions were productive. But for the aid afforded by that house, the Government of the Nizam could not have stood. In my opinion, the assistance given by Messrs. Palmer and Company contributed, in no common degree, to the benefit both of the Nizam's government and that of the British. Without their assistance, the Nizam could not have brought his troops into the field at all — much less could he have brought them in that state of discipline which enabled them to co-operate effectively with the British forces. With the advances derived from Messrs. Palmer and Company, I was enabled to raise and equip a body of troops for the Nizam under the command of English officers, which served with distinguished honour throughout the campaign — which secured the internal tranquillity of the Nizam's country, and facilitated the introduction of retrenchment and reform, and which, at this very moment, when a war is raging beyond our frontier, will enable the Government to send our own troops against the enemy, and trust their interests at Hyderabad to the troops of the Nizam. In spite, therefore, of all that has been alleged against them, I will affirm that the members of that house are entitled to the liberal consideration of the East India Company. On the subject of the question immediately before the Court, as it affects the character of the Marquis of Hastings, I can have no personal feeling or interest whatever. I never saw the noble Marquis in my life, nor ever had any intercourse with him but what arose out of my official duty. But, Sir, I will never remain silent when the honour of that noble person is assailed, or when it becomes a question whether his services to his country were entitled to reward. The Court may certainly withhold from him the merit that he has earned, but they cannot, without injuring themselves, pass any vote which will have the slightest imputation on the character of the noble Marquis. There are, however, other and much larger interests involved in this question; and I implore the Court, before they adopt the amendment, to examine its real purport; to mark the end for which it is designed, and the result to which it may finally lead. I call upon them to look at it not only in its immediate effects, but in the remote consequences with which it is likely to be attended. I trust that nothing will be done to shut the door against future redress. The Company's counsel, in the opinion to which I have already referred, declares that there are no means of legally punishing Messrs. Palmer and Company, but he says that the Court of Directors have the means of punishing them in their own hands, by withholding payment of their claims. The amount of the penalty thus recommended to be inflicted is no longer problematical; for the authorities in India have acted in anticipation of the advice of the Company's counsel, and have already mulcted the house in the enormous sum of 500,000*l.*, by interposing their authority to prevent their recovering their outstanding demands to that amount. Is it to be tolerated that such a power is to be exercised in a free country? Is punishment to be inflicted in this arbitrary manner? If so, and if such as that here assumed does reside in any hand in England, it is high time for English gentlemen to take refuge under the freedom and security of the Inquisition. Honourable proprietors cannot conscientiously give a vote which involves considerations of this magnitude, — which may destroy not only the fortunes but the characters of indi-

viduals occupying an honourable station in society, — and
which may reduce hundreds of innocent persons to beg-
gary and destitution, without carefully, diligently, and
dispassionately examining both sides of the question, and
without weighing what the house had said in its defence,
as well as what had been advanced against them. Gentlemen's minds must be very differently constituted from
mine, if, before they have heard both parties, they can
give a blind vote on such a question as this, and then go
home and lay their heads quietly on their pillows."

But the house failed. The Court of Directors wrote to
Calcutta to see that justice was done to that house, but
in a spirit so cold and tame as one can easily understand
after a perusal of the *Mandamus Papers*, where, for the
second time in the history of the Court of Directors, they
were obliged to do the thing they did not desire, in
subscribing the letter dictated by the Board of Control.
That letter publicly admits an *amende* due to the house of
William Palmer and Company; but the Indian councillors
never acknowledged it, and if they did transcribe their
instructions for the information of the Resident, it was
understood they were never to be acted upon. Mr.
Russell's vindication of his character, as well as that of
the firm, is sufficiently clear; but it is necessary to know
what an Indian banker of that day thought of the rate
of interest imposed by Messrs. William Palmer and Company; and I therefore give the speech of Sir Charles
Forbes, the eminent banker of Bombay : —

" Sir Charles Forbes. — I shall trespass, Sir, on the
Court with but a very few words. I have certainly been
at the head of a banking house in India for many years;

and I must say that, in 1818, such was the scarcity of money, that the Government opened the Treasury at 9 per cent. They raised the interest to 9½ after that, and so it continued for nine months. It was afterwards reduced to 6 per cent. No doubt higher rates were given in other parts, but this was in Bombay. There is one observation I have to make here, which I think of the utmost importance to this Court; and it is, that much as has been said of the interest taken by Palmer and Company on this loan, there is not a man here who would not agree with me, that he would have been sorry to have exchanged situations with that house on that occasion. I declare, upon my honour, I would not at any period, before or after, have entered into such an engagement as that which Palmer and Company did, even for a higher rate of interest, because it was interest stipulated for, but never received, and perhaps never will be received. I would, Sir, at any time, prefer lending money at 9 per cent. to Government to lending it at 24 per cent. to the Nizam. But it has been said this house had a guarantee; it was not the case.

" Mr. Stuart.—I said they had the sanction of Government, which was equivalent to a guarantee.

" Sir Charles Forbes. — I hope that guarantee will be fulfilled; but, Sir, such are the consequences of that unfortunate loan, that I am sure no man envies their situation, even with that guarantee. I must here say, I have not done that which I ought to have done before I troubled this Court with any observations. I have not read the voluminous book containing these papers; but I have read enough to satisfy my mind on this point, that the terms made by Messrs. Palmer and Company were moderate compared to those made by other persons. A great deal

lms been said about native powers, but there are no such
things. No Englishman would be found to place himself
in the power of the Nizam. On one occasion, indeed, I had
an opportunity of placing myself in the power of the Government of India. Soon after the arrival of the Marquis of
Wellesley in 1798, and when preparations were making
for the Nizam war, the credit of the Company was falling
rapidly. Such was the difficulty of getting money, that
every means were used by the Marquis of Wellesley to accomplish that necessary object, previous to his entering on
the war. One of them was this : — "On the 18th August,
1798, an advertisement appeared in the *Bombay Courier*,
under the signature of the Secretary of Government. It
is very short ; and as it is important, I will read it : —

"' The Honourable the Governor in Council will receive
sealed proposals, on Tuesday the 21st instant, from any
person desirous of paying money into the Treasury, for
the Honourable Company's promissory notes on the General Register, bearing interest at 6 per cent. per annum,
for any amount not exceeding 100,000 rupees, on the
following conditions : —

"' The money tendered to be paid into the Treasury at
such time as may suit the lender, provided the same be
on or before the 20th day of September next.

"' On payment of the money, a promissory note will be
granted for the amount, which, according to the terms of
the General Register, will be transferable at par to the
Bengal Register debt, or may be subscribed for bills on
England, at the exchange of 2s. 2½d. the rupee, payable
eighteen months after date.

"' The Governor in Council engages that, excepting
what is tendered under this advertisement, no other promissory notes of the same description shall be issued

during the period stated, viz., before the 21st day of September next, unless the same be at least 2 per cent. below the lowest offer made.

" 'The tenders to be made in the following form : —

" ' On the terms of the advertisement, dated the 14th August, 1798, I do hereby tender the sum of   rupees, to be paid into the Honourable Company's Treasury, on or before the 20th September next, for which I agree to receive promissory notes on the General Register, bearing interest at 6 per cent. per annum, at the rate of rupees for every hundred rupees so paid into the Treasury.'

" 'The tenders to be superscribed, "Tenders for promissory notes," and to be delivered to the Secretary, or sent into Council, at 12 o'clock on the 21st instant.

" ' Published by order of the Honourable the Governor in Council.

" ' ROBERT RICHARDS,
" ' Secretary to Government.

" ' 14th August, 1798.'

" Well, Sir, what do you think were the terms? How much do you think was paid in? On the 30th August, on the 3rd September, and on the 17th September, three different periods, the enormous sums of 18,000 rupees were paid in ; 10,000 rupees was the second sum, and 3,100 was the next sum paid into the Treasury ; at the rate of 120 paper for 100 cash, being added to the 8 per cent., and 6 per cent. being added for one year ; and this was the exchange between Bombay and Calcutta. We only tendered 18,100 rupees, upon these very moderate terms of 34 per cent. per annum. Our money was worth that ; and, in fact, it was worth more, for it was all we could spare. If we had gone on feeding them, perhaps we could have *screwed* out better terms; but this is a fact to which I pledge my honour. I have a right, then, to call upon this Court to do justice; and, if they do not, I trust it will be found elsewhere. And now, Sir, I beg leave to say, I have no connection whatever with these parties. I did, about thirty years ago, see Mr. William Palmer; but, except that, all the parties are totally unknown to me, from the Marquis of Hastings downwards, excepting Sir William Rumbold, with whom I became acquainted only within the last fortnight. Now, Sir, I have a letter in my pocket at this moment, from Calcutta, which states that while some of the houses there are refusing money at 4 per cent., others are getting 12 per cent., with a bonus of 10 per cent. for three months. This is fifty-two per cent. per annum. I should like to know.——(*here a violent knocking in the hall disturbed the hon. Proprietor*). I have but one word more to say; I have heard a great deal about a conspiracy, and opinions have been read on this subject. With what object those opinions were read I do not know; but I think they were most favourable documents, because they show the utmost possible anxiety to fix on these parties a conspiracy. I have said thus much. I will only add one word more. The question before us refers to the Hyderabad transactions, and to them alone, as I conceive. Upon that subject, and upon that alone, I am come here to give an opinion. I am not prepared to approve fully and entirely of every act of Lord Hastings' administration, nor will I do so; but with respect to the Hyderabad question, not only do I conceive there is nothing to find fault with in his Lordship's conduct, but I think it has been highly meritorious. It appears to me that the transactions in question could not have been

more beneficially conducted for the interest of the Government, which seems to have been always the end which
his Lordship had in view. What was the situation in
which his Lordship was then placed? We were threatened with a general war, and the native princes would
have been glad to find an opportunity of turning against
you. How then was his Lordship to get the necessary
money for paying the Nizam's troops? I am of opinion
that if he had resorted to a public sale, as the Government did with respect to the 6 per cent. paper in 1798, he
would not have raised the money on such advantageous
terms as those upon which it was obtained from Messrs.
Palmer and Company. I am borne out in that opinion
by the letters which I have received from India, describing the state of the money market at the period in
question. One word more with respect to the troops of
the Nizam, as they are called. The changes have been
rung upon that part of the speech of the hon. Proprietor
(Mr. Russell) in which he said that if he held up his
finger the troops of the Nizam would have turned against
us. All that I understand the hon. Proprietor to mean
by that expression was to express that such was his
influence with the Nizam, that he was able to avert the
danger with which the interests of the Company were
threatened. That is what I understood to be meant by
the phrase, and it is not fair to attempt to give it a forced
construction. How is it possible that a man with a grain
of common sense could commit himself as it had been
insinuated that Mr. Russell had done by that expression,
much less an individual who has himself so much honour
both in and out of this Court, by that admirable speech
which has delighted all who heard or have read it? I
have been in public life now fourteen years, and can

safely declare that I never before heard a speech so clear in detail, or so able and convincing — I may say so unconquerable — in reasoning as that of the hon. Proprietor. I never heard, in the House of Commons, so clear and luminous an address. A late member of the Bengal Government (Mr. Stuart) has stated that the Resident objected to the raising and maintaining of the troops. I can believe that, because he perhaps thought that their troops might, as I believe they will, be turned against ourselves; — yes, the very troops which we have raised, clothed, and paid. I cannot forget what happened at the battle of Poona. The British character was tarnished by what took place on that occasion. This is the first opportunity I have had of expressing my opinion on this subject, which I had hoped would have been made the subject of discussion elsewhere. I do not intend to detain the Court, but I can assure the gentlemen behind, who are expressing their impatience, that there are members of the Court of Directors who give themselves very little trouble about the business of the Court, and are easily induced to concur in the measures which are proposed there. This, however, is a question on which I think we ought to have the declared opinion of every individual Director, that we may know who are friends of Lord Hastings and who are not. I should not hesitate to give my support to any resolution conveying thanks to the Court of Directors, that might be proposed subsequently to the passing of the original motion ; but to the amendment, in its present form and at the present time, I cannot agree. I would support an amendment which would not destroy the whole effect of the motion, and which would not bind us, as the present amendment does, to approve of what I never can bestow my approbation upon — namely, the political despatches of the Court of Directors. If I had nothing else to support me in the opinion which I entertain of these despatches but the protest of an hon. Director (Mr. Pattison), whom I have in my eye — which out of Court has made a great impression, and been treated with the consideration it deserves — I never could consent to give my vote in approval of them. Besides, the amendment does in fact commit us with respect to the whole future question. That is a very important consideration. The case of these unfortunate men, Messrs. Palmer and Company, would be concluded by the amendment. The Marquis has been the game which it was hoped to run down, but those unfortunate men have been made the victims. Feeling as I do strongly on this point, I would not on any consideration give my approbation to a proposition like the amendment, which would commit me with respect to these unfortunate gentlemen, and preclude me from advocating the claim which they undoubtedly have not only upon the justice of this Court, but upon that of the British nation. For the reasons which I have stated, I will give my vote for the original motion."

Time wore on, and the Nizam's ministers once more renewed the pension to Mr. Palmer and his family; and one would have thought that after his disasters, and with increasing years, some consideration would have been had for the circumstances of the old gentleman; one is surprised to find that, even so late as General Fraser's time, Mr. Palmer is again called upon to explain the grounds for the pension 'and to state the amounts so received by him. I cannot do better than give Mr. Palmer's reply : —

Major-General J. S. FRASER, *Resident, &c., Hyderabad.*

Sir,—I have the honour to acknowledge the receipt of your letter of the 6th instant, and I thankfully and gladly avail myself of the opportunity afforded me to communicate to you all the information I possess upon the several points alluded to in your letter to the Minister.

2. The accompanying schedule* comprises a statement of those awards of the city Udhalut which have not yet been finally disposed of, specifying the dates of those awards, their respective amounts, and the payments which have been received on each respectively.

3. Only a part of the numerous claims of William Palmer and Company were brought into court. Several of the principal claims, and such as were most easy of adjustment, were the first that were carried before the court, and all which were so carried before it prior to 1830 were every one of them, I believe, finally adjudicated.

4. It was ascertained, however, about the middle of 1829, that Oobeed-ool-Hussain, the moonshee of the then Resident, Mr. Martin, was using all his influence to defeat the claims of William Palmer and Company—a fact which received strong subsequent confirmation from the discovery of the striking circumstance (the proofs of which were established before Colonel Stewart when subsequently investigating the matter under instructions from Lord William Bentinck) of his having received from Mooneer-ool-Moolk *Rs.* 50,000 by way of earnest money, with the further promise of a lakh of rupees in addition, as soon as the matter should be brought to bear. In consequence of this state of things, the representatives of

---

* Omitted here as not necessary.

William Palmer and Company ceased from that time to prosecute their claims. They prosecuted the Resident's moonshee, however, whose conviction and dismissal are now matters of record.

5. At the end of 1829 ill-health compelled me, who had conducted the prosecutions in the city courts, to go to the Neilgherries, where I remained till the middle of 1830.

6. No effect had been given to the awards up to the period of my return, and, after I had done so, found that our importunities to the Nizam's government to enforce their performance were utterly unavailing, unless where backed by some show of interest in our affairs on the part of the Supreme Government.

7. The occasional inquiries which the Supreme Government were pleased to make into our affairs led to partial payments being made on these awards. The payments exhibited in the schedule were generally (indeed, with hardly a single exception) obtained in this manner.

8. The experience of the past gave the representatives of William Palmer and Company but little hopes as to the future, and they ceased to agitate their claims except only at such periods when fresh orders or inquiries from the Supreme Government gave them fresh hopes that those claims would be attended to by the Nizam's government.

9. In regard to the allowances received by myself and some members of my family, I beg leave to state that about a year after the failure of the house of William Palmer and Company, being wholly destitute and without any resource for my future subsistence, I solicited maintenance from the Minister, and he was pleased to restore to me and to my brother the allowances which we had formerly derived from the Nizam's government.

10. At that time we were not informed whether those allowances were paid us from the private purse of the Minister or from the funds of the State ; but subsequently, when a reference on this subject was made to the Minister by Colonel Stewart, we were informed that the Minister had paid us these allowances from his own private purse. The result of Colonel Stewart's inquiry is to be found in a letter from the Honourable Court to the Bengal Government, under date 31st October, 1832, given in page 213 of the *Mandamus Papers*, from which I annex an extract :—

" If the Government of the Nizam had continued to be carried on under the direct control of the Resident, it would have been that officer's duty absolutely to prevent by all means in his power the continuance of any payments, either open or disguised, from the resources of the State to any member of the late firm ; but under present circumstances we can only direct that he should shape his conduct in such a manner as to give no encouragement, either intentionally or through inadvertence, to the belief that the firm either has or will ever have any influence with the British Government or its representative. When the Nizam or his Minister shall cease to entertain any persuasion of this sort, they will have no motive for diverting any of the resources of the State to the emoluments of these individuals."

11. Subsequently to the receipt of this despatch from the Honourable Court I had reason to suppose that I had been transferred to the public establishment of his Highness's government. I concluded that the Minister had made this change in my position in consequence of understanding (from the above-quoted despatch) that the Honourable Court had no longer any desire to interfere

with or to prevent his honouring me with any recompense which he might deem suited to my past services; so long as it was clear to them that he was not induced so to do by any misconception as to the real extent of my credit or power, but was fully aware of the fact, that I neither did possess nor was ever likely to possess the slightest influence with the Supreme Government.

12. I am unable to state positively whether his Highness the Nizam is aware of the allowances received by me and my brother, but so far from conceiving that any reason existed for concealment on this point, I solicited the Minister (as soon as ever the interdiction of intercourse formerly imposed on us was removed by Lord Auckland's government) to present me to his Highness at his durbar.

13. The Minister promised to comply, but in so cold a manner that I was deterred from pressing upon him a request which it was possible might not have accorded with his views as regarded other matters.

14. I however took occasional opportunities to present nuzzurs to his Highness, who was pleased to receive them; and even if this did not mark, as in my case and according to the custom of the country it did, the acknowledged homage of a servant to his sovereign, it at least afforded his Highness an opportunity of satisfying himself as to my real position, had any objection to it existed on his part.

	Rs.
I receive per month	2500
My brother	1000
My son, Mr. W. Palmer	600
My nephew, Mr. H. Arrow	400

15. My nephew, Mr. Edward Palmer, whose success in his profession (the medical) has acquired him some repu-

tation in the city of Hyderabad, is the medical adviser of the Minister's family, and has several times attended the Minister himself and many of his relations through dangerous illnesses, and his services are always at the Minister's disposal. For this he receives *Rs.* 500 a month.

16. My son, as you are aware, is employed in the district. My nephew, Mr. H. Arrow, is absent on leave for ill-health, but is shortly expected here. The junior branches of the family (I have made no direct inquiry upon the subject) I have always considered as belonging to the public establishment. Whether my allowances are derived from the coffers of the State or the private purse of the Minister, it is-plain in the first place that they are purely voluntary, in the second that they cannot possibly be attributed to any supposed secret influence on my part with any of the British authorities, inasmuch as not only are the events of the last twenty years a lamentable proof of my total want of any such influence, but as, moreover, those allowances have been continued to us notwithstanding the recorded wishes to the contrary of the Directors and their positive and express declaration, " that I neither had nor ever would have the slightest influence with the British Government."

17. If, therefore, the Minister and the government whom I have served are pleased to consider my services as not undeserving of reward, I trust that the Supreme Government will not, after a lapse of eight years, think it necessary to interfere to prevent its continuance.

18. If it be demanded why an allowance is given to me, I would refer it to the fact of my having been a servant of the Nizam so far back as 1799,—a position from which, I would beg to remind you, it was not the displeasure of the Nizam's government that drove me. I

would refer it to the Minister's recollection of services
(frequently of a confidential nature) in which I had been
employed, to the zeal with which he knew I had always
served his interests, and, in one important matter (a
detail of which I annex in a postscript) to the benefit
which I had been fortunately instrumental in securing
for his Highness's government; to the kindness which
naturally grew out of our respective positions, and which
certainly was not impaired by the formation of a house
of business, which, whatever others may have thought,
the Minister considered and mentioned as having afforded
him valuable assistance in the carrying on of his government at a somewhat critical period.

19. If these opinions were ever entertained by the
Minister (and I have ample proof that they were, in the
very nature of the services I rendered him), nothing could
be more natural, especially to a man like Rája Chundoo
Lall, than that he should have provided for my maintenance.

20. I would fain hope, if my affairs could be dispassionately discussed, that the nature and manner of the
grant of these allowances could lead to no other result
than an admission that the Minister, as far as his own
feelings were concerned, was only doing an act of liberal
justice towards me. The Rája himself, and I presume
most other people, would have considered that, to allow
me in the decline of life to struggle with destitution and
poverty, would have been to act in a manner consistent
neither with generosity nor with good faith.

21. It is deeply painful to me to be obliged to trumpet
forth my own services: it was so even formerly, but it is
doubly so now that the lapse of years has removed almost
all those companions of my military and political services,

whose personal testimony I could once have commanded;

and still more so, when the Directors' despatch of 1832, and the eight years which have since elapsed, without any departure from its tenor, had led me fondly to imagine that, as far as the Supreme Government and the Residents were concerned, the subject was at rest for ever, and that I should be permitted for the remainder of my years to enjoy, without molestation, the rewards which those who had profited by my services had been pleased to confer upon me in consideration of them.

22. As far as his Highness's government was concerned, I presume to believe that the Raja might, and gladly would on many occasions have employed my services advantageously for its interests, and not less so for those of his own administration, which labours, I really believe, under undeserved imputations as to the motives which dictate his revenue arrangements, had he not been deterred by the belief that my frequent intercourse with himself which the employment of my services would have necessarily occasioned, would have given positive offence to the Supreme Government.

23. Could such objection, if it still exist, be removed, and I would fain hope that it is not the intention of governments liberally constructed, like Lord Auckland's, to proscribe me from obtaining maintenance under the Nizam's government, under which my whole life has been passed. No possible objection could then have existed, nor could now exist, were I employed under the Nizam's government, to my enjoying my present allowances.

24. I regret that I am not able to state the aggregate amount of payments made to me, having kept no regular account of them. Such as I did keep for a time shall be submitted, if necessary, for inspection. Had I any idea

that the subject would again have been made matter of discussion and inquiry, I might have been more particular.

25. For a detail of the services on which I was employed I beg to refer you to an annexed copy of a letter in page 835–9 of the Hyderabad papers, and I earnestly solicit your attention to the statements therein contained.

26. I shall here content myself with a brief recapitulation of the principal events in which I was then engaged, when my services were used equally by the Nizam's government and by the local British authorities.

27. When Colonel Stevenson commanded the subsidiary force in the field in 1803–4 against Scindia and the Raja of Berar, I accompanied his force, and was selected by him to act as his Brigade-Major to the Nizam's troops.

28. When, subsequently, during the same campaign, I was left in military command of the frontier town of Aurungabad, I communicated with General Wellesley, by his desire, respecting the movements of the enemy.

29. At the end of the war I was employed to take military possession of the districts ceded by the enemy to the Nizam.

30. When Mohiput Ram, in 1808, rebelled against the Nizam's government, I was selected, conjointly by the Resident, Captain Sydenham, and the ministers, Meer Allum and Chundoo Lall, to negotiate with him on the part of the Minister; and by the Resident's desire I corresponded directly with him, and referred to him all my negotiations.

31. I was in the subsequent action where the Nizam's troops were defeated, and when Mohiput Ram afterwards fled, pursued by a detachment of the subsidiary force

under Colonel Montresor, Mr. George Sydenham, the
Persian Interpreter, being absent, I was employed in his
room, and placed in charge of what is called, I believe,
the Intelligence Department, that of the Hurkarus, employed to bring information of the enemy's movements.

32. My next service was performed subsequently to
the establishment of my house of business. A mutiny
broke out among Mr. Gordon's troops, and I was employed to bring them over. Failing in the attempt, a
detachment, under Colonel Hopetoun Scott, was sent to
intimidate them into submission, and I was employed
under him to communicate with the mutineers and also
with the Resident. It was at length resolved to attack
the mutineers, and General Conran having taken the
command of the detachment, I was placed in command of
the Nizam's troops acting in conjunction with him, and
volunteered in the capacity of guide, to lead the attack
on the Choultry, in which the mutineers were posted.

33. On this occasion I was honoured with the approbation of Lord Minto's Government, conveyed to me
through the Resident, Mr. Russell.

34. After the surrender of the mutineers I was appointed President of a Court Martial to try the ring-
leaders. Captain Beckett, commanding the Russell
Brigade, and several officers of the Russell and Aurungabad Brigades, were members of the Court Martial.

35. Subsequently, in 1812 or 1813, I believe, when
the conduct of Captain Beckett, then employed to reduce
the foot of Bhoowaneepeit, had been disapproved by both
the Minister and the Resident, I received a commission to
supersede him in his command, and proceeded to his
camp at Ellareddypeit for that purpose. Captain Beckett,
however, having made the *amende* which I was desired

to call for at his hand, was not superseded ; had I superseded him, I should have been placed over the Company's officers,—Mr. Meikle, Lieutenants Holroyd and Currie.

36. I mention these facts, not from any exaggerated estimate of their importance, but simply to show that I was *bonâ fide* in the service of the Nizam, and that my services were real and actual. I was prominently and frequently employed in his Highness's service, and at no time did I meet with disapprobation.

37. My son and nephew came into the service subsequently to the restoration of mine and my brother's allowances; they were from the very first placed upon the public establishment of his Highness's government, and they are employed and attend the Minister's Durbar regularly and avowedly as the servants of the State.

38. I presume it will not be said that there has been any concealment with respect to the restored allowances received by myself and brother since the departure of Sir Charles Metcalfe ; but I have no other means of proving this fact than by referring not to an original letter, for I unfortunately have no copy of that, but to a letter referring to that original, and which will show that on Lord William Bentinck's arrival in the country, I requested my brother, Mr. John Palmer, of Calcutta, to inform his Lordship that I was maintained by the bounty of the Minister. This was accordingly communicated to his Lordship, not indeed by my brother, but by Sir William Rumbold.

39. I subjoin extracts from my letters of the 13th November, 1829, to Sir William Rumbold, referring to the previous letter addressed to my brother, Mr. John Palmer :—

" Since the cessation of the house, the Minister has renewed to me and to my brother the allowances formerly

given — 2500 rupees to me and 1000 to my brother."
" You know from what I have repeatedly expressed, and
from my letter, I believe to John Palmer (perhaps to
yourself), in the first case written before your arrival in
this country, that I was most anxious to communicate to
Lord William that I was maintained by the Minister."

40. I have been anxious to be employed by the Minister when I considered he could employ me, but I found
a perpetual obstacle in the Minister's belief that he was
not at liberty to employ me in any way without the Resident's express sanction — a' sanction for which he was
reluctant to ask.

41. You are aware that he for a long time refused
employment to my son, until he was satisfied, by repeated
explanation, that there was no objection on your part.

42. I hope I may have been fortunate enough to have
given all or most of the information required by your
letter. I shall gladly afford whatever more may be
wanted at my hands, but I cannot too much deplore the
precarious and harassing nature of my present situation,
and deprecate a continuance of the irksome position in
which I am placed by this unexpected renewal of discussions personal to myself.

43. I had hoped that the considerable length of time
which had been permitted to elapse without any com-
ments respecting either my allowances or my position
had secured some sort of permanency for them, and that
I might continue to enjoy them without molestation.

44. I need hardly remark that to remove me now from
a position in which I have been stationary for more than
forty years, would be an infliction of no common severity.

(Signed)   W. PALMER.

Hyderabad, 18th March, 1840.

Postscript first.—1. In 1819 Mr. Russell, the then Resident, had drawn up a plan for the internal administration of the Nizam's country, which he was about to submit to the Supreme Government. The main feature of this plan was that Mr. Russell proposed to place the several districts of his Highness's country under the management of English collectors, in order to introduce a good system of management, which he thought it would be possible to accomplish in a few years, when the English Collectors might be gradually withdrawn.

2. Before forwarding this plan to Calcutta, Mr. Russell sent it to me, desiring to have my opinion upon it.

3. I was at this time ill in bed. I at the first glance saw weighty and numerous objections to Mr. Russell's scheme, so far, at least, as the Nizam's government was concerned, and accordingly requested him to wait for a day or two, until I could commit to paper my ideas on the subject. He said he could not make any delay, and as I saw it was a case of emergency, I left my bed, ill as I was, and arranged my ideas as best I could.

4. I remonstrated strenuously against the introduction of any English Collectors. I said that it would prove but the first step to the Company's taking the entire country into their own hands. I pointed out that they had but the preceding year overthrown the neighbouring native governments of Poona and Berar; that they already possessed the exclusive command of the military force of this government; that if English Collectors were introduced, there would inevitably be frequent collision between them and the Nizam's officers; that the appeal of the former would always be to the Resident, who in the majority of cases would naturally see with the eyes of his own countrymen, and accordingly support them

by force, if necessary; that this course of depriving the
Nizam of every shadow of real power in all departments
of his state would leave him a mere cypher, who could
not long avert the fate of other native princes in the
Company's hands, and that when once the English Collectors were fixed in their places, and supported by the
influence of their friends in the Supreme Government
and in the direction, the task of removing them would be
found one of no small difficulty.

5. I proposed that the Resident should have the power
of appointing and removing native collectors, and pointed
out that Chundoo Lall, who confided implicitly in Mr.
Russell, was perfectly ready to be guided by his advice,
and accomplish the proposed reforms without any English
interference with the details.

6. This paper I submitted to Mr. Russell, and by .his
permission I subsequently forwarded it to Sir William
Rumbold, who laid it before Lord Hastings, who was
pleased to agree in the views I had expressed and to
cause a letter in accordance with its tenor to be written
to the Resident, Mr. Russell.

7. Many persons may doubt, perhaps with reason, whether this act of mine was really beneficial or the reverse to
this country, but I submit that there can be no reasonable
doubt as to the opinion which any native prince, like the
Nizam and his minister, must have entertained of my zeal
to avert from them their degradation to the class of
state puppets.

8. Accordingly, as soon as the result of my plan was
known, I requested Mr. Russell's permission to communicate the above facts to the Minister, in order that I might
reap the benefit of my services, and the gratitude of the
Minister literally knew no bounds. He sent a message to

me by three of my native friends to name my own reward. I refused anything for myself, but the subject
having been renewed for several days, I at last solicited
the Minister to give my two sons, then in England, a
salary of *Rs.* 500 each. The Minister rejected this as too
little, and at last I so far yielded to his offers as to accept
from him for each of my sons a salary of *Rs.* 1200, which
he continued to pay until all our allowances were revoked
by orders from the Supreme Government.

9. I appeal for confirmation of what I have just advanced to Mr., now Sir Henry Russell, Bart., to Captain
Jones, Mr. Jeffries (formerly Residency Surgeon), and to
Mr. French (now acting in the Sudder Dewany Udhalut
in Calcutta). Mr. Dighton is the only English gentleman
now here who is acquainted with the circumstances.

Postscript second. — 1. Since writing the foregoing part
of this letter I have been unremittingly occupied in an
endeavour to lay my hands on some of the old letters referring to the important service which in paragraph 18
of this letter I mentioned I had been fortunate enough to
render to this government, and the sketch of which, given
in the preceding postscript, is taken entirely from memory.

2. These letters, I was convinced, must still exist amongst
my heaps of old documents, and I have been fortunate
enough to find four, which I append to this letter marked
Nos. 2, 3, 4, and 5.

3. No. 2, as far as my recollection serves me, is *not* an
accurate copy of the paper which I transmitted to Lord
Hastings. I feel convinced it must have been a rough
draft of that paper. No. 3 is the letter which I wrote to
Sir William Rumbold when I transmitted to him that
paper to lay before Lord Hastings. For the despatch sent
by Lord Hastings, in consequence of that letter, to Mr.

Russell the Resident, see page 87 of the *Hyderabad Papers*.

4. No. 4 is my letter to my brother, Mr. John Palmer, of Calcutta, written some months after, in consequence of the Minister's most liberal offers made to me when he learned what I had done and the effect my letter had produced. Mr. Russell felt himself at the time obliged to indicate some opposition to the Minister's liberality, but he consented to refer the question to Mr. John Palmer. I could not object to such a course — hence this letter, No. 4, which speaks for itself.

5. I have not as yet been able to discover Mr. Russell's letter to me on this occasion, admitting in a most gratifying manner both my services and the Minister's *right* to reward them as he pleased, without question or interference. Should I find it, I shall do myself the honour of forwarding it to you to be appended to this letter. I however annex another letter of Mr. Russell's, No. 5, written some years before for the purpose of proving that while he (who better than any other English functionary knew the real extent of my services) was always pleased to speak of them in a manner as honourable to himself as it was gratifying to me, he was the very reverse of being disposed, as his successor was pleased to insinuate, to permit me *even the appearance* of enjoying the *slightest private influence* with himself, though he kindly expressed his readiness at all times to bear *public* testimony to my services.

(Signed)   W. PALMER.

Mr. William Palmer still lives, enjoying a green old age.

CHAP. VI.

CHAP. VI.

Provincial Divisions. THE principality of Hyderabad comprises the following different circars or provinces :—

Berar, including the Payeen Ghaut and Balla Ghaut.

Aurungabad, with part of Bujapore.

Bedur.

Hyderabad.

Governing officers. The governing officers are a soobah for Aurungabad, and talookdars in the other provinces, who are supreme in their respective talooks in all revenue and police cases. Lately six zillahdars have been appointed to supervise the police, and to put down, *vi et armis*, the Rohillas and other marauders. These Rohillas consist chiefly of Mekranees and Wuhilatees who have moved south from the Punjab ; they have hitherto occupied the fastnesses about Berar ; but as they are now to be summarily treated as dacoits, the country will soon be rid of these predatory characters.

Soil. The soil in general is extremely rich and fertile ; and, except where the tanks have been allowed to fall into decay, the country is well watered. In favourable situatious, two crops of rice are produced within the year from the same ground. Juwaree, bajree, wheat, barley, and chenna, are the principal produce of the country. Rice is grown in particular parts only, and in sufficient quantities for the consumption of the inhabitants. The poorer classes subsist chiefly on juwaree and bajree; the higher classes eat rice and wheat.

The population of Hyderabad (city) is supposed to be about 250,000; of which, perhaps, 150,000 may be within the walls, and 100,000 in the suburbs. Of the population within the. walls, the Hindoos are perhaps about 40,000, the remainder being Mahommedans. In the suburbs, about 60,000 may be Hindoos, and 40,000 Mahommedans. There are no means of computing the whole of the Nizam's population with any certain approach to accuracy. In estimating the population which the capital bears to the rest of the country, if the comparatively small number of inhabitants in a city which has no trade or manufactures be allowed to counterbalance the reduction made by bad government in the number of inhabitants of the country, the population of Hyderabad may be about a tenth of the whole population of the Nizam's territories, which will give a total of two millions and a half. At the capital, the Mahommedans have been computed at 150,000, and the Hindoos at 100,000. In the country, the Mahommedans are not, perhaps, above a tenth of the population. This, therefore, will give, exclusive of the capital, 2,025,000 Hindoos, and 225,000 Mahommedans; or altogether, 2,125,000 Hindoos, and 375,000 Mahommedans. The cultivators of the soil are chiefly Mahrattas, Telingas, Canarese, and other Hindoos.

There is but little commerce in the Nizam's territories;

and of what there is, the balance is very much against them. From the adjoining country they import copper, broadcloth, velvet, silk, muslins, chintz, calicoes, ornamented clothes, sugar, drugs, spices, sandalwood, and salt. From Cashmere they import shawls; from Malwa, opium; from Marwar, camels and blankets; and a good deal of salt is also imported from the Konkan. They export wheat, steel, cotton, and a considerable quantity of excellent teak timber which grows on the banks of the Godavery, below Momul, and is conveyed down the river to Coringa. The principal marts in the Nizam's country are Oomrawuttec and Omnabad, near Bedur. The usual interest of money at Hyderabad is two to three per cent. per month. The lowest rate at which the Minister negotiates loans for the Government, even when the amount is secured by assignments on the revenue of the country, is twelve per cent. per annum.

The Nizam's country did produce, in considerable numbers, the finest horses in the Deccan. The breed still exists, but the produce is very much diminished. Before the year 1800, an officer was stationed at Hyderabad to purchase horses for the Madras cavalry, and they were procured in considerable numbers; and, till very lately, an officer of the commissariat was employed to purchase them for the same purpose. The number purchased by him during the year 1815 was 354. The horses are produced chiefly in the western districts, bordering on the river Beema. An annual fair is held for the sale of them at Maligaum, in the Nandeir district.

The original provisions for the administration of justice are fair and rational under the Nizam's, as they are under most other governments. At Hyderabad the Soubah is the chief civil magistrate, and the Kotwal the chief criminal magistrate. Their duty is to receive and investigate all complaints. They refer the result of their inquiries to the Chief Cazee of the city, who pronounces the law; and his decrees again are applied and executed by the magistrates respectively. In all criminal cases the Mahommedan law prevails; in civil cases the Mahommedan law is applied to Mahommedans only. In disputes between Hindoos, the matter is referred to a Punchayet of Hindoos, to decide according to their law or practice; and, except in cases of manifest injustice, the Soubah is bound to adopt their award. When the Nizam takes the field, he is attended by a separate Cazee and Kotwal, who are called the Cazee and Kotwal of the army. The Nizam himself, or his minister, acts as civil magistrate in the camp. In the country, the administration of both civil and criminal justice is in the hands of the Aumul, or manager of the district, whether he be a farmer on his own account, or a collector appointed by the government. There is, however, a cazee in each district, to whom the aumul ought to refer in cases relating to Mahommedans; in those relating to Hindoos, he ought to refer to a punchayet. But as the office of cazee in the country is mostly hereditary, it seldom happens that the person who holds it is qualified to exercise the duties, and he is scarcely ever employed but to perform marriages or to authenticate documents with his seal. All these provisions, however, have fallen into total disuse. Both at the capital and in the country disputes are settled by force or favour, and even the forms of justice are openly neglected and defied. Until the Resident interfered, in 1814, to procure the infliction of capital punishment in cases of murder, not a single reference has been made to the chief cazee of the city in a criminal matter

CHAP.
VI

Justice.

for many years. The office of the soubah has fallen into total disuse, and the Kotwal acts only as the head of an inefficient and oppressive police. · Perhaps the only case in which anything like justice prevails is where a dispute takes place between two Hindoo merchants of equal rank, and is referred by mutual consent to the decision of a punchayet. The persons composing a punchayet are generally ignorant beyond their own immediate habits, but their awards are for the most part fair in their intention. No redress is ever to be had by an inferior against a superior, unless he purchases the assistance of a person still more powerful than his antagonist.

Hyderabad, the present capital of the Nizam, is situated on the south or right bank of the river Moosey, and is about six miles in circumference. It is merely surrounded by a single stone wall, flanked with small bastions and without any ditch; but it must have fully answered the purpose for which it was originally intended, that of keeping out the predatory Mahratta horse. · It was founded in 1556 by Mahommed Koolee Kootub Shah, the fourth king of the dynasty which rose in 1512 with four others on the ruins of the Bahmanee empire, and was destroyed by Aurungzebe in 1685. It was originally called Bhaug-nuggur, after Bhaugmuttee, a favourite mistress of the founder, and it is still known by that name, especially among the Hindoo inhabitants. The wall was built by Nizam-ool-Moolk, the great ancestor of the present Nizam.

Of the five Mahommedan kingdoms of the Deccan which Aurungzebe added to the dominions of Delhi, the capitals of three are still in the Nizam's possession,—Golconda, Bedur, and Ellichpoor. The other two—Beejapoor and Ahmednugger—also did belong to him. But Beejapoor was ceded to the Mahrattas in 1760 with a tract of country yielding sixty lakhs of rupees a year, and has now become by conquest the property of the British from the Peishwa. Beejapoor seems to have been one of the largest and finest cities in India under the Adil Shahee dynasty which reigned there, and the ruins of it are still very striking. The cupola on the tomb of one of the kings is only ten feet less in diameter than the cupola of St. Peter's. Sir James Mackintosh, who visited Beejapoor in 1808, called it the Palmyra of the Deccan. Ahmednugger was surrendered to the Mahrattas by the treachery of the Killadar in 1759. This also now belongs to the British.

Golconda is a place of considerable antiquity. Before the building of Hyderabad it was the seat of government under the Kootub Shahee kings, and it has ever since been considered as the barrier of the capital. It is about six miles west of Hyderabad on the high road leading to Poona. The inner fort, which is on a hill about 250 feet high, is now entirely abandoned, and appears to have no strength, either natural or artificial. The outer fort is on the plain. It is about six miles in circumference, and consists of a single wall flanked by bastions. The rampart of the wall is very narrow. There are altogether eighty-four bastions, on the largest of which there are two or three guns, and on the smaller only one. The ditch is seldom deep or wide. It is double on a part of the south face and single everywhere else. There is a glacis. The fort is by no means strong, and with European troops might probably be taken by escalade. There are still remains of two stone barriers on the high road to the westward, within two miles of the walls. The garrison consists nominally of 1200 men, but there are not probably above half that number. The tomb of the Kootub Shahee kings are within 600 yards of the wall, and would afford cover for at least 10,000 men. They were occupied by Aurungzebe when he besieged Golconda. The Nizam and several of his principal Ameers have their houses in the lower fort. The diamond mines of Golconda derive their name from being in the kingdom of Golconda, and not from being near the fort. They are at the village of Purteeall, near Condapilly, about 150 miles from Hyderabad on the road to Masulipatam. The property of them was reserved by the late Nizam when he ceded the Northern Circars to the English Government. They are superficial excavations, not exceeding ten or twelve feet deep in any part. For some years past the working of them has been discontinued, and there is no tradition of their having ever produced any valuable stones.

Bedur is eighty miles north-west from Hyderabad, on the high road to Jaulnah. It is said to have been founded by a Hindoo prince of the same name, who lived at the time of Alexander's invasion. The tenth of the Bahmanee kings removed the seat of government there from Goolburga in 1434, and it continued to be the capital until the termination of the dynasty and the division of their dominions. Bedur did not preserve its independence above forty years, its territories being swallowed up by its more powerful neighbour. It has since followed the destiny of Hyderabad. The remains of the city are still very fine. The walls are about four miles in circumference; they are of stone, massy, and well flanked, and in some parts there are three or four distinct lines of works. The ditch is deep and wide, and there is a glacis. If it were in good repair and well garrisoned it would be one of the strongest places in the Nizam's country.

Ellichpoor is about 320 miles to the northward of Hyderabad, and about 140 to the westward of Nagpoor. It is built between two small rivers—the Beechun and Serpen—which unite below the town, and after joining the Chundaburga, fall into the Poorna a little below Derriapoor. The fort, which is small and very much out of repair, is situated within the town, or rather the village, for it is now little better. Salabut Khan, who held the neighbouring districts in Jagheer, resided in the town which is surrounded by a single wall. Ellichpoor was the capital of the kingdom of Berar, which began in 1489 and ended in 1574, when it was absorbed into the kingdom of Ahmednugger.

Warangele, properly Wurungal, the ancient Hindoo capital of Telingana, now belongs to the Nizam. It is about 100 miles north-east of Hyderabad. It was founded in 1067, and continued to be the seat of the Roys of Telingana until it was finally reduced in 1523 by an army sent from Delhi by the emperor Toghlukh Shah. The city and suburbs were contained within three enclosures, of which the ruins only can now be traced. Their extent is considerable, but they have not been accurately measured. The only striking remains in their present condition are the four gateways of the palace, which are of grey granite, highly carved and polished; but the extent of the ruins and the magnitude of their dimensions denote a capital of the first class.

Aurungabad, the modern capital of the Nizam's domi- nions north of the Godavery, was founded by Aurungzebe, in 1657, on the site of a village called Khurkee. It is surrounded by a single wall measuring six miles, exclusive of two enclosed suburbs immediately adjoining, and forming, in fact, a part of the city, of which, therefore, the external circumference is upwards of ten miles. The present population of Aurungabad is about one hundred thousand. Nearly a thousand hand-looms are employed here in the manufacture of silks and brocades, of which the quantity annually fabricated is estimated at about three lakhs of rupees. Aurungabad is regarded as the first Moglaee possession in the Deccan, but otherwise not with particular sanctity, though there is a popular belief among Europeans to this effect. Here, however, are interred the mortal remains of the great Asoph Jah, and here, also, is that beautiful mausoleum, after the design of the Taj Mahal at Agra, over a daughter of Aurungzebe, who was buried in the place. The white marble screen round the tomb is said to be surpassingly beautiful; but so little do the local government reverence this place, that they have refused, on the score of expense, something very small to restore one of the minarets struck by lightning some years ago.

Dowlutabad, a place of great celebrity, is eight miles to the westward of Aurungabad. Its original Hindoo name was Deogur, and it is conjectured to be the Tagara of Ptolemy. It was reduced by the Mahommedans just before Wurungal, and appears at that time to have been the capital of the old Mahratta country, of the extent of which, as of Telingana, we have now no means of judging, unless we take the limits within which the Mahratta and Telinga languages respectively are spoken.

The Mahratta language now extends from the Injadree or Sautpoora mountains, which form the northern boundary of Khandesh nearly to the Krishna, and from the sea on the west to a waving frontier, on the east of which the general direction is indicated by a line drawn from Goa to the river Wurda, near Chanda, and from thence along the river to the Saulpoora mountains. The Telinga, vulgarly called the Gentoo language, from a corruption of the word Gentile, occupies the space to the eastward of the Mahrattas, from near Chicacole its northern, to within a few miles of Pulicat its southern boundary.

Early in the fourteenth century the Emperor Toghlukh Shah removed the seat of government from Delhi to Deogur, to which he gave the Mahommedan name of Dowlutabad. The fortress is a stupendous work, but its strength is an object rather curious than useful. The principal fortress is on a rock about six hundred feet high, the edge of which has been scarped away so as to leave a precipice all around fifteen hundred yards in length, and varying from two hundred and fifty to three hundred feet in perpendicular height. At the foot of the scarping there is a ditch near fifty feet wide and forty-five deep. The entrance is from the inner of four forts that are built one within the other upon the plain, and lies over a narrow bridge across the ditch into a small door, from which a shaft ascends spirally through the heart of the rock and issues by an iron trap-door in the centre of the work above. This shaft is about three hundred yards long, about seven feet high, and ten wide. The lower forts consist of stone walls flanked by bastions. They have little strength, and even the upper works, which are confined and have not much cover, might perhaps be bombarded.

The celebrated excavations of Ellora are six miles from Dowlutabad, and are evidently the work of the same age.

Moongee Puttun, also called Pytun, and supposed to be the Pytanæ of the Greek geographers, is situated on the Godavery, a little distance beyond Aurungabad. Although it has much declined, it still contains a population of about thirty thousand. It has a peculiar manufacture of embroidered cloths, in which near six hundred looms are employed. The annual value of the commodity fabricated is about two lakhs of rupees.

Coolburga, properly Goolburga, was the capital of the whole of the Mahommedan possessions in the Deccan under the Bahmanee kings from the establishment of the dynasty in 1347, and continued so until 1434, when the seat of government was transferred to Bedur. It is about one hundred and twenty miles west of Hyderabad, and fifteen east from the river Beemah. The town has fallen into decay, but the fort, which is extensive, is still in tolerable repair. The tomb of Syud Bundeh Nuwaz, who lived in the beginning of the fifteenth century, and is still worshipped by both Hindoos and Mahommedans as the tutelar saint of the Deccan, is at Goolburga.

The objects of curiosity not already noticed, like the tombs of Golconda, are the country palaces of some of the nobles. The buildings, perhaps, are not so grand, nor are they so extensive as those to which we are accustomed in Europe; but the interiors are elaborately got up, and expense is not an item that has been had in consideration. The ruins of mosques and mausolea arrest the eye in every direction; but this is the natural condition of a country where there are only two classes of people, individuals of which at any moment change places. There is, also, no respect for antiquity. In illustration, I may notice the beautiful mausoleum, after the design of the Taj Mahal at Agra, erected over the daughter of the emperor Aurungzebe, which the local government refused, on the score of expense, and that expense something very small, to restore one of the minarets which was struck by lightning four years ago. And yet individuals have spent enormous

sums of money in the construction of tanks, from the
childish desire which the natives generally have of per-
petuating their names for beneficence. There are tanks
all over the country, and pretty legends connected with
each and every tank. The tank of Meer Allum, a little
outside of the city of Hyderabad, is charmingly situated
among mountain, and plain, and wood; but for the Oriental character of the tombs by, and the native dwellings,
the scene might be believed to lay in the South of Europe.
The present Dewan, however, is giving another character to
the Hoosain Sagur Tank, by having connected it with the
river Moosee by a channel thirty-six miles long, at a cost
of about 25,000*l.* sterling. The superficial area of the
tank is roughly estimated at about 1400 acres; the number of cubic feet of water that can be stored at 15,000,000;
the average velocity of the channel is set down at four and
a quarter miles per hour; the discharge off into different
tanks, when there is three feet of water at the head sluice, is
between twelve and thirteen thousand cubic yards per hour,
and when the channel is full, it has an average width of
seven yards, and is two feet deep. This work not only
supplies Hyderabad, but Secunderabad, with water; it has
enabled tracts of country, abandoned for want of irrigation,
to be brought under cultivation; and it promises, if properly maintained, to avert those fearful seasons of want
which brought both fear and death to every door, but
specially that of the poor.

At Surroo Nuggur is the park of the Nizam, abounding in game of every variety, but not open to the public, and
to private individuals only by special permission. Amongst
the zoology of the principality of Hyderabad, interesting
to the naturalist and the sportsman, may be found the

Indian bison (*bos caviformis*) the tiger, leopard, cheetah, bear, wolf, hyena, and wild boar; the sambhur, nielghye (blue cow), cheetul, antelope, and the *bakir corona*, or four-horned antelope; the wild dog (which is said to run down its prey hunting in packs, even attacking and killing the tiger), the jackal, lynx, wild and civet cat, fox, porcupine, ichneumon, and hare, are plentiful. Here also is to be found the grey flying squirrel, with a body as large as a cat, covered with thick slaty-coloured fur; the monkey, peafowl, and jungle-fowl. There is no part of the peninsula of India which so abounds in sport, and which at the same time is so little known, as Hyderabad, excepting Mysore.

The distance between Bombay and Hyderabad—a little more than 450 miles—is now accomplished within four days. Yet it took Sir John Malcolm, in 1799, 18 days to travel from Hyderabad to Poona, within 112 miles of that distance. This rapid travelling now is owing, not only to the railway, which has been constructed as far as Sholapore, 276 miles, exclusive of the break across the Bhore Ghaut of six miles, but a splendid made road between Sholapore and Hyderabad, with resting-houses at convenient distances of between ten and fifteen miles. From the Administrative Report, sent to the Government of India, I gather that the Government undertook this road as a military work, in December 1857, for the transmission of troops, as they can now be pushed forward, on an emergency, at all seasons of the year, to Hyderabad, between eight and ten days at the rate of a hundred men a day; whereas, formerly, they would have taken fifteen days to march from Sholapore, and from twenty-five to thirty from Poona, and then could have travelled at this rate only in the fair season. The result of this road has been that the traffic between Bombay and Hyderabad has materially increased, and the proposed branch line of railway will do still more.

Mr. James J. Berkley, the Chief Resident Engineer of the Great Indian Peninsular Railway, upon his first arrival in Western India recommended the construction of this branch line from Sholapore to Hyderabad as one of those feeders that could prove both useful and profitable. By one of those strange coincidences peculiar to India, the Government objected to this, and made a halt at Sholapore, just where a halt should never have been made, in the same spirit that they have carried the Madras line of Railway away from all principal towns. The Government of India have, however, recommended, though the Home Government have for the present disapproved of, a survey of the line proposed between Sholapore and Hyderabad, but it is to be hoped that even this preliminary measure will not be attended with vexatious delays. Considering that both oil and fibrous plants are now being rapidly raised in this neighbourhood, the construction of this branch should be hastened; for its completion will affect not only the revenue of the Nizam's country but the income of the railway; and the sooner that line is constructed, the more advantageous to all parties. For the ability and foresight which he has ever shown in the interests of the country as well as of the railway, Mr. Berkley is deserving of the highest encomiums of the State. I may, in exemplification of what I say, quote the following from a Bombay newspaper of the 20th April last, as pertinent:—

"It has been calculated that, of the manufactured goods consumed in India, not more than 10 per cent. are of British production, and that in Bengal these only find their way to the borders of the great trunk roads. Large as our trade with this country is, it is yet only in its infancy, and this consideration might convince Government of the impolicy of checking, by a 10 per cent. duty, our difficult competition with the native looms. The great increase which has taken place during the last few years in the Import trade of India is in no small degree attributable to the improvement of the means of transit. The engineer is the pioneer of commerce in Hindoosthan. Over every pathway he hews out, trade eagerly passes. He is the missionary of civilisation, levelling the barriers which have so long retarded the march of knowledge, and kept the dense Indian population for centuries ignorant and benighted. The European trade, which is now limited to the borders of the great Indian highways, would speedily diffuse itself over the whole country, were there but the means of traversing it. Instead of wasting time and energy in fruitless and theoretical encouragement of cotton cultivation, if the commercial bodies directed their efforts to such measures as irrigation and the construction of roads in India, the results they more immediately seek would sooner be realised. A limited tenure of office seems to have many of the disadvantages of a limited tenure of land. Ministers will not take the responsibility, or endure the odium of expenditure, which may enrich their successors, but only straitens themselves. A light budget in the present is of greater importance in their eyes than a well-filled treasury in the future; but this is a kind of penny-wisdom and pound-foolishness which ought to be abandoned. Our forefathers did not scruple to make expensive wars, and leave us a heavy national debt to defray them, but it would be a more glorious inheritance to leave behind us great public works, such as we have described, which must eventually return a hundred-fold the capital laid out, and not only abundantly provide raw material for British industry, but immensely extend the consumption of British manufactures, and increase the glory and happiness of a great empire."

There is no country perhaps, so little known to the European as the Nizam's, and yet for facilities in respect of obtaining land, together with fertility of soil, it is unequalled. The superior descriptions of sugar may be imported into the principality, but sugar of the best description is grown all throughout Hyderabad, except in the very wildest districts. Persian silk has been largely manufactured, though the real silkworm has never been met with in the country. The mulberry, it is thought, will not grow in the Nizam's dominions, except in the Sautpoora range of hills, sufficiently luxuriant for the food of the worm, as the country is not moist enough; the coarser kind of worms certainly do exist in the country to the eastward of Hyderabad, in the jungles adjoining the Godavery.

A silk carpet was sent to the Exhibition of 1857 manufactured at Wuruugal, where cotton and woollen carpets of the most brilliant colours are manufactured. Common cotton carpets are made in all the large towns, especially Berar.

A private individual, Mr. Mulhera, has commenced coffee planting in the Sautpoora range, between Ellichpore and the Taptee. It has been a noble country, but is now very unhealthy except in the hot season, when Chikuldah (which is in the district, and has been regarded as a sanatarium, and therefore built upon of late years) is frequented by officers of the Hyderabad contingent in the neighbourhood. The Sautpoora range of hills is about 3000 feet above the level of the sea.

The district of Berar is notorious for cotton, and while it was found difficult, even for experimental purposes, to get natives in British territory to grow from New Orleans' seed, in the Nizam's country the trial was made without hesitation by his Excellency Salar Jung, and with success. The Oomrawuttee cotton, — the name by which it is familiar to Manchester people — though not quite equal to Dhollerah, will, I have no doubt, soon take that position, and even surpass it.

In 1848 there was a report, accompanied by specimens submitted to the Government of India, showing that the Chenoor coal was of the same formation as the English carboniferous species. The examination carried out at Calcutta showed that the specimens exhibited abundance of black flakes, as commonly occurs in bituminous shale, but no marks of structure. The appearance, supposed to be of scales of a lepedodandrous plant, turned out to be enamel dermal plates of an extinct placoids fish. There is no doubt that, before long, important discoveries will be made in the Nizam's dominions, as it has hitherto proved a sealed volume, but the Nizam's minister is not the man to allow this seal to last much longer, either for his master's benefit or that of the public generally.

I may here quote the opinions of two different medical officers of two distinct parts of the country. Dr. Bradley writing of Dowlutabad says :—" Though a very considerable proportion of the surface has been occupied by mountainous tracts and soil of a barren nature, still, allowing for this deduction, it contains much land of a very superior nature, manifested in the luxuriance of the growth of the cane and poppy, and heavy corn crops raised throughout the Circar. The cultivated soils are of two descriptions : that prevailing in the higher tracts is generally of a heavy, rich, aluminous character, whilst in the plains it is principally a light and fertile loam; in either case of no great depth, and resting upon a rocky substratum. These two soils are derived from the wearing away of the surface of rocks; the basalt going to form the stiff dark soil, whilst the amygdaloid wacken disintegrates into a friable earth, the lime and sandy particles of which, mingling with the stiff aluminous soil, counteracts its tendency to contract in the hot weather, as well as giving it higher powers of absorbing moisture. On the other hand the wasting of the basaltic rocks, mixing with light friable earth, converts it into rich loamy lands, diminishing its radiated powers and causing it to be more retentive of moisture. Such is the exuberant fertility of basaltic rocks in general that some are said to bear wheat crops for thirty years in succession without a fallow — the secret rests in the knowledge that those inorganic substances plants require for their healthy condition are lavishly afforded by the decomposition of these rocks, which year by year are undergoing chemical changes by the alternate influence of heat, moisture, light, and air, and thus unseen are constantly restoring to the soil those inorganic substances the crop has been consuming. In the absence of these facts, it would be difficult otherwise to conceive how such fertility could exist in such a wretched looking soil; but here appearances are no criterion of its quality."

Dr. Walker in an official report says :—" The black soil country comprehends the greater part of the Doab between the rivers Krishna and Tumboodra, a large portion of the Mulkair Circar, and the northern division of the Shorapore State. The subjacent rock here is partly granite, partly lime-stone, and partly trap. The population here is much denser than in the granitic soil. There is a good deal of traffic, too, in these districts. This soil is in some parts saliferous, yielding not only subcarbonate of soda but common salt. A tract, twenty-five miles east of Sherapore, is of this nature, where there are several brine wells which afford very good culinary salt. At one of the villages I observed this salt to be particularly pure, and it was to be had for a farthing a pound.

" The sandstone country of the Godavery extends west and east from the neighbourhood of Peddapully, in the Ramgeer Circar to Palooncha, and north and south from Chenoor to the Pakhal lake, is covered by a soil almost entirely of sand, on which a forest jungle is rooted. The population here is very sparse; in some districts, as in the Koorwah pergunnah of the Wurungal Circar, not amounting to more than two or three inhabitants to the square mile."

What this country can produce, or rather what it will be when its productive resources have been worked, is just one of those Utopian ideas in which the enthusiast may indulge; there is at least the possibility that even now it may be made to produce a great many more staples, and of an improved character. But with the drain upon the cultivating classes to construct the line of railway to Nagpore, and a like drain southward towards the completion of the railway workshops at Sholapore, I was surprised to see within a period of six months the amount of land that was brought under cultivation for oil-seed plants, between Sholapore and Hyderabad, and if this spirit should continue, I have little doubt that many of the vast tracts of country now lying fallow will be tilled. Lord Wellesley saw the policy of a commercial treaty more than half a century ago with the Nizam. That treaty has had its advantages, but we must look to

Nuwab Salar Jung for more substantial advantages than
exist at present.

I am indebted for the following interesting paragraphs upon the · military medical statistics of the
Nizam's country, to a valuable little brochure prepared by Dr. Riddell, late Superintending-Surgeon for
General Fraser, and published by the Nizam's government.
I have extracted only those portions which would interest
the general reader.

" The cantonment of Bolarum and head-quarters of the
Hyderabad division Nizam's army is situated about twelve
miles north of the city of Hyderabad, and about five north
of Secunderabad. There is a good road between the two
stations. Though at so short a distance from Secunderabad, and only sixty feet more elevated, still Bolarum has
always been remarkable for its salubrity and freedom from
the periodical visitations of fever, so prevalent at the head-
quarters of the Hyderabad subsidiary force. Dysentery
also, which is so formidable a disease at Secunderabad,
very rarely indeed assumes a serious type in this locality,
in fact all the cases generally seem most amenable to
treatment. The granitic ridge on which the station stands
is 1890 feet above the level of the sea. This ridge, though
of some extent, and forming an open plain on the higher
and eastern side of the cantonment of six or seven miles
in circumference, is surrounded on all sides by paddy
fields, and there are several small tanks about the neighbourhood. The gardens produce most kinds of European
vegetables in perfection, besides the common Indian fruits.
Mangoes, pineapples, and strawberries grow here in great
perfection. The range of the thermometer throughout
the year may be stated at from 50° to 90° in the shade,
although in the hot months it sometimes rises much

higher. The winds are westerly in June, July, August, and September; during October, November, December, January, and February, they blow from the east; and in March, April, and May, the north-westerly breezes are frequent. The annual fall of rain may be considered as from twenty-eight to thirty-two inches, which occurs principally during the south-west monsoon, that is between June and October. In the north-east monsoon there is sometimes a fall of some four or seven inches.

" The cantonment of Wurungal was formed in the year 1847. It is situated on a low plain near the bottom of some high rocky granite hills. The soil is partly black and partly composed of red sand. There is no jungle of any consequence within four miles of the place. Tanks are in great numbers in all directions, and rice cultivation is carried on extensively close up to the bounds of the cantonment.

" From the proximity to the rocks the temperature may be two or three degrees higher than that of Bolarum. During the greater part of March and April a fresh cool breeze blows from the south-east, which the natives call the " salt wind," and consider very healthy.

" The face of the country in this neighbourhood presents a striking similarity to that in the vicinity of Hyderabad. There are the same rounded dark-coloured herbless eminences, solitary, or in groups of inconsiderable range, rising to the height of 300 or 400 feet, with the same ruinous appearance of the lower hills and the fantastic piling of one boulder of rocks on another.

" The cantonment of Linsoogoor is situated in latitude 16° 9' North, and longitude 76° 35' East, ten to twelve miles south of the river Krishna, here running in a north-easterly direction. It lies two and a half miles to the north of the village of Lingsoogoor, upon the north-east corner of a tank, about three-quarters of a mile in length and three-eighths of a mile in width.

" The surrounding country is flat, with a few low scattered hills, usually composed of masses of granite irregularly piled one upon another.

" The soil immediately around the cantonment is of a reddish colour, loose, sandy, and of no great depth, with a substratum of rock, which in many places shows itself above the soil, and of which loose blocks are everywhere scattered over the surface.

" At the time of the formation of the cantonment this soil was covered with a low open jungle. This, however, has since been almost entirely cut down, giving the country a bleak and barren aspect. About five miles towards the north and west, where the soil is of the same description, low open jungle again makes its appearance, and extends as far as the Krishna. ·

" After the rains the soil in this jungle becomes speedily covered with a luxuriant crop of grass, which, on being cut and dried, forms hay of excellent quality, and hence are drawn the supplies for the cavalry karkhana and store departments.

" At a short distance from the cantonment, to the south and west, the soil consists of a rich black mould, producing abundant crops of wheat, gram, jowarree, and other grain.

" The winds are frequently high, occasionally blowing almost a hurricane. They are at the same time variable, frequently veering half round the compass in the course of a few hours.

" The following table gives the fall of rain during the last five years : —

	Fall of Rain up to 31st August.		Total to 31st December.	
	Inches.	Cents.	Inches.	Cents.
1847	13	14	19	17
1848	11	91	20	50
1849	22	56	34	27
1850	8	81	25	60
1851	8	58	17	67

"Mominabad, otherwise Amba or Ambajoghai, situated on the high table-lands of the Balla Ghat, at an elevation of 2500 feet above the level of the sea. It is the highest spot on the Balla Ghat-Dharoor, about twenty miles to the west excepted.

"The town of Ambajoghai is in latitude 18° 45' North, longitude 76° 40' East, and contains about 15,000 inhabitants. A nullah runs over a rocky bed on the west and east side of the town. All superfluous water is carried off by this outlet during the rains, and it is seldom dry during the hot months of the year.

"The village and cantonments of Mominabad, the head-quarters of the cavalry division, are in a hollow, surrounded by low hills, the village occupying the north-east corner of the basin. It is surrounded by a stone wall (breached in several places) about two miles in circumference, and has no ditch. The soil is mostly black, alluvial in the hollow, but on the surrounding high ground there is much trap rock and decayed trap. Amba is almost encircled by nullahs which, during the monsoon, render travelling, except on horseback, almost impossible.

"The climate is very superior, enjoying a delightful medium between the extremes of heat and cold experienced in the upper provinces of Hindoostan. The hot wind during the latter end of March and the months of April, May, and the beginning of June, does prevail, but never to the extent to make it extremely disagreeable to expose yourself to it, and it is always followed by cool and refreshing breezes soon after sunset. In the cold season the climate is by no means severe, but much more congenial to an Anglo-Indian than excessive cold. The monsoon usually sets in about the middle of June, and ceases about the end of September; and this is altogether the most pleasant season of the year.

"Gulburga, at present a place of little note, though famous in former times as the capital both of a Hindoo and Mahommedan sovereignty, lies in latitude 17° 20' North, longitude 76° 54' East, and about 120 miles west of the city of Hyderabad. The cavalry cantonment is situated three-quarters of a mile to the south of the native town, in a hollow space of black cotton soil, surrounded by low hills, distant on the north and west sides about a mile and a mile and a half, and on the south and east from three to five miles.

"The climate may be characterised as that of the Deccan generally. The maximum of thermometer (suspended in an open verandah fronting the north-west) as taken for the year 1850, was 103°, minimum 52°; and for the past year 106° maximum, 54° minimum; average fall of rain, twenty-nine inches. During the four months of cold weather, the atmosphere is dry and bracing, the nights very cold, and the whole day delightfully cool and pleasant. The prevailing diseases of this part of the country are fever, guinea-worm, urinary calculi, and psora. Fevers are of the ordinary intermittent type; their only peculiarity being an extreme tediousness of convalescence and a strong tendency to relapse. Dracunculus rages almost epidemically at certain seasons, and the natives of this place have a strong conviction that the worm is generated as much by eating particular kinds of vegetables as by water.

"The small walled village of Booldanah is situated on an elevated table land, on the Lackenwarra and Adjunta range of hills. It is subordinate to Saklee (Kusbah), and is four miles north-north-east from Davulghaut and fifty north from Jaulnah, in latitude 20° 34' North, longitude 76° 24' East.

"The height of this extensive plateau has not been ascertained, but being considerably higher than Adjunta, and appearing more elevated than the Aurungabad hills, (the latter is estimated to be 667 feet above the plain), it may be assumed to be not less than 700 feet above the plain of Berar. Its breadth varies from two to three miles, terminating on its northern side in precipitous falls and in projecting spurs, until it reaches the valley of Berar; and to the southward in a narrow but higher valley, the probable depression of which may be from 150 to 200 feet. This valley is very fertile, and has numerous villages situated on the course of the Paim Gungah, which takes its rise at a distance of about twelve miles westward, and winds its way about one and a half miles from Booldanah.

"To the north at a precipitous descent flows a little spring, taking its rise near to the village of Booldanah, and which forms the source of the Isva Gungah in Berar. On the declivity of this, as well as other ravines, and on the north side of the plain, it is somewhat jungly, but it has never been known to be unhealthy.

"The climate of Booldanah is salubrious; and from its

mild dry temperature, pure air, and cool nights, even during the hottest part of the year, is well adapted for a sanatarium, possessing as it does military protection and medical aid.

"Hingolee is a Kusbah or market town in the district of Mahore, province of Berar, situated on the north, or left bank of the river Khar, which runs a few hundred yards in front of it.

" Hingolee stands in latitude 19° 43', longitude 77° 0'. It is 247 miles viâ Gunga Kheir from Hyderabad, and 224 miles viâ Nandeir, being distant 60 miles from the former, and 40 miles from the latter place.

" It was selected as a military station in 1819, soon after the siege of Nowah, as a more centrical position than the former cantonment of Rissoor, situated 32 miles north-west of Hingolee.

" The climate is said to be favourable.

" The Ellichpoor cantonment is placed on both banks of a small river, named Sampam, about 21° North latitude and 77° East longitude, with an elevation, according to Colonel Waugh's measurement, about 1300 feet above the level of the sea. This small river, coming from the mountain range to the north of the cantonment, is sometimes swollen to a rapid torrent, and at other times it is nearly dry. Both banks of the river are almost flat, like all the other parts of the neighbouring valley of Berar, admitting of no proper drainage of the Sepoy's lines or cantonment. This circumstance of the water-lodging in the black cotton soil, and the bad situation of the canton-ment in general, is more severely felt, from the cool air being excluded by the range of hills on the north, which is at a distance of about four miles from the cantonment. It is as well to make a few remarks on these hills, which

s 4

have such an influence on the climate of this place. The base of the hills in this direction appears to be chiefly of sand-stone with lime-stone superimposed, both being sedimentary rocks, are regularly stratified, and are more or less elevated and thrown out of position by the upheaving of the trap rocks, of which these hills are chiefly composed. This picturesque range of hills is allowed by all to exercise a pernicious influence on the climate of this place, particularly during the monsoon, preventing a free circulation of air, to carry away the malaria, which no doubt then prevails, from the great number of fever cases that occur at that season of the year. In a country of a cotton soil in the vicinity of a range of hills, and consequently so liable to be cut up by a multitude of mountain streams, it may be imagined that no site for a cantonment more eligible could be chosen—but this is partially the case and applicable solely to the latter circumstance. For with all black soils, whatever be their substratum, there are invariably associated banks (if we may use a marine phrase for what appears by every sign to have been subaqueous) of calcareous tuff of greater or less extent; these tracts, when they exist, unite the advantage of slight elevation with its concomitant dryness of surface to the cause by which they have been produced, a much smaller capacity for the absorption and retention of moisture than is found in the black soil.

"The calx also containing a small proportion of magnesian earth, the vegetation of such spots is much less luxuriant than that of the surrounding country.

"Such sites and those too fitted in extent, and every other circumstance requisite for a cantonment, are to be found in the neighbourhood of Ellichpoor; of these the more remarkable are, one at the village of Burgaom, six miles to the east of Ellichpoor, and another at Chumuk, eight miles to the south; the latter was the encamping ground of General Dovcton's force in 1818–19.

The cantonment is admired for its appearance from the refreshing perpetual green foliage on the trees; the Sepoy's lines are situated on the right bank of the river, a short distance behind the officers' bungalows; they are found fault with from their defective construction and improper drainage; these faults are, at present, proposed to be remedied as far as practicable. The cavalry lines are situated on the left bank of the river, a little higher up, and more elevated than the infantry lines. The hospitals are placed close on the left bank of the river, opposite the infantry lines, and having the bazaar between them and the cavalry lines. The staff hospital is of a very superior construction.

"Chikuldah is situated on an undulating table-land, near to and somewhat higher than the Fort of Gawilghur; according to Hamilton's Gazetteer, this latter is situated in about latitude 21° North, and longitude 77° East, and by the measurement of Colonel Waugh, of the Great Trigonometrical Survey, the height of the Gawilghur Fort above the plain is 2300 feet, thus it will be 3600 feet above the level of the sea; since, according to Colonel Waugh, this part of the Berar valley is 1300 feet above the sea, Chikuldah is on the Vindhya, or as some call it, the Gawilghur range of hills, and is about twenty miles from the cantonments of Ellichpoor.

"The plateau of Chikuldah is not above three-quarters of a mile broad, and about a mile in length; but though thus limited in size, it has easy access to the surrounding table-lands and valleys, that renders its contracted space of little moment. The form of the plateau in outline, when viewed from the west, bears a fanciful resemblance to a map of the British Isles. The cool breeze which prevails at the Sanitarium during the hot months is a proof that the elevation must be considerable, and many invalids can bear testimony to the sudden relief they have experienced there from the suffocating heat usual at Ellichpoor during the hot months. Ladies and children in particular seem to derive much benefit from the place. The varied and extensive scenery commanded from this elevated spot is both graceful and romantic, exhilarating the mind by the grandeur of its precipitous ravines with their bluff fronts and bold projections. The more gentle scenery of a vast sylvan tract is seen trending away towards the north, covered with high grass and forest trees, in a series of undulating steppes, all connected one with another, and diminishing in altitude as they recede: embosomed amidst which are lying innumerable verdant and secluded valleys. Good roads have been made along the irregular plateau, commanding fine views of the neighbouring most picturesque country, and giving every facility for taking air and exercise, without the fatigue of wandering in the jungle or descending into the deep ravines near which the roads pass.

" As the slope of the mountains inclines towards the north, a more pleasing character presents itself in this direction than towards the south, where the face of the mountain stands denuded as a bold, precipitous, and cliff-like barrier, admitting only at intervals of winding pathways, steep and difficult of ascent, up its craggy front. It was through some of these passes that the first Moslems penetrated into the Deccan, led by the enterprising but murderous Ala-a-Din, of the house of Khilge. Upon the south the whole valley of Berar is seen spread out be-

neath the gazer's feet ; during the hot months it is generally shrouded in a sullen-looking mist, that seems to hang
oppressively over the valley ; but when the air is clear
and bright, as at other periods of the year, the extensive
champaign of Berar is seen across its entire breadth, and
sometimes far beyond, the hill fort of Mahore being at
times very distinctly visible."

APPENDIX

APPENDIX.

A.

No. I.

Earl CORNWALLIS's *ultimate Instructions* to Captain JOHN KENNAWAY, *deputed to Hyderabad.*

Fort William, June 16th, 1788.

Sir,—Being extremely desirous to act with every degree of moderation and respect to the Nizam, that may appear to be compatible with the requisite means for the effectual accomplishment of the object of your mission, I am now of opinion, after very mature deliberation, that it will be most expedient to postpone the delivery of my letter to the Nizam, and the full explanation of our intentions respecting the Guntoor Circar, till after your arrival at Hyderabad.

You will therefore continue your journey with as much expedition as the season and other circumstances will admit, acquainting Sir Archibald Campbell and me and Meer Mahommed Hussein from time to time with your progress.

I trust that you will find the Nizam sufficiently well inclined to show all the necessary and usual external marks of civility in his reception of you; and my wish will be that, as soon as the visits of ceremony are over, you shall proceed, with as little loss of time as possible, to the business of your deputation. For that purpose you will, as soon as may be consistent with decency, demand an audience of the Nizam for the purpose of delivering

my letter containing the demand of the Guntoor ; and conformable to the reasons which are stated in the instructions that you
have already received, you will accompany the formal demand
with an explicit declaration that the Company's troops will
march into the Circar within fourteen days after the date of that
conference.

You are already apprised that the Nizam will probably express much discontent at this determination.

So far therefore it may be proper to authorise you to suspend
the declaration relating to the Company's troops at the time of
your audience, lest in the first moments of disappointment and
vexation the Nizam should be tempted to form some violent
resolution, and express it by any act of intemperance.   Of this
you will judge, but I cannot by any means consent to your
postponing the declaration beyond three days after your audience, which may be notified to him by letter.

But whilst you cannot relax in any part of the substance of
the measure, I must repeat my recommendation that you will
be prepared with every conciliatory argument that has been
pointed out in your instructions, or that may be suggested by
your own prudence and good sense, to endeavour to prevail
upon him to preserve an amicable appearance in yielding his
acquiescence to it.

Should he determine to refuse a voluntary surrender of the
Circar, some unpleasant scenes may be unavoidable, though the
troops, in taking possession of it, will be directed to abstain as
much as possible from injuring individuals, and from all acts of
violence whatever.

It is also probable that, in the event of our being forced to
execute this measure without his consent, the Nizam's temper
will not for some time be sufficiently cool to give you credit for
the liberal principles on which you will offer to proceed to the
adjustment of the public account.

A little reflection, however, upon the danger of losing entirely
and immediately a large sum of money of balance, besides the
future payment of the peshcush, by declining all friendly discussion, may in a short time render him more accommodating;

but whatever signs of ill-humour or discontent, short of hostility or actual insult, may be shown on his part, you will be particularly careful to conduct yourself with the greatest moderation of manner, and to manifest an uniform disposition to negotiate and terminate the whole transaction with the utmost fairness and liberality.

In whatever manner the possession of the Circar may be obtained, the Nizam, when he proceeds to a statement of accounts, will probably make several charges for stores or balances due by renters in the Circar, exclusive of the sum that may be admitted to be due to him upon the adjustment of the general account between the two governments.

You will pay a civil attention to all such claims; but I wish the settlement of them, as a matter of local detail, to be left to Sir Archibald Campbell. You may, however, agree to transmit them to Sir Archibald Campbell, and you will follow such directions as he may think proper to give you for bringing them to a final and satisfactory settlement.

Sir Archibald Campbell will receive a copy of all your instructions, and of my letter to the Nizam; and a copy of that letter will also be transmitted to Messrs. Malet, Palmer and Foster, that they may be able to give a distinct explanation, where they respectively reside, of the nature of our present negotiation with the Nizam, and of the principles upon which we have preferred our demand of the Circar.

For the reasons which have induced me to leave little time for intrigue to the Nizam, between the declaration of our intention and the term which we fix for the surrender of the Guntoor, I do not wish to communicate to any of the Mahratta chiefs the real object of your mission until our design is ready for immediate execution, but at the same time it will be most proper that they should receive the first notification of it from the Residents of this Government.

In order, therefore, to give the necessary information on your part, you will prepare separate letters directed to Sir Archibald Campbell, to Mr. Malet, Major Palmer, and to Mr. Foster, as soon as you can mention to them the precise day on which the declaration will be made; and you will despatch them by different cossids forty-eight hours before the day named by the Nizam for a formal audience, which will enable you to execute that part of your instructions.

From the present political appearances, both in this country and in Europe, it seems at least highly improbable that any circumstances will arise between this time and that of your arrival at Hyderabad which would induce this Government to alter our present determination upon the business in question; and indeed I should hardly consider any reason short of a rupture with any of our neighbours upon other grounds, or an immediate war being an almost certain consequence of our making this demand, as sufficient for postponing it

I have confidence enough in you to be persuaded that your own judgment would suggest the necessity of suspending the execution of your orders in the event of very important incidents occurring that could probably not be known by this Government; and should there be reasonable grounds, contrary to all reasonable probability, to apprehend circumstances of the description to which I allude, you will confine yourself to a civil intercourse with the Nizam, and to general professions of friendship, until you can receive further instructions for your guidance.

I am, &c.
CORNWALLIS.

No. II.

Earl CORNWALLIS *to the Secret Committee.*

Fort William, November 4th, 1788.

Gentlemen,—Of the political occurrences in this country since the last sea conveyance, the most important has been the resolution which the Board adopted at my recommendation, and which has been communicated to you by an express overland, dated June 5th, to execute your orders for demanding possession of the Guntoor Circar for the Honourable Company, according to the terms of the treaty concluded_with the Nizam Ally Khan in the year 1768; and I have now very sincere pleasure in congratulating you on his Highness's having acquiesced in the justice of our demand, and surrendered the Circar to the officers of the Government of Fort St. George.

Being sensible of the value of the Circar, on account of its situation, to the Honourable Company, I should have been happy if I could have carried your commands upon that head into execution at an earlier period; but I trust that the reasons which induced me to delay making this demand upon the Nizam, and which have been partly enumerated in the overland despatch, will appear to you to have been founded on sound policy, and a due consideration of your real interests.

The general state of political affairs at the time of my arrival in this country rendered it, in my opinion, a season particularly improper for agitating the point in question, because the Nizam being then engaged in a dangerous war with Tippoo, we could not take any step which wore the least appearance of being unfriendly to him, without giving an advantage to Tippoo, which would have been neither conformable to our interest nor to our inclination.

The nice and delicate ground on which at that time we stood with his allies the Mahrattas was likewise deserving of very serious consideration. Respect for the legislature and a regard for your credit rendered it indispensably incumbent upon me to lose no time in recalling the offer which had been so inadvertently made by the preceding Government of furnishing them with the assistance of a body of troops from Bombay; but however necessary this measure might be on our part, I concluded that it could not fail of exciting considerable irritation with them, and perhaps some doubts of our national sincerity and good faith.

It was also in my recollection that the demand of the Guntoor had, under nearly similar circumstances, on a former occasion induced the same powers to lay aside their own quarrels and unite in a dangerous confederacy against your interests; and it therefore appeared to me for every reason to be prudent to allow

the claim to lie dormant, until by conciliatory communication
and an uniform adherence to the principles of justice and moderation, we could gain the confidence of the Mahrattas, and until
we could in every respect have grounds to believe that we could
assert it with reasonable hopes of success, and with less hazard
of involving your possessions in war. The appearances of hostile
designs which Sir Archibald Campbell perceived in Tippoo
during the course of the summer of 1787 were sufficient to prevent my forming any intention of touching upon a subject which
I believed at any time would be unpalatable to the Nizam. We
have every reason, however, in the mean time to be satisfied with
our progress in cultivating a good understanding with the
Mahrattas, and I considered it as a circumstance by no means
unfavourable to our interests that Scindia's power and influence
suffered about that time a considerable shock in the Upper Provinces of the empire. Whatever may have been Tippoo's real
designs in the first part of the season, it appeared towards the
end of that summer that he had no immediate plan of hostility
against the Carnatic. But although this circumstance, as well
as all other political appearances in India, would have been
sufficiently encouraging to me to consider the period as proper
for demanding of the Nizam the full accomplishment of the
treaty of 1768, our knowledge of the alarming dissensions in
Holland deterred me from taking any step which could give
umbrage to any of the native powers, from a belief of its being
very possible that the convulsions in the Dutch Republic might
in their consequences involve England in a war, which would
soon have extended to your possessions in this quarter of the
globe.

And as it appeared to me that the state of the political affairs
in Europe rendered an immediate interference from the French
or any other European power in the internal affairs of India, at
least highly improbable, I considered that a more favourable
opportunity could never be expected for opening a negotiation
with the Nizam, for the purpose of obtaining from him the full
accomplishment of his treaty with the Company. I therefore
proposed immediately to the Board, as you have been informed

by the former despatch, to depute a proper person without loss of time to Hyderabad. But although we had a right to expect that the honour and good faith with which we were determined to execute on our part the stipulations of the treaty, would tend to induce the Nizam to acquiesce in the justice of our demand, yet from the unwillingness which he had so frequently manifested of parting with the Circar, I could not suppose that these considerations alone would on this occasion influence him to relinquish it. The duplicity of his character and his talents for intrigue being likewise generally admitted, I considered myself as called upon by public duty to take every precaution of your Government against the disgrace of disappointment, and I thought it therefore equally prudent and necessary to leave him but a very short time, after making the requisition, for consulting with any of his neighbours on the means of opposition, and to direct that a good body of troops should be assembled near the Circar under other pretexts, to be ready to act if necessary in support of our demand of his performance of the terms of the treaty. Captain Kennaway, one of my aides-de-camp, was at my recommendation appointed to the deputation as a gentleman well acquainted with the country languages and customs, and in whose ability and prudence I could place an entire confidence, and he left this place in the beginning of May, though the rains and bad roads rendered his journey so unavoidably tedious and difficult that he did not arrive at Hyderabad till the latter end of July.

I shall beg leave to refer you to the despatch from the Board, for the copies of his instructions and of the letters with which he was charged from me to the Nizam. He was received by his Highness with every proper mark of attention and respect; but their intercourse for some time was necessarily confined to ceremonials and general expressions of civility. As the insult and demand which one of Tippoo's tributaries, the Raja of Cherika, had made upon Tellicherry whilst Captain Kennaway was upon his journey, had created doubts of that prince's pacific disposition, we could not venture on any step that might disgust the Nizam until it should clearly appear that we should not be forced into hostilities with Tippoo. Distressing as a war would be to your affairs in this country, it cannot be admitted to be so great an evil as the injury which you would suffer in your honour and ultimately in your substantial interests, by appearing to that prince to be apprehensive either of his enmity or his power. Upon that principle, and believing that the Raja of Cherika would not have dared to stir but by his instigation, I thought it indispensably necessary to write to him upon this occasion, and to declare explicitly that as on one hand it would be my constant study to act on the part of the Company with the greatest moderation and with the most scrupulous regard to the faith of treaties with all the princes of India, I was on the other equally determined not to suffer the least injury or insult to ourselves or our allies from any power whatever to pass unresented; and notifying to him that with these resolutions I had sent orders to punish the Raja of Cherika, and expressing my expectations that as the Raja was one of his tributaries, he would lend his assistance to force him to make ample reparation for his conduct. Tippoo's answer to me, as well as to letters which Sir Archibald Campbell had written to him about the same time, giving no reason to apprehend that his mind was prepared for an immediate rupture with us, Captain Kennaway was directed to proceed to the execution of the principal object of his mission, and I am persuaded that you will see with pleasure in his correspondence, which will be transmitted by the Board, the proofs which he has given of good sense and address in this transaction; and that Sir Archibald Campbell's judgment and exertion, in directing the measures of co-operation which depended upon him, will give you the highest satisfaction.

Although the Nizam acquiesced in our demand with sufficient decency of manner, we cannot venture to flatter ourselves that he did it without considerable real reluctance. It will be my earnest desire from my own inclination, as well as in compliance with your instructions, to impress his mind with a conviction of its being our fixed determination not only to act in the most liberal manner in the adjustment of the present account between him and the Company, but also to continue the payment of the peshcush in future with the strictest honour and regularity; and as I believe Captain Kennaway to be well calculated for gaining his good-will and esteem, and at the same time to discover any intrigues that may be meditated, I propose to leave him some time longer at Hyderabad to keep a watchful eye upon his Highness's conduct, and to endeavour by every means in his power to establish a confidential and friendly communication between the two Governments.

I am, &c.
CORNWALLIS.

No. III.

The GOVERNOR-GENERAL *in Council to* Captain KENNAWAY.

Fort William, May 31st, 1790.

Sir,— . . . I am fully aware of the importance of giving the Nizam every encouragement in our power, especially since we have reason to doubt the sincerity of the Mahrattas, and I approve therefore of the articles of agreement which you have signed relative to the Bengal detachment, understanding it of course to be considered by the Nizam to he no further binding than may be compatihle with previous military arrangements, which from circumstances cannot now be altered.

I enclose copies of the letters that I have written to Colonel Brathwaite and to Lieutenant-Colonel Cockerell, from which you will be enahled to explain in a satisfactory manner to his Highness the principles on which my orders are necessarily given, and I am persuaded you will be able without difficulty to make him sensible of the dangerous consequences that might attend my sending positive and unconditional orders to the troops, which are placed under the immediate command of General Medows, without giving that General time to prepare against the ill effects which such orders might produce to his general plan of operations.

By the time this letter reaches you, his Highness will either have passed the Kristnah, or he will have determined not to pass it till after the rains. If he should have passed it, and the Mahrattas still hang back, and there should really be reason to apprehend that Tippoo could send a formidable force against him, he must, at all hazards, be supported without loss of time, and without regarding the distress which the troops will suffer by making a long march at that season. But if he should not have crossed the Kristnah he can have nothing to fear from Tippoo before the breaking up of the rains, and I really think that in that case it would be for the safety and advantage of the common cause, that Cockerell should be employed for the defence of the Carnatic till that period, when he might, without much risk, leave a country in which the rains would soon be expected to commence, and when, unless a powerful co-operation on the part of the Mahrattas should render it unnecessary, the Nizam may depend upon being joined by so considerable a body of our infantry as to enable him to advance with confidence against the enemy. . . .

I cannot help thinking, notwithstanding the present doubtful appearances, that the Mahrattas will ultimately perform their engagements and take part with us, but, if I am too sanguine in this opinion, I can never believe that they would adopt a contrary line, and assist their inveterate enemy, Tippoo, whom they have so much cause to hate and dread. It is, however, possible that the apprehensions of the Nizam and his ministers of their hostile intentions, may again revive on the present occasion, and although I should wish you to avoid a discussion of this delicate subject if it was practicable, yet, if you find them seriously alarmed, you may repeat in the most explicit terms, that so long as his Highness acts heartily with us and fulfils his engagements, we shall think ourselves bound to defend him against attacks from any quarter whatever. . . .

I am, &c.
CORNWALLIS.

Marquis CORNWALLIS *to the* NIZAM.

Calcutta, April 12th, 1793.

I have been honoured with your Highness's letter in reply to my address on the subject of Kurnool. APPENDIX A.

In the commencement of this business when your Highness did me the honour to desire my opinion, I considered myself bound by the ties of personal friendship and political regard, to weigh the circumstances of the case in all their relations as affecting the rights of your Highness and Tippoo Sooltan, or as involving in their consequences the interference of the allies, and after the most mature deliberation on the subject in which so many important interests were concerned, I could not hesitate upon the ground of justice and policy to recommend to your Highness to desist from interfering in the affairs of that district. It appeared to me that your interference might involve serious consequences to your Highness's government alone, as no engagements existed by virtue of which the Company could unite with your Highness, nor any, as far as I was informed, between your Highness and the Peishwah, that could warrant the assistance of the Mahratta state in support of such measures.

The respect which I entertain for your Highness's wisdom and character, as well as the sincere regard which I possess for your Highness and the interests of your government, have induced me to reconsider what I before wrote, and to weigh and compare the reasons which I afford to your consideration in support of my opinion, with the arguments which you have urged in reply to them; and I should be wanting in that friendship and esteem which I profess for you if I did not candidly and explicitly declare, that the more I have deliberated upon the subject the more my opinion is confirmed that you should leave the discussion of the succession to Kurnool and the demand for the peshcush to be settled by the sons of Runmust Khan and Tippoo Sooltan, and that it is for your Highness's dignity and interest to withdraw your interference.

The proper time for discussing the claims of Tippoo Sooltan

to the peshcush from Kurnool, was before the conclusion of the peace with him. At the conferences upon this subject your Highness's ministers objected to the insertion of the peshcush in the schedule of Tippoo Sooltan's revenues, and denied the existence of any agreement under the signature of Runmust Khan to pay the peshcush. Here the matter rested, affirmed by one party and denied by the other, and your Highness's minister, although importuned by the sons of Runmust Khan to obtain an adjustment of the business, did not prosecute their objections and bring the point in dispute to a final decision; thus the opportunity of deciding this affair was lost, and the right of Tippoo Sooltan to the peshcush of Kurnool, which he and his father had exercised at different times for upwards of twenty years, was not rejected by the allies when they had the power to reject or admit what they pleased. I request, therefore, your Highness to consider with what justice this right can now be contested, or with what equity Tippoo Sooltan can now be called upon to produce the agreement of the Nabob of Kurnool. It is my duty and determination, as well as that of the English nation, to adhere inviolably to the faith of their treaties and the terms of their agreements. When it pleased the Almighty to crown the arms of the allies with success, they demanded what they thought proper from Tippoo, and whatever they did not exact must be considered as his property, which they have no right to demand at this time. It is certainly probable that at the period of the negotiation for peace, if a proper attention had been given to the affair of Kurnool on the part of your Highness's ministers, the amount of the peshcush or a territorial equivalent would have been required by the allies; but since from haste, inadvertence, or other cause, the matter remained then undecided, and no claim on this account was made upon Tippoo Sooltan, he would have just reason to complain of an infringement of that amity which has been established by the treaty of peace, if a demand were now made upon him.

These are the reflections which have occurred to me, and which I have already communicated to your Highness, who on this occasion, as in all others, will act agreeably to the dictates of wisdom and justice. Your Highness, adverting to the mode by which Hyder and Tippoo acquired their present power, and rendered the Nabob of Kurnool tributary to them, seems to consider it as no foundation of right on their parts; but every page of history, in which your Highness is so well instructed, shows that the Almighty Disposer of events bestows kingdoms and victory, and raises and depresses according to the inevitable decrees of His eternal wisdom, and that most of the great monarchies now existing were founded, under the permission of His providence, by the power of the sword; and in fact, unfortunately for the peace of mankind and for the prosperity of states, the rights of sovereigns are too often decided by an appeal to force instead of being settled by amicable counsels and reciprocal conciliation. It was by taking advantage of the times that Hyder Alee, as your Highness observes, established his power, and such is also the foundation of other great powers in Hindostan. By the blessing of God peace is now everywhere established, and my endeavours, as well as those of successors to this Government, will be constantly exerted to render it perpetual.

Your Highness proposes to engage for the payment of the arrears of peshcush to Tippoo Sooltan, and of the peshcush itself in future, when the amount is ascertained by the production of the agreement of the Nabob of Kurnool. Permit me to state to your Highness, that on this point it has occurred to me that in fact it would be to make your Highness tributary to Tippoo Sooltan, and I request that you will reflect that even if you could submit to such degradation, by making a private agreement of that nature with Tippoo, the country of Kurnool can never be considered by the allies in the same light as the other dominions of your Highness, for the guarantee of which against the attacks of Tippoo Sooltan the faith of the allies is mutually pledged.

I have complied with the duties of friendship in communicating without reserve what has occurred to me on this subject, and I trust that your Highness will be persuaded that in doing so I have been actuated by the most sincere concern for the interests of your government. Your Highness, in calling for my opinion, has imposed this task upon me, and I should have been happy if my sentiments on this occasion had coincided with those of your Highness, as it is my earnest wish to act conformably to your inclination; but the obligations of friendship indispensably require that I should write what, after the most mature consideration, appears to me dictated by justice and policy. The decision rests with your Highness's wisdom, which will no doubt suggest what is proper and right.

No. IV.

Earl CORNWALLIS *to the Secret Committee.*

Fort William, 12th April, 1790.

Gentlemen,—I am persuaded that you will observe with satisfaction that by the means of the powerful preparations which we have made on our own part, and by the apparent hearty disposition of the Nizam and the Mahrattas to co-operate with us in this war, there is very reasonable ground to expect that we shall be able to exact ample reparation from Tippoo for his insolent and flagrant violation of the late treaty of peace.

Every personal consideration rendered it peculiarly desirable for me to take all means that were honourable to prevent an interruption of the public tranquillity, because many of the effects of my earnest endeavours since my arrival in India to restore order to the Company's finances must be counteracted by the unavoidable expenses of a war, and it may likewise be the cause of detaining me another year in this country, which I shall feel as a severe disappointment. But at a crisis when Tippoo's enmity and ambition prompted him to commit a decided act of hostility against one of our allies, I should have deservedly incurred the contempt and censure of my country if a pusillanimous anxiety for the continuance of peace had induced me to endeavour to delay an open rupture with him by abandoning the dominions of that ally to ruin and devastation, or if I had even hesitated in resenting so daring an insult, according to the clear dictates of sound policy, honour, and justice.

The cordial reception which the Nizam and the Mahrattas gave to the propositions that I have made to them to avail themselves of this opportunity to revenge the many injuries that they have suffered at different times from Tippoo or his father, by joining us in the war, have been highly gratifying to me, and you will see from my correspondence with Mr. Malet and Captain Kennaway, that we have good grounds to expect that we shall obtain an early and vigorous co-operation from both these powers upon very advantageous terms.

You will be informed by the despatches to the Court of Directors that I have been extremely dissatisfied with the conduct of the late Government of Fort St. George, and I am still under great apprehension that many fatal consequences may follow from their criminal disobedience of our orders, which directed them to consider Tippoo as at war with the Company, if he should attack any part of the ancient possessions of the Raja of Travancore, and to make preparations accordingly for carrying it on with vigour.

I trust that it is not yet entirely impossible that Tippoo may be deterred from prosecuting his designs against Travancore, by the accounts which he must constantly receive of our military preparations, or, at least, if he should penetrate into Travancore, that he will be obliged to evacuate that country, and to employ his troops in the defence of his own dominions, when General Medows, according to the present plan, shall be enabled to commence offensive operations against the country of Coimbatoor.

There are hardly any circumstances that could be supposed under which an expensive and a dangerous war would not be to a certain degree a distressing event to the Company's affairs. But as we know that Tippoo's enmity to the British name and interests is avowed and implacable; that he put himself to the expense of sending an embassy to our formidable European rival to propose an offensive alliance against us ; that, exclusive of repeated pressing general applications to the Nizam and the Mahrattas to join in a league with him to subvert our power, that there is at this moment an embassy from him at Hyderabad for the express purpose of soliciting his Highness to join with him in attacking our dominions, or those of our allies, and consequently that we must have looked upon a war with him as constantly impending over us, and if it could have been avoided at present, absolutely certain at some future and perhaps early period, I do not think it unreasonable to expect that it may ultimately prove fortunate both for the Company and the natives, that by a most flagrant breach of a solemn treaty we have been forced, by adhering to the principles of honour, justice, and good faith to our allies, to come to a rupture with him at a juncture which offers to us so many considerable and evident advantages.

Should the war prove successful, we shall have a variety of interests and political arrangements to adjust with our confederates, and should the Nizam and the Mahrattas continue to act with the same fairness and openness that they have hitherto manifested in the preliminary negotiations, they will have the strongest claims to a liberal share of the advantages that can be secured for the Confederacy by a treaty of peace.

I am, &c.

CORNWALLIS.

No. V.

Earl CORNWALLIS to Captain KENNAWAY.

Camp at China Baleporam, 2nd April, 1791.

Sir,—After the communication contained in your letters, I must acknowledge that it was with the utmost astonishment and disappointment that I received, on the 31st ultimo, a letter dated the 23rd, which enclosed a copy of Raja Teige Wunt's

letter to me of the 22nd, conveying an account of the most
absurd and unfounded information that he stated to have been
received by him, of the measures that Tippoo had taken to prevent the junction of his Highness's cavalry with this army, and
informing me that, regardless of my requisition, and of his
master's public orders, he had determined to remain at Wini-
pilly, a place not above the distance of two moderate marches
from Gungycotta, until he should hear from me that I had sent
a detachment of infantry and guns to meet him at Chittagong.

Appendix A.

As the Raja must have had good grounds to suppose that
his letter would reach me at the critical period of my being
engaged in the siege of Bangalore, in presence of Tippoo at the
head of his whole army, I am under the necessity of viewing the
dilatoriness of his progress and his motives for writing that
letter in the most disadvantageous light; and though I wish it
to be done in guarded language, I must desire that you will on
this occasion express my dissatisfaction to his Highness and the
minister in the strongest terms.

You will state to them that, after the most deliberate reflection upon the Raja's conduct, it has appeared to me that it
can only be accounted for by one of the three following reasons:—1st. That his public orders have been counteracted by
private instructions; 2ndly, that his Highness has entrusted
the command of a large part of the force of the state to a man
who is no soldier; or 3rdly, that the Raja has been actually
corrupted by Tippoo's money. But you may assure them that
my mind has immediately rejected all attention to the first supposition, though the impression that remains upon it of the
probable existence of one or both of the latter causes, leaves me
little reason to hope that I can ever confide in the Raja for
giving me a hearty support in carrying on this war.

You will at the same time, after desiring them to call to their
recollection the openness and fairness of the whole of my public
conduct towards his Highness, the vigour with which I have
commenced the operations of the present campaign, and the
celerity and success with which I took my measures after the
reduction of Bangalore to prevent Tippoo from disturbing the

march of his Highness's cavalry, clearly give them to understand, that I will not tamely submit either to evident breach of engagement, or to strong marks of deception, and that, in the present case, unless, instead of receiving frivolous excuses, I shall soon see the most satisfactory grounds to expect the speedy junction of the above-mentioned body of cavalry, I shall not waste time in waiting for them, but proceed with this army to the execution of my own plan of operations, without placing any further dependence upon their assistance.

I am, &c.

CORNWALLIS.

Earl CORNWALLIS *to* Raja TEIGE WUNT.

8th May, 1791.

The army having now reached the open country, I consider it as a duty which I owe to the interests of the common cause, and to the honour of his Highness the Nizam's arms, to call upon you to bring the large body of cavalry under your command into activity, that it may assume the degree of superiority over the enemy to which it is entitled both by its numbers and by the zeal and spirit of its chiefs, and by that means contribute in the manner which was intended by his Highness to promote the success of the campaign.

As Tippoo has on all occasions since the commencement of the war carefully avoided an action with British armies of very inconsiderable numbers, and in particular would not attack this army when a large part of it was employed in carrying on the siege of Bangalore, there is not the least probability that he will now hazard a battle with the strongest army that was ever brought into the field against him; it therefore falls to the share of the infantry to proceed with the artillery according to the plan which has been settled to attack Seringapatam; and it is the duty of the cavalry to overrun the country, to cut off Tippoo's communication with his capital, and to prevent the approach of his small detachments of light horse to disturb the troops that will be employed in the siege.

To answer these purposes I desire that you will immediately detach a body of his Highness's cavalry of any number that you may judge advisable, and under the command of such chiefs as you may think qualified for executing the service, into the open country to the north-west of the present encampment, with orders to drive the enemy's small parties from the neighbourhood of the army and to intercept everything going to or coming out of Seringapatam on the roads leading to it from Corapatam and Treagunga.

Tippoo was by the last accounts at a great distance from hence with the main body of his army, and there is no reason to believe that there is at present any considerable body of his cavalry near our front; but whatever the situation of the enemy may be, the detached corps should leave its heavy baggage with the army, and move into the country as lightly equipped as possible, which will enable it either to avoid with facility any detachments of the enemy that may be furnished with infantry and guns, or to attack them with success if a favourable opportunity should offer, and if it should at any time be pressed by superior numbers it will find perfect security in falling back to the army.

I shall order further detachments to be made as the army advances; and I think it right at the same time to state to you that it is only by their own activity and exertions that it will be possible for the cavalry under your command to procure forage for their horses or subsistence for themselves, and that to continue, as has hitherto been the practice, to encamp with their followers in the rear of the line of infantry, would certainly occasion great distress to the whole army and ruin to the cause in which we are engaged.

I must likewise request that you will take effectual measures to restrain the troops under your command from insulting or forcing sentries belonging to the English regiments, and to oblige not only the cavalry, but also the baggage and followers, to remain in the situations which are allotted to them by the general order of march.

I am persuaded you will see the necessity for using your utmost authority to prevent a repetition of both these irregularities, when I inform you that by the rules of the English discipline it is the duty of a sentry to put any man to death who attempts to force him upon his post, and that, exclusive of the great inconvenience which has been experienced from the multitudes of the cavalry and their followers, who have broken in upon the line of march of the columns of our infantry and artillery, the English troops are exposed to great danger, and have already suffered considerable loss by the similarity of appearance of his Highness's and the enemy's cavalry, which renders it impossible for the officers and soldiers of our army to distinguish the one from the other, and which enables the enemy to mix with the stragglers of the Nizam's cavalry, and to watch for favourable opportunities to attack individuals on the line of march or upon their arrival at the new encampments.

I am, &c.

CORNWALLIS.

Earl CORNWALLIS *to* Captain JOHN KENNAWAY.

Camp, eight miles north of Seringapatam, 31st May, 1791.

Sir,—The different enclosures of this despatch, consisting of copies of letters to Sir Charles Oakeley and to Mr. Malet, and of my late correspondence with Tippoo, will give you the fullest information of all the material circumstances that have occurred since the date of my last letter, and of the influence which they have had upon my decisions, and will also convey to you a general outline of my future intentions.

You will deliver a copy of the correspondence with Tippoo, and communicate the substance of the other papers to the Nizam and the minister, and you will, according to the direc-

tions contained in my letter to Mr. Malet, avail yourself of that
opportunity to assure his Highness of my determination to per-
severe in a vigorous prosecution of the war until the objects of
the confederacy can be obtained, and of drawing their particular
attention to the pressing advances that Tippoo has repeatedly
made to me on account of the Company, and of the uniform
steadiness with which I have constantly declared to him that I
could listen to no propositions for opening a negotiation except
in concert and with the consent of the other members of the
confederacy.

APPENDIX
A.

I do not at present see any great reason to believe that
Tippoo's power is in his own opinion reduced so low as to render it necessary for him to make the sacrifices for peace which
the allies will think themselves entitled to demand, but as I have
engaged to him to recommend to the Nizam and the Peshwa
to send deputies with full powers to Bangalore to meet persons
that may be named by him for the purpose of opening a negotiation for the re-establishment of peace, I trust that his Highness
will lose no time in nominating his deputies, and should the
proposed meeting actually take place he may depend upon me
for showing a due regard to his interests.

Although I have been unwilling to express myself to his
Highness in harsh terms respecting his cavalry, it is right that
you should know that ever since the first ten or twelve days after
their junction they have given me numberless reasons to be dissatisfied with their conduct, and that our late distresses for forage
and provisions, which have had so material an influence on
the operations of this army, are principally to be attributed to
them.

The uncertain state of political affairs in Europe made me
anxious to use every means in my power to bring the war with
Tippoo to a speedy termination, but I should not have ventured
to have undertaken the enterprise against Seringapatam so late
in the season if I had not expected that so numerous and
powerful a body of cavalry would have been sufficiently able to
have procured forage for our cattle and to have secured supplies
of provisions for the troops.

They proved, however, regardless in almost every instance of my orders, and deaf to my representations after my near approach to the enemy's capital, and instead of spreading themselves in the country to secure our communications and to cut off those of the enemy, they could hardly ever be prevailed upon to go beyond our picquets even in search of forage and provisions for themselves, but persisted in remaining close in our rear in an unwieldy mass and in a state of the most unaccountable inactivity and apathy, until they were reduced to the greatest want and misery, whilst they at the same time consumed great quantities of forage and provisions which would have properly fallen to the share of this army, as being within its power and reach, and even in a great measure actually within the bounds of its own encampment.

I can hardly allow myself to suppose that this behaviour of the cavalry, which has given me such ground for complaint, has proceeded from a premeditated criminal design in any of the chiefs; but it may, perhaps, be more properly ascribed to the incapacity of Rajah Teige Wunt for such a command, and to the discontented and unmanageable disposition of Assud Ali Khan, who appears to engross his entire attention.

Having long relinquished all hopes of deriving any advantage to the common cause from the services of that cavalry, and the Raja and the other chiefs having also frequently applied to me for permission to quit the army, I had about a week ago agreed that the whole body shall return to their master, but the Raja having since the junction of the Mahratta armies earnestly requested to be allowed to remain with a few thousand of those that are in the most serviceable condition, I have, from an unwillingness to do anything that might be disagreeable to the Nizam, as well as from other political considerations, consented to it; and Assud Ali Khan with the sick and lame horses of the whole, and with his own troops and those of several of the inferior chiefs, has this day commenced his march to the northward, leaving with the Raja, Mahomed Ameen, of whom I must, in justice, say that I have always had reason, as far as I can judge, to be satisfied with his conduct.

It is only necessary to add, that as the Raja appears at present to be in a tractable temper of mind, and as I think he may profit from the advice of Mahomed Ameen, I do not desire that he should be removed from the command, but that in case his Highness should send a reinforcement of cavalry, my wish is that Assud Ali Khan shall never again be of the party.

You may take proper occasions to convey to his Highness and the minister, in the most moderate terms, part of my sentiments of dissatisfaction with the cavalry; but in justice to my own conviction of the Nizam's intention to give me a powerful support, you will always in such conversations give the strongest assurances that, far from looking upon the misconduct of the cavalry as in any degree imputable to him, I remain perfectly persuaded of his earnest desire to fulfil his engagements, and to do every thing in his power to promote the success of the alliance against the common enemy.

I am, &c.

CORNWALLIS.

Earl CORNWALLIS *to* Captain KENNAWAY.

Camp near Bangalore, 10th July, 1791.

Sir,—I read with the greatest surprise the copy of the letter from Raja Teige Wunt to the minister Azim-ool-Oomra, dated the 17th May. The gross falsehood of every syllable of this letter is so easily to be proved, that no person but so weak a man as the Raja could have hoped that it would have protected him against the displeasure of his master, when the heavy complaints that I had to make against him were fully stated to the Nizam. I must now withdraw the request which I made to you in my letter, dated the 31st of May, that you would convey in the most moderate terms part of my sentiments of dissatisfaction with the cavalry; in refutation of so much misrepresentation and falsehood it is necessary that you should tell the whole truth. I shall now only think it necessary that you should tell the whole truth, and take notice of a few of the most striking points in the Raja's letter, to show that I felt much more concern than he did, for securing supplies of provisions for his Highness's troops. I pressed him in the most earnest manner (when we were encamped at Vencatagherry, twenty-four miles from Amboor) to send all his Brinjarries to that fortress, where I assured him they would be supplied with as much rice from our magazine as they could carry away, on the most reasonable terms, and that the payment of it should not be required until it suited the Raja's convenience. I likewise explained to him that if he missed that opportunity it would be impossible for me afterwards to afford him any assistance. When the army halted in my camp, I recommended, what is I believe practised by all cavalry, that the Raja would send detachments of his troops to cover his foragers in procuring forage and grain from the villages in the rear of our position, where no force of the enemy could be apprehended except some parties of his looty horse; and in marching days, instead of requiring him to send his cavalry four or five coss for forage after they came to their ground, I requested of him, but in vain, that he would order his numerous foragers to forage in the villages on his flank during the march, where they would be protected by our line which always moved between them and the enemy, and where they would find much more forage and grain than in the villages adjoining to the road, instead of pursuing their constant practice of pressing forward between the head of our column and our advanced guard, and before our line arrived in camp, stripping the villages that were within its limits of the only forage that it was possible for us to procure for the support of our numerous cattle, and specially of the bullocks that were employed in dragging the battering train, and by that means most effectually defeating the great object of the march, which was the attack of the enemy's capital. In answer to his ridiculous complaint of marching double the distance than I did, I would submit it to his Highness's decision whether it would have been practicable, if I had been capable of wishing it, to have given them so unreasonable a degree of fatigue, and in cases where it became necessary to march by different routes whether the cavalry or the four-and-twenty pounders should have taken the shortest road.

The very circumstance, which the Raja describes so little to his own credit, at the head of twenty thousand horse, " that the enemy's looties patrolled round our camp," induced me to give orders, which after the first few days were either directly disobeyed or almost totally eluded, for detachments of his · Highness's cavalry to extend during our marches a few miles on our flank that was next to the enemy; and the Raja well knows that on the particular occasion to which I conceive he alludes, when knowing that the body of the enemy's army was at a considerable distance I directed him to send three thousand horse four or five coss into the country, in order to assert that superiority which so large a body of cavalry ought to have maintained, the small corps, which accompanied them under Captain Dallas, was not meant as a proportional force that was to be given by our troops for that service, but merely to prevent their being mistaken for the enemy on their return to the army.

The Raja's rhodomontade, respecting his behaviour in the action of the 15th, is really so absurd, that I cannot bring myself to enter into a serious refutation of it. The truth is, the cavalry showed on that occasion a better countenance and more good-will than I had expected from them, and I was induced to express my satisfaction, in the hope that it would operate as an incitement to their acting with more spirit in future than they had previously manifested; but it so happened that the victory was completely decided and gained before his cavalry came up, and, instead of his contributing to render it more complete, he placed his troops directly in front of a body of our infantry that I was exceedingly anxious to push forwards on a piece of broken ground in which cavalry could not have acted with advantage, and prevented their pressing the enemy in their retreat at a crisis when it would have been most particularly desirable. The Raja cannot possibly forget that just at that time I sent Captain Dallas to him to desire that he would make a movement with his cavalry to the left, that he might not impede the advance of our infantry.

After having been driven to the necessity of desiring you to lay the above statement of the Raja's conduct before the Nizam and the minister, you will easily conceive that I cannot by any means approve of his being continued in his present command. Although I have long known him destitute of every military qualification that was requisite for the station in which he was placed; yet being in hopes, when I wrote my letter of the 31st May, that he would in future be tractable, and probably fall into the hands of better advisers after the departure of Assood Ali Khan, I was unwilling to be the immediate cause of his being publicly disgraced; but having now found him to be capable of acting so falsely and treacherously towards me in his representations to his master, I must desire that you will request his Highness, in my name, to recall him. I wish that I could accompany this request with a recommendation of a successor; but I freely confess that I do not look upon any of those that have been with us qualified to fill a station of so great importance. I have a very good opinion of Rochum Vihan; but his bad health renders him incapable of exertion of any kind Mahommed Ameen appears to have several good qualities; but he is by no means a fit person for the chief command; and you are to recollect that if by any accident Assood Ali Khan should be thought of, I put the strongest negative upon his appointment, for very substantial reasons, which perhaps I shall explain to you more particularly hereafter.

I shall therefore only request, in general, that the Nizam and the minister will, in the selection of a successor to Raja Teige Wunt endeavour to send me a person in whom, for the interest of his master as well as the other confederates, I may safely confide; and if the idea should occur to them of placing the Nizam's son in that situation, attended by so able an adviser as Meer Abool Cossim, you may readily assure them that the measure will be most perfectly agreeable to me, and that I shall receive him with the most distinguished marks of attention and kindness.   I am, &c.

CORNWALLIS.

B.

No. I.

To the Right Honourable HENRY DUNDAS, *President of the Board of Control, &c.*

Cape of Good Hope, 23rd February, 1798.

My dear Sir, — Amongst the subjects which you recommend to my early consideration upon my arrival in India, you particularly urged the necessity of my attending with the utmost degree of vigilance to the system, now pursued almost universally by the native princes, of retaining in their service numbers of European or American officers under whom the native troops are trained and disciplined in imitation of the corps of Sepoys in the British service. By accident I found at this place, on account of his health, Major Kirkpatrick, lately Resident at the Court of Hyderabad, and formerly at that of Scindia, and I have endeavoured during the period of my detention here to collect from him whatever information he could furnish respecting the European or American officers and the corps commanded by them in the service of the Nizam. For this purpose after several conversations on the subject, I requested Major Kirkpatrick to return detailed answers in writing to several questions which I drew with the intention of bringing under your observation not only the actual strength, but the original object of this part of the Nizam's military establishment, its rapid increase, the consequences to be expected from its continuance or further growth, as well as the means which either had been or might be suggested for averting any danger which those consequences might threaten to our interests in India. I transmit with this letter a copy of my questions and of Major Kirkpatrick's answers*, and although I am aware that the substance of both must be familiar to you, yet imagining that it may hitherto have come under your notice only

APPENDIX
B.

* See Appendix A.

incidentally in detached despatches and advices from India, I think it may be useful to lay before you, in a more regular and connected form, a view of this most material and (in my judgment) formidable branch of the system to which you have directed my attention. In this letter, I shall endeavour to recapitulate the most important facts stated by Major Kirkpatrick, adding such observations as have occurred to me upon them, in the hope of receiving from you at an early period, your instructions upon such points as the materials before you can enable you to determine.

It appears that the Nizam had recently at different periods retained in his service, exclusive of our detachment, three distinct corps of Sepoys under the command of European or American officers: one commanded by a Frenchman of the name of Raymond, another by an American of the name of Boyd, and a third by an Irishman of the name of Finglass, for some time a quarter-master in the 19th Regiment of Dragoons.

The corps of Boyd and Finglass were taken into the service of the Nizam during the residence of Azeem-ool-Oomrah at Poona, at the suggestion of our Resident at that court, acting under the sanction of the Government of Bengal. This measure was taken by our Resident and by that government principally with a view of forming a counterpoise to the corps of Raymond. Boyd's corps consisted of about 1800 men, it is no longer in the service of the Nizam, and has probably passed into that of the Mahrattas. Finglass' corps still remains at Hyderabad, but consists of only one battalion of about 800 men. Both these corps appeared to be well affected to our interests, as may be judged by their willingness to assist our detachment in repelling an expected attack from the corps of Raymond. The corps of Raymond had been in the service of the Nizam before the last war with Tippoo-Sooltan, and in 1792 its strength was not more than 1500 men at the highest estimation. At the battle of Khurdlah in 1795 its strength amounted to no less than 11,000 men; it now consists of 10,000 men, and the order has actually been given for augmenting it to the number of 14,000. Attached to this corps is a train of artillery of about thirty field pieces, and a troop of eighty native dragoons. The discipline of the corps does not appear to be by any means good, and accordingly it has never yet rendered any distinguished service in the field.

The pay of the corps is now secured by the assignment of a large district of country, part of which borders the Carnatic. At this particular station is a fortified post, and constant communication is maintained between it and the port of Narpilly as well as with Ongole and other parts of the territories of the Company and of the Nabob of Arcot. The corps is recruited, in the proportion of one third of its total numbers, from our territories and from those of the Nabob of Arcot, and partly from deserters abandoning our service. The chief officers are Frenchmen of the most virulent and notorious principles of jacobinism; and the whole corps constitutes an armed French party of great zeal, diligence and activity. The efforts of this party are continually directed to the object of magnifying the power, resources, and success of France in the eyes of the Court of Hyderabad, and of depreciating the character, force and credit of Great Britain by every possible means.

The detachment of this corps stationed on our frontier has been very assiduous, with great success in seducing from their duty our Sepoys quartered in the neighbourhood: a considerable desertion lately took place in one of our native regiments on its march from Masulipatam to the southward, and many of the deserters on that occasion are to be found in Raymond's corps. No positive proof has yet appeared of a direct correspondence between the leaders of this corps and the French Government, but it seems to be unquestionably certain that they communicate with Tippoo-Sooltan and with the French corps in his service. Whatever may be the discipline or military skill of this corps, it now forms by far the most considerable part of the Nizam's military establishment. In this corps consists the main strength of the army of our ally; and it possesses the influence which usually belongs to an army in the councils of the native princes of India. This influence seems to have alarmed Azeem-ool-Oomrah the first minister of the Nizam; neither the origin nor the subsequent augmentations of this corps appear to have been at all connected with any hostile disposition in the Court of Hyderabad towards the British interests.   The institution of the corps proceeded from an admiration of the successful policy of Mahdajee Scindia, and the subsequent augmentation was directed principally if not solely against the Mahrattas. There is reason to believe that the orders lately given for a further increase of the corps to the number of 14,000 men arose from a desire in the mind of Azeem-ool-Oomrah of drawing us into a more intimate connection with the Nizam, by exciting our jealousy of the growing influence of the French party at Hyderabad.

Such is the state of the leading facts communicated by Major Kirkpatrick.   The result in my mind is a decided opinion that the continuance, and still more the further growth, of the corps of Raymond ought to be prevented by every means within our power, consistent with the respect due to the Court of Hyderabad, and with the general principles of moderation and justice which ought to form the rule of our conduct in India.   The dangers to be apprehended from the existence of this corps are not to be estimated by a consideration of its actual state of discipline, or even of its actual numbers, or degree of present influence over the councils of the Nizam.   I consider it as the basis of a French party in India, on which, according to the opportunities of fortune and the variation of events, the activity of the enemy may found a strength of the most formidable kind either in peace or war.   If we are to look to the settlement of peace, can it be possible to provide a more ready channel for the intrigues of France, than would be offered by the existence of a body of 10,000 men, united by military discipline, and stationed in the dominions of one of our principal allies, and on the borders of our own?   If the war is to continue in Europe without extending to the continent of India in the first instance, the danger of French intrigue acting with such an instrument as I have described, would be greatly aggravated.   But if the war should extend to the continent of India, and if we should be under the necessity of calling forth the strength of our allies

to assist us in any contest with Tippoo, what assistance could
we expect from the Nizam, the main body of whose army would
be officered by Frenchmen or by the agents of France, and the
correspondents of Tippoo himself?* In such a situation it would
be difficult to determine whether our danger would be greater
from an entire desertion of our cause by the Court of Hyderabad,
or from our acceptance of the only species of support which its
military force could offer us in the field. But I confess I carry
my opinion upon this subject still farther. I have no doubt that
the natural effect of the unchecked and rapid growth of such a
party at the court of one of our principal allies must be in a
very short period to detach that court entirely from our interests,
and finally to fix it in those of our enemies, to subject its councils
to their control, and its military establishment to their direction.
However despicable the corps of Raymond may be now in point
of discipline or effect in the field, would it be wise to leave a
large body of men in readiness to receive whatever improvements the ability, assiduity, and zeal of French officers, sent from
Europe for that express purpose, might introduce into the constitution of a corps so prepared by correspondent principles and
objects to meet the most sanguine expectations of their new
leaders? Under these circumstances, the corps, which perhaps
now has little more efficiency than that of a political party,
might soon become in the hands of our enemy as efficient a
military force as it is now in that view wholly useless either to
the Nizam or to us.

I desire to add one more consideration; must not the continuance of such a corps in the service of our ally tend to raise the
hopes of Tippoo, and in the same proportion to disparage us in
the eyes of all the native princes of India? That it has tended
to encourage Tippoo, I have no doubt, and his correspondence
with the leaders of the corps will sufficiently show in what light
he views them. Perhaps I have dwelt too long on this part of
the subject, where the proof of the weak policy of suffering such

* The correspondence of M. Raymond with Tippoo was subsequently
proved by means of a letter found in
the palace of Seringapatam, among
the other papers, after the death of
Tippoo.

an evil as I have described to increase without check or disturbance seems to require no labour of argument.

A more interesting and difficult consideration will be to devise for remedying this evil some means which shall not expose our interests to as great a danger as that which we wish to avoid. In the paper transmitted with this letter, four distinct measures are proposed for consideration, with a view to the desirable object of subverting the French party at the Court of the Nizam. The first is to introduce British subjects, or others (being the subjects of friendly powers) into the military service of the Nizam, for the purpose of forming a balance against Raymond's corps. This measure has already been partially attempted by the introduction of the corps of Boyd and Finglass at Hyderabad, but it has failed of success in the case of Boyd, who upon some quarrel with the court has left the service of the Nizam. I do not think this measure likely to be effectual to any good purpose, and it might even aggravate the evil which it is proposed to remove. A party so consolidated and united as that of Raymond's, which has been strengthening itself for a period of several years at Hyderabad, and has established the means of recruiting and augmenting its members, will not be counteracted by the irregular and desultory opposition of such adventurers as might be induced by our encouragement to seek employment in the service of the Nizam; persons of this description (and we cannot expect that any other will engage in such an undertaking) would want the system and concert necessary to give vigour to their operations.

It is also difficult to suppose that the Nizam would at once retain in his service such a number of these persons as could in any degree enter into competition with the numerous corps of Raymond and his adherents. But even if these objections did not exist against the introduction of a crowd of European adventurers at Hyderabad, there would remain a difficulty which appears to me insuperable — the impossibility of finding a sufficient number of such adventurers on whose principles any reliance could be placed. In such circumstances our attempt to subvert the French party at Hyderabad might only serve to furnish it with additional recruits of other nations; and I much fear that many British subjects might be found in India whose spirit of adventure would rather direct them to seek a new order of things, than to contribute to the maintenance of our power. Lord Hobart has declared his objection to this measure; but, as well as I recollect his letter, his principal ground is the danger of improving the military discipline of the armies of the native princes by furnishing them with European officers: unfortunately, this objection now comes too late; the system which Lord Hobart very justly dreads has been suffered gradually to gain such a strength, that there is scarcely a native court in India without its establishment of European officers.

The second measure proposed in the annexed paper, is nothing more than that we should endeavour by representation and demand to induce the Nizam to disband Raymond's corps. I recommend Major Kirkpatrick's observations on this head to your particular attention. Certainly no representation from one friendly state to another could ever be more solidly founded than ours might be to the Nizam in the case before us. But besides that Major Kirkpatrick expects no benefit from representation and demand unconnected with the offer of some advantage to the Nizam, I doubt whether our manifesting, in the first instance, the extent of our anxiety for the dismission of Raymond's corps, might not embarrass us in the progress of the most effectual measures for that desirable end. At present the Court of Hyderabad seems willing to purchase a closer connection with us by great sacrifices, and if that connection should not appear objectionable on other grounds, it may probably take place on much more advantageous terms to us, if we grant it as a matter of favour to the solicitation of the Nizam, than if we commence the negotiation by demanding the dismission of any part of the Nizam's military establishment. This observation will be better understood when I come to take notice of the fourth measure proposed by Major Kirkpatrick. Before I leave this article, I must however remark, that I should not be satisfied by obtaining the modification hinted by Major Kirkpatrick, namely, that the French officers and other Europeans in Raymond's corps should be dismissed, and their places filled by British subjects nominated by us. This modification would leave the corps precisely in its present form, with the exception of the European officers only. Although the European officers are certainly the most objectionable part of the establishment, it may be doubted whether the habits and dispositions of the native officers and Sepoys formed under French leaders would be at once broken by a mere change in the command, while every other circumstance of the corps remained the same. Seeing, then, no prospect of success from official representation or demand alone, and thinking it imprudent to anticipate the expected application of the Court of Hyderabad for a more intimate connection with us, by urging to them at this period any proposition the concession of which they might deem a favour, I proceed to examine Major Kirkpatrick's third suggestion. This he states to be of a nature justifiable only by the case of an actual rupture with the Nizam, or of open violence on the part of Raymond against us. The measure is no other than to induce Raymond's officers, by pecuniary compensation, to abandon the corps. On this measure it is unnecessary to say anything, because the cases alone to which it is meant to apply neither have existed, nor are now likely to happen. I own that I should never think it worth while, even in the cases supposed, of a rupture with the Nizam, or of an attack from Raymond, to repel the aggression by corrupting the officers of the hostile enemy. I trust that, in either case, we should soon find à more certain as well as a more honourable mode of effectually destroying this French party and its adherents.

The fourth proposition contained in Major Kirkpatrick's paper, is that to which I wish to call your most particular attention.

The desire of the Court of Hyderabad to obtain from us an increase of our detachment now serving the Nizam, and also an extension of the power of employing the force furnished by us, has appeared on several occasions, and you will find allusions to this disposition in the last secret despatches from Bengal. There seems to be no objection to the first part of this propo-

sition, provided our consent to it shall secure to us equivalent
concessions on the part of the Nizam. In another letter which
I shall forward to you, on the general subject of the political
state of India in the present moment, you will find my reasons
for entertaining · an opinion that it would be a wise policy for
us to check, by timely aid, the rapid declension of the Nizam's
weight among the powers of Hindoosthan. This could be done
in no manner so effectual or unobjectionable as by furnishing
him with a large increase of our force now in his pay, the
pay of the augmented force to be secured in the manner best
calculated to prevent future discussion and embarrassment. In
granting this force to the Nizam, we ought not only to stipulate
for the disbanding of Raymond's corps, but we ought to take
care that the officers should be immediately sent out of India.
There are, perhaps, other points which on this occasion might
be obtained from the Court of Hyderabad. The great difficulty
which would obstruct such an arrangement, would be, that the
Nizam would probably be unwilling to part with Raymond's
corps, which he has the power of employing against any enemy,
unless he could obtain powers equally extensive with respect to
the employment of any force furnished by us. You are aware
that the British detachment now in the pay of the Nizam is not
only restricted from acting against the Mahrattas in any possible
case, but also from acting against certain poleegars, tributary both
to the Mahrattas and to the Nizam, and even from passing, without a formal permission, certain parts of the Mahratta territory
which are intermixed with the dominions of the Nizam. The
object of the Court of Hyderabad would, of course, be to obtain
our guarantee of its possessions generally, against the Mahrattas,
accompanied with the assistance of a large force, to be employed
with the same extensive powers as now apply to the corps of
Raymond. For this object, I have little doubt that the Nizam
would sacrifice the whole French party at his court, and even
the peshcush now paid by us on account of the Northern Circars.
But such an alteration of our connection with the Nizam would
naturally rouse the jealousy of the Mahratta powers, and might

involve us in discussions of a very disagreeable nature, if not in a war with them. The result, therefore, of this view of the subject, would lead us to inquire, whether some arrangement might not be framed, founded on a modification of the views of the Court of Hyderabad, and comprehending certain favourite objects of the Mahratta States, which, while it secured for us the destruction of the French party at Hyderabad, should tend to restore to the Nizam his due weight among the Indian powers, without exciting the animosity of the Mahrattas against the British Government.

It appears to me that the only effectual mode of eradicating the French party at Hyderabad would be to furnish to the Nizam such a force as should be a just equivalent to Raymond's corps; considering the superior discipline of our Sepoys, I believe that 3000 men under British command not only would be, but would be deemed by the Court of Hyderabad, a force fully equal to that of Raymond in its present state.

The instruction by which our detachment is prevented from acting as the troops of the Mahrattas and of the Nizam now act against the poleegars, who pay joint tribute to the two powers, might probably be removed by a full previous explanation with the Mahrattas; as that restriction does not appear to be founded on any solid principle, nor could the removal of it open the way to any real inconvenience or danger to the interests of the Mahratta State.

The power of mutually passing their intermixed boundaries is now constantly exercised by the troops both of the Mahrattas and of the Nizam; and there is no reason to suppose that a formal permission would have been refused to our detachment for the same purpose, had it ever been demanded. But the Nizam never would allow any application to be made for a permission to do that, which he held to be his right, and which was constantly done without question both by his own army and by that of Poona. It is very improbable that we should find great difficulty in engaging the Mahrattas to place our detachment in this respect on a footing with the other branches of the Nizam's military force, and with their own; nor can I foresee any tenable ground of argument on which this point could be maintained against us.

The settlement of these two points only would, I understand, be considered as a great acquisition by the Nizam, and would go a great way towards inducing him to substitute a British force in the room of Raymond's corps.

The third point is of much more importance, and of much greater delicacy and danger; I speak of the desire of the Court of Hyderabad to obtain our guarantee of their possession against the Mahrattas, as well as against Tippoo, together with a right of employing defensively the troops furnished by us against the former as well as against the latter of these powers. This point, perhaps, might be reconciled with the interest of the Mahrattas, if it were thought prudent to enter into similar engagements with them, or, in other words, to guarantee their possessions against any attack from the Nizam. The effect of such an engagement with both powers would be to place us in the situation of arbitrators between them; and perhaps their mutual apprehensions of our interposition in the case of any aggression on either side, might tend to restrain the resentment and ambition of both. In this view, such a system of treaty with the Mahrattas and with the Nizam, so far from being liable to the objection of an undue interference in the disputes of the native powers of India, or of that description of officiousness and intriguing spirit which tends to foment divisions and to occasion war, might be deemed the best security for the maintenance of the peace of India, as well as the strongest pledge of our disposition to preserve it from disturbance. It would also tend to preserve unimpaired the strength and resources of the two powers on whose co-operation we must depend for assistance against any future attempt on the part of Tippoo. It cannot be a wise policy to suffer the Nizam and the Mahrattas to weaken themselves by repeated contests, while Tippoo remains at rest; and any measure deserves attention the tendency of which is to restore to the Mahrattas and to the Nizam their respective consideration and power as they stood at the conclusion of the Treaty of Seringapatam.

You will find by the last secret despatches from India[*] that some opening has been given for our arbitration in settling the disputes between the several Mahratta chiefs, and that the Government of Bengal has agreed to undertake the mediation proposed, under the condition of a previous formal agreement signed by all the parties, binding themselves to accept our award as final and conclusive upon their respective claims. If any such proceeding should take place, it will give a natural opening to such further engagements as may appear advisable.

The same despatches will inform you of the anxiety of the Mahrattas to obtain our agreement to a general defensive treaty against Zemaun Shah. The Government of Bengal has postponed the consideration of this proposition to a period of time which I confess I should think the most unfavourable for the examination of this difficult question, and still more unseasonable for the negotiation of a treaty with such a power as the Mahratta States; this period of time is no other than the moment when Zemaun Shah shall again approach the frontiers of Hindoosthan. Without giving any decisive opinion on the wisdom of entering into the treaty proposed, I shall certainly think it my duty upon my arrival in India to proceed without the delay of one moment to the examination and decision of the proposal made by the Mahrattas; if it should appear expedient to engage with them in a defensive system against the threatened invasion of Zemaun Shah, there is no doubt that such a measure would tend greatly to reconcile to them any propositions which we might wish to offer with respect to the arrangements at the Court of Hyderabad.

The inclination of my opinion at present rather leads me to think, that a general defensive alliance between all the existing powers of Hindoosthan (Tippoo perhaps alone excepted) against the expected invasion of Zemaun Shah, would not only be the best security against the success of such an invasion if attempted, but might have the effect of deterring that prince from an undertaking which must end in his own disappointment and ruin,

---

[*] The opening of these despatches is explained in letters Nos. 2 and 8.

if our government in India, and our allies do not neglect to make seasonable preparations of defence. If a treaty can be formed at an early period, so as to unite the Mahratta powers with us in a cordial and systematic plan of vigorous opposition to the supposed projects of Zemaun Shah, without binding us to advance farther from our own frontiers than the real exigency of the case may appear to demand upon his approach, I should think such a treaty a solid acquisition of strength in the present critical situation of India. You will observe from this detail, that I consider the fourth measure suggested by Major Kirkpatrick to be the only one from which it is reasonable to hope that the effectual destruction of the French army at Hyderabad can be accomplished, but that I view that measure as connected with considerations of the most serious nature, and involving consequences of the utmost delicacy and importance. I have laid before you the whole train of my thoughts on this subject, as I shall think it my duty to do on every question affecting those interests which I know to be not only highly valuable in your estimation, but the most particular and anxious objects of your unremitting solicitude and care. I will conclude this long letter by stating the precise questions on which I wish to receive your instructions, and by submitting to you the plan of measures which I propose to pursue, with relation to this subject, in the interval which must elapse before I can receive your opinion.

In the first place I wish to be informed whether you think a closer connection than at present subsists between us and the Nizam advisable for our interests on general grounds, provided such a change of our engagements with the Nizam can be rendered acceptable to the Mahrattas.

Secondly, whether you would approve of our entering into treaties both with the Mahrattas and the Nizam, guaranteeing the dominions of each power respectively against the aggression of the other.

Thirdly, whether you would approve of our taking measures for acting in concert with Azeem-ool-Oomrah in support of the succession of Secunder Jah, the eldest son of the Nizam?—whether we should endeavour to obtain the co-operation of the Mahrattas in securing this succession?—and what should be our conduct, if the Mahrattas should differ from us in the choice of the successor to the Nizam?

Fourthly, whether you would approve of a general defensive treaty against any invasion from Zemaun Shah, and what limitations would you propose to the powers which the other allies might require of employing our troops beyond our own frontiers?

You will observe that the determination of all these questions is necessary, in my view of the subject, in order to enable me to carry into effect the only measure which I can rely upon as a sufficient check to the growth of the French interest at the Court of Hyderabad, and as a permanent barrier against any future revival of that interest in the same quarter.

But I am aware that I cannot receive your opinions for a long time. In that interval circumstances may compel me to decide some of these important questions upon my own judgment; my wish, however, is to reserve them all for yours, and with this view, I propose to pursue a system of measures which, while it shall leave all the most delicate parts of the situation of affairs in India open to your decision, shall tend to check in some degree the progress of the French party at Hyderabad, and to furnish me with such materials as shall enable me to form a competent opinion of the effects to be expected from any decision of the points reserved for your judgment.

I propose to direct the Resident at Hyderabad to suffer no augmentation of Raymond's corps to take place, if it can be prevented by the strongest and most pointed representations. This step may probably check the increase of the corps, although from this step alone I cannot hope for its final annihilation.

I mean also to direct that any proposals from the Nizam's ministers for an increase of our detachment shall be favourably received; and I shall increase the detachment accordingly on the first practicable occasion; but I shall stipulate that for every man we grant, there shall be a proportional reduction made in Raymond's corps. This proportion shall be calculated upon the relative estimation of our Sepoys (in the opinion of the ministers of the Nizam themselves) when compared with Raymond's corps; and I believe that on this ground, I shall not find it difficult to contend that a reduction of 3000 men should be made for every 1000 men granted by us. In reducing the army of Raymond, I shall endeavour in the first instance to disband the most obnoxious and dangerous officers with their corps. I have reason to believe that I may be able to effect this species of partial reduction of Raymond's corps, without entering upon any of the difficult points involved in the general questions stated in the letter. In the meanwhile, however, I shall direct the Resident, at Poona and with Scindia, to ascertain as speedily as possible the views and dispositions of those powers with respect to the same points, and especially with respect to any alteration of our connection with the Nizam, to his eventual successor, and to the proposed defensive engagements against Zemaun Shah.

In submitting the whole of this extensive subject to your consideration, I have been obliged to leave many parts of it open to doubt, for want of the information which may be expected from the Residents with Scindia and at Poona; I believe, however, that it will not be difficult for you to answer the questions which I have proposed, framing your answers, in such a manner as may admit of any variation of opinion which the information from those courts may require.

The state of the military establishment of the Mahratta powers did not properly come under Major Kirkpatrick's view, and I propose to transmit to the Resident at Poona and with Scindia a copy of my questions to Major Kirkpatrick, with such alterations as the several cases may require, in order to obtain for you a full statement of the corps disciplined by Europeans or Americans in the service of the Mahrattas. I am at present able to give you no fuller information on this part of the subject, than that Scindia employs about 20,000 Sepoys disciplined by Europeans or Americans. The commander is named *Perron*, a Frenchman, most of the officers are British subjects. The discipline of this corps is said to be superior to that of Raymond's, but the disposition of its officers to be much more favourable to the British than to the French interests.

This was De Boigne's corps, whose history you probably know:
De Boigne was lately in London; if he should not have left it,
he can give you the fullest information of the state of Scindia's
army.   There was a small corps of about 2000 men, commanded
by European officers in the service of the Peishwa, and another
of about the same number in that of Tuckagee Holkar; they
are both inconsiderable, if they still exist, and the dissensions
which have broken out between Holkar's two sons since the
death of their father, have left that branch of the Mahratta
power in a situation from which little danger is to be apprehended. · There is a fourth corps commanded by a Frenchman
of the name of D'Agincourt in the service of Azeem-ool-Dowlah
at Hyderabad.   This corps is paid by the State.   It consists of
1500 men.   The commander is a determined Jacobin.   ·

The Raja of Berar is said to have a corps in his service commanded by British officers; it is said to consist of above 2000
men.   I am, my dear Sir, &c.,

                                              MORNINGTON.

QUERIES *proposed by* LORD MORNINGTON *to* MAJOR KIRKPATRICK,
with the ANSWERS *of the latter (referred to in the Governor-
General's Letters from the Cape of Good Hope, p. 2).*

Question 1st.—What was the origin of the corps disciplined
by European officers now in the service of the Nizam?

Answer.—The corps disciplined by European officers in the
service of the Nizam consisted during the Mysore war of 1792
of no more than two battalions, and had been raised not long
before the commencement of that war by its chief commander,
Raymond, a French adventurer, formerly belonging to the
corps of Lally.   Du Boigne's and some other regular bodies of
infantry (with field pieces attached) had been formed ante-
cedently to this period both by Scindia and Holkar; and it
was probably in consideration of the important and abundantly

obvious advantages which the former of these chiefs in particular had derived from such an establishment, that first suggested to Azeem-ool-Oomrah the expediency of a military institution. Raymond's battalion served during the war principally
in conjunction with the detachment of the Company's troops
furnished, according to treaty, to the Nizam.

· *Question* 2nd.—What has been the augmentation of that
corps? At what periods of time has that augmentation taken
place? To what causes is it to be attributed? And is there
any ground for believing that either the formation or augmentation of that corps proceeded from any hostile disposition
towards the British interests?

Answer.—There is no precise information of the terms or
the extent of Azeem-ool-Oomrah's original agreement with Raymond, but probably it went to the establishment of more corps
than were immediately raised. Be this as it may, the Peace of
Seringapatam had not been long concluded when the Minister
authorised, and afterwards from time to time frequently urged,
Raymond to complete his corps, with all possible expedition, to
fourteen battalions or regiments, of 1000 men each. Such a
large augmentation might in some measure appear expedient,
on account of the great extension of territory obtained by the
Court of Hyderabad through that peace: it sprung principally
perhaps from a desire of preparing for that contest with the
Mahrattas, so long before in contemplation of the Minister, and
which accordingly followed soon after. There is no reason to
suppose that the measure was connected, either immediately or
remotely, at the least in the mind of Azeem-ool-Oomrah (whatever might be the case in regard to Raymond), with any views
of a nature hostile to British interests.

Although the corps was thus directed to be augmented to
14,000 men, Raymond had not been able to complete it to this
establishment when the Nizam took the field against the
Mahrattas. Its strength at the affair of Khurdlah hardly
exceeded 11,000 men; but that he should have been able to
increase it, even to this amount, within so short a period as
two years, is a circumstance that no doubt evinces the activity

and resources of himself and officers to have been very considerable.

Some time after the return of the army to Hyderabad from the unfortunate expedition just alluded to, a nominal reduction of Raymond's corps took place; that is to say, the acting minister, in a fit either of economy or of temporary dissatisfaction with its commander, directed the recruiting for it to be discontinued; in consequence of which, its remains were compressed into ten battalions or regiments of 1000 men each.

In this state it appears to have continued till the return of Azeem-ool-Oomrah to Hyderabad; when that minister once more augmented it to at least its formerly intended establishment of 14,000 men, either on some particular suggestion of Raymond, or with some sinister view of thereby working upon the British Government, in jealousy of that Frenchman's growing power. For if he had really judged an increase of the regular infantry of the State necessary, his purpose would heve been equally well answered by making the requisite augmentation upon the rival corps of Finglass. This, too, is the step which he ought rather to have taken consistently with his own spontaneous professions on the subject of Raymond to the Assistant at Hyderabad, immediately upon his return thither from Poona, when he affected at least, if he did not feel, considerable uneasiness at the conduct and dispositions displayed by that Frenchman in his absence, and no less solicitude to circumscribe within very narrow limits, if not altogether annihilate his power. Neither the fact, however, upon which the present reasoning proceeds (that is to say, the actual augmentation of the corps), nor the still more important one of the annexation of Kummun to the already enormous territorial assignments held by Raymond, is sufficiently established to permit of our building any strong conclusions upon one or the other. It may, nevertheless, be allowable to observe in this place, that there will be but too much ground for fearing, should either or both of the points in question turn out to be true, that Azeem-ool-Oomrah must have been moved to proceedings so offensive (as he well knows) to us, and so much at variance with his own recent declarations, by a notion of the possibility, not to say probability, of the "French nation" acquiring, at no distant period, decided ascendency in India, as well as in Europe. There was no doubt of the unceasing endeavours of the French party at Hyderabad to instil this notion into every one about that court; and when it is considered that they had from 10,000 to 12,000 tongues, by means of which they could diffuse among a people, prone, from the highest to the lowest, to believe the marvellous and striking, their true, false, or exaggerated accounts of the successes and projects of their nation, it will not, perhaps, be wondered at that the efforts of the Residency to expose their misrepresentations, or counteract their views in them, should not always be successful.

Question 3rd.—What is the present strength of the corps, the state of its discipline, and the number of European officers? Of what nation is the majority of those officers composed? And what are the characters and principles of those who bear the chief command?

Answer.—In addition to the ten battalions or regiments already alluded to, the French had besides a field train of artillery, consisting of about thirty pieces, and on the whole pretty well appointed; there was attached to the corps a troop of sixty native dragoons. With the exception of an European officer to each battalion or regiment and a sort of second to a few of them, all the other Europeans, to the number of about fifty, constituted, at one time, a separate corps. Subsequently they were attached to the Artillery, or distributed in the character of serjeants among the several regiments; an alteration found to be an important improvement in his system. These men consisted of various nations, and among them there were many English, deserters from the Artillery, who had been often but fruitlessly reclaimed. The parade appearance of the corps was, in general, good; that of Perron's regiment particularly so. In other respects, however, its discipline would not seem to be very strict; which probably was the powerful inducement with many of the natives of the Company's as well as the Nizam's country, to prefer the services of Raymond to that in any way connected with the British. Whatever may be the cause, this Frenchman had greater facility in recruiting than the British Carnatic officers experienced.

The number of the officers, properly so called, did not exceed twelve; and the whole of these were Frenchmen, with the exception, perhaps, of one or more jacobinised Germans. Raymond had formerly a Hanoverian of some professional merit in his corps, who had been an ensign in his Majesty's service. This man, however, was soon dismissed, and afterwards assassinated by a furious Demonah in the employ of the chief of the Pungahs. He had also with him at one time a French gentleman who had been an officer in the regiment at Pondicherry, but openly professing his attachment to royalty, he likewise speedily lost his situation, and was finally obliged to quit the country. The best disposed man in the corps is, or was some time since, one Salnave, commandant of a regiment, and supposed to be secretly averse to the democratic party. With the exception of Perron, Baptiste, and perhaps one or two more favourites, the officers were represented to be dissatisfied with Raymond on account of his hardness and want of liberality in pecuniary matters. But as they would nearly all appear to be of the jacobinical stamp, and have no prospect of bettering themselves elsewhere, this circumstance alone will hardly induce any of them to leave him, especially as he has contrived to make it very difficult for them to do so without his consent. Besides, he possesses a resource (such as it is) for replacing any he may lose by desertion or otherwise, in his rank of serjeants, most of whom are just as likely to be qualified for the command of corps as the majority of those at present holding them.

Raymond himself would not appear to be a man of vigorous mind, or, in any respect, of a very decided character. He has never shown himself to be much of a soldier; but he is artful, seems to have an arranging head, and is sufficiently conciliating in his manner towards those he has to deal with. He is an undoubted republican in principle; but I don't know that he is a violent one. I should rather suppose from the general mould of his character, that he was not. I take him to be about forty-five years of age.

Perron, who is his second, is a native of Alsace, and several years younger than his chief. He appears to be a far more enterprising and active man than the latter, and to be particularly fond of the military profession. I understand he is an outrageous Jacobin; as some proof of which it may be mentioned that he sent, not long since, to his namesake and countryman, the successor of Du Boigne, in the service of Scindia, a silver tree and cap of liberty; the acceptance of which, however, is said to have been declined by the latter. Perron, at the head of two regiments, was with Azeem-ool-Oomrah during the latter part of that minister's stay at Poonah; on which occasion he would, of course, not neglect to cultivate his namesake, or to disseminate his own principles as well as he could among the officers belonging to him. It happens, however, either that Scindia's Perron is lukewarm in his politics, or that having several British subjects in his corps (introduced into it by Du Boigne), one of whom, named Sutherland, commands a brigade of six or seven battalions, he does not yet consider it safe or prudent to countenance any movements of this nature.

Baptiste, who stands next in rank to, is not a less bitter Jacobin than, Perron; but he is very much his inferior in point of military endowments. What he wants, however, as a soldier, is made up for by a certain gasconading manner that suits very well the genius of the Court he belongs to, by great activity and cunning, and above all, by a large stock of that unprincipled sort of address so useful in the management of low intrigue, and the conduct of pecuniary transactions with the classes he has usually to deal with. He is also eminently and peculiarly serviceable to Raymond, as the main link of his correspondence with Pondicherry, Tranquebar, and Marpilly; and as his agent for enticing French and other deserters, both native and European, and facilitating their escape to Khummum; where, just at our doors, as may be said, this bustling emissary of seduction and procurator of all material supplies any way connected with or depending on the Carnatic, has established his head-quarters.

I consider both Perron and Baptiste as much abler men, that is, more equal to the purposes of mischief, or such purposes as the French Government may be supposed to machinate against us in the Hyderabad question, than Raymond; and should accordingly be sorry to see his command devolve on either of them.

Question 4th.—In what mode is the corps paid and recruited? Of what nation are the ranks composed? Where is it stationed? What have been its operations? What effects has its existence already produced upon the British interests at the Court of Hyderabad or elsewhere? And what dangers are to be apprehended to those interests from its continuance?

Answer. — Till the period of Azeem-ool-Oomrah's captivity the corps had always been paid either immediately from the treasury at Hyderabad, or by occasional tunkhaws, on the revenue collectors, with the exception only of a permanent assignment, on the revenues of Khummum proper, which he had previously obtained as a fund for the payment of a particular division of his corps, nominally distinguished by the appellation of Solyman Jah's Risalah. During the administration, however, of the Roy Royan, he contrived to procure, on a still better footing, the whole Circar of Maiduck, a fertile district, computed to yield about eighteen lakhs of rupees; and fully adequate, I believe, to the total charges of his corps, as fixed by agreement. This was among the financial arrangements of the Roy Royan in the absence of Azeem-ool-Oomrah that appeared to give the latter the most displeasure, as placing the corps in a higher and more independent view than it had hitherto been his own policy to assign to it. We have nevertheless since heard of his being prepared to follow the example of the Roy Royan in this particular, by granting to Raymond another extensive district (namely, Khummum-mait), in addition to what he already held.

The corps is recruited more or less from all the provinces of the Nizam's dominions, but from none so much as Aurungabad; partly, I believe, from the adjacent Mahratta districts; and but in too great a measure from the dependencies of the Carnatic, particularly the Northern Circars. The majority of the native officers would, more especially, appear to be natives of the latter; and of these a large proportion have been educated in the military service of the Company. I had taken some measures before my departure from Hyderabad for ascertaining, as well as possible, the names and birth-places of all the men of this corps, but in particular of its native officers, with the view of thereby obtaining some hold, through the medium of their families, on such as might prove to belong to the Company's dominions. It may be observed in this place that the pay of the coast sepoy in garrison, or cantonment, is less by a rupee (I believe) than that of Raymond's sepoy, whose duty too is easier. If it were raised a rupee, the effect would, probably, soon appear both in the decrease of desertion, and in a greater facility of recruiting than is experienced at present. A proclamation too might be issued, forbidding the natives of our territories, under certain penalties, from entering into the military service of foreign powers.

The station of the corps has varied according to circumstances, Raymond seems averse (and several reasons for this may be conceived) to its being divided; and its usual head-quarters are in the vicinity of Hyderabad, where he has established a sort of cantonment for it. Its professional services have hitherto been very inconsiderable. I have already glanced at those performed by what may be called the root of it, in conjunction with one detachment last war; and which principally appeared in the siege of Kopul. At Khurdlah (in 1795) the corps certainly gathered no laurels; but if it did not acquit itself on that occasion with spirit, the Nizam himself as well as his minister displayed still less. The rebellion of Rachore, headed by the late Darah Jah's son, was subdued by one detachment; for two regiments of Raymond employed on that service, under the command of the Mons. Salnave, mentioned above, had but little share in the business. In the insurrection of the late Jah, it happened, fortunately for Raymond, that the Prince directed his flight to a quarter whither he could not be pursued by our troops without the consent of the Mahrattas. Raymond by simply following him to Aurungabad, where the Prince submitted without further struggle, acquired the credit of having

crushed a formidable conspiracy. The military actions of
neither party in the course of this short contest, were of the
least importance. For the rest, the services of the corps have
been much of the nature of those performed elsewhere by
Sebundy or Purgunnah troops.

The principal effects hitherto produced, or likely hereafter to
be produced, by this corps upon the British interests, are refer-
able to the circumstance of its being commanded by men belonging to a nation, and very probably devoted to a government
which, we have abundant reasons to believe, have nothing so
much at heart as the destruction of our power in India. It
cannot, I am persuaded, be requisite to enlarge on the dangers
liable to proceed from such a source, or to expatiate either on
the probable or possible consequences of so constant, intimate,
and unrestrained an intercourse as must necessarily subsist, in
the case before us, between the agents of Jacobinism, and under
the implacable enemies of Great Britain, and the court of one
of our principal allies — that court, too, never distinguished for
the inviolability of its engagements, and certainly governed less
by views of honour, sound policy or justice, than by the variable motives of supposed safety, of low prudence, of personal
ease, and of immediate advantage. It is plain that so close
and mutual a relation between the Nizam and the notorious
rivals of the English is but too well calculated, in the present
conjuncture, to excite doubts in many of the sincerity of his
Highness's friendship for us, and to encourage a notion of the
probability of the French regaining their former ascendency at
Hyderabad. Nor is the natural tendency of such a persuasion
to promote the purposes and aid the operations of Raymond, by
gaining him many useful instruments and adherents, so little
obvious as to need being further insisted on.

There is, however, one particular danger connected with the
point immediately under discussion, of such an aspect as to
challenge the most serious consideration. What I allude to is
the predicament we should be placed in supposing a war with
Tippoo to break out, by the unquestionably hostile dispositions
of Raymond and his officers in general, seconded by the enter-

prising spirit of some individuals among them, which might, in such a case, become more or less transfused into the commander himself. It is manifest that though his corps constitutes the chief, nay, almost the sole strength of the Nizám's army, we should, notwithstanding, be unable to employ it against the common enemy, except at a risk, to which its total inactivity would be far preferable. But it is likewise obvious that we should not be altogether safe in leaving it behind us; since upon any sinister accident to our arms, or in the possible (happily no longer probable) event of a French armament appearing at such a crisis in India, the temptation to Raymond and his officers openly to attempt something against us might become very powerful. If time permitted, yet it would not, perhaps, be necessary to pursue this consideration further; the bare mention of the matter seeming sufficient to suggest the whole train of its consequences. Whether the evil admits of any eligible remedy short of the radical one of entirely annihilating the corps in question, is a point on which different opinions may be entertained. My own, however, is, that under the existing circumstances with respect to us and France — circumstances, too, to the continuance of which no period can be assigned — it does not. Another prejudicial effect of this corps upon our interests, and which, though not of the same political importance as the one just noticed, is, nevertheless, of sufficient magnitude to claim attention, has already been touched on, and consists in the inducements it holds out to our European and native soldiery on the coast, and in general to those classes of the inhabitants inclined to a military life, to join its standard; giving birth, by this means, to numerous desertions from the Company's army, and rendering it extremely difficult to raise recruits for supplying even the ordinary casualties of the service. This is a mischief that, no doubt, might be corrected in a material degree, as far as regarded Europeans particularly, by suitable arrangements of precaution and vigilance; while, with respect to the natives, some augmentation of the sepoy's pay, followed by such a proclamation as before suggested, would be found a still more effectual remedy. The evil, however, can never, perhaps, be completely removed while we have such a neighbour as Raymond.

Question 5th.— Have you any reason for believing that Raymond is in correspondence with the French Government in Europe, or that of the Isle of France, or with Tippoo Sooltan ?

Answer. — I have no very substantial proof of Raymond being in correspondence either with the Government of France, or with that of the Mauritius ; though whispers to this effect have reached me from his camp. The strongest circumstance I know of, indicating such an intercourse, is his having fired a salute about two years ago on occasion, as was at least given out in his party, and reported to me by one of them, of his having recently received the commission and uniform of a general officer from the French Government in Europe. Considering, indeed, the great activity of that Government — the obvious interest it has in attaching Raymond to its cause, and the dispositions of the latter and his officers, nothing certainly can be more reasonable than to suppose such an intercourse subsists between them.

The proofs of the existence of a correspondence between Raymond and Tippoo Sooltan will, perhaps, be deemed less vague, when one of these is stated to be the discovery, a few months ago, by the Assistant at Hyderabad, of a secret intercourse between him and the wukeel of the latter (Medina Saheeb), residing at the Nizam's court. It was conducted through the medium of a third person, who, it is remarkable, disappeared immediately after his name had been confidentially communicated to Azeem-ool-Oomrah by Captain Kirkpatrick.

It is also a fact sufficiently well established that the last secret agent deputed by Tippoo to Hyderabad (namely, Kadir Husain Khan) had charge of some letters for Raymond ; but whether they were from the Sooltan himself or only from Vigee's (formerly Lally's) corps in the service of Tippoo, I had not the means of ascertaining.

Question 6th.— Does Raymond occupy any fortified posts, either on the Company's frontier, or elsewhere? and if he does, what is their strength and garrisons; and what are the advantages he derives, or disadvantages we suffer, from his possession of them?

Answer. — Raymond occupies two or three small forts in the district of Maiduck, of which, as has already been mentioned, he is in some sort the renter. They are, however, of but little importance in a military view, and are in a quarter remote from the Carnatic.

The only post he holds in our neighbourhood is Khummum, where Baptiste (otherwise Talihard) has commanded for several years, and where a regiment of the corps has usually been stationed. The fortifications are not, I believe, considerable, but they have been improved, I understand, by Baptiste. It serves Raymond as a magazine; the stores he from time to time procures from the Carnatic, being in the first instance deposited here, and forwarded, as occasion requires, to Hyderabad. It is also conveniently situated for communication with Narpilly (formerly a French post in the Guntoor), where Raymond has a store-house (ostensibly belonging to the Nizam) in charge of a Frenchman of the name of L'Empreur. This is also the point whence Baptiste's emissaries issue for the purpose of inveigling deserters, and procuring recruits from the adjacent districts of Ongole, Guntoor, &c. It is likewise the principal link in Raymond's communication with Pondicherry; most of his messengers to and from thence, all the French fugitives, and many recruits obtained in the same quarter, pursuing the route by Kurpal and Khummum.

It is presumed that this hasty sketch of the advantages which Raymond derives from the possession of this post will sufficiently show the detriment it is of, and may be to us.

Question 7th. — What measures have been suggested for the purpose of inducing the Nizam to disband this corps, and what have been the objections to the adoption of any measures suggested for that purpose?

Answer. — I suggested some time in 1795, in a private correspondence with the Governor-General and Lord Hobart, under sufficient encouragement to disband this corps received

from the Nizam, through the medium of Meer Allum, the
expediency of introducing some select British subjects into his
Highness's employ, for the purpose of raising and disciplining
for his services such a body of troops as would, in the first
instance, have served as a counterpoise to the corps of Raymond, and perhaps ultimately have led, by gradual reforms, to
its complete reduction.   At the same time that I started this
idea, I fully admitted the mischievous tendency, in an absolute
view, of the general measure, offering it simply in correction of
an evil that already reached to an enormous height, that bore,
for obvious reasons, a particularly threatening aspect at Hyderabad — that called for a speedy remedy in that more pressing
than in any other quarter; and that did not admit, as well as I
could judge, either of a prompter or more certain one than that
which I, or rather Meer Allum (not to say the Nizam himself),
had recommended. The Governor-General seemed to be sensible
of the necessity of the experiment, and even to have fixed, at
one time, upon a person every way qualified, I believe, for
conducting it to a favourable issue.   In the meanwhile, however, Lord Hobart declared himself to be decidedly averse to
the measure; insomuch that I thought it would be no longer
easy or prudent to pursue it.   Here, then, it dropped for the
present.

I cannot call to mind, at this time, the particular arguments
publicly opposed by Lord Hobart to the measure; but I recollect that I myself furnished him with the objection that had all
along appeared to me (though with him it was only of secondary
consideration) to be the most forcible of the whole; and that
was the offence it might possibly give to the Mahrattas.   Yet
neither was this an insuperable obstacle, since the circumstance
of there being several British subjects in the service of the
Mahrattas themselves, would have furnished (if the affairs had
been conducted as I proposed) a sufficient answer to any dissatisfaction they might have manifested on the occasion.

But though I cannot detail Lord Hobart's reasoning on the
subject, I have not forgotten that it comprehended all the topics
obviously adverse to such a question considered absolutely; and

that though he did not, in my judgment, demonstrate the inexpediency of the thing, as an insulated measure, yet he abundantly proved its danger, as a general one, of which truth no person indeed could be better satisfied than I myself had always been.

The Governor-General continuing to deem it extremely desirable to oppose the best check that circumstances might admit of to the growing power of Raymond (which, indeed, daily became more and more alarming), thought proper to authorise the Resident at Poonah to promote, but with due precaution, the introduction into Azeem-ool-Oomrah's (or rather the Nizam's) service, of certain Europeans at that place, who appeared disposed to engage in it, and to be of a description likely to answer as some sort of counterpoise to that Frenchman. The consequence was, that an American named Boyd, and a British subject of the name of Finglass, were entertained by the minister; the former bringing with him a ready-formed and experienced corps of about 1500 men; but the latter only a small body, which it was settled should be (as it since, I believe, has been) considerably augmented. Mutual disgust, however, soon arising between Mr. Boyd and the Court of Hyderabad, he quitted the service. Mr. Finglass proving more tractable, appears to be rising in favour with the ministry. I am not qualified to speak from my own knowledge of this man; but Mr. Uthoff, the Assistant at Poonah, has reported favourably of his character. He was formerly, I think, quartermaster of His Majesty's 19th Regiment of Dragoons.

It may not be amiss to mention in this place, that on occasion of an alarm somewhat hastily taken, in August last, by our detachment at Hyderabad, in consequence of a report of Raymond's designing to attack their camp, both Mr. Boyd and Mr. Finglass, on being apprised of the circumstance, instantly prepared their corps, and signified their determination in the supposed event, of supporting the Company's troops.

I shall close this head with remarking, that if a fair trial of the project suggested (as above related) in 1795, had been made, I think there is a considerable probability that Raymond's would, by this time, either have ceased to exist, or, at least, to be an object of the reasonable solicitude which it excites at present.

Question 8th.—What measures now appear to you to be the best adapted to the object of inducing the Nizam to disband this corps?

Answer.—The pressing importance to the British interests in India, of effecting (and with as little further delay, too, as possible) the subversion of this party, though a point only incidentally considered before, and by no means anywhere urged with the force of which it is susceptible, may be presumed (as it is, indeed, by the question supposed) to be fully established. It only remains then to inquire how this desirable object may be best obtained.

The most attentive examination I have been able to bestow on the subject, has suggested to me nothing better than the four following modes of proceeding :—

1. By introducing, with every possible previous attention to their characters and principles, British subjects (or other Europeans, being the subjects of friendly powers) into the service of his Highness, with a view, in the first instance, to balancing the French corps, and of ultimately completely suppressing it.

2. By pointed and firmly demanding the dismission of the corps, and signifying the determination of our Government to withdraw itself, in case of refusal, from its existing engagements with his Highness.

3. By holding out suitable inducements to the European and principal Native officers, as well as to the European serjeants of the corps to quit it, and retire into the Company's dominions, a measure which, if tolerably successful, would necessarily either bring about the entire dissolution of it, or at least, reduce it to a state of comparative insignificance.

4. By meeting the wishes so often expressed by the Nizam's Government, for a closer connection with the Company; and for such an augmentation of the detachment of our troops already allowed his Highness by treaty, as should in some measure preclude the necessity of retaining Raymond's corps.

I shall consider each of these expedients in order.

1st. Regarding the first of them, however, little remains to be said, the subject being nearly exhausted in the reply to query the 7th. It would, no doubt, under present circumstances, although a foundation for it is already laid by the establishment of Finglass's corps, be of slow operation. Besides, the inclination of Azeem-ool-Oomrah, to countenance the measure farther, is at least uncertain. He may possibly imagine that by manifesting a backwardness in this respect, we may be the more readily induced to do what he would like still better — that is, augment our detachment and take off some of the restrictions under which it had hitherto acted. It may be added, that the Government at home, having thought proper to discourage the measure immediately under consideration (though on what grounds is not known to me), it is the less necessary to enlarge on it at present.

2ndly. With the exception of the Peishcush, which, perhaps, no circumstance short of an open rupture with the Nizam, would warrant our withholding, there seems nothing in the measure suggested in this article that might not be vindicated both to the world at large and to the other member of the triple alliance (or the Mahratta state), by a variety of forcible arguments deducible from the absolute impossibility of our ever acting together, under any critical state of things, with the confidence and concord necessary to the success of our joint operations, or even with entire safety to ourselves, composed as his Highness's principal military force virtually is, and swayed as his councils are, or may be, by the inveterate enemies of our nation. But however defensible, or reconcileable with the spirit of treaties, such a step might be, I very much doubt whether it would at any time, and especially in the present conjuncture, produce the desired effect. The proud spirit of this Court (still proud under its recent humiliations) would revolt at such a capitulation; and, most probably, hazard much rather than subscribe to it. It would talk, as it has already done, more than once, on occasion of some temperate and distant expostulations on the same head, of its independence; of its right to employ and favour whom it pleases; of its reliance on the fidelity and attachment of its French servants, and of the unreasonableness of our entertaining any distrust of men entirely at the devotion, and the mere creatures of a friendly power, having no interests but what are inseparable from ours. But these arguments, plausible as they are, do not constitute the sole, or perhaps principal difficulty in the present case. One of the consequences of Raymond's corps (and besides Raymond's corps there is another consisting of from twelve to fifteen hundred sepoys, commanded also by Frenchmen, attached to the Risalah of Umjid-ool-Dowlah) has been a material reduction of every other description of military force; insomuch that excepting the regular infantry of the state, it has few other troops of any estimation. Were it then to comply with the proposed demand, it would be left without sufficient means not only of defending itself against foreign attack and domestic insurrection, but of collecting its revenues; for it is not to be supposed that our small detachment would be adequate, even if there subsisted no objection to its being applied, to all these purposes. The experiment failing (as I am of opinion it almost necessarily must), and we following up our provisional resolution in that case, the consequence, it is natural to suppose, would very soon be a closer connection than ever, if that should be practicable, between this court and the French; and at all events, such an understanding with Tippoo as would hardly fail to give him that ascendancy in its councils which he has long been endeavouring (more sedulously than artfully, perhaps) to acquire.

It may be thought that the abominable tendency of French principles (in whatever view considered), and the evil consequences which have resulted to almost every power that that nation has drawn into its alliance, if properly exposed and illustrated, ought to have the effect of exciting, at the different courts of India, such a detestation of the one and dread of the other as to render any connection between them next to impossible. But though these are topics which have not been neglected, and though they doubtlessly seem well calculated to produce the sort of impressions to be wished for, yet it would be wrong to place any great reliance in considerations which unfortunately have not always had the weight they were entitled to with European powers better qualified, in general, to appreciate their force (as being more conversant in systematic and prospective politics), more immediately liable to suffer from a coalition with the new republic; and, finally, more interested to oppose its aggrandisement than any of the princes or states of India can be. It is true, that a French connection would be dangerous even to Tippoo Sooltan; but remote and speculative danger is often overlooked in favour of immediate, and, perhaps, only apparent, benefit. With regard to the Court of Hyderabad in particular, I may venture to say, that its political views hardly ever embrace a very distant period, or any combinations having the permanent advantage of the state for their object.

I have dwelt the longer on the consideration of the expedient suggested in the present article (from the subject of which, however, the whole of the preceding paragraph must be owned to be a digression), because I apprehend there may be some persons capable of imagining our political position in India, as ascertained at the peace of Seringapatam, to be so commanding as to enable us to carry a point of this kind with little or no difficulty. No doubt we were placed by that event, or rather by the political sagacity and military skill which conduced to it, on higher and more respectable grounds than we had ever before occupied in India; but we shall, nevertheless, do well always to bear in mind, that it is an envied eminence we stand on; and to beware how we forfeit or hazard, by a domineering spirit, what a spirit of moderation so much contributed to our gaining.

Before we dismiss the consideration of the measure suggested in this article, it may be proper to notice a modification of which it may be thought susceptible, and which presents itself in a limitation of its operation to the European part of the corps, and an offer of replacing this immediately by British subjects. But though the main obstacle to the measure, namely, that of depriving the state of its principal military force, would by this means be got rid of, yet it would, at the same time, become liable to much of the objection lying against the first expedient, from which it would not then materially differ in the chief feature.

3rdly. I shall confine myself to observing, with regard to the suggestion contained in this article, that although I have little doubt of the general efficacy of the measure, yet its adoption would not seem to be warrantable or prudent in any other cases than those of an absolute rupture with the Nizam, or of some strong and open act of hostility on the part of Raymond himself. Such cases have, in some degree, been secretly provided for, but not to the extent that would probably be requisite. For though a simple pecuniary douceur might answer in some instances, yet in others it might be necessary to hold out something like a permanent provision, if not even employment.

4thly. It has long been a favourite object with the Court of Hyderabad to make the defensive engagements subsisting between it and the Company general instead of particular, or, in other words, that we should guarantee its possessions against the Mahrattas as well as Tippoo Sooltan. It has also long sought to prevail on us to relax from the strictness of that article of the agreement of 1789 with Lord Cornwallis, conformably to which we have always not only restrained our detachment from acting against certain Polygars tributary to the Mahrattas as well as to the Nizam, but also carefully prevented it from passing the Mahratta boundaries, whenever this has appeared necessary (as owing to the mingled nature of their respective dominions has sometimes happened), in order to reaching the point where its services were required. Such, for instance, was its situation towards the close of the rebellion of Alee Jah, whom it was obliged to decline pursuing to Aurungabad, because this could not be done without its occasionally entering the Mahratta territory, and because the Court of Hyderabad either would not apply for, or could not obtain, the consent of the Poona Government for that purpose.

By complying with the wishes of the Nizam's ministers in these respects, and agreeing to such an augmentation of the detachment at present employed with his Highness as might be judged necessary, there is little doubt but we should obtain our object with regard to Raymond to whatever extent we pleased; to say nothing of other advantages that we might either expressly and previously stipulate for, or subsequently derive from the ascendancy which we should, in this case, acquire at the Court of Hyderabad.

Perhaps even something short of these compliances might procure us our main object. But as perfect confidence is not likely to subsist for any long time together between the Courts of Hyderabad and Poona, and as apprehensions of future encroachments by the latter will ever continue, most probably, to be entertained by the former, who, on this account, will always deem it necessary to be prepared for such a contingency, it may be presumed that it will scarcely consent to part with Raymond's corps, without our undertaking, in some shape or other, if not by express defensive engagements, to secure it against that danger. It would be to no purpose, as to this particular, that we replaced that corps by an adequate body of our own troops, if those troops, in case of an invasion of his Highness's territories by the Mahrattas, should not be at liberty to assist in repelling it, which, however, is the predicament that our detachment stood in during the late contest between these two powers.

There is, probably, one point, at least, that Azeem-ool-Omrah would consider as an indispensable condition in such an arrangement as we are now contemplating, though he were even to waive insisting on a general defensive alliance against the Mahrattas, and that is a positive engagement to support the succession as it might be settled by the nomination of the Nizam (or, in other words, by himself), against all opponents whatsoever. Now, such an engagement might happen to place us in opposition to the Mahrattas, who, upon the Nizam's death, might be disposed to favour some other pretender to the musnud, and, persisting to maintain his cause, make it extremely difficult, if not impossible, for us to avoid a war with them. Here is an impediment that deserves to be well considered, and weighed against the advantages of the measure immediately in question.

In regard to the restrictions under which our detachment has hitherto served, I am of opinion that, without their being removed, no body of troops that we might supply to replace Raymond's corps, would compensate to the Nizam for its loss, since, while they continue, they must operate, as hitherto, to deprive him of its services in cases, perhaps, of the first importance in his estimation. Besides, though these restrictions were properly enough established by us, yet they are considered, and not entirely without reason, as great hardships by the Court of Hyderabad, between which and the Government of Poona there subsists a sort of tacit convention, whereby the forces of his Highness have not only occasionally passed through the other's territories, but even acted against the Polygars tributary to both states (as those of Shorepoor and Gudwaul), without any visible objection on the part of the Mahrattas. We certainly could not now relax from the rigidness of our practice in these particulars, without giving offence and furnishing a just ground of complaint to the Government of Poona; but, on the other hand, the peculiar nature of the case would appear to warrant a hope that the difficulty might be surmounted by means of a suitable representation to the Court of Poona, made in concert with that of Hyderabad.

But however practicable it should be to obtain the acquiescence of the Mahrattas in these points, or with whatever indifference they might view our determination to interfere in the settlement of the succession to the musnud of Hyderabad, it can scarcely be doubted that such an extension of our defensive engagements with the Nizam, and such an augmentation of our detachment serving with him as above spoken of, would excite in them considerable jealousy and alarm. The consequences to which sentiments of this kind might lead are not difficult to conceive; and though they are not, perhaps, inevitable, yet in measuring the advantages against the disadvantages of the proceeding under discussion, it may be right (and will, at least, be the safest way), to take these last in the extreme. And here it is proper I should acknowledge my own incompetency, and the superior means of the Residency at Poona to appreciate,

APPENDIX.   333

with due exactness and greater certainty, the extent of the APPENDIX
effects capable of being, or likely to be, produced on the Mahratta Government by the different measures in question. That
Residency, also, will be best able to ascertain how far, and to suggest in what manner, it may be possible to reconcile it to those
measures. On this last head I shall, for my own part, only venture to hint, that perhaps an offer to admit it to a participation
of any advantages granted to the Court of Hyderabad, might
conduce to remove its objections to the arrangement, and that
though the Mahrattas are not likely ever to stand in need either
of our troops, or our guarantee against the Nizam, yet they
might not be unwilling to accede to the projected treaty with
his Highness, on condition of our agreeing to a defensive alliance with them against Zemaun Shah and the Seiks, which it
may sooner or later be advisable for us to do, with other views
besides that of propitiating them in regard to the objects of the
present inquiry.

In conclusion, and on an attentive review of all that has been
advanced, I have no hesitation in declaring it to be my opinion,
that of the four different modes which have been suggested for
arriving at our object with regard to the corps of Raymond, the
one calculated to accomplish it with the most promptitude and
efficacy, and the least liable to failure, is the fourth, or last. It
must, at the same time, be confessed, that owing partly to a
certain unaccommodating and illiberal spirit in the Government,
and partly to the generally disordered state of its finances, our
present detachment suffers inconveniences on the score sometimes of pay, and at others of provisions, that would, as well as
the unpleasant expostulations and discussions to which they occasionally give rise, be but too likely to increase with any considerable augmentation of its numbers. The most effectual
way of preventing these difficulties under a new arrangement,
would probably be by procuring the assignment of one or more
districts known to be adequate in point of revenue to the discharge of the subsidy, and, in their other resources, to supplying the remaining wants of the troops. Kurpah alone, if not
entirely, would yet, in a great measure, particularly well answer

these purposes, at the same time that our possession of it would, on account of its local position with regard to the north-eastern parts of Tippoo Sooltan's dominions, add considerably to the security of the Carnatic, and especially of the Sircars. Whether the jealousy and discontent which that Prince would no doubt conceive at our gaining even a footing of so limited a nature in Kurpah, ought to make us waive so great an advantage, is a point for the consideration of others.

It would likewise, in the event of such a connection between us and the Court of Hyderabad as the one in contemplation, particularly behove us to be on our guard against the arts which the latter might be but too apt to practise for the purpose of provoking an attack from the Mahrattas, and with the secret view of prosecuting, in that case, by our means, some project of resentment or aggrandisement.

The only remaining precaution that occurs to me as particularly necessary to be taken in case of a material augmentation of our troops at Hyderabad, respects the selection of not only their commander, but of all the principal officers, in whom it would be desirable, for obvious reasons, that temperate and conciliatory manners, a just solicitude for the maintenance of the national character, together with a competent knowledge of the customs and language of the country, should be joined to the qualifications more properly professional.

No. II.

The Earl of MORNINGTON *to* J. A. KIRKPATRICK, Esq., *Acting Resident at Hyderabad.*

(Secret.)

Fort William, 8th July, 1798.

Sir,—I transmit to you an authentic copy of a proclamation published by the Governor-General of the Isle of France during the residence of two ambassadors from Tippoo Sooltan on that island. The proclamation purports to be a declaration of certain propositions communicated to the French Government in the name of Tippoo Sooltan, by his ambassadors then upon the spot.

It enumerates those propositions with a particularity of detail which would not have been hazarded in the presence of the ambassadors, had it not corresponded with the substance of the communications made by them to the French Government.

In addition to the arguments founded in the nature of the proclamation, and in the facts of its publication under the eyes of the ambassadors, I am in possession of evidence which leaves no doubt upon my mind of the concurrence of the ambassadors in every part of the proclamation, and I cannot suppose that they would have ventured to exceed the limits of their instructions from Tippoo Sooltan in a matter of such serious importance as the conclusion of offensive and defensive engagements with the French Government. Under this proclamation 150 officers and privates were actually raised in the Isle-of France for the service of Tippoo, and for the purposes avowed in the proclamation, and that force has since been landed at Mangalore, and received into Tippoo's army with peculiar marks of honour and distinction.

This circumstance is sufficient to prove that the proceedings of the ambassadors have obtained the sanction of their sovereign, who has thus confirmed and avowed the propositions made through them to the enemy by a solemn, public, and personal act. Having thus entered into an offensive and defensive alliance with the French Government; having collected, in conjunction with that Government, a force openly destined to act against the British possessions; having avowed, through his public ambassador, that he has actually made preparations of war for the express purpose of attempting the subversion of the British power in India; and having declared that he only waits the effectual assistance of France to prosecute his design, Tippoo Sooltan has violated the treaties of peace and friendship subsisting between him and the allies, and has committed a direct act of hostility against the British Government in India.

That he has yet obtained no formidable assistance from the enemy is undoubtedly a fortunate circumstance for the British interests,. but the temerity and consequent ill success of his councils in no degree palliates the offensive nature of an aggression so unprovoked, and of a violation of faith so public and undisguised. It is not improbable that he may still expect to receive a more effectual succour from France; but there is every reason to hope that any attempt to furnish him with assistance from that quarter would be frustrated by the vigilance and superior power of his Majesty's fleets.

It is, however, difficult to ascertain the precise motives which may stimulate the violence of his temper to action; and his late embassy to the Isle of France is a sufficient proof that revenge against the British nation in India is an object which he is capable of pursuing with more zeal than discretion.

Under such circumstances it is prudent to be prepared to repel the attack which he has openly menaced; and as our future security, our reputation, and our honour demand that he should be reduced to the alternative, either of making such satisfaction to the allies as they may hereafter require for the injury which he has committed, or of risking another contest with the British power, it is advisable to arm for the purpose of supporting whatever requisition we may deem it necessary to make to him when our respective preparations shall be sufficiently advanced to enable us to act with effect.

The 10th and 13th articles of treaties of alliance between the Company, the Nizam, and the Peishwa, provide that "if Tippoo should molest or attack either of the contracting parties, the other shall join to punish him, the modes and conditions of which shall be hereafter settled by the three contracting parties."

I desire that you will immediately communicate to Azeemool-Oomrah in a formal manner the accompanying proclamation, and explain to him the nature of the propositions which it contains; you will also notify to him the landing of the French force at Mangalore, and declare to him in my name that I consider the whole transaction as a violation of treaty, and a direct act of hostility on the part of Tippoo, and that I claim the assistance and co-operation of the Nizam under the 10th article of the treaty of Paungul. You will, however, add, that although I should feel myself completely justified in making an immediate attack upon the territory of Tippoo, my disposition to preserve the tranquillity of India induces me in the first instance to afford him an opportunity of restraining the excess of his violence before it shall have involved him in the calamity of war.

With this view you will apply to Azeem-ool-Oomrah to signify to the Nizam my wish that he should now express his disposition to concur with the Peishwa, and with me, in making a demand of satisfaction from Tippoo Sooltan; the nature and extent of the demand, as well as the time of making it, to be hereafter concerted between the allies. You will inform Azeem-ool-Oomrah that a similar application has been made to the Peishwa: the Resident at Poona will be directed to communicate to you the progress of his proceedings at that Court under the instructions which he will have received from me. As soon as you shall have received from Poona the notification of the Peishwa's concurrence in the propositions made to him on this part of the subject, you will send me immediate advice of it.

If Tippoo Sooltan, in the career of his ungovernable passion, should refuse to make the satisfaction which shall be demanded of him by the allies, hostilities will become inevitable; and you will signify to Azeem-ool-Oomrah that I have already taken the necessary precaution of assembling the forces of the Company with a view to that event, entertaining no doubt that in such a contingency the Nizam will be ready to afford to the common cause of the allies the effectual co-operation of his force.

Although I have thought it expedient to communicate my instructions to you in the foregoing order, I am sensible that their effectual execution will be impracticable, unless some previous measures be taken for restoring the independence of the Nizam's government, by delivering it from the influence of the French party, and from the hostilities menaced by Scindia, as well as from the danger of future attacks on the part of the Mahrattas.

The present crisis demands a serious and dispassionate review of the relative interests of the powers united by treaty for the purpose of securing an effectual barrier against the inordinate ambition and implacable revenge of Tippoo Sooltan.

It has been painful to observe that since the conclusion of the treaty of Seringapatam, two great branches of the triple alliance have been engaged in mutual contests, of which the result has terminated in their mutual weakness; whilst the common enemy has remained at rest, improved his resources, and increased his strength. The unfortunate animosity between the Courts of Poona and Hyderabad, while it has tended to foment and aggravate the distractions in the former Court, has contributed to reduce the latter to the lowest degree of weakness and humiliation. In the meanwhile the French faction at the Court of Hyderabad has grown to such a formidable degree of power, as to control on many serious occasions the councils of that state, and to menace an ascendant influence in the eventual succession to the throne of the Nizam.

Although the death of Monsieur Raymond and the resumption of the jaghire which had been granted to him, have in some degree reduced the political influence of the French army at Hyderabad, it now forms the only efficient part of the Nizam's military strength; its numbers have been lately increased; its discipline considerably improved, and it possesses sufficient activity and power to attempt and accomplish objects of the most prejudical nature to the independence of the Court of Hyderabad, to the common interests of the Nizam and of the Peishwa, as well as those of the British nation in India. In event of a war with Mysore, there can be no doubt that the wishes and interests of this part of the Nizam's army must be favourable to the cause of Tippoo Sooltan, more especially under the actual circumstances of his having concluded an alliance with France, and having admitted a body of French troops into his service. If the French troops of the Nizam did not afford Tippoo open assistance, at least they could not be brought into the field against him without the utmost danger to the cause of the allies; nor could they be suffered to remain in the Deccan during the continuance of the contest, unless checked by the presence of an equally powerful force, which must in the case be diverted from the common objects of the war, and must operate as a positive diminution of our effective strength in the field.

It appears, however, nearly certain, that in the present weak state of the Nizam's government, the French corps in his service would openly join Tippoo Sooltan, and by a sudden blow endeavour to seize the Nizam's territories and to secure them to the dominion of France, under an alliance offensive and defensive with Tippoo Sooltan.

It is scarcely necessary to observe that the success of such a design must be highly injurious to the interests of the Court of Poona, especially when it is considered, that it must be the interest and inclination of Scindia (who entertains a large body of infantry in his service, under the command of a French officer) to engage with Tippoo Sooltan and the French, upon conditions fatal to the existence of the Peishwa's authority, and even of his office. The junction which might thus be effected between the French officers with their several corps in the respective services of the Nizam, of Scindia and of Tippoo, might establish the power of France and India upon the ruin of the states of Poona and of the Deccan. The Court of Hyderabad, therefore, in its present condition, is more likely to prove the source of additional strength to the common enemy of the Nizam, of the Peishwa and of the Company, than to afford useful assistance to any branch of the triple alliance.

From my letter to the Resident of Poona, of which I enclose you a copy, you will observe that I have instructed him to state to the Peishwa the arguments of prudence and policy which should induce him to view the restoration of the Nizam to a just degree of consideration and power, as an object intimately connected with the Peishwa's own emancipation from the undue influence by which he is now oppressed, as well as with his future security against the violence of Tippoo Sooltan and of Scindia.

I refer you to the same letter for the particulars of my instructions to Colonel Palmer, and of the measures which I have

z 2

authorised him to pursue for enabling the Peishwa to fulfil his engagements under the triple alliance.

I am persuaded that the Azeem-ool-Oomrah will at once perceive the advantages which must result to the interest of the Nizam from the restoration of the due authority of the Peishwa, accompanied by the arrangements which I have proposed. Under these arrangements the power of the Peishwa would operate as a constant restraint upon the motions of Scindia, of Tippoo, and of the French, who are equally the enemies of the Peishwa and of the Nizam, and who menace equal danger to the tranquillity and independence of both.

Immediately upon receiving this despatch you will communicate to Azeem-ool-Oomrah the whole of the proposed arrangements with respect to the Courts of Hyderabad and Poona, as detailed in this letter, and in that addressed to Colonel Palmer; and you will explain to him fully the principles upon which the arrangement is founded, the various objects which it embraces, the means by which it is to be carried into effect, and the ends which it is intended to accomplish, with relation to the interests of all the parties concerned.

You will at the same time apprise him without disguise, that the execution of the whole, and of every part of the plan, must depend upon the mutual consent of the Nizam and of the Peishwa. You will further express to Azeem-ool-Oomrah that although I have viewed with great concern and anxiety the progress of the calamities which have disturbed the tranquillity of the two Courts, it is now a matter of cordial satisfaction to me to perceive that the result of those misfortunes promises an union of sentiment between the Nizam and the Peishwa, and affords a prospect for re-establishing the triple alliance on its original basis. You will also urge to Azeem-ool-Oomrah the credit and honour it would reflect on his administration, if through his means the Nizam and Peishwa should be enabled to derive reciprocal advantage and permanent security from a state of confusion which appeared to threaten their common ruin.

I rely upon your ability and zeal for the public service to state the details of these important measures to Azeem-ool-Oomrah with every circumstance of advantage. Your communication should be unequivocal and unreserved; no part either of the principles or details of the arrangement requires any degree of concealment, my object being to unite all parties on the firm ground of their genuine interests.

You will at the same time declare to Azeem-ool-Oomrah that the recent conduct of Tippoo Sooltan having rendered it my right and duty, in conformity with the laws of my country, to take effectual measures in concert with the allies for the mutual defence of our respective possessions, I am now at liberty to express my sincere disposition to attend to the propositions which he has so frequently made for the extension of our subsidiary engagements with his Highness; and you will signify my anxious desire to interpose the friendly mediation of the Company for the adjustment of the unfortunate differences which have so long subsisted between the Courts of Poonah and Hyderabad and Dowlut Rao Scindia.

You will further state, that I have authorised you to enter into an immediate negotiation with Azeem-ool-Oomrah for increasing our present detachment with his Highness to the number of 6000 men, including those now serving with his Highness under the following conditions:—

I. That the services of the increased detachment be subject to the same conditions of limitation and restriction as the present detachment, unless the Peishwa, at the instance of the British Government, should hereafter consent to any variations in those conditions.

II. That satisfactory and effectual provision be made for the regular payment of the detachment, and that the arrears of the Peishwa on the part of the Company be regularly balanced against the arrears of subsidy on the part of his Highness.

III. That the whole corps officered by Frenchmen, and which was named the corps of Raymond, and is now commanded by Monsieur Piron, be immediately disbanded. The French officers and privates to be conveyed to Europe at the expense of the Company, in ships to be provided for that purpose, by the Government of Fort St. George, at a convenient port, to be named by that Government. For this purpose the officers and privates are to proceed to the place appointed by that Government, which will stipulate to treat them with every degree of consideration due to their rank : they will not be subject to any further restraint than such as is absolutely necessary for effecting the purpose of conveying them to Europe. A stipulation to be entered into by the Resident in my name, that the officers and privates so embarked shall be sent to France as soon as possible after their arrival in any port in Great Britain, and not be detained for any cartel or exchange of prisoners, nor be considered as prisoners to any other effect than the security of their return to their native country. Such of the native officers and privates as the Nizam may wish to retain in his service to be drafted into the corps of Mr. Finglass, or into any other corps in his Highness's service under the command of British, or of officers of any country but France. The European and native deserters from the Company's army on the coast to be excepted from this part of the arrangement, and to be delivered up to the Government of Fort St. George.

IV. His Highness to stipulate for himself, his heirs, and successors, that the natives of France shall be for ever excluded from his armies and dominions.

You will urge to Azeem-ool-Oomrah in the strongest terms the necessity of his taking every precaution to prevent the propositions for the dismission of the French party from. transpiring; and you will suggest to him the propriety of dispersing the corps in. small parties, for the purpose of facilitating its final reduction, and of preventing the officers and privates from passing into the service of Tippoo or of Scindia. If the French officers should obtain information of the measures in agitation with respect to them, and should be allowed to unite themselves into one body, there is every reason to apprehend that they would endeavour to excite commotion, or that they would attempt to retire with their corps into the service of the enemies of the Nizam.

You will consider the Nizam's acceptance of my arbitration, between the Courts of Poona and Hyderabad and Scindia, upon the principles stated in my letter to Colonel Palmer, as well as his Highness's consent to the proposed arrangements at Poona, and to the several conditions stated in paragraph No. 25, of his despatch, to be necessary preliminaries to the measures which I have authorised you to take for delivering the Nizam from the power of the French faction established in his dominions. Should Azeem-ool-Oomrah consent, in the name of the Nizam, to the proposed conditions, you will then require the march of the troops from Fort St. George, or from such station as the Government of that Presidency shall have appointed for the detachment, with a view to its speedy march to Hyderabad.

It would be useful for me to learn your sentiments with respect to a new treaty of general defence with the Nizam, and to any new objects which it might embrace with relation to our interests at the Court of Hyderabad; to this treaty I should wish the Peishwa to be a party.

You will inform Azeem-ool-Oomrah, that under the circumstances of Tippoo's preparations of war against us, and of the hostilities with which Scindia menaces the dominions of the Nizam, the British detachment at Hyderabad will have orders to protect his Highness's person, and to support his authority against any attack which Scindia may make upon either, as well as against any attempts of the French party; and you will understand it to be my intention to vest you with full powers to direct the employment of the troops in both cases, in such manner as circumstances may render advisable, provided that in the opinion of the commanding officer, the strength of the detachment shall be deemed adequate to the performance of the service required. You will, however, apprise Azeem-ool-Oomrah, that it is my wish to mediate between Scindia and the Courts of Poona and Hyderabad, under the condition detailed in my letter to Colonel Palmer; and you will consider the provisional agreement of the Nizam to this offer of mediation between his Highness and Scindia as another necessary preliminary to the increase of the British detachment at Hyderabad.

The whole scope of my views is to re-establish our means of defence against the avowed designs of Tippoo, by restoring to our allies that degree of consideration and strength which they possessed at the conclusion of the treaty of Seringapatam, and which it was the object of that treaty to secure on solid and permanent foundations; an object inseparably connected with the security of the British possessions in India.

Since the conclusion of the peace of Seringapatam a material change has taken place in the situation of almost all the states of India, both with relation to each other and to the interests of the British Government. The revolutions at Poona have impaired the influence of the constitutional head of the Mahratta empire, and deranged the whole system of the balanced powers and the interests of the several confederate Mahratta states.

Both the Peishwa and the Nizam, whose respective power it was the object of the treaty of Seringapatam to strengthen and uphold, are now depressed and weakened; the former by the intrusion of Scindia, and the latter by the threatened hostilities of the same chieftain and by the establishment of a French faction in the centre of the Deccan. The co-operation of these two members of the triple alliance has been rendered impracticable by the progress of their mutual contention and intrigues, while the internal convulsions of each state has diminished the resources of both.

In this scene of general confusion the power of Tippoo Sooltan alone (to restrain which was the policy of all our alliances and treaties) has remained undisturbed and unimpaired, if it has not been augmented and improved.

The final result to the British Government is the entire loss of the benefit of the treaty of triple alliance against Tippoo Sooltan, and the establishment of a French army of 14,000 men in the dominion of one of our allies, in the vicinity of the territories of Tippoo Sooltan, and on the confines of the Carnatic and of the Northern Circars.

It is now become an urgent duty to make an effort for the arrangement of a system, the disorder of which already menaces our safety by exposing us to the hazard of a war without the aid of an ally; while, on the other hand, the influence of France acquires daily strength in every quarter of India under the progressive system of introducing French officers into the armies of all the native powers. The principles of justice, good faith, and moderation, enjoined by Parliament and by the orders of the Honourable the Court of Directors, must form the basis of those comprehensive measures the execution of which is demanded by the exigency of our present situation and is favoured by the peculiar circumstances of the moment. Pursuing no schemes of conquest or extension of dominion, and entertaining no projects of ambition or aggrandizement either for ourselves or for our allies, it is both our right and our duty to give vigour and effect to our subsisting alliances and treaties by restoring to our allies the power of fulfilling their defensive engagements with us. Through the means of moderate and pacific representations, confirmed by the force of our own example, it must also be our policy to convince the several powers of India that their real interest consists in respecting the rights of their neighbours and in cultivating their own resources within the limits of their several territories. To these efforts we must add a firm resistance against the intrusion of any foreign power which shall endeavour (to the prejudice of our alliances and interests) to acquire a preponderant influence in the scale of Indian politics, either by force or intrigue; but the primary object of all our vigilance and care must be the destruction of every seed of the French party, already grown to so dangerous a height and still increasing in the armies and councils of the Nizam of Scindia and of Tippoo. The exclusion of the influence of France from the dominions of the native states is not more necessary to the preservation of our own power than to the happiness and prosperity of this part of the world.

In this first communication with you, I have thought it advisable to apprise you of the leading principles which will regulate my conduct towards the native powers, and I have taken a general view of the actual state of our political relations in order to enable you to act with more confidence and despatch upon such questions of detail as may occasionally call for the exercise of your judgment in promoting the objects of your mission.

In pursuing the various topics connected with the subject of this despatch, I shall add my instructions with regard to the conduct to be observed by the British detachment in the event of the death of the Nizam.

If the question involved nothing more than the performance of our obligations under our subsidiary engagements with the Nizam, it would be sufficient to direct that the detachment should remain neuter until the succession should be finally decided, and that it should then be placed under the orders of the prince who might establish himself on the musnud.

But in the present state of India, our interests and those of our allies are materially concerned in the principles and connexions of the person upon whom the succession of his Highness may devolve, and consequently no time should be lost in determining the part which we shall take on the occasion of the Nizam's decease.

The cases for which it is necessary to provide may be reduced to four.

I. The formal nomination of Secunder Jah to the succession.

II. The death of the Nizam without any formal nomination of a successor.

III. An attempt (in either of the preceding cases) of one of his Highness's younger sons, or of any other competitor, to usurp the musnud in exclusion of Secunder Jah.

IV. An actual or asserted nomination of any of his Highness's younger sons to the exclusion of Secunder Jah.

In the first, second, and third cases the right of Secunder Jah would be indisputable.

From the natural right of Secunder Jah, founded on the priority of his birth, added to his having been admitted by the Nizam to the personal exercise of a portion of the sovereign authority, under circumstances equivalent to a virtual nomination, I trust there is little apprehension of a nomination of any of the younger sons, whilst his Highness shall retain the full possession of his faculties.

It is far from improbable, however, that the enemies of Secunder Jah, of Azeem-ool-Oomrah, and of the British interests at Hyderabad, aware of the importance of inducing his Highness to nominate a successor of their selection, may avail themselves of the weakness of his last moments to prevail on him, by misrepresentation or other acts, to nominate one of his younger sons; or in the event of his Highness's death during the absence of Azeem-ool-Oomrah and of the friends of Secunder Jah, the enemies of Secunder Jah may assert that his Highness had made a nomination of one of the younger sons, and under such circumstances the falsehood of that assertion may be difficult of proof.

It is not my wish to interfere in the succession to the throne of the Nizam, in repugnance to the established law or customs of India. On the other hand, I hold it to be my absolute duty to prevent the regular order of the succession from being disturbed, either by domestic faction, or by foreign intrigue or force, to the prejudice of a prince, the establishment of whose right is so intimately connected with the security of the British interests in India.

Although primogeniture may not be considered to give the same absolute and exclusive right to succession in India as it does in Europe, it is invariably deemed the strongest title, and is rarely superseded excepting in the cases of disaffection or of positive disqualification.

So far from these, or any other grounds of objection being applicable to Secunder Jah, it is well known that his Highness has given the strongest indications of his favourable intentions towards Secunder Jah, by entrusting that prince with his seal, and empowering him to perform certain acts which are reserved exclusively for the sovereign.

Sufficient proof has already appeared of the interest which Tippoo and the French take in the exclusion of Secunder Jah, and of their determination to interfere in the succession to the throne of the Nizam. During the absence of Azeem-ool-Oomrah at Poona, when the French army at Hyderabad was neither so formidable in point of numbers or of discipline as in the present moment, Monsieur Raymond obtained the most decided influence over the councils of the Ministers then in power; a permanent establishment was given to the French in the Deccan by the grant of a large jaghire to Monsieur Raymond; the British detachment was dismissed; and a considerable body of Tippoo's troops was encamped on the Nizam's frontier; a close correspondence was established between Tippoo and Imtiaz-ool-Dowlah through Medina Sahib; the enemies of Secunder Jah openly sought the assistance of Tippoo, and of the French, with a view of influencing the succession; and according to the opinion of the Resident at Hyderabad, the event of the Nizam's death in that crisis would have left the throne absolutely at the disposal of Monsieur Raymond.

A similar plan may be again attempted, and its success would necessarily involve the destruction of Azeem-ool-Oomrah and of Secunder Jah, together with the consequent annihilation of the British influence at Hyderabad; all hope of re-establishing the balance of power in India as it existed at the peace of Seringapatam would then be precluded. The countries of the Nizam would in such an event become in effect a dependency of France; and the partizans of that nation, in conjunction with Tippoo and with the body of their countrymen lately received into his pay, would have the means of endangering the existence of the British power in India.

That danger would be greatly aggravated by the approach of Zemaun Shah, who has formally announced to me his intention of invading Hindostan.

The moment is arrived when we must either determine to support the rights of Secunder Jah, founded on priority of birth and on the virtual nomination of the Nizam in full possession of his faculties, against any actual or asserted nomination of any of the younger sons under all the circumstances of suspicion which must attend such a transaction, or we must submit to the certain establishment of the influence of Tippoo and of France in the Deccan, and to the equally certain destruction of our own.

. I have therefore no hesitation in declaring my firm determination to support the succession of Secunder Jah, as being essentially connected with the security of all the interests committed to my charge. The execution of this determination will be attended with little difficulty should his Highness's death be protracted until after the proposed augmentation of the subsidiary engagements with him shall have taken place. The French party at Hyderabad will then be no longer in existence, and so powerful a body of our troops as will then be in the service of his Highness will be sufficient to preclude either foreign or domestic opposition.

It is more than probable, however, that his Highness's death will take place before the proposed engagements can be carried into effect.

With a view to the probability of this case I have resolved to direct the Government of Fort St. George immediately to station a force, consisting of not less than two regiments, in whatever position may be deemed most eligible for affording you the necessary assistance in supporting the right of Secunder Jah; and I authorise you, in the event of the death of the Nizam, or whenever you may understand from Azeem-ool-Oomrah that the death of his Highness is likely to take place within a very short period of time, to order the commanding officer of this force (who will be directed to obey your instructions) to march directly to Hyderabad.

Considerable advantages might arise from your communicating this determination to Azeem-ool-Oomrah; but as it is to be apprehended that he would avail himself of such a communication to serve his private purposes; and as a disclosure of my determination on this point, either to the Nizam himself, or to the Mahrattas, or to Tippoo, might lead to very serious inconveniences, you will take every possible precaution to prevent this part of my instructions from transpiring until the death of the Nizam, or the certainty of the near approach of that event, shall render it necessary to impart my determination to Azeem-ool-Oomrah.

Having received overtures of a very friendly nature from the

Raja of Berar, who has requested the presence of a British Resident at his court, I have despatched an ambassador to Nagpoor, with full powers to ascertain the precise nature of the Raja's views. You will make such use of your knowledge of this circumstance as you may think most advantageous in the present state of affairs; without deciding what benefits to the common cause of the allies may result ultimately from this embassy, it may be expected that the appearance of an established intercourse between this Government and that of Berar, may lead Scindia to form serious reflections upon his own situation, and may tend to give additional confidence to the adherents of the Peishwa and of the Nizam.

Although the previous consent of the Peishwa to the arrangements intended to be made at Hyderabad is highly desirable, and is therefore in the first instance to be stated to Azeem-ool-Oomrah as a necessary preliminary to the increase of our detachment, yet should Colonel Palmer inform you that the plan detailed in this letter has failed at the court of Poona, either from the Peishwa's rejection of the proposed conditions, or from the success of Scindia's operations in that quarter, or from any other cause, you will notwithstanding proceed with all practicable despatch to carry into effect such parts of these instructions as shall appear to you practicable at the court of Hyderabad. Reserving always to the Peishwa the power of acceding hereafter to the new system of alliance, and that with the view of continuing in the new subsidiary treaty with the Nizam, the restrictive terms of our present subsidiary engagements with his Highness. The arrangements will indeed be very incomplete without the restoration of the Peishwa's authority, accompanied by his full concurrence in the measures to be taken at Hyderabad; but as the great danger to be averted is the growth of the influence of Tippoo and of France in India, it is evident that the failure of the proposed plan at Poona would increase the necessity of providing for the existence of the Nizam, and of destroying the French party at his court.

From your reply to the further information required of you respecting your passport for Hybut Rao, I am not altogether certain whether you considered this Government as pledged to exempt him and his followers from the payment of the duties at Gya. If you should be of opinion that this indulgence would materially conduce to conciliate his son, Ragotim Rao, and to render him favourable to the British interests at Hyderabad, I authorise you to assure Ragotim Rao that Hybut Rao's payments on account of the persons who actually accompanied him shall be returned to him at Hyderabad as soon as the amount of those payments can be ascertained. I rely upon you, however, to render this concession the source of advantage with respect to the proposed arrangements, and also to provide effectually against any future attempt to convert so peculiar an indulgence into a precedent for further applications of a similar nature. I entirely approve of your repeated representations to the Court of Hyderabad on the subject of the surrender of the deserters; in the present moment, however, it would not be advisable to agitate this question otherwise than as it is connected with the instructions already detailed in this despatch; but if the proposed engagements with his Highness should not take effect, I desire you will, without delay, insist peremptorily on the surrender of all the deserters from our army, whether European or natives, now entertained in the service of his Highness.

Having your whole correspondence now under my consideration, I shall shortly furnish you with orders on such points of detail as require a reply.

MORNINGTON.

Proclamation at the Isle of France.

Liberty.   Equality.

THE FRENCH REPUBLIC.

One and indivisible.

———

PROCLAMATION.

Anne Joseph Hyppolite Malartic, Commander in Chief and Governor-General of the Isles of France and Reunion, and of all the French establishments to the eastward of the Cape of Good Hope.

Citizens,

Having for several years known your zeal and your attachment to the interests, and to the glory of our Republic, we are very anxious, and we feel it a duty to make you acquainted with all the propositions which have been made to us by Tippoo Sooltan, through two ambassadors whom he has despatched to us.

This prince has written particular letters to the Colonial Assembly, to all the generals employed under this government, and has addressed to us a packet for the Executive Directory.

1. He desires to form an offensive and defensive alliance with the French, and proposes to maintain at his charge, as long as the war shall last in India, the troops which may be sent to him.

2. He promises to furnish every necessary for carrying on the war, wine and brandy excepted, with which he is wholly unprovided.

3. He declares that he has made every preparation to receive the succours which may be sent to him, and that on the arrival of the troops, the commanders and officers will find every thing necessary for making a war, to which the Europeans are but little accustomed.

4. In a word only he waits the moment when the French

shall come to his assistance, *to declare war against the English,* *whom he ardently desires to expel from India.*

As it is impossible for us to reduce the number of soldiers of the 107th and 108th regiments, and of the regular guard of Port Fraternité, on account of the succours which we have furnished to our allies the Dutch; we invite the citizens, who may be disposed to enter as volunteers, to enrol themselves in their respective municipalities, and to serve under the banners of Tippoo.

This prince desires also to be assisted by the free citizens of colour; we therefore invite all such who are willing to serve under his flag to enrol themselves.

We can assure all the citizens who shall enrol themselves, that Tippoo will allow them an advantageous rate of pay, the terms of which will be fixed with his ambassadors, who will further engage, in the name of their sovereign, that all Frenchmen who shall enter into his armies shall never be detained after they shall have expressed a wish to return to their own country.

Done at Port North West, the 30th January, 1798.

(Signed) MALARTIC.

No. III.

The Earl of MORNINGTON *to* Captain KIRKPATRICK.

(Private.)

Fort-William, July 14, 1798.

Sir,—I return you many thanks for your several private communications, and I am happy to avail myself of an early opportunity to express my approbation of your diligence and activity in the discharge of the important duties of your mission. I shall always acknowledge with gratitude the assistance which I received from the extensive knowledge, experience, talents, and integrity of Major Kirkpatrick, during the period of my continuance at the Cape. As he expressed a desire of being near my person, it is my intention of offering to him the situation of my Military Secretary, whenever he shall arrive in India; and as it is probable that he may touch at Madras, I mean to despatch a letter to meet him at that Presidency, suggesting to him the service which he might render to the public, by adding the exertion of his talents to yours in the present crisis of affairs, and by visiting you for a short time, if his health should admit of such a journey.

My detailed instructions to you and to Colonel Palmer, which accompany this letter, will make you fully acquainted with the whole plan, of which the abstract was forwarded to you on the 8th of this month. A few points remain to be recommended to your attention.

It is very desirable that a body of the Nizam's troops should be stationed upon the frontier of the Peishwa's dominions, for the purpose of co-operating with our detachment in the restoration of order at Poonah. You will urge this measure to Azeem-ool-Oomrah, but you will not advise the march of the troops until you have learned from Colonel Palmer that such assistance is both necessary and acceptable to the Peishwa.

In framing the new subsidiary engagements with the Nizam, I desire you will endeavour to restrict the employment of the British troops within his Highness's dominions to those important cases in which his person or authority shall really be endangered, and that you will provide effectually against the use of the British force in those disgraceful services against petty renters and Zemindars, which more properly belong to Sebundy corps; this is an essential point. Your own discretion will sufficiently warn you of the caution and secresy to be observed in the first step towards the proposed general plan. Above all, you must take care to provide for the effectual dispersion of Perron's corps at the earliest possible period. The Government of Fort St. George have my orders to apprise you of the station appointed for assembling the two regiments intended for Hyderabad. The officer who will command the regiments sent from Fort St. George will be senior to Lieutenant-Colouel Hyndman, and will take the command of the whole force.

I am, &c.,

(Signed)   MORNINGTON.

No. IV.

The Earl of MORNINGTON *to* Captain KIRKPATRICK.

Fort William, July 18, 1798.

Sir,—I take the earliest opportunity to acknowledge your two very interesting letters No. 57 and 58.

The intelligence which they contain corresponds in a striking manner with the view which I had taken in my instructions to you and to Colonel Palmer of the 8th instant, of the actual state of affairs at the Courts of Poona and Hyderabad, and leads me to form a confident expectation that my proposed arrangements for restoring to us the benefit of the triple alliance, will be brought to a successful issue, unless my endeavours should unfortunately be frustrated by the success of Scindia's designs upon the power of the Peishwa before Colonel Palmer can have received my despatches of the 8th instant. In your letter, No. 58, you relate a singular instance of the penetration of Azeem-ool-Oomrah, who, as you will have observed, has anticipated nearly the whole principle and object of my instructions of the 8th instant. Although I consider this coincidence of sentiment as a very favourable circumstance in many points of view, I am apprehensive that it may be difficult to convince Azeem-ool-Oomrah of the fact of my first instructions to Colouel Palmer having been despatched on the same day with those addressed to you.

think it necessary to authorise you to declare that I have had no correspondence whatever with Colonel Palmer previously to my despatch of the 8th instant. You will naturally observe to Azeem-ool-Oomrah, that he has foreseen nearly the whole of my plan with this material exception, that the fundamental principle of my instructions, both to you and Colonel Palmer, is an unreserved communication to each Court of the propositions to be made to the other; and that the full previous knowledge and consent of all parties forms an essential condition of the whole arrangement. This circumstance will afford sufficient proof of my sincerity; and, indeed, I cannot conceive what possible motive could be assigned for my preferring the interests of the Peishwa to those of the Nizam, or for my undertaking any negotiations at Poona without his Highness's participation.

But I repeat it, the best answer to any such suspicion is to be found in the whole tenor and spirit of my instructions to you and to Colonel Palmer.

I shall wait for your reply to my letter of the 8th of July before I furnish you with my instructions upon any other points stated in your last despatches.

I have the honour to be, &c.

MORNINGTON.

The Earl of MORNINGTON to Captain J. A. KIRKPATRICK, *acting Resident at Hyderabad.*

Fort William, 11th August, 1798.

Sir, — I have received your letter of the 24th July, to which I now return my answer.

By referring to my detailed instructions of the 8th July, you will perceive that the arrangements which I propose are not limited to a mere enlargement of our existing subsidiary engagements with the Nizam.

I collect from your letter, that Azeem-ool-Oomrah would be likely to require three conditions in addition to those stated in the abstract of my instructions of the 8th July, before he would consent to accede to my propositions.

The first, engagement to support the succession of Secunder Jah.

Secondly, the power of employing the British detachment in carrying into effect various measures of internal reform in the Nizam's dominions.

Thirdly, the extension of my proposed arbitration of the existing differences between the Courts of Poona and Hyderabad, to any cases of difference which may hereafter arise.

It is my decided intention to support the succession of Secunder Jah. But I have directed you to conceal that intention from Azeem-ool-Oomrah for the present, under an apprehension that the disclosure of it might excite suspicion and jealousy in the mind of the Nizam.

If, however, you should be of opinion that this communication could be made to Azeem-ool-Oomrah without any danger of the nature which I apprehend, I authorise you to act according to your own discretion in this respect.

With regard to the employment of the British detachment within the Nizam's dominions, it appears to me that I have already laid down the rule with sufficient clearness in my letter of the 14th July; in which I have directed that the employment of the British troops, in his Highness's dominions, shall be restricted to those important cases in which his person or authority shall be endangered, and shall not be extended to those services which more properly belong to Sebundy corps.

This rule would certainly admit of the employment of the detachment in the cases stated in your letter of the 24th July, nor am I aware of any objection to the use of the British troops, under the direction of the Nizam's ministers, in services connected with the introduction of a system of internal reform into his Highness's dominions.

If the Courts of Poona, and Hyderabad shall concur in accepting my arbitration of their subsisting differences, there will be every reason to hope that they would be prepared to receive a similar security against the effects of any disputes which may hereafter arise. It never was my intention to confine my interpositions to the circumstances of the present moment, my object being to unite the interests of the two courts upon a permanent basis.

My wish unquestionably is, that the Company should for the future be placed in the situation of a mediator between the other two branches of the triple alliance, and should hereafter by a timely interposition of good offices prevent them from engaging in contests, which must eventually impair the strength of both parties, and defeat the ends of the triple alliance.

I am, &c.
MORNINGTON.

No. V.

The Earl of MORNINGTON *to* Captain KIRKPATRICK.

Fort William, 14th August, 1798.

Sir,—I have received your private letter of the 30th ult. Your communications relating to Colonel Kirkpatrick give me great pleasure, and I am happy to find that the situation in my family which I have left open for him is likely to prove acceptable to him.

Azeem-ool-Oomrah's reception of my propositions has afforded me the highest satisfaction; nor could it be expected that he should pledge himself to a greater extent on the first communication of a plan embracing so many complicated interests.

In directing the Government of Fort St. George to hold two regiments in readiness to march at your requisition to Hyderabad, I desired that those regiments might be accompanied by the ordinary proportion of field artillery; and my intention is that the artillery which may be sent with those regiments shall be permanently stationed with the Nizam, he, of course, paying the charge attending it. If the proportion of artillery sent with the detachment from Fort St. George should appear insufficient, Azeem-ool-Oomrah will find me sincerely disposed to accommodate that point to his wishes by making any addition which may be deemed requisite.

I shall hereafter take into consideration your observation respecting the exchange at which the pay of the Bengal troops serving at Hyderabad is now issued. I think it proper at the same time to acquaint you that it is my intention ultimately that the corps stationed with the Nizam shall be composed entirely of troops from the establishment of Fort St. George.

The total inability of the Nizam to extricate himself from the power of the French party without our assistance formed one of the primary considerations which induced me to propose to him the extension of our subsidiary engagements.

The anxiety with which Azeem-ool-Oomrah presses for the arrival of the additional subsidiary force from Fort St. George, as an indispensable preliminary to the destruction of the French party, is a sufficient confirmation of the opinions which I had formed of the dangerous strength of the party, and of the absolute necessity of our interference for the purpose of restraining its overbearing influence.

It could never have been expected by me that the minister should take any other step towards the dismission of Peron's army, previously to the arrival of our regiments, than that of dispersing the corps of which it is composed, so as to prevent their forming a junction, either with a view of exciting a commotion in his Highness's dominions, or of retiring into the territories of any other power. It is indispensably necessary, indeed, that the intended dismission of the French party should be kept secret, until the minister shall possess the means of attempting it with a certainty of success. With the aid of the additional force which we have agreed to furnish, I should hope that he will be enabled to carry this part of the plan into execution, without any material difficulty. Perhaps even a smaller British force might be deemed adequate to this service; if you should be of opinion that it can be successfully accomplished by the Bengal troops now serving at Hyderabad, and a part of the additional force ordered to march thither on your requisition (supposing that any unforeseen obstacle should impede the immediate march of the whole of the two regiments from Fort St. George), you have my sanction to make the attempt with the smaller force.

For the reasons, however, stated in my letter to you of the 25th ult., it is indispensably necessary, at all events, that the Nizam should, without delay, formally bind himself by a written engagement to my propositions respecting the French party, as well as to every other preliminary condition of the proposed arrangements, leaving the mode and time of carrying those arrangements into effect, to be determined by the arrival of our additional subsidiary force.

I consider such preliminary articles to be the basis of a definitive treaty which shall comprehend the general interests of each branch of the triple alliance. On the signature of such articles you must insist, before you despatch your orders for the march of the additional detachment. The actual disbanding of Peron's corps will, of course, follow the establishment of our troops at Hyderabad.

The nature of these measures requires great despatch, the ordinary delays of an Asiatic Court would defeat the whole system.

I am, &c.
MORNINGTON.

No. VI.

(By express.)

The Earl of MORNINGTON *to* Captain KIRKPATRICK.

Fort William, 20th August, 1798.

Sir,—I have received your letters of the 31st of July and 2nd of August.

I shall forward to you by the next post a public letter containing my observations on their contents. But I cannot delay the communication of my anxiety on some points contained in the Persian paper delivered by you to Azeem-ool-Oomrah.

From the tenor of that paper it would be supposed that war with Tippoo was in my opinion become not only inevitable but desirable.

The primary object of all my present measures is to prevent war, by convincing Tippoo, on the one hand, that we are perfectly prepared to meet him in the field, and on the other, that we are equally ready to accept of a just and moderate satisfaction for his late infraction of treaty.

The manner in which that paper states my determination to use compulsory measures against Scindia is very different from the spirit of my instructions to Colonel Palmer. My wish and expectation always has been that measures of conciliation might effect all that I require from Scindia with considerable advantage to his own genuine interests, and I have authorised Colonel Palmer to resort to compulsion in the last and, I trust, improbable extremity. But from your Persian paper it would be inferred that I expected a contest with Scindia, and that I was not desirous of conciliating that chief.

You will bear these observations in mind, and you will endeavour to remove impressions from which I apprehend the most serious mischief.

Without at present adverting to the propriety of your having made any alteration in the propositions which I directed you to make to Azeem-ool-Oomrah, I shall confine myself to apprising you that I do not feel any material objection to any alterations which you have made in the substance of those propositions excepting that which respects the permanency of the new subsidiary engagements. Such a proposition appears to me likely to create jealousy in the mind of the Nizam without securing any possible advantage to us. You will therefore withdraw it if it should have occasioned any objection.

I do not yet think it prudent to disclose the nature of the demand of satisfaction which I have it in contemplation to make from Tippoo, and I am therefore anxious that you should take

an early occasion of removing any impression which may have
been made by your suggestions on that subject.

You will not delay your application for the force from Fort
St. George in consequence of any difficulty which may have
arisen respecting the security for the pay of the new subsidiary
force.   The great object is to effect the dismission of the French
force as speedily as possible.

I am, &c.

MORNINGTON.

No. VII.

The Earl of MORNINGTON to Captain KIRKPATRICK.

Fort William, 31st August, 1798.

Sir, — The general tenor of the late advices from Europe
convinces me that the rumours of the approach of peace which
had reached me in the last month were entirely void of foundation, but my recent intelligence leads me to apprehend that the
attention of France is now earnestly directed towards India, and
that at least a part of the armament fitted out in the Mediter-
ranean may have been destined for an expedition to India, not,
as has been professed, through Egypt and the Red Sea, but by
the ordinary passage round the Cape of Good Hope.   With
these opinions, I am extremely anxious for the immediate conclusion of my proposed engagements with the Nizam, and for
the consequent dismission of M. Piron's corps and the arrest of
the officers.   If, therefore, any delays at Poona should have
prevented untill this time the termination of the negotiation
entrusted to you, I desire you will endeavour to conclude it,
with all practicable despatch, under the limitations suggested
in the 55th paragraph of my detailed instructions of the 8th

July.[*] You will, according to the spirit of that paragraph, take care to stipulate that the Peishwa shall have an option of acceding hereafter to any engagements concluded with the Nizam.

In the case which I have supposed, of the completion of the arrangements at Hyderabad being delayed by the Court of Poona until this letter shall reach you, it will be necessary to agree to the proposal of Meer Allum, for securing the inter-position of the Company in all future differences between the Courts of Poona and Hyderabad, under the condition that the Nizam shall bind himself to fulfil all his engagements with the Peishwa, and to abide invariably by the award of the Company on every point of dispute which may hereafter arise between his Highness and the Government of Poonah.

My letters from Bombay incline me to doubt whether that Government will be able immediately to furnish the number of troops requisite for the service of the Peishwa. Whenever, therefore, the Peishwa shall have acceded to my propositions, and whenever the disbanding of the French force at Hyderabad shall have been accomplished, I desire that you will endeavour to prevail upon the Nizam to permit one of the British regiments to march directly to Poona; and I authorise you to direct the march of the regiment accordingly. The regiment sent to Poona will be replaced as soon as possible.

The *Bombay* frigate is to touch at Masulipatam, where she is to land our marine battalion about the middle of September, from thence she will proceed to Madras, and will return to Masuli-patam about the end of September, where Captain Sutherland will be directed to remain until he shall receive your orders, or shall be driven away by the monsoon. My wish is, that all such French officers and privates as may be delivered up to you at Hyderabad, shall be embarked on board the *Bombay* frigate for this Presidency, where they can be more securely guarded, and from whence they will find a readier passage to Europe than at Fort St. George.

[*] Wellesley's Despatches, vol. i. p. 94.

You will consign the French party to the charge of the commanding officer at Masulipatam in the first instance, and you will take care to provide a sufficient escort for their safe conduct to Masulipatam.

You will direct Captain Sutherland to treat such French officers and privates as may be committed to his charge, with a due consideration of their respective ranks, and with all the attention and kindness consistent with the security of their persons; and you will not fail to use all your influence at Hyderabad, for the purpose of securing the property of such officers or privates as may be delivered to you from the rapacity of the ministers, and of preserving it for the use of the just proprietors.

I am, &c.
MORNINGTON.

No. VIII.

The Earl of MORNINGTON *to* Captain J. A. KIRKPATRICK,
Resident at Hyderabad.

Fort William, 2nd Nov. 1798.

Sir,—I consider it as an object of the utmost importance that every practicable precaution should be taken to prevent any jealousy from being conceived by the Court of Hyderabad in consequence of the great increase of our subsidiary force.

For this purpose it is extremely desirable that the conduct of our troops in their intercourse with the natives of the country, and particularly with the officers of his Highness's government, should be of the most conciliatory nature, and should be so regulated as to form the strongest contrast with the arrogant and contumacious spirit of the French corps. You will, therefore apprise Lieutenant-Colonels Roberts and Hyndman of my particular anxiety on this subject; and you will signify to them my expectations that they will take effectual measures to prevent any such irregularities or misconduct in the officers or men under their respective commands, as might tend to create distrust and jealousy. My wish is that the Company's army in his Highness's service should conduct itself with the utmost degree of mildness towards his subjects, and of respect towards himself and his ministers; and that it should manifest the most prompt obedience to his orders, according to the tenor of the late subsidiary treaty.

I am, &c.
MORNINGTON.

No. IX.

The Earl of MORNINGTON *to* Captain J. A. KIRKPATRICK,
Resident at Hyderabad.

Fort William, 9th Nov. 1798.

Sir,— I am happy to express my entire approbation of the judgment, firmness, and discretion which you have manifested during the important transactions which have passed since the ratification of the new subsidiary treaty with the Nizam, and which have terminated so satisfactorily in the complete execution of the secret and separate articles of that engagement.

Your conduct in the negotiation of the treaty has already received my approbation.

I desire you will signify to Lieutenant-Colonel Roberts, and to the officers and men under his command, the high sense which I entertain of the important service which they have rendered to the British interests, and to the Honourable the East India Company, by the prompt execution of your instructions.

To Lieutenant-Colonel Roberts the greatest degree of public gratitude and applause is due for his skilful and judicious disposition of the troops under his command, and for the temper and humanity of his conduct towards the French officers in his custody.

You will also express my approbation of the service rendered by Captain Scohy, in obedience to the orders of Lieutenant-Colonel Roberts.

The entire reduction of the large French force lately in the service of the Nizam, and the complete subversion of the dangerous influence of that nation at the Court of Hyderabad, place his Highness at length in a position which will enable him, in the event of a war between Tippoo Sooltan and the allies, to co-operate in the vigorous prosecution of it with considerable efficacy. But though neither the ability nor the disposition of the Court of Hyderabad to contribute materially to the support of the common cause can any longer be doubted, yet it must be obvious that without a full and precise knowledge of the extent and nature of the assistance which we may confidently rely on receiving from the Nizam, it will be impossible for us to concert with his Highness any plan of general operations, or even to decide satisfactorily on the practicability of attacking Seringapatam in due season, should the refusal of Tippoo to comply with the demands which may be made by the allies render that measure expedient.

For this reason it is of the utmost importance to ascertain without delay, and with every possible degree of correctness and certainty, the following points : —

1. The greatest amount of the force in cavalry, infantry, and field ordnance which the Nizam will positively furnish; not as an army to act separately, or in the way of diversion, but to join ours, and to proceed with it directly against the capital of the enemy.

2. The earliest period at which the force to be so furnished can move from Hyderabad.

3. The place where the Nizam may desire that this force should effect a junction with our army.

4. The route by which the Nizam would wish this force to

marcñ for the purpose of effecting such junction with the greatest facility and despatch.

5. The speediest period at which we may safely expect the junction to take place.

6. The person to whom the command of his Highness's forces is to be entrusted.

7. The means or resources applicable by the Nizam to the due and regular supply of provisions, whether for the consumption of his own forces or for the use of the united armies.

These are the principal heads of inquiry to which it is necessary to direct your immediate attention.

Upon these points I am anxious to obtain the earliest and most accurate information.

From these leading points arise several questions of a more minute description, to which it will also be proper to give due consideration. I proceed to state the most important of these, in the order in which they result from the preceding propositions.

As the reduction of Seringapatam, in the event of a war, must constitute the sole object of the allies, it is impossible not to feel a desire that the whole of our subsidiary troops should be comprehended in the contingent to be furnished by his Highness for the purpose of acting with our army. These, with the addition of 6000 of Mr. Finglass's corps, and a suitable train of field ordnance, and joined by a body of from 8000 to 10,000 of his Highness's best cavalry, under the command of Risaladhars of approved zeal and fidelity, would form as large a force as it would, perhaps, be necessary to require from him. But if any of the Company's subsidiary troops are to be withholden, although their place will be ill supplied by any others in his Highness's service, the number of the latter must be proportionably augmented.

When you are informed, however, that the army before Seringapatam in February 1792 amounted to 30,000 fighting men (exclusive of five native battalions in different parts of the enemy's country, and four battalions with the Nizam and the

Mahrattas), that an equal force is now deemed requisite for the siege of this place, and that even with the aid of the whole of the subsidiary troops now at Hyderabad we should with difficulty draw together so considerable an army, you will perceive the necessity of urging the Nizam by every argument in your power, to acquiesce in the arrangement here suggested.

In the last war with Tippoo the whole of the subsidiary British force was absent from Hyderabad. No reason occurs to me which should induce his Highness on this occasion to retain any part of it about his own person; nor am I aware of any other ground of objection to the employment of the whole of it against the common enemy, which must not equally have existed in the last war. I therefore entertain a sanguine expectation of his Highness's ready consent to the proposed measure.

I must not dismiss this article without instructing you to be particularly careful, as far as may be in your power, to obtain the exclusion from every sort of command or trust in the Nizam's contingent force of all those Sirdars whose conduct during the last war furnished a just suspicion of traitorous correspondence with the enemy. If necessary, you must formally protest against the employment of those individuals on the present occasion.

With regard to the second object of inquiry, or the period at which the Nizam's contingent can move, I need only observe that, as it will have a considerable distance to proceed before it can effect a junction with the army of the Carnatic (whatever place of junction may be appointed), it is absolutely necessary that it should commence its march as soon after your receipt of this as possible, observing, however, the caution, that it shall not anywhere in its progress pass into the dominions of Tippoo Sooltan without further notice from me. The interval, I trust, will not be long; since no doubt his Highness's preparations for enforcing the demand of satisfaction and security, which it was agreed by the allies to make upon Tippoo Sooltan, have kept pace with those of the Company's government.

As to the third point which relates to the place of the junction, although it is necessary to consult the pleasure of the

Nizam upon the subject, yet I am willing to believe you will have no difficulty in proving to him the expediency of leaving this article to be ultimately adjusted between the Commander-in-Chief of the Company's army and the commanders of his Highness's contingent force, including the commanding officer of the subsidiary troops.

With respect to the route to be taken by the Nizam's troops, although this cannot be completely ascertained until the place of junction with our army be determined, and therefore must be left in a great measure to the discretion of the Commander-in-Chief, exercised in concert with the officers commanding his Highness's division, yet there appears to be no difficulty in fixing some general direction during the earliest stages of the march. Thus, whether the place of junction should hereafter be appointed in the vicinity of Amboor Ryacottah, or Coveriporum, it will be equally convenient that his Highness's troops should proceed by Kurpah. To this point, therefore, it cannot move too soon: and before it can arrive there, the Commander-in-Chief will be able to determine on the best direction for its further progress.

It is of peculiar importance to ascertain the fifth point, or the speediest period at which the junction can be effected, with the utmost accuracy possible.

It being understood that unless the united armies could arrive at Seringapatam by the middle of February, the siege and capture of that place before the setting in of the monsoon would hardly be practicable: to guard against such a disappointment it is absolutely requisite that the army, with its battering train, should not be later in moving from Amboor than the end of January; of course the Nizam's force ought to reach that place (supposing it to be the appointed rendezvous) not later than the middle of that month. For this purpose it is stated to me that his Highness's troops should be in motion by the 5th of December: but as in order to render the junction as secure as possible, a circuitous route from Kurpah to Amboor (probably by Dalmacherry and Chettoor) may be deemed advisable, it is evident that they cannot commence their march too soon.

It is certainly extremely desirable that Azeem-ool-Omrah should put himself at the head of the Nizam's forces; and if no substantial objection should arise to his leaving the person of his Highness, I wish you to urge Azeem-ool-Omrah, by every possible argument, to proceed with the army. It is not, perhaps, of much consequence whether he is accompanied by one of the princes or not; but in this arrangement I see no necessity for your interference. If any solid reason should arise for the minister's remaining with the Nizam, or if he cannot be prevailed on to proceed with the troops, care must be taken to select for the command a person whose zeal for the common cause shall be accompanied by a due share of personal weight and authority. These qualities in the commander of the Nizam's forces are to be sought in preference to military knowledge and experience, which perhaps it would be difficult to find in any considerable degree among the Omrahs of the Court of Hyderabad.

In the case of Azeem-ool-Omrah's proceeding with the Nizam's force, I should think it advisable for you to accompany him, leaving your assistant to attend on his Highness. But in the event of the ministers remaining behind, it will be proper that you should continue at your station, and that Captain Malcolm should accompany the troops, according to the same arrangement under which Lieutenant Stewart was employed in the last war, when assistant to Sir John Kennaway.

Although I fear that the declining state of the Nizam's health, joined to his increasing years, is but too likely to obstruct the measure, yet I cannot help expressing a wish that his Highness may be able, if not immediately, yet early in January, to advance in person to the banks of the Kishna, where his position during the last war, if it no otherwise contributed to the success of the general operations, tended to inculcate the belief of his serious disposition to second them.

With regard to the point remaining to be considered, namely, the regular supply of provisions, it appears to me that no time should be lost in storing as large quantities of grain as possible in Ganjecottah, Sedhout, and all the other forts on the southern frontier of his Highness's dominions in which such supplies may be safely deposited. It is also extremely desirable that the minister should give the most effectual encouragement to the Brinjaries to accompany and follow the army; and I should think you could not better inculcate the great advantages of a liberal arrangement with those people, than by referring him to the result of Lord Cornwallis's proceedings on this subject, of which he was himself an eye-witness. I likewise authorise you to co-operate with Azeem-ool-Omrah in the useful measure of engaging the cordial services of the Brinjaries, by making such advances of cash, on behalf of the Company, as you may judge advisable or necessary for this purpose, not exceeding, however, the sum of 50,000 rupees, and taking sufficient security from them for the repayment of the same within a reasonable time.

As in the event of Tippoo Sooltan's compelling the allies to attack him, by refusing the security proposed to be demanded of him, the immediate siege of his capital will constitute the sole object of their operations; the consequence of this plan must be, that all the supplies for the army to be drawn from the Nizam's country must, for greater security, pass from Kurpah through the Carnatic by the way of Damalcherry, Chittoor, Amboor, &c., or such other routes as may best suit with the circumstances of the moment. It will not be necessary, however, to communicate this arrangement to the Brinjaries, who, when they perceive that it is not our intention to occupy any posts in Tippoo's country on the direct line between Kurpah and Seringapatam, will naturally follow the army by the route just mentioned, as the only one affording them equal security.

The actual state of the Company's troops serving in the Nizam's country, with regard to field equipment of every description, is a subject which demands immediate attention. Whatever deficiencies may exist, no time should be lost in supplying them. You will, therefore, ascertain these immediately, and, as soon as possible, privately advise Lord Clive of them, who will have my instructions to issue the necessary orders for forwarding in due time, to the place of rendezvous of the allied army, whatever articles shall be wanting to complete the equipment of the subsidiary troops for actual service.

Having, in a former part of this letter, supposed Mr. Finglass's corps to form part of the Nizam's contingent, and not having hitherto, in any of my letters to you, touched on the subject of that party, I will now give you my sentiments and instructions respecting it.

On general principles of policy, I am sensible of the danger of admitting the establishment of corps of this description among the country powers, even under the command of British subjects; but the numerous military establishments of French adventurers in the service of the different States of India, suggested the necessity of opposing some counterpoise to their dangerous influence and growing power. Hence arose the introduction of Mr. Finglass into the service of the Nizam, and the subsequent augmentation of his corps. This, however, was a very inadequate security against the danger which existed at Hyderabad, and which could never have been averted by any other means than the complete subversion of the French army in the service of the Nizam.

This object having been happily accomplished, it becomes a question how far it is advisable for this Government to permit or countenance the continuance of Mr. Finglass's corps. Our right, under the treaty lately concluded between the Company and the Nizam, to require the dismission of all Europeans in his Highness's service is unquestionable; but would it be prudent, or politic, or even just, to exercise it in this instance?

It would perhaps be unjust, because the dismission of M. Piron's corps, and the articles of the new treaty under which the restrictions of the former subsidiary troops shall remain in force, joined to those stipulations which limit the use of the Company's troops to cases of important service, have absolutely deprived the Nizam of all means of executing a variety of military duties of an indispensable nature, unless his Highness be allowed to retain Mr. Finglass's corps in his service.

It would be impolitic, first, because it would naturally excite great dissatisfaction in the mind of the Nizam; and, secondly, because it would deprive the common cause, at a very critical period, of a body of troops which, though not to be compared with the Company's, may be capable of rendering considerable service in the event of war.

On the whole, therefore, my opinion is, that it is expedient to encourage and support this corps (Mr. Finglass's), to such an extent as may place it in a condition to act with effect in conjunction with our own troops.

For this purpose I mean to permit Mr. Finglass (on the usual application from the Nizam) to purchase from time to time, at Fort St. George, any quantity of ordnance, ordnance stores, and muskets, which shall appear to you necessary to the efficient equipment of his corps for actual service. But as the opportunities of procuring such articles are precarious, I am also willing that any moderate supply of them which may be required for the use of any division of the corps, actually proceeding as part of the Nizam's contingent to join our army, should be issued at your requisition from the Company's arsenal at Fort St. George; and I shall instruct the Government of that Presidency accordingly. The Government of Fort St. George will, however, be empowered to exercise its discretion with regard to the quantity of the several articles above mentioned, which can at any time be spared with safety from the demands of their own military service; I think it probable, however, that the magazines belonging to the late French corps may be found sufficient to the supply of most of the articles in which Mr. Finglass's corps is now deficient.

But while I consent to extend to this corps the degree of encouragement which I have described, I must particularly enjoin you to use the utmost vigilance for the purpose of preventing the admission of any others than British subjects, not only into commands, but into any rank or station in the corps. You will also take care that such British subjects retain their attachment to their native country, and to its laws and constitution; and that they shall not, under the shelter of their British origin, protect the growth of French influence at the Court of the Nizam.

The sixth article of the late treaty furnishes you with ample means of obtaining the dismission from this corps of any individual whose conduct or principles may render him a just object of suspicion. I conceive, however, that the commanding officer of this party is not likely in any such case to reduce you to the necessity of asserting the right of the Company under the treaty.

It is proper you should be particularly careful so to regulate your occasional intercourse with the corps of Mr. Finglass, as to prevent its exciting any jealousy or dissatisfaction in the mind of the Nizam or his ministers. On this principle it is peculiarly necessary that, except when your opinion or interference shall be expressly desired by his Highness or by Azeem-ool-Oomrah, you should avoid taking part in any discussion which may arise between that corps and the Durbar, whether relating to the pay of the party, to the nature of the duties and services required of them, or to any other point whatever.

I must except, however, from this general instruction, the case of any division of Mr. Finglass's corps which shall happen to compose part of the Nizam's contingent, acting with the Company's army: for it will at all times be incumbent on us to see that due measures are taken by his Highness's ministers for securing the regular payment of whatever troops may form that contingent, whether they shall be those of the Nizam, or the Company's subsidised force; I accordingly desire that you will exert yourself to effect a satisfactory arrangement for this purpose with Azeem-ool-Oomrah.

My anxious desire that Azeem-ool-Oomrah, in person, should accompany the Nizam's contingent, is founded on my opinion that, from his presence a greater degree of security would be derived, not only for the punctual payment of the troops, but for the prompt obedience and efficient co-operation of their commanders.
I am, &c.

(Signed)   MORNINGTON.

No. X.

The Earl of MORNINGTON *to the* RESIDENT *at Hyderabad.*

Fort St. George, 22nd Jan. 1799.

APPENDIX
B.

Sir, — It is of the utmost importance to ascertain the causes which impeded the operations of his Highness's cavalry during the last war, and to consider how these causes can now be removed.

I am informed that for the most part his Highness's cavalry were sufficiently well mounted and armed; and I have never heard that they manifested any peculiar deficiency in point of personal courage. Their unwillingness to engage the. enemy during the last war must, therefore, have arisen from other causes.

During the first campaign of Lord Cornwallis, the commander of the Nizam's cavalry was not zealous in the cause of the allies, and some of the risalahdars were strongly suspected of having been corrupted by the enemy. These circumstances may reasonably be supposed to have contributed, in a great degree, towards their disgraceful inactivity.

At present his Highness's contingent is commanded by a person of very different disposition from Raja Jaiz Wunt; none of the suspected risalahdars are now employed with it, and no reason exists to justify a suspicion of the faith of any of those now attached to it.

Notwithstanding these advantages, certain radical defects remain in the system of his Highness's cavalry which require correction.

The principal of these defects consists in the want of due encouragement to the silahdar, or hired cavalry (of which description the Nizam's contingent of cavalry is, I believe, almost entirely composed), to expose their horses in action. For the horses being the property of individuals, and sometimes constituting the whole fortune of the horseman, no risk will be incurred unless a previous indemnity be provided against the accidents of the field. Engagements to this effect are sometimes formed with silahdar horse by the native powers, but these engagements are frequently violated.

Another defect in the constitution of the silahdar cavalry is, that although a horseman should be disabled for life in action, no provision is made for him; he, therefore, is unwilling to expose his person.

The remedies for these defects are sufficiently obvious. The Nizam ought to engage to pay the proprietor for every horse killed or disabled in action, according to its rated value, and his Highness ought also to make a suitable provision, during life, for such horseman as shall be disabled in actual service.

You will, therefore, take an early opportunity of stating to the Nizam, and to Azeem-ool-Oomrah, the great advantages which would result to his Highness's service from the adoption of regulations of the nature here suggested; and you will endeavour, by every argument in your power, to induce the Minister to pursue the true interests of his sovereign on this occasion.

I am aware that his Highness will not readily adopt the proposed improvements to any useful extent; but if he will only signify his approbation of the plan, and will promise to adopt it, I am disposed (on the strength of such general assurances) to authorise Captain Malcolm, in concert with Meer Allum, to pledge the Company's Government for the faithful performance by his Highness of whatever promises might be made to the horsemen in his name.

Without the guarantee of the Company, it is not to be supposed that any vague assurances from his Highness would produce the desired effect. That guarantee would of course be given with every degree of respect and consideration for his Highness.

It is possible that the whole expense resulting from the proposed measures might ultimately fall on the Company. But the advantages of the arrangement to the Company, as well as to the Nizam, would probably be very considerable, and might be of the most decisive nature in the approaching war.

I am, &c.

(Signed)   MORNINGTON.

No. XI.

The Earl of MORNINGTON *to the* RESIDENT *at Hyderabad.*

Sir,—I have received a letter from Captain White, in which he informs me that 6000 of the Nizam's infantry had halted on the banks of the Kistna, and refused to proceed; and that Meer Allum was doubtful of being able to prevail on them to follow the army.

The deficiency which may be expected to take place in his Highness's contingent in consequence of this event, does not appear to menace evils of so serious a nature as those which may be apprehended from the continuance of a body of disaffected troops in his Highness's dominions, during the absence of our military force.

These troops lately constituted a part of M. Peron's army, and although deprived of their European officers, their discipline is still superior to that of any other corps in the Nizam's service: they are well armed, and have a train of field artillery attached to them. Under all these circumstances, the greatest mischiefs are to be apprehended from their disposition and power. They may either desert in a body to Tippoo Sooltan, who might immediately replace their late officers by others of the same nation, or they may raise the standard of revolt in the heart of his Highness's country. The Nizam and Azeem-ool-Oomrah must, without delay, take any practicable measure for preventing either of these dangers.

My decided opinion is, that these troops ought immediately to be disarmed and disbanded. At the same time I am aware that his Highness may not possess the means, in the absence of the Company's troops, to effect this desirable object. In this case it will be necessary to temporise with the revolted troops, and to endeavour to break them into small parties. They must be withdrawn, without loss of time, from their present station, and on no account be employed to the southward. Their guns

should be separated from them as speedily as it may be practicable to attempt the measure with a prospect of success.

You must call upon the Nizam to supply the existing
deficiency in his contingent, arising from the desertion of these
troops, by a reinforcement of at least 4000 cavalry, who must
be ordered to join Meer Allum, by the route of Budwail and
Dornal pass immediately.

I am, &c.

(Signed)   MORNINGTON.

The Earl of MORNINGTON *to the* RESIDENT *at Hyderabad.*

Fort St. George, 17th May, 1799.

Sir,—Although his Highness the Nizam has unreservedly committed the interests of his Government in the final adjustment
of the concerns of the triple alliance to my charge, yet being
desirous of consulting him in the present important conjuncture
of affairs, as far as is consistent with a prompt and efficacious
arrangement, I desire that you will, without delay, intimate to
his Highness and the Minister my wish to be informed of their
sentiments, not only with respect to the general arrangement
of affairs in Mysore as affecting the combined interests of the
triple alliance, but also with regard to his Highness's particular
views and pretensions. You may assure his Highness of my
entire disposition to meet his wishes to the utmost extent compatible with the general object and interests of the alliance; and
that it is with a view to consult his wishes, as far as may be
practicable, that I now solicit his sentiments and opinion. You
will obtain his Highness's and the Minister's reply as early as
possible, and forward it, in duplicate, to me to Fort St. George,
and to Seringapatam.   I am, &c.

(Signed)   MORNINGTON.

The Earl of MORNINGTON *to the* RESIDENT *at Hyderabad.*

Fort St. George, May 23rd, 1799.

Sir,—I am apprehensive that the extraordinary tide of success which attends us in Mysore may so elate Azeem-ool-Oomrah as to raise the pretensions of his court beyond all bounds of discretion. I rely on you to correct very appearance of such a disposition as well as every symptom of an inclination to hostilities against Scindia or the Peishwa. My wish is that the whole arrangement of our conquests should be left implicitly to the Company's Government, but I should be glad to be furnished with a general outline of the views and pretensions of the Nizam, which his Highness may be assured will form an anxious object of my attention in framing any new distribution of territory or power. I am, &c.

(Signed) MORNINGTON.

The Earl of MORNINGTON *to* Captain J. A. KIRKPATRICK, *Resident at Hyderabad.*

Fort St. George, June 30th, 1799.

Sir,—I now proceed to furnish you with such observations as occur to me to be necessary for your guidance in discussing the several articles of the Treaty of Mysore with the Court of Hyderabad, if, contrary to my hope, any such discussion should arise. In the first place, I wish to state distinctly the fundamental principles on which I have framed the new settlement. I have always been disposed to pay not only every attention to the just pretensions of his Highness the Nizam, but even to exceed the limits of his strict rights in allotting the measure of his participation in the advantages of our late conquests, but I cannot admit the claim of his Highness to an equal partition of all or any of those advantages to be founded on any principles of justice or reason. His Highness cannot avail himself of the Treaty of Paungul to maintain this claim, because the article of that treaty relating to an equal partition of conquests could not be construed to apply to the late war. No other written or verbal engagement existing to support such a claim on the part of his Highness, I have endeavoured to estimate his rights under the alliance by an entirely different, and, in my opinion, more equitable standard. My view has been to distribute the recent acquisitions of revenue between the two states in a due proportion to the efficient share which each has borne in the expense and hazard of the war, as well as to the security which each is likely to derive from the assistance of the other in maintaining their common interests, and in consolidating the basis of the peace.

Although I have assumed this principle as the general foundation of the whole settlement, I am persuaded that a fair review of the details of the Treaty of Mysore will convince any impartial mind that I have made concessions to the Nizam far exceeding the limits of the rule which I had thus prescribed to myself as the just measure of his Highness's rights. It is unnecessary to enter more minutely into this part of the subject; you will find no difficulty in applying these observations to the articles of the treaty.

The preamble of the treaty requires no remark.

The first and second articles leave to the Nizam and to the Company shares of territory, as nearly as is practicable, of equal value, after deducting from each the charges for which they have reciprocally engaged to provide on account of the maintenance of the families of Hyder Alee Khan and Tippoo Sooltan, and although on account of the Jaghire of Meer Cummur-ud-Deen, it may be observed, on the part of the Nizam, that, under the power reserved to the Company in the sixth article, the Company may derive a greater benefit from its share of territory than that which now appears upon the face of the treaty, because the Company, having reserved the power in certain contingencies of diminishing the allowances of the deposed family, is not to be accountable to the Nizam for any such contingent advantage. On the other hand, it is apparent that the Nizam will be entitled to similar advantages with regard to the Jaghire of Cummur-ud-Deen, which his Highness, under his rights of sovereignty over Cummur-ud-Deen, will at any time possess the power of limiting or suspending, although no such power be expressly reserved in the treaty. His Highness also is exempt from the charge of any contingent increase in the expense of maintaining the deposed family, a contingency by no means improbable.

Meer Allum having objected to the operation of the sixth article, I offered on the part of the Company to render annually to the Nizam an account of the expense of maintaining the deposed family, and to divide equally with his Highness any contingent saving within the sum stipulated by the treaty for their annual maintenance, provided his Highness would consent to pay one-half of any eventual excess beyond the stipulated sum. Meer Allum declined this equitable proposal, and agreed to the articles in their present form.

It appears that the Nizam is desirous of retaining a part of Tippoo Sooltan's family within his Highness's territory. The objections to such a plan must be obvious to every friend, not only of the British interests, but of the alliance between his Highness and the Company. The residence of the deposed family in the territory of the Company can never be an object of jealousy to the Nizam. Within his Highness's dominions it might become an object not only of jealousy to the Company, but of serious danger to the stability of the new settlement of Mysore. In addition to this observation, I must also remark that the separation of the different members of the family of Hyder Alee and Tippoo Sooltan would be heavily felt by them as an unnecessary act of severity. It has been my duty to mitigate the rigour of this sudden change of their fortunes, and having been apprised that any separation of the several branches of the families would greatly aggravate the unavoidable pressure of their actual condition, principles of humanity, as well as of policy, forbid me to adopt the plan suggested by Azeem-ool-Oomrah.

The whole of the deposed family will therefore be settled at Vellore, under the care of Lieutenant-Colonel Doveton, and no reasonable expense will be refused by me which can contribute to their comfort or accommodation on a munificent scale, suited to the rank in which they were born.

Before I quit the first and second articles, I think it proper to repeat that a mistake has arisen in enumerating the districts of Coimbatore, retained by the Company, the district of Kanjam having been omitted in the Schedule A.

The necessity of the third article is evident, as without that article Seringapatam would never become an efficient military post in the hands of the allies. I am persuaded that the Nizam will soon feel and acknowledge the security which he is likely to derive from the establishment of a large British force at Seringapatam.

The fourth article contains the basis of an arrangement founded on the strongest principles of justice, humanity, and policy. It does not appear to me necessary to state anything further on this or the fifth article. You will naturally observe that, if the Nizam's claim to an equal partition of territory had been founded in right, and consequently admitted by me, this adjustment, so honourable to the moderation, generosity, and wisdom of the British character, would not have taken place.

I have already remarked the operation of the sixth article, on the interests of the Nizam, its necessity with a view to those of the Company is obvious. The policy of the seventh and eighth articles, I should trust, would not be disputed even by the illiberal, rapacious, and vindictive spirit of which I have perceived so many disgusting symptoms at Hyderabad ever since the fall of Seringapatam.

That the new settlement of Mysore should be rendered as acceptable as possible to all the powers contiguous to the respective boundaries of the allies, is a principle founded on the soundest maxims of prudence, as well as of generosity. The conditions which I have annexed to the provisional cession of territory to the Mahrattas, will, I trust, satisfy the Court of Hyderabad of my sincere disposition to promote the interests of the Nizam by every effort compatible with the laws of my country, and the rules of public faith and justice.

You have already been apprised through my correspondence with Colonel Palmer, of the general outline of the conditions which I propose to require from the Peishwa, as well as of those which the Peishwa has proposed to me; I trust I shall be able, in the course of to-morrow, to forward to Colonel Palmer the draft of a treaty founded on his late communications. The despatch prepared for Colonel Palmer will pass through your hands, and you will communicate its contents to the Nizam, conformably to the stipulations of the treaty of Hyderabad. I desire that you will furnish me and Colonel Palmer, by the speediest conveyance, with such observations as may occur to you relative to the adjustment of affairs between the Peishwa and the Nizam.

The ninth article of the Treaty of Mysore is intended to form the foundation of a connection of the most intimate nature between the Company and the Raja of Mysore; you will inform me whether this arrangement is likely to excite any degree of jealousy in the mind of the Nizam. It is my decided determination not to admit of any relation between the Raja of Mysore and any other power otherwise than through the Company's Government. I am persuaded that in this determination I have made the best practicable arrangement for the interests of the Raja, the Nizam, and the Company. The Nizam will not be a party to the subsidiary treaty with the Raja. I have not yet determined, however, whether a treaty of general guarantee between the three states, to which the Peishwa hereafter may be invited to accede, would not be an advisable measure.

With regard to the two separate articles of the Treaty of Mysore, the nature of the first has already been explained in my observations on the sixth article of the treaty. The second requires some further remarks; it was proposed by Meer Allum as a mode of removing all jealousy from the mind of the Nizam, and of reconciling the Court of Hyderabad to Meer Allum's conduct in signing the treaty without having received powers from his court.

The article appears to me to be perfectly nugatory, unless it be supposed that the Court of Hyderabad possesses sufficient influence with that of Poona to prevent the Peishwa's consent to conditions which might otherwise prove acceptable to him, or unless it be intended insidiously to favour some unreasonable pretensions of the Nizam against the Peishwa. I shall, however, pursue through the whole of the negotiation the course which shall appear to my judgment to lead to the ends of reason and justice, and I will not suffer myself to be diverted from those ends by any intrigues at either court.

It is difficult to express to you the degree of disgust which has been occasioned in my mind by some of the late official documents from Hyderabad. It is evident that Meer Allum, notwithstanding his obligations to the British Government, and personally to myself, has employed every art to create discontent against both, by the tenor of his unfounded complaints, addressed to Azeem-ool-Oomrah, from Seringapatam. I am credibly informed that the cause of Meer Allum's conduct is no other than his disappointment at not having personally shared in the distribution of the spoils of Seringapatam; and I understand that he has the imprudence to proceed so far to hint his right to a share in the prize, equal to that allotted to Lieutenant-General Harris. The rejection of this unreasonable claim was immediately followed by the most marked symptoms of a discontent, which has never since been removed. This is a proceeding unworthy of his character, inconsistent with his professions, and incompatible with his obligations to the British Government; from this moment he will ever be, in my opinion, an object both of suspicion and contempt. The conduct of the Nizam and of Azeem-ool-Oomrah is of a similar character. Nor can I conceive any attempt more despicable in principle, or indiscreet in policy, than that which they have made, to deprive our army and the Nizam's of the just and customary rewards of their gallantry and honourable labours.

I will transmit to you by an early opportunity copies of the orders of Lord Cornwallis, during the last war, respecting the right of the army to property found in places taken by assault.

I will add copies of my late orders on the same subject. You will remark that Lord Cornwallis' opinion proceeds far beyond mine on this subject, although practically our determination has been the same. The plain truth is, that the claims of the army under such circumstances have never been resisted in his Majesty's service, nor do I think they could have been resisted at Seringapatam on any grounds of justice or policy, unless the amount of the captured property had been so enormous, as that its distribution must have affected the discipline of the army. The Nizam's force formed so small a proportion, either in point of number or efficiency, of the whole army, that it would have been the height of injustice to have admitted his Highness's claim to an equal participation of the whole prize, an admission which would have deprived our army of its reasonable advantages, without serving that employed by his Highness. No other principle, therefore, could be adopted but that of allowing his troops to share rateably with ours; excepting always his cavalry, the irregular construction of which rendered such an arrangement impracticable. For his cavalry, therefore, a compromise was made with Meer Allum. Whether Meer Allum defrauded his Highness's infantry of their share of the prize money, and reserved it for his Highness's private use, to the prejudice of those who had so well earned it in the field, is a question which I confess freely it never occurred to me to ask; nor will I degrade the character of the British Government by mixing in such a transaction, although the consequence of my refusal should be the total loss of his Highness's alliance.

When Lieut.-General Harris communicated to me Meer Allum's requisition to be admitted, on the part of the Nizam, to make a valuation of the treasure, I immediately gave my assent to Meer Allum's proposition, with some expressions of surprise, that the Commander-in-Chief should have thought any reference to me necessary. Subsequent information, however, has convinced me that the Commander-in-Chief not only acted with propriety in declining Meer Allum's original proposal, but that he has also been completely justified in suspending the execution of my orders; for it now appears that the Court of

Hyderabad, as well as the whole army, would have construed the concession into a formal recognition of the personal right of the Nizam to one half of the captured property.

I shall close this letter with some general reflections arising out of the recent conduct and language of the Nizam, Azeem-ool-Oomrah, and Musta Keem-ool-Dowlah.

It is with infinite regret that I perceive throughout the whole tenor of the reports of their recent conversations, a spirit extremely dangerous to the stability of our connection with the Court of Hyderabad. The language of Musta Keem-ool-Dowlah is particularly offensive, and as he is nearly connected with Meer Allum, it is not difficult to trace the source of his insolence and boldness in the disappointed avarice of his patron and kinsman; it appears, however, that the language which he used had been previously concerted with Azeem-ool-Oomrah, a circumstance which renders it the more deserving of animadversion. I desire that you will take an early opportunity of bringing Musta Keem-ool-Dowlah to a distinct explanation of his statement of the powers which the Nizam had vested in me. That statement is, if possible, as false and absurd as it is disrespectful to the supreme power of the British Government vested in my hands. His Highness the Nizam, since the fall of Seringapatam, on two distinct occasions declared, in the most positive terms, that he would not in any degree interfere to restrain those plenary powers which he had requested me to exercise with respect to all his interests in the conquest of Mysore. I desire that you will take an early opportunity of reprimanding Musta Keem-ool-Dowlah, in the most public and pointed manner, for the disrespectful terms in which he has spoken of the British Government, and that you will deprive him of his pension if you should deem it necessary to proceed to such an act of severity; at the same time, you will take an opportunity of signifying to the minister the extreme concern with which I have learnt that he has suffered any of his servants to utter with impunity expressions so unwarrantable. It may not be useless to embrace this occasion of awakening Azeem-ool-Oomrah to a just sense of the extensive advantages which have been acquired by the Nizam's Government, within the last year, by means of his connection with the British power. Within that short space of time the Nizam has been delivered from the violence and arrogance of an armed party in the centre of his dominions, which menaced the independence, if not the existence, of his throne. His enemies have been deterred by the intervention of the British power from prosecuting against his Highness's kingdom designs which he possessed no means of resisting, and which probably would have terminated in his destruction. His most formidable enemy has been utterly destroyed, with scarcely any expense to his Highness's treasury; and in place of that enemy has been substituted a power, connected with him by all the ties of interest and public faith, and affording perfect security to his dominions in that quarter, formerly the most vulnerable. He has acquired a large accession of territory and revenue, as well as of reputation and glory, by the conduct of his troops under the direction of British officers during the war.

Finally, from a weak, decaying, and despised state, he has recovered substantial strength, secured the means of cultivating and extending his resources, with power and honour at home and abroad, and resumed a respectable posture among the princes of India. These have been the consequences of his connection with the British power, acquired without effort or hazard on his part.

It is for his Highness and Azeem-ool-Oomrah to determine whether these benefits are all counterbalanced by our adherence to the invariable practice of our military service, and by our justice to the merits of that army which has secured his tranquillity as well as ours. Perhaps it may occur, as a prudential consideration, whether his Highness's disappointment at not being permitted to lay hands on rewards appropriated by the custom of the British Government to encourage the zeal of those who risk their lives in the public cause, should be so far indulged as to hazard any interruption of that friendship from which he has derived advantages so solid, substantial, and honourable.

The Treaty of Mysore appears to me to be highly favourable to his Highness's interests. If, however, he should object to the basis and fundamental principles of it, he will not excite an emotion of alarm or uneasiness in my mind. I am perfectly prepared to carry the new settlement into effect by the aid of British arms alone; and his Highness must be aware of the advantages which he will open to the Court of Poona if he should compel me to resort to such extreme measures. But if his Highness should object merely to partial details or particular stipulations of the treaty, I trust he will not hesitate to ratify it, relying upon me to remove all such objectionable parts, unless they should appear, upon examination, either to be necessarily connected with the whole arrangement, or counterbalanced by advantages which had escaped his Highness's observation.

I am, &c.

MORNINGTON.

The Earl of MORNINGTON to Captain J. A. KIRKPATRICK, Resident at Hyderabad.

Fort William, 6th November, 1799.

Sir,—The general state of the Nizam's health for some time past, and the communications which I have lately received from. you on that subject, joined to the great changes recently produced in the political state of India by our conquest of Mysore, have suggested to me the necessity of revising the principles which regulated my instructions to you of the 8th July, 1798, with regard to the conduct proper to be pursued by the Company's Government in the event of his Highness's death. If we neglect to interfere in settling the succession upon the death of the Nizam, the Mahrattas will not fail to avail themselves of our inactivity, and will establish a preponderant, if not an exclusive influence at the Court of Hyderabad.

The establishment of the exclusive influence of the Mahrattas at Hyderabad would be equivalent in its operation on our interests to the absolute subjugation of the Deccan by the arms of

the Mahratta power; and it should be no less our care to prevent the Mahrattas from governing the territory of the Nizam
in the name of a prince elevated to the musnud by their interference, than to check the progress of any hostile attempt which
they might make to extend their dominions at the expense of
the Court of Hyderabad. It is, therefore, now as necessary
that the succession to the Soobahship of the Deccan should be
settled by the Company's authority as it was in July 1798.

In every view which I am enabled to take of this question,
it continues to appear to me desirable that we should raise
Secunder Jah to the musnud in preference to any of his brothers.
The right of primogeniture is in his favour; his connections are
among those persons best affected towards our interest; he is
the only son of the Nizam who has ever maintained any authorised intercourse with us, or who has ever manifested any desire
to cultivate our friendship. Alee Jah was disposed to connect
his views with those of Tippoo Sooltan. Feridoon Jah has
carried on intrigues in the same quarter; and Jehander Jah has
been suspected of endeavouring to engage the Mahrattas to take
him under their protection.

In favouring the pretensions of Secunder Jah, we must not
overlook what is requisite to the improvement of our connection
with the Court of Hyderabad, and to the establishment of that
connection on a basis of the most solid advantage and of the
most permanent security.

No obligation of treaty binds us to take part in any contested
succession, arising either from the total silence of the Nizam
respecting his intended successor, or from a disputable declaration of his Highness's intention on the subject. Even in the
case of an unequivocal nomination of a successor by his Highness, we should not be bound by the treaty of September 1798,
or by any other obligation, to support that successor against
any rival whose cause might be espoused by the Mahrattas.
Whatever secret or political motives, therefore, may exist to
induce us either to interpose our influence in the settlement of
the succession, or to prefer the pretensions of Secunder Jah, our
faith is not pledged to raise that prince to the musnud, or un-

conditionally to support him upon it against any effort of the Mahrattas, or of any other power, in favour of another candidate.

Having stated the general principles which should govern our conduct in the conjunction under contemplation, I shall proceed to furnish you with an outline of the particular conditions on which I am willing to support the succession of Secunder Jah against all competition.

These conditions are as follows:—

1. The treaty of September 1798 shall be confirmed by Secunder Jah, for himself and his heirs, in all points not expressly altered by the new treaty.

2. The subsidiary force shall be augmented to four regiments of native infantry, two regiments of native cavalry, and three companies of artillery, including a proportionable increase of gun-lascars.

3. The additional force shall be subsidised at the same rate as that now serving in the Nizam's dominions.

4. A territory, to be selected by the Company, producing a net revenue at least adequate to the payment of the whole subsidy (under the treaty of 1798 as well as under the new engagement), shall be assigned to the sole and absolute management of the Company: the Company to account to the reigning prince for any surplus of revenue exceeding the amount of the subsidy which may be realised from the said territory under their management.

5. The peshcush at present payable by the Company to the Nizam on account of the Northern Circars shall be remitted for ever.

6. If the number of troops stipulated to be subsidised should at any time appear to be inadequate to the purpose of securing Secunder Jah on the musnud against the attempts of any competition, whether supported or not by the Mahrattas or by any other power, the Company will augment the subsidised force to such an extent as the Company may judge necessary; and Secunder Jah shall in that case defray the expense of such temporary addition of force.

7. 'All rahdary duties on goods passing to and from the respective territories of the contracting parties shall be abolished. No articles of merchandise shall pay duty more than once, and a proper tariff shall be established for the regulation of the single duties to be so levied; and a treaty of commerce shall be concluded between the two States, on just and equitable principles of reciprocal interest and common benefit.

8. Secunder Jah shall engage to pay at all times the utmost attention to such advice as the Company's Government shall occasionally judge it necessary to offer to him, with a view to any objects connected with the advancement of his interests, the happiness of his people, and the mutual welfare of both states.

Such is the outline of the terms upon which I propose to support and maintain the succession of Secunder Jah, whether he should obtain the previous nomination of his father, or not; or even if it should be pretended that his Highness had declared in favour of some other of his sons. You will prepare, without delay, an instrument in the Persian language, in conformity to the foregoing outline, in order that Secunder Jah (at the moment of his father's death, or whenever that event shall appear to approach) may be apprised of the terms on which we are ready to support his cause, and may be enabled by immediately executing a formal instrument, to accede to my propositions in a regular manner.

I think it necessary to permit you either totally to suppress or to modify the 8th article according to your discretion; apprising you, however, that I consider it be of great importance to obtain such an ascendancy over the councils of the Nizam as is described in that article.

Secunder Jah must not be allowed to procrastinate his determination. If at the end of a stated and short period of time he should not determine to accept the proffered treaty, you will proceed, in concert with Azeem-ool-Oomrah and Meer Allum, to place one of the younger sons of the Nizam on the musnud; previously stipulating that the prince succeeding to the musnud shall fulfil all the conditions of the treaty proposed to Secunder Jah.

I am aware that the objects proposed might be obtained from Secunder Jah with less difficulty previously to the death of the Nizam, and that it would on that account be desirable that a negotiation should be opened immediately with Secunder Jah. But many objections occur to deter me from such a step. The attempt if it should transpire (either by accident or design) would probably lead to mischievous consequences. I am therefore of opinion that no such attempt should be hazarded until the Nizam shall be at the point of death.

It is manifest that our power of settling the succession in the manner described, and of obtaining the advantages which I have enumerated, will depend in an eminent degree, if not absolutely, on the local position of the subsidiary force at the time of his Highness's death. It is, therefore, of the last importance that the force should not only be kept together, but stationed as near as possible to the residence of the Nizam; and I accordingly direct you to adopt every practicable means of accomplishing these most desirable and essential objects without delay.

I am, &c.

MORNINGTON.

No. XII.

The Marquess WELLESLEY *to the* RESIDENT *at Hyderabad.*

Fort William, 15th June, 1800.

Sir,—I have received your despatch, No. 79, dated the 20th ultimo, transmitting to me the treaty executed on the same day by his Highness the Nizam, and by you. I have also received your letters, numbered and dated, as noted in the margin.

The Persian translator regularly laid before me translations of the several reports (dated and noted in the margin) which you had received from the moonshee, Azeez Oollah, of his conferences with Azeem-ool-Oomrah during the course of the negotiation.

You have assigned the necessity of despatch to justify this mode of communicating to me the progress of the treaty. Admitting such a mode of communication to have been the most expeditious, it has produced considerable inconvenience by leaving me in ignorance and doubt with respect to various important points of the negotiation. Your observations and explanations, transmitted in the usual manner, would have enabled me to form a more accurate judgment of the real temper of the Court of Hyderabad, with regard to the present treaty, than can be founded on the unconnected, incomplete, and unexplained materials now before me.

Defective as those materials are, they are sufficient to prove that you have not stated to the Court of Hyderabad, with adequate force, the great advantages which his Highness the Nizam would derive from the proposed alliance; and that you have conceded to Azeem-ool-Oomrah with more facility than was prudent, a point which has long and justly constituted the object of his most anxious desire and solicitation.

Being fully apprised of the importance justly attached by the Court of Hyderabad to a general defensive alliance with the Company, against all enemies, I had foreseen the earnestness of the Nizam to obtain such an engagement; and accordingly I had authorised you eventually to yield to his Highness's wishes. But you were not empowered to concede this important benefit unconditionally, or without obtaining a just equivalent. You were empowered to concede it if the concession should appear likely to secure in return the consent of his Highness to the whole, or to any of those articles which, under the project of a limited guarantee, I had authorised you to suspend.

But the treaty which you have concluded concedes to his Highness the Nizam the full benefit of the general guarantee without securing to the Company any of those advantages (the augmentation of the subsidiary force excepted), the whole of which I had declared necessary to constitute a reasonable equivalent for a limited defensive engagement.

It appears by the conferences between Azeem-ool-Oomrah and moonshee Azeez Oollah, that the Court of Hyderabad sincerely intends to commute the subsidy for a territorial grant to the Company; and the territory to be ceded to the Company is generally described in the fifth article of the treaty. But the fourth article of the treaty expressly reserves to the Nizam the option of discharging the subsidy either from his treasury, or by an assignment of territory, according to his Highness's pleasure. And in your letter of the 26th of May, you admit that the court of Hyderabad actually understands the concluding clause of the fourth article to empower the Nizam to exercise this option whenever his Highness shall think proper. Under such an engagement, if the ratifications of the treaty had been exchanged, his Highness would be at liberty to declare his determination to discharge the subsidy regularly in money; and the territorial grant might be at once avoided. His Highness, under the indefinite terms of the fourth and fifth articles, would also possess full power to modify the grant of territory by any qualifications or conditions which he might prescribe, either with respect to its duration, to the nature or extent of the authority to be exercised by the Company within the assigned districts, or to any other point affecting the stability or efficiency of the assignment.

The proposition for the territorial grant originated with Azeem-ool-Oomrah, and was received by you with judicious reserve and caution. The manner in which this proposition was introduced by the minister, as well as the actual state of the countries intended to be assigned, induce me to believe the Court of Hyderabad to be sincerely disposed, and even secretly anxious for a commutation of the subsidy. But my conjecture may be erroneous; and in a matter of such importance nothing should be left to conjecture, or to the precarious will of the Court of Hyderabad. If the Nizam, upon the ratification of the treaty, should declare his resolution to discharge the subsidy in money, and should refuse to cede the countries to be assigned, in the complete and absolute manner indispensably necessary to their proper arrangement, the Company would stand pledged to the general guarantee without having acquired any equivalent benefit or compensation.

It is evident, therefore, that, by this treaty, the Court of Hyderabad would secure all its objects, while the situation of the Company would be rather injured than improved. For, if it be admitted that the augmentation of the subsidiary force would add in some degree to our political consideration in the Deccan, as the additional troops furnished by the British Government would require to be replaced by new levies, the arrangement would be productive of no pecuniary relief or advantage to the Company; and the security for the regular discharge of the subsidy would become more precarious in proportion to the increased amount of the subsidiary payments. The treasury of his Highness would be subjected to increased embarrassment; or, if territory should be assigned, the cession might be burdened by conditions absolutely precluding such a system of management as must be adopted to render the assigned revenues equal to the maintenance of the troops. Any expression in the grant calculated to raise a doubt of its permanence, or to limit the power of the Company's internal government of the countries, or to favour the Nizam's right of resumption, would evidently prevent us from concluding any settlement worthy of our character, or advantageous to our interests.

In paragraph four of your despatch of the 26th of May, you plainly admit that the Court of Hyderabad understands the fourth and fifth articles to have secured to the Nizam an arbitrary right of resuming the districts subsequently to the intended assignment; and you endeavour to remove this insurmountable objection to these articles by alleging your construction of their exposition to be different from that maintained by the Nizam and his ministers. It is painful to me to be compelled to remark that your argument in this paragraph is founded on principles incompatible with the maintenance of public faith, and exploded by the wisdom, justice, and integrity of the law of nations. To introduce ambiguous phrases into formal instruments designed to constitute the basis of public obligations between two great States, is a practice repugnant to the policy, honour, and dignity of the British nation. The perspicuity of our expressions in all acts of obligation upon our national faith should be as manifest as the superiority of our power. If it were possible for me to afford my countenance to a contrary system, common discretion would preclude me from such a course in the present case, when you distinctly avow that the ambiguous phrases on which you propose to rest the future claim of the British Government against its ally, are at this moment, previously to the ratification of the treaty, construed by that ally in a sense directly contrary to that which you desire to maintain. Your further arguments on the article under consideration serve only to prove that the Nizam might be embarrassed in the exercise of the right which he intended to reserve to himself. If your reasoning on this part of the question·be admitted, the result would be not an amicable, firm alliance, founded on clear, distinct, and indisputable principles, but an ill-defined state of perpetual jealousy, controversy, and animosity of doubtful claims, and of incompatible rights.

When I received Azeem-ool-Oomrah's draft of a treaty, it was my intention to have examined separately each article of that extravagant project. I have already expressed my animadversions on several of his propositions; I shall now consider such principles only of that project as have been adopted with or without modification in your treaty, upon the several articles of which I now proceed to state my ideas.

The general tenor of the preamble to the treaty received from you is perfectly conformable to my views ; the terms of it appear susceptible of improvement. A draft of the preamble, which I should prefer, accompanies this letter in English and Persian.

Article 1. — The first article requires no remark.

Article 2. — This article is principally objectionable on account of its unqualified spirit of hostility. If the contracting parties should have just grounds to apprehend an attack on their territories, or on those of their allies and dependants, it would be reasonable and necessary that they should prepare to repel it. But such preparations are not to be occasioned by every trivial dispute on the borders, or by every desultory, and perhaps unauthorised, depredation of armies, whose licentiousness and rapacity are the necessary consequences of defective discipline and irregular pay. Still less would it be either prudent or justifiable to resort to arms whenever (according to the words of the treaty) any act shall be committed incompatible with friendship and good understanding. In your letter No. 80 you have anticipated this objection, and endeavoured to diminish its force.

It is the essence of a defensive alliance that a sincere desire to avoid an appeal to arms should constitute its most prominent feature. But this article is entirely silent with respect to the propriety of employing any endeavour to adjust subsisting differences by measures of amicable explanation and discussion. From the first mention of aggression, the article proceeds directly to stipulate for punishment and war.

Article 3.—No material objection exists to the expression, and none to the principle of this article.

Articles 4 and 5.—These articles must be considered together.

It appears by your letter No. 80, that the amount of subsidy fixed for the cavalry belonging to the subsidiary force is inadequate to the expense of those troops; it is not stated how this deficiency was occasioned; but I cannot suppose his Highness the Nizam to be disposed to avail himself of any error of calculation which subjects the Company to pecuniary loss. In adjusting the amount of the general subsidy, you might, therefore, have corrected any error of account which had occurred in the original settlement. This point will be of no consequence, under the arrangement which I mean to propose for the full and permanent satisfaction of the Company's claims on account of subsidy.

The further discussion of this point will be unnecessary in the event of the Nizam's acquiescence in my proposed arrangement. But the considerations here suggested, as well as those arising from the insufficiency of the cavalry subsidy, constitute powerful arguments, and may be advantageously urged in support of the main article of that arrangement, by which I have stipulated for the absolute cession in perpetuity of the whole of his Highness's acquisitions from Mysore in the two last wars, adding some modifications with relation to exchanges of territory for the convenience of the respective frontiers of the two States.

The revenues of the countries acquired by the Nizam, under the Treaty of 1792, are acknowledged to be greatly injured, and I have no satisfactory grounds for believing that those of the districts acquired by his Highness under the Treaty of Mysore are now equal to the amount stated in the schedules of that treaty. It appears to be highly probable that the resources of the countries in question have materially declined since those countries came into the possession of his Highness. They have been ravaged by various insurgents, and it is to be feared that they have been managed on principles which must impair their future prosperity, whatever immediate advantage may have been extracted from those unhappy districts by their rapacious governors and managers.

Article 6.—Requires no remark.

Articles 7 and 8.—These articles require to be considered together. Notwithstanding the observations stated in your letter, No. 80, these articles require alteration.

The specification of the force to be furnished by the Nizam at the commencement of hostilities, for the purpose of immediate operations with the Company's subsidiary troops, is extremely proper and necessary; but the terms of the 7th article imply that this specification is to define the full extent of the Nizam's exertions, in point of force, during the whole course of the supposed hostilities, with the single qualification stated in the 8th article. The 7th article is objectionable in this respect. The specification of the local limits in the 7th article, within which his Highness shall be bound to co-operate against the common enemy, is not expressed with sufficient accuracy.

These articles proceed on the presumption that the Company is as likely as the Nizam to be attacked by an enemy; but this supposition is manifestly contrary to reason and probability.

The Nizam, in every view, is more exposed to hostile aggression from various quarters, as well as less able to repel it, than the Company. The eventual exertions of the Nizam against the common enemy should not in any case be limited, either with respect to the amount of troops, or to the theatre of the war. A fair view of the nature and objects of the proposed alliance must demonstrate the justice and reason of requiring that the Nizam, in every case of war, should employ his utmost efforts against the enemy. The Company cannot in policy, and will not in practice, contract the scale of their operations in the event of hostilities, whether directed against their own territories, or against those of the Nizam. This limitation of the number of troops to be employed might be reasonable, if the Nizam's interest, in the issue of any supposed contest, could be deemed remote, or temporary, or doubtful. But no contest can occur in which the Company shall be deeply engaged, without involving the existence of the Nizam's kingdom; the probability is, that, in every case, his Highness would be the first object of attack.

For these reasons, while I consider it to be proper to specify the number and description of his Highness's troops which shall be furnished immediately at the commencement of war, to act in concert with the subsidiary force, I deem it to be necessary that his Highness should also be bound, in every case of hostility, to employ his utmost efforts (if required by the nature of the war), against the common enemy.

It may not be useless to observe, in this place, that, even if the seat of war should be on the other side (as the treaty expresses it), or to the northward of the Nerbudda, it is not probable that any junction of the Nizam's forces with those of the Company in Hindoosthan proper, would ever be expedient or requisite. In such a case, a powerful diversion by his Highness, which would not lead his troops beyond the Nerbudda, would, perhaps, be the most useful operation in which they could be employed.

Article 9.—This article merits my entire approbation; it requires, however, a slight alteration in the expression. You have rendered a considerable service to the Company's interests in India in establishing, by treaty, a right to the use of the Brinjarries of the Deccan in time of war.

Article 10.—This article is likewise highly satisfactory to me. It is, however, necessary to observe (and it may be proper to apprize the Nizam and Azeem-ool-Oomrah), that I consider the operation of this article to prohibit any correspondence with any of the dependants of the Honourable Company, excepting with the knowledge and consent of the British Government. The intercourse at present maintained by the Court of Hyderabad with the Raja of Travancore, the Nabob of Arcot, and other dependants of the Company, would necessarily cease from the period when this article shall take effect. But whatever may be the issue of the depending negotiation, I think it proper to direct you to insist on the immediate discontinuance of the correspondence occasionally maintained between his Highness the Nizam and the allies or dependants of the Company described in this paragraph.

Article 11.—I consider this article to be of the greatest value and importance, it certainly counteracts in a considerable degree many of the objectionable parts of the treaty. It does not, however, remove the objections which apply to the 4th and 5th articles.

Articles 12 and 13.—The provisions of these articles are properly of a secret nature, and ought to have constituted separate articles. It would have been sufficient, in the body of the treaty, if the contracting parties had declared their disposition to admit the Peishwa and Ragojee Bhonslah to the benefits of the alliance, on such conditions as might hereafter be mutually concerted.

Article 14.—This article requires no remark.

On the separate articles of the treaty I must generally remark, that you have not discussed them with Azeem-ool-Oomrah in a manner suitable to their great importance, nor have you availed yourself of a proper extent of the valuable concessions which they convey to the Nizam.

Article 1.—The engagement comprehended in this article relative to the zumeendars of Shorepoor and Gwulwal, and to the Nabob of Kurnool, is rendered extremely delicate by the tributary relation of those chieftains to the Mahrattas' government, as well as to the Nizam; on this account we have hitherto uniformly refused to permit the Company's troops to assist the Nizam in coercing those chieftains. The proposed defensive alliance with the Nizam does not require our unconditional departure from this principle. At the period of negotiating the Treaty of Hyderabad, Azeem-ool-Oomrah laboured with equal assiduity to accomplish an object so important to the interest of his sovereign. At that time I refused the concession, not because I saw any considerable objection to its principle, but because it was of too much importance to be granted gratuitously to his Highness, and because I wished to reserve so great a favour for an occasion when I might be able to derive from it a proper return of advantage to the Company. This occasion is now arrived, and it is reasonable to require a return correspondent with the magnitude of the object.

I entirely approve the clause introduced into this article, by which the British Government is authorised to investigate and to determine the merits of all disputes arising between the Court of Hyderabad and the tributaries in question.

Article 2.—Nothing can be more repugnant to the true spirit of a defensive alliance than the terms of this article; they also indicate a distrust of the justice and honour of the Company's Government, which ought to have been repelled in the first instance.

I entertain no views of conquest upon the territories of Dowlut Rao Scindia, or of any other native power of India; I cannot, therefore, consent to a formal arrangement for the division of spoils which I have no wish to acquire. If Dowlut Rao Scindia, or any other power, after the conclusion of the defensive engagements between the Company and the Nizam, should be guilty of any unprovoked aggression against either party, and war should appear inevitable, in concerting the operations to be undertaken against the aggressor, the allied States may proceed with propriety to adjust the division of such conquests as might appear attainable during the progress of hostilities, and convenient to be retained at the conclusion of peace.

It is evident from the 11th article of Azeem-ool-Oomrah's project, that no rational principles were consulted by him in the plan of partition which he had imagined. It may, therefore, be proper plainly to apprize Azeem-ool-Oomrah, if he should appear dissatisfied with my modification of this article, that I can never consent to regulate the division of our eventual conquests or acquisitions by any other standard than the actual share of expense and exertions in military operations which each contracting party shall have contributed towards such conquests or acquisitions.

Article 3.—The stipulations of this article belong properly to a separate and secret engagement. But it does not appear necessary that the Company and the Nizam should concert, by any formal previous instrument, the conditions on which they will admit the Peishwa and the Raja of Berar to the benefits of the proposed defensive alliance. My mind, however, being satisfied with respect to the general terms on which it would be expedient to admit those powers to the alliance, I am not unwilling to gratify the Nizam by recognising the specific terms of the eventual admission of the Peishwa and the Raja of Berar to the proposed treaty in the form desired by his Highness.

The review which I have taken of the several articles of the treaty in question, must have convinced you that I cannot ratify it without departing from many leading principles of the policy, interest, and reputation of the British Government. The copy of the treaty transmitted to me is accordingly returned to you in order that it may be regularly cancelled, together with the counterpart which you have delivered to his Highness.

Notwithstanding my determination not to ratify this treaty, the discussions which it has produced, and even your conclusion of it, under all the circumstances of the case, have contributed to lay the foundation of extensive improvements in our connection with the Court of Hyderabad. In the progress of the negotiation, many important points have been gained for the Company, many inveterate prejudices injurious to our interests in the Deccan have either been absolutely destroyed or considerably weakened, and the whole scope of the extravagant and absurd policy of Azeem-ool-Oomrah and of his court has been disclosed. In this view of the subject, I consider you to have rendered essential service to the British interests at the Court of the Nizam; and although in this despatch I have animadverted on some of the principles which you have stated, as well as on some passages in the management of the negotiation, I am happy to be able to express my general approbation of your conduct in this important transaction. The animadversions contained in this despatch are not intended to operate as a censure on your proceedings, but to furnish you and your successors in the Residency at the Court of the Nizam, with rules for your guidance on any similar occasion.

My anxiety to conclude a general defensive alliance with the Nizam, on reasonable conditions, continues unabated; and I now transmit to you in English and Persian the draft of such a treaty with his Highness as you are at liberty to execute immediately on the part of the Company.

I entertain a sanguine expectation that the observations which I have made on the treaty concluded by you will enable you to reconcile the Court of Hyderabad to my rejection of that treaty. I am equally confident that the explanations and remarks with which I shall now accompany the treaty herewith transmitted to you, will afford you the means of convincing the Nizam and Azeem-ool-Oomrah that the true interests of his Highness require their immediate acceptance of this engagement.

In the new treaty a very material object of the Court of Hyderabad is more distinctly and more effectually secured than in the treaty already executed by the Nizam. A long period of time must elapse before the territory which I require as a security for the subsidiary payments can become equal to their discharge; it is even doubtful whether the produce of the countries required will ever exceed, in any considerable degree, the amount of the subsidy. If the net revenues of the districts specified in the new treaty should hereafter exceed the charges of the subsidiary force, or if the present nominal revenue of those districts (a revenue which, under the management of his Highness's officers, never has been realised, and under the same management never can be rendered more productive) should be realised under a more wise and prudent system, enforced by the abilities, experience, and integrity of the Company's officers, it would be reasonable that the increased resources of those countries, now verging to ruin, should be turned to the advantage of that power under whose happy auspices the improvement had been carried into effect. The augmented revenue might justly be claimed by the Company on various grounds.

1st. Because the Company must suffer immediate pecuniary loss and embarrassment by the commutation of the subsidy in the actual declining condition of the districts to be ceded.

2nd. Because the expenses incident to the Company's system of management far exceed those incurred by the Nizam's administration, consequently the probable amount of the surplus which may be realised by the Company is not to be estimated by the standard of charges usually authorised by his Highness's government.

3rd. Because an acknowledgment is due to the Company for the inestimable advantages of protection and security acquired by the Nizam under the general guarantee. In this respect the benefits of the treaty cannot be deemed reciprocal. The Nizam's present hazard far exceeds that of the Company; and even in the event of an attack upon our possessions his Highness could not assist us with means of defence bearing any proportion to those with which we should furnish him in a similar exigency.

4th. Because in the event of an attack being made on the Nizam the expenses of the Company, over and above those of maintaining the subsidiary force, would far exceed any charge which could fall upon his Highness in the event of any attack being made on the Company's dominions.

5th. Because this treaty grants to the Nizam, without any specified equivalent, the new and extraordinary benefit of the

Company's aid in repressing the refractory spirit. of such tributaries and dependants as owe a mixed allegiance to him and to the Mahrattas. In this view it may justly be expected that the resources of the territories retained in his Highness's hands may be improved to an amount proportioned to any excess in the produce of the countries to be ceded to the Company.

But whatever view may be taken of this subject by the Court of Hyderabad, it is my determination not to grant the Nizam the complete protection and support which he solicits on any conditions less advantageous to the Company than those comprehended in the new treaty. I accordingly direct you not to admit any alteration in that treaty which shall affect any of its principles; mere verbal alterations you are at liberty to receive.

You will not press the Nizam to accept this new treaty with any appearance of solicitude or earnestness. You will confine yourself to a distinct explanation of the reasons which have compelled me to refuse my ratification of your treaty, and to such an illustration of the articles of the new engagement as this despatch will enable you to furnish. You will then leave the whole subject to the calm and deliberate decision of the Nizam.

In the course of the late negotiation for the purpose of undervaluing the separate and limited guarantee against Scindia, Azeem-ool-Oomrah affected to consider the Company to be already engaged to protect the Nizam against any attack from Scindia, because during the course of the late war I had declared my determination to support his Highness against such an attack. The weakness of this argument ought to have been instantly and plainly exposed, for which purpose a distinct statement of facts would have been sufficient. With a similar view of depreciating the value of a guarantee against the Mahratta empire, Azeem-ool-Oomrah may affect to suppose me to be at present prepared to force the arbitration of the British Government upon the Peishwa. Any such insinuations or errors on the part of the Court of Hyderabad must be repelled or corrected as being equally at variance with the true intent and meaning of the Treaty of Hyderabad, and detrimental to the

favourable issue of the present negotiation. The Court of
Hyderabad must be sensible of the powerful advantage which
it would derive from the general guarantee; but it is absolutely necessary to convince Azeem-ool-Oomrah and his Highness
that I am equally well apprized of its great importance and
value to the Nizam; that I know the precise nature and extent
of our obligation under subsisting treaties to interpose between
his Highness and his enemies; that I will not suffer that obligation to be stretched beyond its just extent; and that I will
not wantonly sacrifice the equivalent due to the Company in
return for the new and important concession of the general
guarantee.

I now proceed to furnish you with such observations on the
different articles of the new treaty as appear to be necessary.

Title and Preamble.—The alterations which I have made in
the title and preamble of your treaty are so inconsiderable as to
require no observation.

Article 1.—This article agrees in substance with your first
article, but it contains the important addition which declares
the friends and enemies of either party to be the friends and
enemies of both. This declaration is contained in a subsequent article of your treaty, but it is not quite so distinctly
expressed nor inserted in its proper place.

Article 2.—This article is substantially the same as the
second article of your treaty. The Nizam, in effect, acquires
by this article all that he would gain by your treaty. The observations contained in the fifteenth paragraph of this despatch
will sufficiently explain to you the necessity of moderating the
hostile tenor of your second article.

Article 3.—This article requires no remark.

Article 4 requires no remark.

Article 5.—No other effectual or satisfactory security than an
assignment of territory can be given by the Nizam for the
regular payment of the subsidy. The present resources of his
country cannot be expected to improve without an entire change
in the system of his Highness's government. Of such a change
no prospect appears. The difficulty experienced in obtaining a

punctual discharge of the existing subsidy will be greatly increased by an augmentation of the subsidiary force, and the risk of failure in the funds necessary to the punctual payment, and consequently to the discipline of the troops, would also be proportionately aggravated.

I have always desired that the subsidy should be secured by a territorial assignment, although the punctuality with which the Court of Hyderabad has hitherto discharged the subsidiary payments has precluded any ground of serious complaint, and any demand from the Company's Government of the security stipulated by the Treaty of Hyderabad. I am of opinion that until the pecuniary payments shall be actually commuted for territory the punctual realisation of the subsidy must ever be extremely precarious.

This consideration involves the security of an important branch of our resources, as well as the continuance of that harmony now subsisting between the British Government and the Nizam. No event could produce discussions of a more invidious nature at the Court of Hyderabad than a failure in the regular payment of our subsidiary troops. These apprehensions are so deeply impressed on my mind, that if all prospect of the proposed general defensive alliance were closed I should be disposed to accept even an inadequate territory in exchange for the subsidy, rather than leave that resource to depend on the defective government of the Nizam, and on the fluctuating state of his Highness's finances. Adverting, however, to the great and positive benefits presented to the Nizam by the proposed treaty, and to the increase of expense which it must necessarily bring upon the Company, the British Government is entitled to require such an equivalent as shall not only preclude any pecuniary loss on account of subsidy, but in some degree defray the extraordinary charges of defending his Highness's country against all enemies.

It may be reasonably apprehended, on a just consideration of the nominal value of the districts required by this article, of the evil government under which they have so long suffered, and of the refractory spirit prevailing in a great proportion of those countries, that their actual produce, deducting all charges of management, will, for a long tract of time, prove unequal to the discharge of the subsidy; and until the net receipts from the country shall be sufficient.for the payment of the troops, the Company must provide the necessary funds for this purpose, —a circumstance which cannot fail to subject their Government to considerable temporary inconvenience.

The fifth article suggests no further observations which have not been anticipated in preceding paragraphs of this despatch.

It is unnecessary to state the obvious objections which exist to the extension of our frontier beyond the Toombuddra in the direction of Kopul, Gugundher, &c. No reasonable objection can be made by the Nizam to the exchanges stipulated by this article. It is, however, necessary in this place to apprize you of the full extent of my views in this proposition.

If we should acquire the territory specified in the fifth article, our line of frontier and our barrier against any sudden incursions of hostile cavalry in that quarter will require that all the country situated to the southward of the Toombuddra and of Krishna should be annexed to the Company's possessions. This cession would include, besides Kurnool, the districts of Adonee and Ghazipore or Nundicud. At present I am ignorant of the value of these districts, and consequently of the proportion which it bears to the revenues of the countries to the north-ward of the Toombuddra. The possession of the whole line of country to the southward of the Krishna and Toombuddra is so essential to the security and compact form of our general frontier that although the districts to the northward should be found more productive than those to the southward of the rivers, I should be willing to cede the former for Adonee and Ghazipore.

The revenues of Adonee, &c., may, however, exceed those of the districts which I propose to offer in exchange, and the Court of Hyderabad may object to the cession of Adonee and Ghazipore, and particularly of Adonee. Whatever may be the difference of value between those districts, it would not be a greater concession than the Company can justly claim in return for the effectual protection. afforded by the general guarantee of the Nizam's

dominions, as well as for other advantages already enumerated
in this despatch. You will urge this argument with the utmost
assiduity; but if it should not be admitted, I would rather
provide an equivalent for the amount of the differences of
revenue in some other quarter than relinquish the proposed line
of frontier. You will exert your utmost efforts to obtain this
line on the principles already stated — Article 5. This object,
however, is not absolutely indispensable; if you should find
that the aversion of the Court of Hyderabad to the arrangement now suggested is likely to endanger the success of the
whole treaty, you will relinquish this point until a more favourable conjuncture shall arise, and you will content yourself with
obtaining an equivalent for the districts to the northward of the
Toombuddra in some other part of his Highness's country contiguous to the Company's possessions.

Article 6. — You are at liberty either to agitate and decide the
question of the exchanges previous to the conclusion of the
treaty, or to defer that question until the treaty shall have been
executed. My wish, however, is to bring the greatest possible
proportion of this extensive arrangement to a definite conclusion
by this treaty.

Article 7. — This article requires no explanation. I have
already stated the indispensable necessity of assigning districts
in perpetuity, to be placed under the exclusive management and
authority of the East India Company. If the subsidy were a
mere temporary charge upon the funds of the Nizam, the perpetual assignment of territory would be objectionable, but as the
subsidy is a fixed and permanent charge, the funds for its
liquidation should be of the same nature, nor would the honour
or dignity of his Highness's government be in any degree compromised by such an arrangement.

Article 8. — The principal design of this article is to close for
ever all questions of account between the Company and the
Nizam with regard to the subsidiary force; and to suggest the
solid reasons which ought to induce his Highness to consent to
this arrangement. The cession will appear both advantageous
and honourable, when his Highness shall reflect, that the do-

minions proposed for cession were acquired principally by the aid of the British arms; that, after the cession, his Highness will possess the same extent of country which he held previous to the war of 1790-1; that he will be enabled, without any pressure upon his finances, to command the services of a large British force; and finally, that he will be effectually protected against all future encroachments of the Mahrattâs.

Article 9. — The necessity of this article is obvious; its omission in your treaty proceeded from the operation of the objectionable clause at the close of your 4th article. If the new treaty should be accepted by the Nizam, you will communicate a copy of it by express to Lord Clive, and you will concert with his Lordship the time and mode of assuming, on behalf of the Company, the districts to be ceded. The object of the clause at the close of this article, is to guard the assigned countries from the depredations of the Nizam's officers in the interval between the date of the treaty and the actual assumption of the countries by the officers of the Company.

Article 10. — This article requires no explanation. It suggests, however, an arrangement of considerable weight to strengthen the probability, that, deducting all necessary charges, the surplus revenue to the ceded districts will scarcely prove equivalent to the subsidy. The establishments and garrisons which it would be indispensably necessary for the Company to maintain in some of the forts, and particularly in Gurrumcondah, Gooty, Ganjecottah, &c., would occasion a considerable expense to the British Government.

Article 11. — It may be necessary to remark on this article, that it is not intended, in every supposable case, that the Nizam should continue to pay the whole of the subsidy, until the Company's officers shall have obtained complete possession of the ceded countries. It must necessarily happen, that some districts will be evacuated by his Highness's officers at an earlier period than others: and it is also possible, that some of the poleegars of those districts may oppose a temporary resistance to the introduction of the Company's authority. In the former case a regular account shall be opened with the Nizam; and he shall be credited for the revenues of every district from the date of its ac- tual delivery to the Company. In the latter case, the resistance of the poleegars shall not operate to the prejudice of the Nizam, and his Highness's responsibility for a proportional part of the subsidy, shall cease from the day on which the disturbed districts respectively shall be delivered to the Company by his Highness's officers.

Article 12. — The first clause of this article is indispensable in a treaty designed not to lay the foundation of future war, but to guard to the utmost extent of human precaution against the return of that calamity. No reasonable objection can be urged against this clause by the Court of Hyderabad.

For the reasons assigned, in the 26th, 27th, and 28th paragraphs of this despatch, the unlimited exertions of the Nizam in the common cause must be secured, with a view to the case supposed.

Article 13.—This is the 9th article of your treaty, with a slight verbal alteration. I repeat my approbation of your prudence in securing by treaty the right of the British Government to the exertions of the Court of Hyderabad, in points so essential to the success of military operations as the timely collection of Brinjarries and the establishment of magazines of grain.

Article 14.— Requires no remark, being nearly the same as the 6th article of your treaty.

Article 15.—The only observation suggested by this article has been anticipated in the 31st paragraph of this despatch.

Article 16.— This is the same as the 11th article of your treaty, of which I have already expressed my entire approbation.

Article 17.—In the 36th paragraph of this despatch I have stated my sentiments with regard to the importance of the concession required by the Nizam in the 1st of your separate articles; it is reasonable that some return should be made by his Highness. The stipulations of this article ought to be deemed objectionable by the Court of Hyderabad. The maintenance of good order and tranquillity in the ceded districts can never be an object of indifference to the Nizam's government; and the present article binds the Company to afford his Highness similar assistance whenever he may require it. It is not intended by this article that the subsidiary force, or any part of it, should be permanently employed in the protection of the ceded countries, or permanently stationed in any of the forts comprehended within the limits of those districts. In the event of any insurrection of the poleegars, or the sudden incursion of any enemy, which the ordinary military force stationed in that part of the Company's territory may not be sufficient to check, it is proposed that a division of the subsidiary troops, although stationed within his Highness's frontier, should be at the command of the Company, until the British Government may be enabled to dispense with its services.

Article 18.—This article comprehends as much as appears to me necessary or proper to be stated in a public treaty on the subject of your 12th and 13th articles.

Article 19.—This article is entirely conformable to the general spirit of the treaty. It has no tendency to weaken any of the stipulations framed with a view to the case of any aggression on the part of Dowlut Rao Scindia. If the Nizam should accept the treaty, you will ascertain as soon as possible, and report to me the conditions on which his Highness would be disposed to admit Dowlut Rao Scindia to be a party to the proposed alliance. At a proper season I shall communicate to you, for the information of his Highness, those conditions which I should demand from Scindia on the part of the Company.

Article 20.—You are authorised by this article to declare the treaty to be complete, whenever it shall have been executed by you and the Nizam, and to act upon it accordingly without delay, in the same manner as if I had formally ratified it in council. I think it necessary, however, to repeat, that you are empowered to make no other than mere verbal alterations in my draft, that no departure from the substance of any one of the articles can be admitted, and that your power of verbal alteration is confined strictly to cases of absolute necessity.

Separate Articles.—I have consented to annex the separate articles to the treaty solely with a view to the gratification of the Nizam's wishes. It is necessary that you should signify these sentiments to his Highness, and inform him that the conditions on which the Peishwa and Rhagojee Bhonslah should be admitted to the present alliance appear to me to be more proper subjects of verbal discussion and arrangement between his Highness and the British Government, than a solemn adjustment by treaty.

Article 1, Clause 1.—The Nizam is not entitled by this clause to more, on the part of the Company, than a just arbitration between his Highness and the Peishwa, founded on the basis of the Treaty of Mhar. Azeem-ool-Oomrah has repeatedly declared that nothing more is desired by his Court. To expect more from the British Government would be an injury to its honour and justice. The Peishwa may possibly advance just claims on the Nizam, entirely unconnected with the provisions of the Treaty of Mhar. Such claims may be compromised through the amicable endeavours of the British Government; but if any just claim of the Court of Poona on that of Hyderabad should be clearly established, we can neither deny nor resist it. The Nizam desires that it should be an express condition of the admission of the Peishwa to the alliance, and the restoration of his authority in the Mahratta empire, that he should previously renounce for ever all claims of chout on the territories of the Nizam, and should fulfil all the stipulations of the Treaty of Mhar. But if the Peishwa shall consent to an adjustment of all his claims of every description on the basis of that treaty, his Highness the Nizam will obtain all that can reasonably be required.

Article 1, Clause 2. — The third separate article of your treaty provided solely for the satisfaction to be given by the Peishwa to the Nizam, but the Company will also be justified in demanding from the Peishwa a just return to them for the services to be rendered by their interposition in the affairs of the Mahratta empire. This clause requires no further observation.

Article 1, Clause 3.—This stipulation requires no remark. It is sufficiently manifest that the acquiescence of the Paishwa in this stipulation is indispensably necessary to enable the Company to restore and maintain his Highness's authority. This stipulation is also essential to the permanent security of the Nizam. The establishment of a British subsidiary force at Poona will for ever preclude all disturbance of the Nizam's possessions by that restless court, and will contribute materially to the preservation of general tranquillity.

Article 2, Clause 1.—The general tenor of the observations applied to the first and second clauses of the separate article is equally applicable to the clause. If the Raja of Berar shall accept the present proposal, the Nizam may be assured the British Government will render strict justice to his Highness's rights.

Article 2, Clause 2.—I have not judged it necessary or expedient to disclose more explicitly on the present occasion the precise nature of my object at the Court of Nagpoor. You are already apprized, however, by my instructions to the Resident at that court, of their general tendency. I wish Rhagojee Bhonslah to accept a permanent subsidiary force from the Company. Such an arrangement would prove his most effectual security against Dowlut Rao Scindia. I also wish to obtain the province of Cuttak, either by a territorial assignment from the Raja in exchange for subsidy, or by an agreement between the Raja and the Company for a reasonable equivalent from the Company either in money or territory. The Court of Hyderabad possesses the means of promoting the success of my views in respect to the acquisition of Cuttak, and I therefore desire you to pay the most particular attention to this object, and to avail yourself of the earliest possible occasion of ascertaining the sentiments and disposition of Azeem-ool-Oomrah on the subject.

The possessions of the Nizam in Berar would probably constitute an ample equivalent with regard to revenue from Cuttak. You will direct your observations to this suggestion, and you will consider the means of inducing the Court of Hyderabad to

excha ̃ ̄ ̄ge the territory in question for Cuttak, with the view to
the ̄ ̄ansfer of the latter to the Company. The cession to
Rhagojee Bhonslah of Ellichpoor and of the other districts of
Berar now occupied by the Nizam would evidently conduce
more than any other possible arrangement to the establishment
and preservation of harmony between those two powers, and
would probably secure from the Raja of Berar a renunciation
of all claims of chout on the dominions of the Nizam. It is
generally understood that the net revenue derived by the Court
of Nagpoor from the province of Cuttak constitutes an inconsiderable branch of Rhagojee Bhonslah's resources.

Secret Article 3. — Any detailed article stipulating rules for
the division of eventful conquests is irreconcilable to the spirit
and object of this treaty. I cannot consent to any such article,
and even in the expressions of the article now under consideration I have made a concession to the Court of Hyderabad to
which it cannot assert any actual right.

It is hardly necessary to apprize you that the latitude allowed
you with regard to verbal alterations to be eventually admitted in
the public articles of this treaty must be exercised with peculiar
reserve and caution in respect to the secret and separate articles.
I shall transmit to you with all practical despatch a draft of a
treaty of commerce to be proposed to the Court of Hyderabad.
The unaccountable indisposition manifested by that court to entertain this subject has suggested to me the expediency of
separating it entirely from the Treaty of Alliance, and of opening a distinct commercial negotiation. The repugnance of the
Nizam to this measure may, I trust, be overcome, since my proposition will not only secure to his Highness a perfect reciprocity
of advantages, but also the free use of seaport and the protection of the British flag. To these concessions it is my intention
to add as a present from the Company to his Highness a vessel
of considerable burthen completely equipped. The artifice
employed by Azeem-ool-Oomrah (and stated in your letter, No.
84, dated the 31st May) for the purpose of anticipating the advantages of the depending treaty, is suitable to his temper and
genius. You will omit no exertion to frustrate the mischievous

effects of this unworthy attempt. He must be distinctly informed that whenever the treaty now proposed shall be finally concluded, Colonel Palmer will be instructed to declare explicitly to the Peishwa, to Dowlut Rao Scindia, that the British Government, from the period of that formal notification, will consider any unprovoked aggression against the Nizam as an aggression against the Company, and accordingly, if the Nizam should execute the treaty, you will communicate the event to the Resident at Poona, together with a copy of this despatch and of the treaty, and you will inform him that it is my order that he should make the proper notifications to the Peishwa and Scindia according to the tenor of this paragraph. You will explain to him that he is not authorised to communicate to the Peishwa and Scindia any other articles of this treaty than the first, second, sixteenth, eighteenth, and nineteenth articles.

Azeem-ool-Oomrah must also be apprized that I will not suffer the slightest deception to be practised on this important subject, and that I have already adopted effectual measures for the purpose of removing the false impression which his unauthorised and unwarrantable communication to the Peishwa's coukeels was evidently calculated to produce. You will take this occasion of signifying distinctly to Azeem-ool-Oomrah that no engagements whatever are to be presumed to be finally concluded merely because the British Resident has expressed his consent to them, especially when the Resident has declared any doubts of obtaining the final ratification of the Governor-General in Council. While the Resident's public acts are declared by him to be exactly conformable to his instructions, a confidence may justly be entertained that no alteration will be made by the supreme authority of the government which he represents. Under any other circumstances the direct sanction of the Governor-General in Council is absolutely requisite to give valid effect to every public instrument.

If you should have any reason to suppose that the Court of Hyderabad will reject the treaty now offered by my authority, you will communicate your opinion to the Resident at Poona,

and you will desire him without delay to declare to the Peishwa ~~Appendix~~
and to Dowlut Rao Scindia, in the most explicit and public <u>B</u>
manner, that the political relations subsisting between the Company and his Highness the Nizam remain on the basis of the Treaty of 1798, and have suffered no alteration whatever.

I am, &c.,

WELLESLEY.

THE END.

Nizam , His History and Relations with the British Government, Vol. 2